Washington L. Sanford

History of Fourteenth Illinois cavalry and the brigades to which it belonged

Washington L. Sanford

History of Fourteenth Illinois cavalry and the brigades to which it belonged

ISBN/EAN: 9783337811006

Printed in Europe, USA, Canada, Australia, Japan

Cover: Foto ©ninafisch / pixelio.de

More available books at **www.hansebooks.com**

FIRST LIEUT. WASHINGTON L. SANFORD, Company I.
(1860.)

HISTORY

OF

Fourteenth Illinois Cavalry

AND THE BRIGADES TO WHICH IT BELONGED

COMPILED FROM MANUSCRIPT HISTORY BY SANFORD, WEST AND FEATHERSON,
AND FROM NOTES OF COMRADES; CAREFULLY COMPARED WITH AND
CORRECTED BY GOVERNMENT PUBLISHED OFFICIAL REPORTS
AND STATISTICS FURNISHED BY UNION AND CONFED-
ERATE OFFICERS. WITH BIOGRAPHIES OF
OFFICERS AND ROLLS OF MEN, AND
EMBELLISHED WITH
PORTRAITS

COMPILED AND PUBLISHED BY

W. L. SANFORD

Late First Lieutenant Company "I," Fourteenth Reg. Illinois Cavalry
Address: Chana, Illinois.

CHICAGO
R. R. DONNELLEY & SONS COMPANY
1898

TABLE OF CONTENTS.

PREFACE 5

INTRODUCTION 7

CHAPTER I.

CALLED TO KENTUCKY.................................13 to 31

First Celina raid. Second Celina raid. Active duty scouting.

CHAPTER II.

MORGAN PURSUIT ACROSS THE OHIO RIVER................32 to 53

Its object. Rebel Gen. Wheeler's statement. Morgan flanks our division. Our brigade prevents his return. Morgan driven across the Ohio river. Pursuit. Our brigade flanks Morgan. Battle of Buffington Island. Final pursuit and capture.

CHAPTER III.

PREPARING TO INVADE EAST TENNESSEE..................54 to 66

Cross the Cumberland Mountains. Capture Knoxville. Capture Cumberland Gap.

CHAPTER IV.

MARCH TO MORRISTOWN, BLUE SPRINGS AND GREENEVILLE..67 to 86

Attack rebels at Kingsport and pursuit. Fight at Blountville. Capture of Bristol. Engagement at Zollicoffer. Second engagement at Blountville. Skirmish on Zollicoffer road. March to Loudon. March back to Knoxville. Engagement at Rheatown. Third fight at Blountville. Second fight at Bristol. Drive rebels into Virginia. Scout to Kingsport under Major Quigg.

CHAPTER V.

LONGSTREET ATTACKS BURNSIDE................87 to 108

    Longstreet's forces. Burnside's forces. Knoxville besieged. Brigade under General Wilcox. Camp near Cumberland Gap. March to Maynardville. Our brigade strength. Skirmish below Maynardville. Rebel attempt to surround brigade. Battle of Walkersford. Rebel forces engaged. Strength of regiment and of brigade. Guy Niles' splendid shot. Skirmish at Powder Spring Gap. Gen. Shackelford in command of cavalry. Sent to watch Longstreet's movement. Reconnoisance to Mooresville.

CHAPTER VI.

LONGSTREET'S FORCES; OUR FORCES.................109 to 126

    Battle of Bean Station. Sanford's description. Connelly's description. Longstreet's report and object. Rebel Gen. Johnson's report. Johnson acknowledges our gallant resistance. Other rebel reports confirm our description. Strength of opposing forces. Second day's fight. Gen. Longstreet acknowledges his failure.

CHAPTER VII.

GENERAL FOSTER IN COMMAND................127 to 142

    General Foster in command. Powder Spring Gap evacuated. Join General Sturgis. Frequent engagements. Severe battle. Intense cold and hard fare. Battle near Dandridge. March to Knoxville. Divided into detachments. Skirmishes and brisk engagement.

CHAPTER VIII.

INDIAN RAID INTO NORTH CAROLINA................143 to 159

    Crossing the mountains. Silently approaching Indian camp. Capture of Indian pickets. Furious charge into Indian camp. Complete surprise and rout of Indians. Results of the engagement. Gen. Sturgis' report. Gen. Grant's dispatch. Parson Brownlow's comment. Reconnoisance above Knoxville. March to Loudon and Philadelphia.

CHAPTER IX.

DIVIDED INTO DETACHMENTS................160 to 169

    Passing a spy through the lines. Indian attack. Organization of band.

CHAPTER X.

START TO JOIN SHERMAN..........................170 to 181

Joined by recruits. Pursuit of rebel parties. Organization of Stoneman's division. Skirmishing. Drive a rebel battery. Rebels driven across the Chattahooche. Burn Moore's bridge. Cross the river to Decatur.

CHAPTER XI.

STONEMAN RAID TO MACON.........................182 to 211

Initial correspondence and orders. Start on raid. Hood discovers movement. Reasons for change of plan. Commands in Stoneman's division. Capture of Monticello and Hillsboro. Davidson's battalion detached. Capron's brigade destroys rail road. Confederate force at Macon. Attack on Macon. Information of strong force in our rear. Retreat toward Wheeler. Skirmishing with Wheeler. Changes by Eighth Michigan. Capron's brigade drives the enemy. Battle line formed. Repeated furious charges on rebel lines. General Stoneman surrenders. Capron's brigade dashes through rebel lines. Retreat; men exhausted. Pursuit and night attack. Terrible fate. Work of Davidson's command.

CHAPTER XII.

ROMANTIC STORY OF ESCAPE.........................212 to 223

CHAPTER XIII.

REMOUNTING AND SERVICE UNDER GEN. THOMAS.........224 to 253

Armed with muskets. Strength of Hood's Army. Reason of change of our orders. March to Pulaski, Tennessee. Gen. Schofield commanding in front. Schofield's force, infantry and cavalry. Hood's force, infantry and cavalry. Hood designs to flank Schofield. Wide belt of country defended by our small cavalry force. Capron's brigade reconnoiter to Waynesboro. Capron's brigade opposes overwhelming force. Four days and nights' perilous service. Capron's brigade saves Schofield's army.

CHAPTER XIV.

FIFTH IOWA CAVALRY JOINS BRIGADE............254 to 291

Capron's brigade at Lewisburg pike. Successfully resists Buford's division. Active work. Wilson's cavalry driven back. Capron's brigade alone resists. Holds the enemy until night. Surrounded by Forrest's cavalry. Engagement at picket post. Headquarters swept away. Final gallant charge of brigade. Capron's brigade again saves Schofield's army. Retreat to Franklin. Great battle at Franklin. A disastrous victory for Hood. Retreat to Nashville. Siege of Nashville. Dismounted and armed with carbines. Reorganization of brigade. Battle of Nashville. Destruction of Hood's army. End of active service. Quietly in camps.

CHAPTER XV.

AT EDGEFIELD AND PULASKI........................292 to 347

Comparative loss of Fourteenth. Synopsis of service. Narratives of comrades. Biographies of officers. Roster of men. Muster out of regiment.

PREFACE.

A regimental and brigade history of Fourteenth Illinois Cavalry, including the services in brigade of the Fifth Indiana Cavalry, the Sixty-fifth Indiana Mounted Infantry, the Eighth Michigan Cavalry, McLaughlin's Ohio Squadron, the Sixteenth Illinois Cavalry, and the Sixth Indiana Cavalry.

INTRODUCTION.

This history began as a daily record of events in the service by two members, W. L. Sanford, of Company "I," and Martin West, of Company "C," neither knowing of the other's work. It was first designed for the information of friends at home. As the record grew in interest, comrades suggested a published history. When this purpose became fixed, Sanford proposed a partnership with Comrade Thomas Featherson, of Company "I," to illustrate the book with views, as Featherson was a fair artist. Sanford, having lost a portion of his notes, searched for notes to supply the lost material, and found that Martin West had also kept full notes and that he was an able writer and diligent in gathering material. On talking the matter over each became convinced that it were better to unite their work. A partnership of "Sanford, West and Featherson" was formed, and when Sanford, in the spring of 1865, resigned, it was arranged that he should write up the history from their notes, and a subscription list of over eighteen hundred dollars was obtained, payable when the book was ready for the press. As the regiment was discharged before its three years' term was completed, the book was not yet ready, and at the muster out the members were so scattered that the means could not be gathered to publish and the project was abandoned. At the reunion of the regiment at Ottawa, Illinois, in August, 1887, the project was revived to publish. Major H. C. Connelly, Captain A. B. Capron and Lieutenant W. L. Sanford were appointed a committee to devise a plan to bring out the history. They at once decided that the history should be revised by combining the first manuscript, sifted and condensed, with all other useful and truthful material that could be gathered, using the Government published official reports of union and confederate officers to verify and add to our record.

It was finally decided that Lieutenant Sanford should compile the work, and finally the whole work was placed in his hands. Comrade Featherson had died and Comrade West consented to relinquish all to Sanford, who began by collecting the official reports and other material. A long time passed before the official records could be gathered, then the examination and culling from ten thousand large pages of these records was a long and laborious work. The compiling, arranging and interweaving with our record and with other notes, and the correcting and rewriting many times to correct and condense to the prescribed limits as new material was received, required a vast amount of labor and consumed much time. An immense correspondence to gather the names and addresses of comrades, and finally to gather the means to secure its publication, and also to gather and provide photo prints of officers and comrades with which to illustrate the book, required much patience and hard labor. We have been greatly aided in the work by Major Connelly by the use of his many valuable published accounts, and by notes furnished, as well as by encouragements and advice. Captain Capron furnished a portion of his father's memoirs from which much has been selected. Captain William R. Sanford, of Company "K," also furnished, in carefully written notes of his services and observations, much that is very valuable. Besides the notes of Sanford, West and Featherson, we have been permitted the use of those of Lieutenant J. H Allen, long acting adjutant, Lieutenant John F. Thomas, of Company "G," and others, which have been used in the body of the work, besides the articles in the last chapter accredited to each writer. Lieutenant Moore, of Company "L," furnished notes for history as well as articles.

The plan of Sanford, West and Featherson's history was from necessity mainly a collection of reminiscences, combined with such historical facts as could be gathered in the field from a knowledge of operations gathered from union sources alone. The authors, especially West, were fluent writers and diligent in gathering facts. Since the publishing of the Government official reports we are enabled to add much of historical facts, as well as to verify or correct, as the former notes required. This has added immensely to the value of the book as a history—indeed, it has made it as nearly perfect, as a history, as it is possible to get. It is, however, greatly to be regretted that the limited amount of funds for publishing has compelled such a condensing of the work as has crowded out some of the finest descriptions of country and scenery, and some individual reminiscences. This will be a disappointment to a few that we cannot avoid, while it will gratify the many, who will thus receive a much more perfect history. Our labor has been an immense task, much more than many, if any, comrades can realize, but we have not been alone in the sacrifice. Had we not been aided to an unexpected extent by willing comrades, the published history would have been an impossibility. First the encouragements, advice and promptings of Major H. C. Connelly, one of the committee, which have been of great value, in addition to his notes and his financial support. It was an absolute essential that we have a custodian to care for the gathered funds. Fortunately we found one perfectly suited to this work, who willingly assumed it, and who has performed a vast amount of work, as well as caring for the funds and contributing more than one-sixth of the whole amount. The history would have been an impossibility without Colonel David Quigg, of Chicago, Illinois. But others, too, have done nobly, and, indeed, we may say that without the aid of other noble comrades it would have failed. In financial aid the next highest to Colonel Quigg is Lieutenant William Moore. The next is Comrade George W. Norris. The next are Major H. C. Connelly, Captain Sanford, of Company "K" (not the writer), and Lieutenant Beckwith, of Company "C." Then follow Lieutenant William H. Puckett, of Company "I;" Major J. B. Dent, Sergeant J. H. Melven, of Company "E," Lieutenant-Colonel D. P. Jenkins, Captain Lord, Peter Vanarsdale, W. C. Callicott, Mrs. Eliza Featherson, Mrs. Ruth Boren, George Q. Allen (son of Lieutenant Allen), William E. McCready and Lieutenant J. W. Sanders.

Captain William A. Lord furnished an able article on the Stoneman raid. This article is valuable, as Captain Lord was on General Stoneman's staff. The narrative of escape from Stoneman's raid by Norris while it is no more valuable as history than other articles furnished, yet is of such a nature that, while truthful and real, it is also highly romantic. We owe much to the financial liberality of many comrades, but most prominent is Colonel Quigg and Lieutenant William M. Moore and Comrade Norris, who, when failure was imminent, determined that failure should not be permitted.

HISTORY
OF THE
FOURTEENTH ILLINOIS CAVALRY.

CHAPTER I.

ORGANIZATION AND SERVICE IN KENTUCKY UP TO THE MORGAN RAID.

Few regiments in the late war began their history under circumstances of as great discouragement as did the Fourteenth Regiment Illinois Cavalry.

In the summer of 1862 Horace Capron obtained permission to raise a cavalry regiment, to be numbered the eighteenth. D. P. Jenkins had also been authorized by Governor Yates to raise a regiment of cavalry, to be numbered the fourteenth. Colonel Hancock also recruited for the fifteenth. Illinois had filled her quota of the call for three hundred thousand for that year, and had raised a dozen regiments in excess ere any number had enlisted in these regiments. The country had been depleted of laborers, and the opinion almost universally prevailed that though "Uncle Sam" had not crushed and masticated the southern confederacy before breakfast, that he now had that tough customer about ready for the noonday meal. The consequence was, in Illinois, the prevalence of a decided opposition to further enlistments, by many now deemed unnecessary. It was autumn when the nucleus of these regiments gathered at their rendezvous camps at Peoria, Illinois, then only to find that they were far from completed.

Many bounty jumpers and deserters from other organizations had crept in. The deserters were reclaimed and the bounty jumpers skipped, and the delay in organization bred discontent, so that desertions depleted about as fast as recruiting strengthened. It was found necessary to consolidate the Eighteenth and the Fifteenth. This consolidation threw out one-half of the prospective officers, which increased discontent, as the men saw favorite officers, under whom they had enlisted and expected to serve, crowded out. Many had left families at home dependent on them for support. Failure to organize and receive some pay deprived their families of support. These combined influences caused further desertions, so that little progress was made toward completing the organization. Finally a further consolidation with the Fourteenth, together with what were gathered by enlistments, enabled the mustering of the first battalion, with Francis M. Davidson as Major, and the second battalion, with David Quigg as Major, on the 7th day of January, 1863; and the third battalion, with Haviland Tompkins as Major, February 6th, 1863. The regiment now mustered little more than the minimum number. The field and staff as first organized were: Colonel, Horace Capron, Sr.; Lieutenant-Colonel, David P. Jenkins; First Major, Francis M. Davidson; Second Major, David Quigg; Third Major, Haviland Tompkins; Adjutant, Henry W. Carpenter; Quartermaster, Samuel F. True; Surgeon, Preston H. Bailhache; First Assistant Surgeon, George A. Wilson; Second Assistant Surgeon, John Ivory Wilkins; Chaplain, Samuel Chase, D. D.; Commissary, Bruce C. Payne; Sergeant Major, Henry C. Carrico; Quartermaster Sergeant, Charles West; Commissary Sergeant, Abner N. Scribner; Hospital Steward, George A. Sumner; Saddler Sergeant, John B. Reed; Chief Bugler, Henry S. Walker; Veterinary Surgeon Alonzo H. Sanborn. In the last of January we received our horses and drew Springfield sabers. February 23d we received from the state a beautiful rich silk banner, which was thankfully acknowledged by Colonel Capron in a stirring and appropriate speech. March 25th received *"our month's advance pay."* The long delay in rendezvous camp caused by impeded organization, afforded ample time which was well improved in every kind of drill essential to cavalry, so that the evils result-

MAJOR HENRY C. CONNELLY.

ing from such delay was compensated in such discipline and drill as made the regiment one of the most effective cavalry organizations in the service. The thorough sifting incident to the hindrances in organization left in the regiment only the most patriotic and determined men, whose ardor could not be quenched by any opposing obstacles. Whether their after history fulfilled the promise of these advantages will best be shown by the following record of their service. Recruits were still gathered in; thorough drill and discipline continued. All dissatisfaction had disappeared, and in its stead grew up an eagerness for the fray.

We shall have occasion to quote or refer frequently to the published reports of the Union and Confederate forces, giving page, volume, series and part. In Series 1st, Part 2d, Volume 23d, page 167, is a message from Major General H. G. Wright, then commanding in Kentucky, to General A. C. Fuller, March 23d, 1863: "I have intelligence that the rebels are entering Kentucky in considerable force, and we shall want all the troops we can get. Please hasten movement of Fourteenth Cavalry as much as possible." Again, on page 170, March 24th, 1863, General Wright to Brigadier-General Boyle, says: "Have again urged Governor Yates to send you the Fourteenth Cavalry." At this time southern and eastern Kentucky was so overrun with the enemy's raiders that it was almost undisputably in their possession. March 25th, 1863, Major General Ambrose E. Burnside superceded General Wright in command of the Department of the Ohio. See Part 2d, page 172. Same page and date, General Halleck instructs General Burnside: "It is important that you immediately carry out my instructions of the 23d, by concentrating forces in central Kentucky to meet the raids of the enemy." March 26th Burnside replies: "I think we can hold the line of the Kentucky (river) until a column can be organized near Lebanon. * * * Our cavalry force is very small." General Joseph Wheeler was assigned the command of the rebel cavalry in Bragg's army (part 2d, page 175). He was posted on Bragg's right wing, with headquarters at McMinnville. His strength in February, 1863, exceeded 10,000 effective present. His work was to guard Bragg's right wing, and to raid Kentucky for supplies (part 2d, page 718). The brigades of Brigadier Generals Wharton, John H. Morgan and Hagan constituted his division (page 650). Morgan's headquarters at Sparta was convenient to raid any part of Southeastern Kentucky. General Humphrey Marshall's command (afterward Sam Jones' command), effective present, Infantry, 1,700; Artillery and Cavalry, 2,467; total, 4,167 (page 638), were posted near Southeastern Kentucky. General John Pegram's brigade, effective present April 1st, 1,644 men (page 733), belonged to Western East Tennessee. All these successively raided Southern and Eastern Kentucky.

Their irregular and more independent cavalry under Colonel John T. Morgan and Major Hamilton, with headquarters at and near Celina on the south side of the Cumberland river, were of themselves guerrillas and, together with the many bands of bushwhackers of that region, ranged the country when and where opportunity offered, by theft, by robbery, and by every means of barbarity, to gather in supplies from Kentucky to their various depots of supply; the principal one being Celina, whence these supplies were carried by boats to Nashville, while the enemy occupied that place; after they were driven back, these supplies were carried by wagons across the mountains to Livingston and other points. These guerrillas and bushwhackers were unprincipled robbers, pillaging, burning and murdering without compunction; they never sought a fair fight, but always avoided it; fleeing to their mountain concealment whenever pursued even by an inferior force; turning on them or ambushing their pursuers when in very small parties. The policy of Bragg was to supply his army as much as possible from within the Union lines (see part 2d, page 776).

This was the situation when our regiment was ordered to Kentucky. Happy were the boys of the 14th Illinois Cavalry when Saturday, the 28th day of March, 1863, came, bringing orders to march to join our noble comrades in the front, to aid in crushing treason, and in bearing aloft our glorious flag, the emblem of the proudest and most glorious nationality that ever blessed the earth.

By 4 p. m. man and horse, with all the habiliments of war, were on the train, which moved out at sunset. Ran all night; passed Joliet early in the morning. March 29th, passed the western boundary of Indiana; reached Michigan City, Indiana, where we were regaled with a cup of hot coffee for each, as breakfast and dinner. Weather cold for the season. At 1 p. m. the iron horse, with his tremendous load, passed out on the Michigan City & New Albany Railroad; passing first through a swampy, desolate region with little improvement. Reached Lafayette about dark. Short halt, then ran all night, reached Indianapolis about 4 a. m. of March 30th. From Lafayette we passed through fine country, which now grows more broken. Reached Jeffersonville, Indiana, on the Ohio river, opposite Louisville, Kentucky, about 7 p. m. Slept on the cars. On our trip down through Indiana we were greeted with one continued display of Union flags and waving 'kerchiefs, as signals of good will and cheer, indicating that we had the earnest prayers and best wishes of all the loyal left behind us. This remembrance of the sympathy of a loyal people, cheered us on many a sanguinary field in our tedious and arduous service. March 31st go into camp a furlong north of town. April 1st, 10 a. m., move camp to quarter mile east of town, near the Ohio river, opposite Louisville; a beautiful camp called "Camp Bright." Remained in this camp until April 7th, then crossed the Ohio river on ferry boat; marched through the city of Louisville, and camped one mile southeast, near the camp of the 25th Michigan Infantry. April 8th in camp; April 9th, grand review; draw Colts revolvers and Burnside carbines. Each man who would take them got two navy revolvers. Our number was now about 800; the maximum being 1,200. On the 11th and 12th the regiment was paid by Major Fell, U. S. A. paymaster. April 12th, before noon, struck tents and marched for southern Kentucky. Each company was furnished with long cable rope to tie the company horses and one wagon to each company, and wagons for headquarters and regimental stores. Camped 12 miles south of Louisville. April 13th marched through "West Point," on the Ohio river 20 miles below Louisville; where were some rebel forts on commanding bluffs, erected to control navigation of the river, but these had been rendered useless by the introduction of our gunboats. We camped on Salt creek, 10 miles south of West

Point; day's march 30 miles. April 14th, reveille before day; marched early, passed through Elizabeth City about noon. This town is on the Louisville & Nashville Railroad and turnpike, 42 miles nearly south of Louisville. Camped 10 miles south; day's march, 21 miles; rained hard day and night. April 15th, marched to Mumfordsville on Green river, 22 miles, and camped after night. April 16th, crossed Green river, which was very high, by swimming. Though the river was a torrent, swimming the river was preferable to crossing the railroad bridge 80 feet above the water on no floor but two planks laid lengthwise and without side supports of any kind, as we were at first ordered. Some of our horses could not swim; these would sink, strike the bottom, then spring up to the surface, and by a series of such springs succeeded in reaching the opposite shore without loss of a man or horse. The crossing occupied several hours when, wet to our armpits, we resumed our march and camped 9 miles south. April 17th, marched early, reached Glasgow, 85 miles south of Louisville, about noon, having marched 11 miles. Found here the 107th Illinois Infantry, the 5th Indiana Cavalry and the Elgin Battery. These comrades all gave us lusty cheers of welcome. We were now brigaded with them.

We expected to rest here at least a short time, but were ordered to provide ourselves rations and ammunition for a raid, having only time to prepare dinner and feed our horses when "Boots and Saddles," "To Horse" and "Assembly" sounded; when 600 of the 14th and 300 each of the 5th and the 107th, under command of Colonel Felix Graham, of the 5th Indiana, accompanied by one section of the Elgin Battery (12 pounders) formed column and marched for the Cumberland river in Tennessee, on our first military expedition. Glasgow had but recently been captured from the enemy. We continued our march through the night, halting at 10 p. m. to feed. Our trains and guns were much impeded in progress by the darkness and the very bad roads. We were halted many times to permit the trains to close up. We now learned the operation of the "vocal telegraph" used to keep a column closed up in a night's march. The commander from the head of the column starts the inquiry, "Trains all right?" which is repeated by officers at proper distances along the column, conveying the inquiry to the rear much more rapidly than could a courier mounted on the fleetest horse After a time comes back the answer conveyed in the same manner: "Trains all up;" when "Forward" is sounded, until the next halt brought a repetition of the same signals. So slow was our progress that it was after sunrise when we reached Tompkinsville, the county seat of Munroe county, Kentucky, 24 miles from Glasgow, and seven miles from the north line of Tennessee. This was a dilapidated village. We halted within a few miles to feed. Passed the state line about 9 a. m.; soon the country grew rougher until we entered a region verging the mountainous, and thinly settled. Few dwellings of a rude sort, inhabited by a poor class, who cultivated small patches of land. One redeeming quality was the abundance of pure, sweet spring water, a luxury to the weary soldier on the march not often obtainable. For miles our road led down a ravine until the collecting spring outlets made a rivulet, growing soon to be a creek walled in by bluffs on either side; the passage often difficult, caused by the dipping or inclination of the rocks that formed our roadbed. About 4 p. m. halted about a mile from the village of Celina; having a range of bluffs to cover us from view of the town. March, 40 miles.

Celina was in outward appearance unimportant, valued only as a depot of supplies from which small river boats carried supplies down the river 75 miles to Nashville; or later by wagons across the mountains. Our present mission was to break up this nest of marauders and cut off this source of rebel supplies. Our column was formed and the order "Prepare to charge," given. The wildest shouts of enthusiasm rang out as the men eagerly prepared for the fray by divesting themselves of everything not absolutely needed in the expected encounter, and forming line eagerly awaiting the order "Forward," "Charge." After a few moments of impatient waiting came instead a new order, or rather, a request for 300 volunteers to swim the river and charge the town. So eagerly did the men of the 14th respond to this call that the officers were compelled to designate who should remain.

The river was high, the banks steep and muddy, and it was said that rebel sharpshooters occupied old buildings near the river to pick off our men as they swam the river, without opportunity to return the fire. Our two guns were planted on an elevation and soon booming shells flew thick and fast. A dense column of flame and smoke shooting heavenward, attested the skill of our gunners. The town was on fire. The enemy raised a white flag. They proposed to surrender the town with 600 prisoners. Instead of the charging column a small party was sent over in a boat bearing a flag of truce to arrange terms of capitulation, but before they reached the opposite shore they were fired upon by those dastardly cowards, who regarded neither the rights of humanity nor the universally acknowledged rules of war. It was now too late to make a further attack, and scouting parties were sent out in various directions.

The first battalion of the 14th, which had been sent up the river to learn whether a rumor that the enemy were crossing to the north side of the river was true, returned about 9 p. m. without having discovered an enemy. Command now bivouacked for the night. April 19th, beautiful morning. We were early in line ready to begin the contest. Company "A," under Lieutenant Horace Capron, and Company "I," under Lieutenant Kilbourn, had been sent up the river on double quick 12 miles, to capture a band of the enemy gathering in supplies. When we reached the point indicated we found two boats laden with bacon and corn for down the river, but the party had fled ingloriously. An old Union lady living near informed us that she had frightened the party by telling them that a large party of Yankees had just passed down. She had told them the truth without knowing it. We took possession of the boats and a party under Lieutenant Kilbourn navigated them down the river, while Company "A" and Company "I," under Sergeant Sanford, returned to camp. These boats became useful in transporting our troops over the river; together they carried 25 men and their horses. Great eagerness prevailed as to who should cross first. Each company of the 14th clamored as to which company should cross first. Colonel Capron ordered the following rotation. First "G," Captain Perkins; "D," Lieutenant Carrico; "K," Captain Sanford; "H," Captain Lord; "C," Captain Dent; "E," Captain Crandel; one battalion under

Major Quigg was out on an important scout, and Companies "A" and "I," though eager to cross, were obliged to be content with another scout after rebels reported to be on north side of the river. A portion of the 5th Indiana was next crossed over. As soon as sufficient had crossed to form line they advanced on the enemy, driving them to the heavily timbered hills, where a sharp skirmish ensued. Major Davidson commanded our right wing, and Major Tompkins the left wing, the 5th Indiana, under Lieutenant Colonel Butler, occupied the center. Our lines continually pressed upon the enemy seeking the advantage of a close range for their revolvers and short range carbines. This did not suit the rebs, as they preferred to hold the Yanks at long range with their longer guns, as the Yanks at short range had the advantage in rapidity of loading and firing. In this manner we pressed them back farther and farther until Captain Dent, with his Company "C," was ordered to charge a strong position, but when his brave company was all expectation for a close contest, they found that the whole line of the enemy was in full retreat for the mountains, where they took refuge in inapproachable cliffs, and mountain gulches.

This was the first engagement for the 14th. Although all fought well, the 14th were the more impetuous; a fact that was common of our new troops. The 5th had been in engagements before. The roar of battle strife was tantalizing to the comrades left north of the river to guard our rear from a large force of the enemy said to be coming to re-enforce Celina. The casualties on our part did not exceed two killed and four or five wounded as far as we could learn. The following Colonel Graham reported to Brigadier General Hobson (see part 1st, page 264) : "I arrived at this place (Celina) at 4 p. m. (18th), opened fire upon O. P. Hamilton's camp, driving him and killing seven. I have possession of Celina. Hamilton's camp is entirely destroyed. The rumors are very conflicting; rebels report 3,000 men back of town. I think 1,100 will cover the entire number all told. I will move after the rebels today (19th). River not fordable." In Vol. 23d, part 1st, page 264, General Hobson to General Rosecrans says of Colonel Graham, that he destroyed Hamilton's camp and killed 7 rebels on 18th and on 19th took possession of town, killing 30; the rebels in full retreat in disorder; our force 1,200 but not all engaged. Rebel force 1,200 to 1,500." On page 263 General Wright says: "The expedition to Celina was entirely successful, they destroyed the town; 100,000 pounds bacon; 10,000 bushels wheat; 10,000 bushels corn; 100 barrels whisky; 100 barrels flour and considerable quantity of sugar, coffee and tea, meats and other stores, and 40 boats used in transporting supplies to the rebel army. Rebels report 90 killed, but Colonel Graham thinks the number greater. This result is highly creditable to the troops engaged; indeed it was a perfect success." General Burnside twice refers to this affair, on page 265, part 2d, and in his general report, page 12. He also there speaks of the constant skirmishing of the cavalry, but no decisive results in April except this expedition to Celina. Our notes give the same amount of property destroyed as is given in the foregoing reports. As to the loss of the enemy, we then had no means of ascertaining, but believe the highest estimate given is below the facts. On page 783, Vol. 23, part 2d, General John H. Morgan reports April 22d, 1863: "Received information from Celina that the enemy had advanced on and shelled that town on 19th instant, partially burning it and causing Major O. P. Hamilton's command to fall back; the enemy's force being about 1,200 strong." On page 785 he says: "The enemy between 1,200 and 1,500, crossed the river at Celina on 19th instant, shelled and burned the town together with the churches; not giving the citizens any warning of their intentions. Major Hamilton had to fall back four or five miles, but being reinforced by Colonel Johnson's regiment, attacked and drove the enemy back across the river." Hamilton's force was reinforced as Morgan says, but our forces were not driven back across the river as he states; they retired as we have stated, after they had driven the enemy to the mountains. Our force in all was 1,200, but not near all engaged. What buildings were destroyed was on the 18th, which, like all sudden attacks or surprises, was made without warning. No buildings except their depot of supplies were burned after we took possession on the 19th. We are confident that no church was destroyed for we took pains to learn at the time; nor do we believe there was a

CAPTAIN ALBERT B. CAPRON, Company A.

building in the town worth two hundred dollars; it was a mere collection of old tumble down shanties valuable to the rebels only as a depot of stolen supplies, and of course the dwellings, humble as they were, were the homes of families, and to be respected as such, which they were. As to the destruction of supplies it was a war necessity, as the longer the rebel armies were supplied and strengthened the greater the loss on both sides, of property as well as of human lives. Then this nest of robbers who had systematically robbed and plundered and burned the dwellings of Union people, as well as murdered them, were the last to have the right to complain that they were now forced to swallow a small portion of their own medicine. On page 270, Vol. 23, part 2d, is the following from Jules Fassett, assistant inspector general: "Louisville Ky., April 23d, 1863, to Colonel Capron: I heartily congratulate you and your command for their conduct in fighting on the very first of their arrival. I went to the Louisville Journal this morning. A true account will be published. I have sent you four howitzers with implements and ammunition." These afterward figured conspicuously in our history. These guns were first manned by a detail of the 14th, commanded by Sergeant Phillips. Soon after they were manned by a detachment from Company "I," commanded by Lieutenant Kilbourne, of that company, and when we left Kentucky to cross the mountains Lieutenant H. C. Connelly, of Company "L," 14th, commanded and manned them by a detachment from his company, in whose hands they remained until the spring of 1864, after they had been disabled in severe but efficient service.

Having heard that the enemy were to be heavily reinforced, a heavy chain guard was placed around our camp at night. Then occurred some incidents which were the source of much merriment in after years after we became veterans in the service. As was common with those new in the service, the true report of expected reinforcements to the enemy set on foot many camp rumors and among them a report that we would be attacked at night by a large force which included a band of Indians. The chain guards completely encircled the camp with the men posted at intervals of about five rods. It was so nearly dark that only the outlines of the next sentinel could be seen as a shadowy form from each comrade. The brown leaves were on trees and shrubs and their occasional waving in a breeze easily excited fancy in the belief that the enemy was approaching. To add to apprehension the men were told that the Indians were expected to slip through our lines by stealth and murder our sleeping comrades in camp. Of course these instructions were given to the soldiers to arouse vigilance. Each sentinel was instructed if he saw an enemy approaching or slipping through the lines, to fire his carbine when the whole line was ordered to fall back three rods and form a new line. After waiting some time a soldier of Company "I," 14th, saw some shadowy form on his right, slipping toward our camp inside of our lines. Somewhat apprehensive that it was the sentinel on that side and not risking the shooting of a comrade though the strict command was to discharge his gun, he fired at space to the front and seizing his revolver fell back as ordered, to a fence in the rear, about three rods. While falling back an exclamation of fear from his comrade on his right, revealed that, contrary to strict orders and military discipline through cowardice he had abandoned his post. With a severe reproof he was told that he ought to be shot. Of course the report of the carbine aroused the whole sentinel line with the apprehension that the enemy were upon us, and fancy easily pictured an approaching enemy in every dimly seen waving bush, and bang, bang, bang was heard at intervals all around the line throughout the night. As the principal cause of this alarm manifested symptoms of insanity and was sent to hospital, where he died, we withhold his name; and as to the other hero in the "drama," his extreme modesty prompts us to withhold also his name, though the honors of that night's fancied battle with the enemy is given where it belongs, to Company "I," of the 14th, as having begun it by firing the first gun. Comrades of the regiment will not be jealous of our honor.

April 20th, pleasant morning. After scouting parties were in, brigade marched at 11 a. m. toward Tompkinsville. Halted several miles out, having heard that the enemy had been reinforced and were preparing to cross the river. The guns, with 300 of the 14th, were sent back. They discovered the rebels in strong force just below the town. Upon our approach they retired down the river. We followed several miles and opened upon them with our artillery, when they retired to the hills beyond our reach. We then returned to the command, which resumed its march about 5 p. m. Continued march through the night, making little progress owing to extreme darkness and bad roads. Halted to feed and breakfast two miles from Tompkinsville at 7 a. m. of April 21st; then marched through Tompkinsville and on to Camp Boyle at Glasgow; where we arrived during a very hard rain, about 9 p. m. Glasgow and Tompkinsville, which had recently been permanently wrested from the enemy, were the most important southern positions held by our forces in southern Kentucky, and absolutely essential to our forces if we would gain and hold the line of the Cumberland; hence Glasgow was made the headquarters of General Judah's division, the third of the 23d Army Corps, now commanded by Major General George L. Hartsuff. Department commander, Major General Ambrose E. Burnside. Our brigade, the first, was nominally commanded by Brigadier General Mahlon D. Manson, though on every active expedition it was commanded by Colonel Graham. Our brigade was now composed of 107th Illinois Infantry, Colonel Joseph Kelly commanding; 23d Michigan Infantry, Colonel Marshall W. Chapin commanding; 5th Indiana Cavalry, Colonel Felix W. Graham commanding, and the 14th Illinois Cavalry, Colonel Horace Capron commanding. The artillery now belonging was, the Elgin, Illinois, Battery, 4 howitzers, 24 pounders, and 6 James rifles, 6 pounders, Lieutenant Andrew M. Wood commanding, and Henshaw's Illinois Battery, 4, 6 pounders and 2 James 6 pounders, Captain Edward C. Henshaw commanding (see appendix to part 2d, page 969). Besides this artillery, the 5th Indiana had 2 Rodman guns, and the 14th Illinois had 4 mountain howitzers, 6 pounders. The situation in Kentucky is shown by official reports. Burnside to Hallack, April 21st (see part 2d, page 265): "Rebel General Humphrey Marshall in S. E. Kentucky with from 1,500 to 4,000. Also about 4,000 cavalry near Monticello. General Marshall reports, April 18th (page 777), that he had moved into Kentucky and had been in 15 counties. In February his total force was

7,667, cavalry and artillery alone, 2,467 (see page 638). On page 773, Part 2d, Vol. 23, is rebel report April 15th, '63, showing Morgan's command at McMinnville with 6,000 or 8,000 cavalry. Wharton's toward Murfreesborough, 2,000; Forrest and Vandorn at Columbia, 10,000. Morgan's (assorted) command still in southeastern Kentucky." This is information from rebel sources. Besides were the commands of Colonel Pegram and Colonel Scott. Burnside well said of this period: "Skirmishing by the cavalry with the enemy was of almost daily occurrence."

Much of our service in Kentucky was the sending out of detachments to scout the country and drive out raiding parties of the enemy; an important and tedious service, as it was of almost daily occurrence; yet as detachment service was seldom reported, we could gather but few details and thus this important service, except on few occasions, is of necessity omitted from our record. We remained in Camp Boyles three days; receiving meanwhile the four mountain howitzers as before spoken of. We now heard that after we returned from Celina, Hamilton's force marched to Tompkinsville and burned the courthouse there, and killed several Union citizens, and committed other depredations (see page 273). Tompkinsville, as well as all of Monroe county, was intensely loyal; the county having furnished but 30 votes to secession and but 30 recruits to the rebel army; hence the intense hatred of the rebels toward them. The enemy were reported in force at Celina and a force was ordered to be sent from Glasgow against them.

April 25th, 350 of the 14th Cavalry, 350 of the 5th Indiana Cavalry, and 200 of the 107th Illinois Infantry and the howitzers of the 14th, again under command of Colonel Graham started for Celina; reached Tompkinsville at sundown; camped near. The rebels had fallen back to Celina.

April 26th, marched to within one mile of Celina and camped; rained hard; sent out scouting parties; day's march, 16 miles. Burnside says, page 277, April 25th: "1,400 cavalry from Glasgow are moving upon Tompkinsville, which I will, if possible, move to Burksville." On same page and date Burnside said to General Boyle: "Tell Graham to look out for a move by Morgan in the direction of Glasgow, and to threaten Burksville and Celina from

Tompkinsville." So it appears that Burnside intended this move more as a feint to divert Morgan from his intended attack on Glasgow.

As the rebel main command at Tompkinsville had fallen back to Celina, it was decided that Graham's main command should proceed there, with a large detachment sent toward Burksville to watch Morgan. On page 279, part 2d, April 26th, Hobson says: "Colonel Graham was at Tompkinsville last night; his scouts near Burksville report Pegram with his force near Burksville and Albany. Scouting parties of the 14th were near Gainsburg; captured 16 prisoners from Morgan's and Hamilton's command. Hamilton and Johnson's forces are in the vicinity of Celina. Wheeler and Morgan are reported near Gainesborough with 6,000 men and batteries. This information is regarded as reliable. Colonel Graham will move his main force to Celina; will keep sufficient force at that point to prevent rebels from crossing the river. Reconnoitering parties will be kept on roads leading to Burnett's ferry and Gainesborough. I have instructed him to blockade all places if rebels advance in large force, and if he is compelled to fall back on Glasgow to give me information of his own and rebel movements. It appears that Graham's force at Tompkinsville and Celina will have all it can do to watch Pegram and Morgan." Pegram had 2,000 and Morgan from 1,500 to 3,000, enough surely to keep us busy without the pestering raids of Hamilton and other Cumberland robbers.

April 27th, sent out scouting parties through the day, who have occasional skirmishing across the river.

Afternoon, Companies "I" and "L," of the 14th, with the howitzers, were sent down the river two miles and discovered the enemy in force across the river. The order was given "Prepare to fight on foot." This order is obeyed by counting off by fours from right to left, then numbers one, two and three throw their halters to number four, who takes charge of their horses. After one, two and three have dismounted the horses are taken to the safest convenient place, while the dismounted men form a new line, counting off again, and are ready for any movement on foot. In this case we marched to the foot of a high ridge which with difficulty we climbed, and formed line on its summit in the hopes that the altitude would enable our shots to take effect. We were now joined by one company of the 5th and one company of the 107th. The carbine shots fell short, only a few reaching to their position. The guns of the infantry were more effective; between them all after some of the rebels or their horses seemed to be struck, they all scampered back to their favorite hills.

We were now in full view of Major Hamilton's dwelling, a large frame house standing on an eminence a little below us and about one mile off. As we had no affection to waste on this robber it was deemed that the better way to get rid of pestiferous rats was to destroy their nests. The howitzers were moved down the river to a point opposite this dwelling and a little target practice was instituted until it was found that with our best efforts the shells fell short. We now received orders to return to camp, which we reached about 9 p. m. Remained in camp until midnight awaiting the coming in of other scouts, then marched toward Tompkinsville in thick darkness and heavy rains. Marched through heavy forests and over broken roads until 8 a. m. of April 28th, halted and camped a half mile east of the road and a half mile north of the state line; called this "Camp Hills." This camp lay in a flat valley between two ranges of hills. We had a heavy rain before noon. Our only protection against it was our ponchos and blankets spread upon poles. Having exhausted our coffee our fare was hardtack and sowbelly while it lasted. Experience had not yet taught us that even this fare in plenty was feasting for soldiers in active service. This lesson was well learned afterward. The sudden heavy rain soon brought a flood rolling down this valley in such quantity and so suddenly that before we were aware our belongings that would swim were floating around us, and with difficulty we saved them by hastily saddling our horses, packing our things and mounting and riding through the rising flood to "terra firma" on the hills. We remained quietly encamped until May 1st, when our Sibley tents arrived from Glasgow; but we were now out of rations. Citizens brought in pies and cornbread for sale. The boys declared that the pies were worth more than the cost to half sole their boots with, and the cornbread could be used in our howitzers in place of shells. Scouting parties sent out captured a few prisoners.

May 3d in the evening the camp was alarmed and the command called out and formed line awaiting an expected attack, but no enemy appeared. Part 2d, Vol. 23d, page 293, Burnside says: "April 29th: Colonel Graham is at Tompkinsville with outposts at Burnett's ferry, Celina, Burksville and other crossings on the river. He has been skirmishing yesterday and today, with results in his favor. Morgan and Wheeler were at or near Gainesborough." And on same page: "Pegram near at hand. Colonel Graham's movements are very satisfactory; let him remain in the vicinity of Tompkinsville, but look out that he is not caught." On page 293 is another favorable reference to his command.

On page 296 April 30th, instructions from Burnside to General Boyle, show the great anxiety for the defense of Glasgow and the importance of the trust assigned to our brigade in its advanced position, in the presence of strong forces of the enemy and in their scattered condition, compelled to watch the enemy at points distant from each other and at the same time to defend the advanced post at Glasgow, now far in our rear. The caution to Graham to "look out and not get caught," was hardly needed by that vigilant officer, with the 14th Illinois Cavalry and the 5th Indiana Cavalry as his scouts.

Page 297, April 28th, General Boyle says: "General Hobson dispatches me that detachments of the 5th Indiana and 14th Illinois Cavalry, on the 25th inst. near Jamestown and Scottsville, captured 23 rebels, 35 horses, 2 mules, 1 yoke of oxen, sundry small arms and some merchandise, and destroyed a mill grinding for General Morgan. Expedition last heard from at Celina." On same page Hobson says: "Colonel Graham in his expedition has captured 30 rebels, shelled the enemy at Celina and drove them from that place, attacked 600 at Bennett's ferry, shelling them at long range, killing one. * * * I fear if he withdraws to Glasgow the scoundrels will come and desolate the country yet. A force should be kept in the works at Glasgow."

May 4th, in camp until 3 p. m. when we moved toward Tompkinsville; hard rains had made the roads heavy and our progress was slow, as we dare not leave trains and artillery far behind. Marched through Tompkinsville and bivouacked a mile from town, about 1 a. m. of May 5th; rained very hard through the night and we got soaking wet, as we had no shelter. At 9 a. m. (May 5th) marched toward Glasgow, reached Camp Boyle at 9 p. m.; pleasant day but bad roads. In the morning May 5th, 15 men of Company "I" were sent back to Camp Hills with ambulances for some sick left near there; they hear many rumors of forces of the enemy near. Citizens warn them to hasten away. They get the sick in the ambulances and return and when near Tompkinsville they are ordered back to Camp Hills for some beef cattle left there. Again they are earnestly warned to hasten; but they take their own time and procure a yoke for the cattle, the easier to drive them. When they reached Tompkinsville they got supper and captured five of John Morgan's men; then marched 8 miles toward Glasgow, put out pickets and camped. The main command marched on the 5th 23 miles; this detachment marched about 32 miles and on the 6th marched 16 miles to Glasgow. Our loss on this expedition was light; that of the enemy only partly known. The main command captured 30. The various detachments full twice as many. A few were killed; their known loss about 100. In part 2d, page 318 are instructions for Graham to keep his forces well in hand, and guard carefully all the fords on the river. Detachments of the 14th and 5th were kept busy driving out raiding parties and scouting the river borders; while the remainder of the brigade was kept at Glasgow for its defense, and ready for any movement that might be needed. Through the remainder of May and June there was a great amount of sickness in Camp Boyle, which depleted our brigade by deaths and disabilities. May 15th the reported effective strength was 800; the 107th was 700, and the 5th 1,000, but soon after the strength of each was greatly diminished. Fortunately for us, our recent success on and near the Cumberland river, had tended to quiet the rebels in that region, or at the least, it rendered them more timid; while standing orders to Generals Burnside and Rosecrans at the first opportunity to move simultaneously into upper and lower East Tennessee, kept Bragg's cavalry constantly

GENERAL HORACE CAPRON

on the alert to guard against that movement, so that during this period of weakness the rebel raids were less in number and in strength. Colonel Sanders' raid into eastern Tennessee with 1,500 cavalry begun June 14th and returning June 24th in which he boldly marched through upper East Tennessee, destroying much military property, railroad and bridges, and strongly threatened Knoxville, caused the enemy to believe that the day of judgment was at hand; and was doubtless the origin of the bold countermovement made soon after by General John H. Morgan. Meanwhile the cavalry at Glasgow able for duty were out almost daily after raiding parties of the enemy, who supposed that the withdrawal of a strong force of cavalry under Colonel Sanders gave them increased opportunities for plunder. The following is from a letter to friends at home, written by one of the authors: "The 14th and the 5th send out scouting parties nearly every day. A short time ago a party of the 5th were out toward Columbia on scout; they allowed themselves to be surprised by a stronger party of Hamilton's band, and a number were captured. Colonel Graham sent out a detachment of the 14th and the 5th, under Major Woolley, of the 5th, who pursued the rebels toward Jamestown. The enemy separated into two parties. Our command also separated; the 5th, under Major Woolley, followed their party to the river where they abandoned pursuit. The 14th band pursued their party to the river and after the rebels crossed, our party also stealthily crossed and learning the location of the rebel camp, they determined to surprise them. They marched rapidly at night and succeeded in surrounding the camp of the enemy, but owing to the premature attack by a portion of our band the rebels were enabled to escape through the gap not yet closed up. Major Hamilton barely escaped by mounting, barebacked, his superb iron gray charger, and riding through a volley of carbine shots, leaving his hat, sword and trunk, containing his private papers, the pay rolls of his command, $15,000 in stolen greenbacks, and $40,000 of Confederate money—worthless rags, except to pay rampant rebels *in their own coin.* Our band succeeded in killing a few and capturing 36, with two small cannon, and several hundred stand of arms, and some wagons, which, with the arms, were burned, and a lot of horses and mules which, with the cannon, were brought to Glasgow. Yesterday (says the letter) a party returned who had pursued a band of rebels that had intercepted a train loaded with broken down U. S. horses that were being sent to Louisville to be recruited up. Our party pursued, and when near Bowling Green, another Union party came out and 25 of the rebels were killed and 50 captured, with all their horses and the captured horses also. The details of such service, could all have been gathered, would, of itself, make an interesting history. The few that are given are fair samples of the many unrecorded. These predatory parties were always driven to their hiding places; but a few hours' rest, and they were ready for another venture. Their facilities for hiding when pursued closely were not only the hills and unsettled regions bordering the Cumberland river, but if very closely pursued, as they were dressed in citizen's clothing, they had only to disperse and hide their arms, when with impunity they could, as they often did, stand in groups by the cabins at the road side, watching our columns as they passed; there being no way of recognizing them as the raiders. Woe to the small parties of Union men who encountered strong parties of these banditti. On more than one occasion were these prisoners shot down in cold blood, with their own guns.

A party of these robbers attacked Scottsville, where was only a small hospital guard to protect our sick soldiers left there; the guard was overpowered and the sick were murdered in their beds.

June 30th, our brigade reported some change in its organization; now composed of 14th Illinois Cavalry, 5th Indiana Cavalry, 107th Illinois Infantry, 23d Michigan Infantry and 111th Ohio Infantry, with the same batteries as before and the same brigade commander.

In Part 1st, page 367, is official report of Colonel Graham, June 12th, 1863, in which he reports the result of an expedition sent to the Cumberland river; 250 of the 14th, 300 of the 5th, with the howitzers of the 14th, under Colonel Capron, left Glasgow June 8th, were joined by 100 men of 14th and 100 of the 5th and marched to Burksville and Rays crossroads; learning of the whereabouts of the rebel camp on the other side of the river, they crossed.

Colonel Graham tells of the attack on Hamilton's men three miles from their camp; of the pursuit and capture of some prisoners; and of the capture of their camp and cannon. The officers of the 14th that Colonel Graham especially mentioned were, Colonel Capron, Major Quigg, Major Tompkins and Captain Sanford, of Company "K," 14th Illinois. Colonel Graham sums up the result of the expedition as the total rout of Hamilton's command, about 40 killed, 36 captured, 2 12-pound howitzers, 7 wagons, 40 horses and mules and 7 head of cattle and a large quantity of flour and corn, and about $10,000 in Confederate notes, and all their camp equipage. The wagons, ammunition and guns were burned, the remainder of the capture was brought to Glasgow. Colonel Graham adds: "I desire to thank all the officers and men of my command for good behavior and prompt obedience to orders." On page 369, Vol. 23, Part 1st, Series 1st, is the following from General Judah, division commander: "Glasgow, June 17th, 1863. Col. Graham and his officers and men are favorably commended to the notice of the Major General commanding the 23d Army Corps." On the same page is report of rebel John H. Morgan: "June 12th, 1863. The enemy surprised Hamilton's battalion at Kettle creek on the 9th inst., capturing two pieces artillery, wagons and stores, and $25,000 public funds, and many men and horses; scattering the entire command. Major Hamilton had been ordered to report to Colonel R. C. Morgan, but refused. There is now no force on the Cumberland river and the entire rear of this flank is exposed to raids, which no doubt the enemy will attempt, and if successful, with most disastrous results."

The raid of Colonel Sanders, before referred to, now occurred. In consequence of Sanders' raid and the routing of Hamilton's force, we had a short period of rest, but it was only the calm that preceded the storm of General Morgan's great raid, the motive of which was doubtless the revival of sinking courage in the rebel ranks, by a bold counter movement. Nothing more of note occurred until the Morgain raid, and we close this, the first chapter of our history, which to us, though disagreeable in the nature of the service, was the very best possible training which led to our future extraordinary success.

CHAPTER II.

THE GREAT MORGAN RAID ACROSS THE OHIO RIVER.

In recording this interesting campaign, in addition to the original notes of Sanford, West and Featherson, we are indebted for important contributons to the following: Lieutenant H. C. Connelly, of Company "L" (afterward promoted); Captain Wm. R. Sanford, of Company "K," and Acting Adjutant Isaac H. Allen. Each of these have contributed much. The government published records, Series One, Volume Twenty-three. Part first, contains nearly 400 reports, references and dispatches pertaining to this important campaign. These have all been carefully examined and the important part relative to our service is embodied. Some fine descriptions and reminiscences have been crowded out for want of room, but not to the exclusion of any historical facts. Morgan never made any report and all that can be gathered from Confederate reports is found in General Wheeler's report, pages 817 and 818. In reporting to Confederate headquarters November 7th, 1863, Wheeler says: "Morgan asked privilege June 14th to take a cavalry force and attack Louisville, Ky., where he said the enemy had but 300 men." Wheeler consulted Bragg, who consented, providing Morgan would take but 1,500 men, and all the artillery he wanted. Morgan said he could accomplish all with 2,000; his object being to destroy the transportation, shipping and U. S. government property at Louisville. Morgan says: "Can I go?" Wheeler and Bragg consented and Wheeler adds: "Not one word was said about his crossing the Ohio river; on the contrary he was urged to observe the importance of his return to our army as rapidly as possible." The real reason for his finally crossing the Ohio river will be disclosed as we proceed, and the number of men with which he crossed will be satisfactorily estimated in the close. Brigadier General Henry M. Judah, commanded third division of the 23d Army Corps, of which our brigade, the first, was posted at Glasgow. The second brigade was commanded by Brigadier General Edward H. Hobson. Brigadier General James M. Shackelford commanded the first brigade of the second division posted at Russellville, about 30 miles south of west from Glasgow. June 22d reports had reached us that Morgan, at the head of a large mounted force, was about to invade Kentucky, and indications pointed to the probability that he would strike Scottsville or Gallatin, west of Glasgow, in penetrating our lines. Page 441 Judah says to Shackelford: "I have Carthage, and shall occupy La Fayette, Tompkinsville and Marrowbone." And he asks Shackelford to throw forward scouts via Franklin, to watch between Scottsville and the railroad. The effective force of our brigade marched at 8 a. m. June 22d, toward Scottsville 12 miles and camped; weather very warm. June 23d marched at 6 a. m., 14th in advance. Camped at 5 p. m. at Scottsville, a small town south of west from Glasgow 25 miles. Most of its citizens were rebels. (See also General Judah's report, page 655.) From 24th to 26th in camp with much rain and small rations. Morgan is now reported to be approaching Carthage, Tennessee. June 26th, marched at 9 a. m. 3 miles (and camped near Barren river. June 28th in camp. June 29th, forded Barren river and marched toward Tompkinsville and camped near Jamestown. June 30th, marched to Tompkinsville, 25 miles, camped near; mustered for pay. July 1st to July 4th in camp. For days the weather has been excessively warm, with many showers. July 2d Major Quigg and Captain Dent, with 150 men of the 14th Illinois, were sent on reconnoissance on the lower Burksville road to Turkeyneck bend. July 4th, marched to Glasgow, 25 miles, and camped on the old ground; our camp there was called "Camp Boyles." Our scout to Turkeyneck bend reported the enemy's pickets in sight at that point, but learned that his main force had moved toward Burkeville farther east. General Judah, page 655, says: "On 3d instant a portion of his forces attempted to force the position at Marrowbone held by my second brigade under General Hobson, and were handsomely repulsed. I determined to attack the enemy at Burksville, moving up my first brigade under General Manson during the night for that purpose. Before the necessary orders could be given word was received from the front that the enemy had disappeared. Although I had every reason to apprehend resistance to his advance at Columbia from the U. S. forces from Jamestown or other points, I dispatched General Shackelford with his brigade, within half an hour in the direction of Columbia, having previously reinforced him by the 12th Kentucky Cavalry from my division. On the ensuing morning I started General Hobson's brigade in the same direction, with orders to move according to circumstances."

From necessity Shackelford's brigade and Hobson's were merged into one command under the command of General Hobson, and so remained until the capture of Morgan's command. Judah says: "Before leaving Marrowbone I ordered my first brigade from Tompkinsville to Glasgow, under General Manson; proceeding there myself." Again: "Upon arriving there I took command in person of its cavalry, consisting of the 5th Indiana Cavalry, under Lieutenant Colonel Butler, the 14th Illinois Cavalry, under Colonel Horace Capron, and the 11th Kentucky, under Major ———, including two 3-inch Rodman guns (of the 5th Indiana), and four mountain howitzers (of the 14th Illinois), in all 1,200 men, and marched for Greensburg."

July 5th, severe sickness at Glasgow had disabled many of the brigade, both infantry and cavalry, so that from these, and from other commands a large number of convalescents there were organized into a convalescent corps, under the command of Major David Quigg, of the 14th Illinois Cavalry. These were to be used, as far as they were able, in defending Glasgow and all southern Kentucky, against rebel raids through that country, in the absence of so much of our effective cavalry now in pursuit of Morgan.

The troops under Burnside then in Kentucky, were a portion of the 23d Army Corps, about 20,000 in all, infantry and mounted forces. These were scattered over the state. At Somerset, Ky., 3,524, being 3 infantry and 4 mounted regiments. At Mount Vernon a brigade, 3,042, being 3 infantry and 3 mounted regiments. At Jamestown, 1,304, 3 mounted regiments. At Russellville, Shackelford's brigade, 2,254, 2 infantry, 2½ mounted. At Glasgow, one brigade, 2,591, 3 infantry, 2 cavalry. At

Marrowbone, 2,435, 3 infantry, 3 mounted. At Carthage, 1,563, 3 infantry, 1 mounted. Of these General Judah had at the front, 3 brigades, aggregating 7,280, more than half of which was infantry, incapable of being moved quick enough to head off a mounted force, so that he had available for this purpose not more than 3,640, and these scattered all along southern Kentucky, as Morgan's maneuvering left Judah in doubt where he would attempt to cross into Kentucky. Considering the secretness and swiftness of Morgan's movements, it was remarkable that General Judah was able to maneuver as well as he did, and as Morgan finally crossed above or farther east than his assigned limits it was but reasonable that he should expect the United States forces farther east to meet him. It was not then anticipated that Morgan would be able to baffle the Union forces as he did. Kentucky was filled with rebel sympathizers that furnished hundreds of young men mounted on good horses, as recruits to his army. And in addition, these rebel sympathizers aided in spreading false rumors, and in tearing down telegraph lines, and in sending false dispatches, and for this last purpose Morgan had with him an expert telegrapher, with all needed appliances by which Union dispatches were intercepted, and bogus messages sent in their stead. By these means he so far succeeded that none but Judah's forces attempted to intercept him; and these he flanked by passing beyond their reach. He then turned westward, passed near the forces at Jamestown and Somerset, and attacked the slender force at Columbia. On July 4th he attacked a small force at Tebbs bend, commanded by Colonel Orlando Moore, and got whipped. He then hastened to Lebanon, and after a hard fight of hours with the small force there, he got possession by a trick, and compelled his captives to keep pace on foot with his mounted forces on double quick for 9 miles, on that extremely hot July day. Three or four of the captives died of over-exertion, or were knocked in the head because they could not keep up. But for a timely shower doubtless all would have died. See pages 647 and 649, Series 1, Volume 23, Part 1st.

Shackelford and Hobson were now pressing up, and other forces were gathering to their support. Because one of our officers reproved them for their inhuman treatment of prisoners, Captain Morgan, a brother of the general, seized him and threatened to shoot him. This was the gallant John Morgan, who, though a coward by nature, was enabled through the greatest amount of cunning ever displayed by a military leader, and through the greatest exercise of barbarity, to accomplish one of the greatest raids ever recorded, but which ended in the destruction of his army and in landing himself in the Ohio penitentiary.

We will now leave our pursuing forces in eastern Kentucky, who have turned Morgan toward the west, and will return to our command under General Judah.

July 5th the choice, able-bodied cavalry of the brigade, 1,200 strong, marched at 7 a. m. on the Louisburg pike a few miles, then turned on a byroad eastward; marched 20 miles and camped near Barren river; no rations for man or horse.

July 6th. All day occupied in crossing Green river, which was very high. Companies "I" and "K" crossed by swimming, and the rest of the brigade by means of a ferry. Marched one mile and camped. Captain Sanford, with 150 men of 14th, advance pickets.

July 7th. Learning that Morgan is turning westward with evident intent to destroy the Louisville & Nashville Railroad, and make his way back to the rebel lines, at 4 a. m. we marched rapidly toward Elizabethtown, avoiding all towns, and camped after dark, having marched 35 miles.

July 8th. Reveille at 4 a. m.; marched early; passed through Hudsonville. A part of Morgan's force had been here the night previous. Arrived at Elizabethtown at 3 p. m.; marched 25 miles. Here we were ordered to leave all clothing not absolutely needed in that extremely hot weather; it was boxed up, but eventually ruined by much rain, and we believe that through some mismanagement the men never received compensation. In Part 2d, page 517, is an order of General Judah dated Elizabethtown, July 6th, assigning Colonel Horace Capron, of the 14th Illinois Cavalry, to the command temporarily of the cavalry brigade composed of 14th Illinois, 5th Indiana, and 11th Kentucky Cavalry. Page 656, Judah says: "Deeming it useless after crossing (Green river) to attempt to join the pursuing forces, I directed my march upon the

LIEUTENANT COLONEL DAVID P. JENKINS.

left flank of the enemy, for the purpose of intercepting him upon his attempt to return, after crossing the Louisville & Nashville Railroad. We remained at Elizabethtown until 9 p. m., then marched in the night toward Litchfield; reached Litchfield much fatigued at 7 a. m. of July 10th. Here learned that Morgan had passed through, and was now near the Ohio river, with the undoubted intention of crossing into Indiana. Camped near the village, having marched 31 miles. All day in camp cleaning arms and washing clothes.

July 11th, 6 a. m. Marched to Elizabethtown; arrived after night after a fatiguing march of 31 miles through deep mud. Hobson and Shackelford are in close pursuit of Morgan. Morgan was so keenly pursued by our cavalry, which gathered strength as it proceeded, that he forgot all about Louisville and its 300, and the nice plunder he expected to pilfer, and began to think of "Home, Sweet Home;" and turning in that direction he found 1,200 resolute men pressing up to give him battle; and though he had nearly four times that force, he had no appetite for a fight unless he could attack a much weaker force than ours. There was now no alternative but to fight or cross the Ohio river; he chose the latter as promising the least amount of fight. On July 8th, at Bradenburg, Morgan captured two steamboats and crossed into Indiana. The United States steamer "Springfield" engaged Morgan, but could not prevent his crossing. The whole country was now in a flutter of excitement, especially the people of Indiana. Messages flew over the wires from the President, and from Governors, and by the hundreds from all grades of army officers. Governor Morton feared Morgan would attack Indianapolis, 120 miles distant; but he attacked Corydon, and then Salem, and then made his way eastward where he supposed he had many sympathizing friends; but the barbarity of his treatment of the people left few sympathizers in his rear. Stores, mills and dwellings were robbed and burned with impunity. Hobson and Shackelford crossed as soon as boats could be procured, and followed as rapidly as the exhausted condition of their men and horses would permit; but now is again displayed the cunning of Morgan that never forsook him. He kept out men five miles on each flank, collecting all the horses fit for service; so that while keeping his men splendidly mounted for rapid and constant marching, he left no horses in his rear by which Hobson and Shackelford could remount their men, while the condition of their horses not only prevented rapid marches, but they were constantly dropping on the route, and could not be replaced except by horses never fit for the service. Nor was this all. He dressed some of his men in citizen's clothes, with instructions where important roads met, to come rushing up breathlessly and, imitating excited citizens, to implore the Union cavalry to hasten to defend certain points upon which they stated that Morgan was marching; thus endeavoring, and often successfully, to deviate from the direct course of pursuit. But on the other hand, not only were many forces of militia called out, but these inexperienced men Morgan swept from his path with ease; but another method of obstruction was more successful. Citizens turned out by scores and hundreds and leveled forests in his path. These of course also somewhat impeded the Union cavalry, but by the aid of citizens this obstructed the Union cavalry much less than it did Morgan's forces.

It now seemed apparent that Morgan was seeking a possible crossing of the Ohio. General Judah was ordered to Louisville to take boats up the Ohio river, to head off Morgan if he attempted to recross the river.

July 11th, night; under orders to take the cars for Louisville; the men are all eager excitement. The 5th was engaged all night in shipping their horses.

July 12th. All day with horses saddled awaiting to take the cars. At 9 p. m. marched to the depot and began shipping our horses, which occupied till midnight. The train started at 1 a. m. of July 13th, arrived at Louisville at 7 a. m.; unshipped and fed our horses, then marched to the soldiers' home where was provided a bountiful repast of substantial food; then mounted and marched out of the city two miles, expecting to camp. It rained hard. We unsaddled, but in a half hour "Boots and Saddles" sounded, and we marched down to the river to be shipped on boats. Boarding the boats occupied the day until 4 p. m., when our fleet of fifteen steamers, containing our brigade, steamed up the river toward Cincinnati, running all of that beautiful moonlight night.

July 14. Still sailing up the Ohio river; reached Cincinnati 3 p. m. We were received with much rejoicing and military display.

July 15. New horses received today. Again boarded the boats; all of our brigade except the 11th Kentucky, which was left behind. At 4 p. m. again started up the river in our flotilla.

July 16th. Still sailing up the river; passed Maryville, 7 a. m.; here several gunboats joined our flotilla. The people along the river were wild with delight. Reached Portsmouth 4 p. m., where we landed and enjoyed a warm reception by the citizens. Every luxury which the rich surrounding country produced, and the commerce of the Ohio river supplied, was furnished us to the full. At 9 p. m. marched up the river to Portland.

July 17th. Halted at sunrise and fed hay in a meadow. We had missed our road in the night, so only marched 12 miles up the river. We rested a half hour, then on again double quick through a very hilly country, being hastily treated to pies, cakes and apples by the overjoyed citizens as we sped quickly by. Four miles from Centerville our artillery was hastily planted in expectation of battle; heard that Morgan was marching on that place. We now increased our speed to a run to intercept him. We galloped through the town and formed line of battle on the side of a hill; planting our batteries on the summit, and waited in line two hours to give Johnny a military reception; then heard that friend John had turned on another road about six miles off. Now ordered into camp, having marched 30 miles.

July 18th. Marched at 4 a. m. toward Pomeroy; leaving Cheshire to the right. Morgan had sent a regiment in that direction to throw his pursuers off the track. On page 656, Judah says: "Early on the ensuing morning (July 18th) I continued my march toward Pomeroy on the enemy's right flank, and between him and the river, with the intention of consummating on the banks of the Ohio what his sudden change of direction prevented me from doing on those of Green river. I remained at Pomeroy long enough to ascertain definitely that the enemy was making (via Chester) for Buffington bar, on the Ohio river." We reached Pomeroy about dark, passed through on double quick, and were greeted from every dwelling with deafening cheers and waving flags. We were bountifully fed by the ladies of the town. Distance from Centerville 30 miles. Citizens of Bridgeport and Pomeroy have been bushwhacking Morgan all day. While we were feasting, the ladies cheered us with their songs, but in the midst of our entertainment is heard the discordant notes of the bugle sounding "To horse" and we speedily mount and onward again up the river road. Marched all night until an hour before day we halted for a short rest.

Sunday, July 19th. Foggy morning; marched double quick and soon our ears are greeted with sounds of musketry in front in direction of Buffington Island. When within a mile of that place our advance drove their pickets in. Our boys were eager for the contest, but coolly executed the needed preparations for battle. In the beginning, however, the fight was against us. General Judah and his body guard of the 5th Indiana were drawn into an ambush which the rebels said was designed to entrap home guards, and they seemed much surprised to find that the attacking party was General Judah's command. When our advance were passing through a lane the enemy rose up from their concealment in front and on either side and poured a hot fire into our advance. In his report on page 656 General Judah describes this affair and says that Major McCook (the father of the famous Generals McCook) who soon after died of his wounds, was mortally wounded, two privates were killed and nearly 30 of his command were captured, including Captain R. C. Kice and Captain Grafton and 10 men were wounded. The advance were roughly handled and were forced to beat a hasty and not very methodical retreat. Henshaw's two guns were planted, but could not be used on the furiously charging foe without destroying the no less impetuously retreating friends. On came the mingled mass plump over the battery, knocking over one of the guns, which fell into the enemy's hands; the other gun was brought safely off. The 14th Illinois now made a vigorous counter charge and drove back the enemy and recaptured our lost gun and one of the enemy's guns with it. The battle now raged with fury; the enemy using all his guns. Henshaw's guns were used, but not so effectually as the howitzer battery of the 14th Illinois, which, under the command of Lieutenant Kilbourne, of Company "I," 14th Illinois Cavalry, secured a good position within its best range—a half mile—and it was here that Sergeant Guy Niles, of Company "I," first displayed his superior skill, which marked him as one of the best gunners in the Union service. All the officers spoke in high praise of the service of the howitzer battery that day. The guns of the 5th Indiana Cavalry also did effective service. In half an hour we forced the enemy to a new position on a high hill. We pressed forward and planted all our guns and began a furious rain of shells in their midst. We now heard the roar of battle on our left, which was the advance of Hobson's division under Colonel Kautz and Colonel Sanders. The worn condition of Hobson's command rendered it impossible for his main force to keep pace with the rapidly fleeing rebels, whom Morgan had kept supplied with fresh horses by his thieving tricks. Colonel Kautz, with 200, and Colonel Sanders, with a few men, the best mounted of Hobson's forces, had pressed forward with all possible speed, and were now attacking Morgan in the rear whilst our attack was on his right flank. See Hobson's report, page 660, and Colonel Kautz' report, page 662, and Colonel Sanders' report, page 664.

Colonel Sanders says: "I found the enemy were retreating soon after my artillery opened, and followed with the 8th and 9th Michigan Cavalry. These troops, and especially the 8th and the 9th Michigan Cavalry, now did excellent service in completing the victory over the enemy and in capturing many of them." Colonel Wormer (page 666) speaks of his men—the 8th Michigan—in the pursuit and of the effective use of their guns, the Spencer (7-shooter) rifles. General Judah had not only the great bulk of our attacking force, being his whole brigade, but we also preceded the attack of Hobson's men by at least half an hour, but this does not in the least detract from the merits of General Hobson's men. Never in the history of wars did any military body perform greater and more long continued and fatiguing service than did Hobson's men in their determined and unflagging pursuit of Morgan. Day and night for nearly one month did they pursue, while their horses, worn down with excessive service, gave out or were compelled to a slow pace; while Morgan's men were kept supplied with fresh horses. It was a great misfortune but yet a very natural result, that Generals Judah and Hobson should have so disagreed relative to the now reunited brigades. Before General Judah sent Generals Hobson and Shackelford's brigades in direct pursuit of Morgan, General Judah commanded the division and though, for convenience in receiving orders, Hobson was placed in command of these pursuing forces, General Judah deemed this only a temporary arrangement and when the brigades were reunited Judah claimed the right to command the whole reunited division, whilst General Hobson claimed that his command was a permanent arrangement. It must have been a perplexing point for General Burnside to decide, as the official reports do not show his decision, further than this, that the subsequent movements all seemed to be placed under the management of General Shackelford, whose brigade had been ordered to reinforce Judah's division in Kentucky. General Judah describes the commencement of his attack (see page 656) : "Traveling all night I reached the last descent to the river bottom at Buffington bar at 5 :30 a. m. the 19th, halting my force and placing my artillery in commanding positions. I determined to make a reconnoissance in person to ascertain if report made to me was true that the gunboats had left, and that the enemy had been crossing all night. A very dense fog enveloped everything, confining the view to a radius of 50 yards." The substance of General Judah's further description we have already given. He says Colonel Basil Duke commanded the force that routed his advance. He also says, that our batteries were then brought into position, which soon silenced the enemy's batteries, and in half an hour broke their lines and drove them in confusion back on Hobson's forces, who engaged them on another road. His prisoners, the piece of artillery they had captured, and his own artillery, five pieces, his camp equipage, transportation and plunder of all kinds, was abandoned and captured, also a large number of prisoners, among them Colonels Basil Duke and Dick Morgan and Allen, and the most of Morgan's staff. Judah says: "After the attack on my advance the gunboats came up and opened a fire upon the retreating enemy." General

Judah speaks in high praise of his officers and men. Many of the enemy attempted to escape across the river. A few succeeded, some were drowned, some were killed by the gunboats and the remainder were driven back.

As to the number of prisoners captured at Buffington Island it is difficult to estimate correctly, because of the double claiming of the various commands. If estimated as apparently reported it would make Morgan's force at least 6,000; but it is doubtless true that the claims of captures by the smaller commands were sometimes estimated in the aggregate of larger commands; but the most careful estimate would make Morgan's whole force to somewhat exceed Burnside's estimate in his general report, which was 4,000. Many of these were doubtless recruits gathered in Kentucky as he passed through, as General Wheeler suggested to him he might do. General Shackelford's report (pages 640 to 642), describes the sharp pursuit of Morgan; he says: "The enemy, finding his way of retreat cut off and being hotly pressed from the front (by Judah's force), fled to an immense bluff for refuge. A flag of truce was immediately sent up, demanding an immediate and unconditional surrender of Morgan and his command. The flag was met by Lieutenant Colonel Cicero Coleman and other rebel officers with another flag. They came down and desired a personal interview with me. They asked for one hour for consultation amongst their officers. I gave them 40 minutes, within which time the whole command, excepting General Morgan, with a detachment of about 600 officers and men who deserted the command, surrendered. It was my understanding and, as I learned, the understanding of many of the rebel officers and men, that Morgan himself had surrendered." Regarding the number of Morgan's force, General Burnside, in his general report (page 14), says: "The loss of Morgan's command, which came to Kentucky 4,000 strong, was a heavy blow to the rebellion and the brave men who followed him so persistently deserve the thanks of their country."

Our notes say: Company "I," of the 14th Illinois Cavalry, detailed for the purpose, buried two or three hundred of their dead. All of their armament and belongings—yes, and much that was not their belongings—fell into our hands. The battle ground was literally strewn with cloths, silks, ready made clothing, stockings, boots and shoes, and even baby clothing, in profuse abundance; the plunder of their many thieving and robbing operations, which included the taking of all the money they could find or could extract as a ransom of dwellings and public buildings which they otherwise would burn. Great pains were taken that everything stolen by them should, as far as possible, be restored to the rightful owners; but the many dwellings, stores, mills and other property, public and private, burned by Morgan's orders, could not be restored from their ashes.

The southern atmosphere of Indiana and Ohio had been much tainted by the miasma of copperheadism; but Morgan's cyclone of iniquity swept all this taint from the region of the path it traversed. No more rebel sympathizing there. We spent the rest of the day in scouting and in gathering up arms and other property, then went into camp, and unsaddled our horses for the first time in six days. If ever men enjoyed rest we did that night, having marched all the night previous, and that day 25 miles, and had a big fight.

July 20th. Company "I," 14th, buried several hundred of the enemy's dead, then by a rapid march rejoined their regiment at midnight, just as they went into camp at Pomeroy.

July 21st. Marched at daylight and reported to General Shackelford; heard that the captures reached 4,600 rebels. Shackelford's report (page 642), says: "On the morning of the 20th I called for 1,000 volunteers who could stay in their saddles as long as I would without eating or sleeping until we captured Morgan. The entire command would have volunteered, but for the want of horses. We could find but about 500 horses in the command fit for service. Colonel Capron, with his regiment, the 14th Illinois, reported to me on the night of the 20th, and volunteered 157 of his regiment (all who had fit horses). Colonel Wolford also volunteered with detachments of the 1st Kentucky and 2d East Tennessee, and 45th and 2d Ohio. We also had small detachments from other regiments. With 500 men, on the morning of the 21st, we

LIEUTENANT-COLONEL DAVID QUIGG.

resumed the chase. Traveling day and night we came up with the enemy the morning of the 24th at Washington. We drove in the rebel pickets and by flank movements drove the entire rebel force out of the town, killing and wounding several of the enemy. One mile east of Washington the enemy made a stand in a dense wood. We formed a line of battle and soon drove him from his position. He fell back two miles, tore up a bridge over a rugged stream and took a position in the woods on a high hill just beyond the bridge. The advance moved upon his left flank, while a portion of the 14th Illinois crossed the stream just above the bridge, and moved up the hill in the face of a heavy fire from the enemy; steadily they moved up and drove him before them. Late Friday evening he burned two bridges over Stillwater, causing considerable delay. At daylight on Saturday morning, the 25th, we came up with the enemy one mile from Athens, marching on a parallel road one quarter of a mile from ours. A half mile in advance the roads formed a junction. We pressed forward to it in time to see the enemy reversing his column and flying to the woods. We shelled him for 30 minutes. At dark on the 25th our main column reached Richmond. We heard that the enemy was moving from Springfield to Hamersville. We saved 5 miles by marching directly from Richmond to that place. At 12 o'clock at night met Major Rue, with 375 fresh men and horses, who was now given the advance. Reached Hamersville at daylight of 26th, proceeded 5 miles in direction of Salineville, heard that the enemy were moving upon Hamersville. Now heard that he was at Salineville. We pressed on for that point. Now heard that Major Way had encountered the enemy and captured 230. Learning that Morgan, with 400, had crossed the railroad and was going toward Smith's ford, we had gone about 7 miles when we learned that Morgan had run into the New Lisbon road, in advance of Major Rue. Then learned that Major Rue had come up with the enemy and wanted reinforcements. The whole column was thrown forward at the utmost speed of the horses. We came to where the roads forked. The enemy had gone to the left, and was between the two roads. My advance had taken the right hand road. I moved my column on the road the enemy had gone. On our approach some of the enemy ran and was fired upon. They were ordered to halt, but refused. A flag now came from the enemy. Morgan wanted a personal interview with me. Morgan claimed that he had surrendered to a militia captain. Morgan stated to me in the presence of Colonel Wolford and other officers that he became satisfied that escape from me was impossible; that he himself might have escaped by deserting his men, but this he would not do. He stated that he did not care for the militia, that he could, with the command he then had, whip all the militia in Ohio; yet he said that since crossing the Ohio he had found every man, woman and child his enemy; that every hill top was a telegraph, and every bush an ambush." When Morgan claimed to Major Rue that he had surrendered to a militia captain, the Major very properly (says Shackelford) "refused to take any action in the premises until I came up." After traveling back about two miles we halted to have the prisoners dismounted and disarmed. General Morgan then desired a private interview. He called three or four of his staff and Colonel Cluke. I asked Colonel Wolford to attend the interview. He claimed that he had surrendered to a militia captain, and that the captain had agreed to parole him, his officers and men. I stated that we had followed him 30 days and nights; that we had met and defeated him a number of times; we had captured nearly all of his command; that he had acknowledged in the presence of Colonel Wolford that he knew that I would capture him; that Major Rue had gone to his right, and Captain Ward to his left, and the main column was moving rapidly upon his rear; that he had acknowledged that the militia captain was no impediment in his way; showing by his own statement that he could, with the force he then had, whip all the militia in Ohio; that I regarded his surrender to the militia captain, under such circumstances, as not only absurd and ridiculous, but unfair and illegal, and that I would not recognize it at all. He then demanded to be placed back upon the field as I found him. I stated to him that his demand would not be considered for a moment; that he, together with his officers and men, would be delivered to Major General Burnside at Cincinnati, Ohio, and that he would take such action in the premises as he might

FOURTEENTH ILLINOIS CAVALRY.   47

think proper." General Morgan afterward appealed to Governor Tod, of Ohio, making the same claim of having surrendered to a captain of Ohio Militia, and asking his interference. That there might be no grounds left for complaint of unfair treatment, Governor Todd took the matter in hand, arranged a regular trial, at which it was proved by many witnesses, and by the alleged militia captain—James Burbick—that he was not a captain, but a private citizen sent to hold an interview about Morgan's passing peaceably through; that Morgan proposed to surrender to him on condition that he, his officers and men might be permitted to go home, and stating that he had a right to surrender to anyone. Not knowing his business, this private citizen accepted his surrender. For some of the proofs see Burbick's statement (page 810), L. W. Potter (page 809), Sheriff Jessee Duke and Wm. Hostetter, C. D. Mans (page 811), Cornelius Curry (page 813), L. W. Potter (page 814). On page 809 is this from Governor Todd to Secretary Stanton: "July 28. I visit General Burnside tonight to settle the question that Morgan raises as to his surrender. From what I can learn of the matter, it is all gammon on Morgan's part." Morgan and his officers were put for safekeeping in the Ohio penitentiary, not, however, as culprits, which their unnatural barbarity would have warranted, but as prisoners of war. Morgan afterward escaped, doubtless through the aid of rebel sympathizers. He succeeded in raising a new command, passed into East Tennesse, where few Union troops then were. While sleeping in a house near Greenville, East Tennessee, a good Union woman gave information to a Union command some miles off, who marched rapidly, surrounded the house and demanded surrender. Morgan's officers surrendered, but he refused, and attempted to escape and was shot dead. Major Rue made claims that Morgan had surrendered to him (see page 808). To this General Shackelford replied (see page 815): "I see that Major Rue still claims the capture of Morgan, under General Burnside. Rue reported to me on Saturday night, was acting directly under my orders, a part of the 1st and 3rd Kentucky Cavalry being in the front with him. Morgan never surrendered to Rue, (when he) came up with him he sent back to the head of the column for reinforcements.

Rue refused to take any action until I got up. In behalf of my command, who followed Morgan 30 days and nights, I appeal to the general, to set this matter right." Rue in his report of campaign (page 668), says: "I was sent in the advance by General Shackelford, to intercept Morgan, it possible, at the junction of the roads." He also says: "Morgan promptly dispatched a flag of truce, which met me in the advance with the demand that I should surrender my force to him. I told the bearer to return at once to his commander and notify him that I demanded the instant and unconditional surrender of his entire force, or I would forthwith open fire upon them. The rebel bearing this flag of truce left with this demand, and in a few minutes Major Steele, of the Confederate cavalry, was brought to me by Captain Neal, of the 9th Kentucky Cavalry, who informed me that Morgan had already surrendered. I then rode forward to Morgan and notified him that matters must remain as they were until General Shackelford arrived." This report of Rue himself settles the matter that he was acting under General Shackelford and that Morgan did not surrender to Major Rue, for he himself confesses that he did not. This, however, shows nothing against the valuable services of Major Rue as a brave, gallant officer.

We add our notes of these movements much condensed.

July 22d. Marched 11 miles, halted, fed; marched to Nicholasville. Citizens overjoyed, furnishing us freely with all needed by man or horse. Marched 36 miles.

July 23d. Marched 2 p. m. through Millertown at sunrise, breakfasted and fed; then crossed Muskingum river 90 minutes behind Morgan; 2 miles farther, halted and fed, then began night's march to Washington.

July 24th. While still marching at 9 a. m., overtook the enemy at Waybout, had a brush with him; he eluded us; we pursued all night.

July 25th. Still in pursuit; discovered the enemy on a hill near Graytown. Opened on him with shell and sent a detachment to cut off his retreat. He now made a concentrated attack, first on our left, then on our right, his movements covered by the woods. He succeeded in charging past our extreme right flank, and rapidly retreated toward the river. The home guards with us were anxious to be with us except when there was fighting. We learned that the 9th Michigan had encountered them, and we pursued on to Richmond. Morgan was two hours ahead. We halted a short time and fed, then at midnight moved on again.

Sunday, July 26th. Continued toward Salineville, made short halt, then on again double quick, overtaking and capturing his whole force on the north fork, at 3 p. m., then marched to Salineville. This pursuit and capture of the notorious John Morgan and his large force of the choice cavalry of the Confederacy, has no equal in the War of the Rebellion, either in the audacity, cunning and cruelty of Morgan and his men, or in the pluck, courage and unflagging energy of his pursuers, who for the space of one month continued the pursuit night and day; often without rations or horse feed for want of time to cook or to feed, and almost without sleep.

In his report (page 644), General Shackelford speaks in the highest praise of all his officers and men who aided in the final pursuit and capture of Morgan. He says: "It is difficult for me to speak of individual officers and men without doing injustice to others;" yet he especially mentions Colonel Wolford, Colonel Capron, of the 14th Illinois, and a few others with the highest praise, and says of all: "They deserve the gratitude of the whole country for their energy and gallantry."

No event of the war attracted the attention of civilians and soldiers of all classes and grades as did this, and none was ever accompanied by the same degree of prolonged excitement, and few great events brought about such important results as this destruction of such a large body of the enemy's best cavalry.

Colonel Capron was greatly aided by his officers that accompanied him. Major Davidson, Captain Dent, of Company "C," and Captain Sanford, of Company "K," on this, as on all occasions, distinguished themselves. Lieutenant H. C. Connelly displayed such ability and courage as rapidly brought him into prominence. Lieutenant I. H. Allen, acting adjutant of the 14th, by his faithfulness and ability earned a far better position than he ever obtained. In reply to a notice sent by Shackelford that he had finally captured Morgan, Burnside replied, July 27th: "The whole country will thank you for your good work. I can not tell you how thankful I am to you and your command."

In Burnside's report of campaign (page 14), is this: "The loss of Morgan's brigade was a heavy blow to the rebellion, and the brave men who followed him so persistently deserve the thanks of their country."

At Salineville, July 26th. General Shackelford, Colonel Wolford and Colonel Capron now left us and went to Cincinnati, leaving Major Davidson in command of the 14th.

July 27th. Marched at 8 a. m. to Richmond; dined, then on to Steubenville, where we joined the rest of Shackelford's pursuing force. A large concourse of citizens had congregated to witness our triumphal entry. We were all anxious to rejoin our full commands.

July 28th. Shipped on the cars for Cincinnati at 4 p. m.; ran all night.

July 29th. Arrived in Cincinnati at noon. Crossed the river to Covington; found the rest of the regiment; all overjoyed to meet again. We were glad of a little rest, having marched 300 miles in 5 days. We record the itinerary of our comrades who were disappointed at being unable to join in the final pursuit.

July 21st. Camped in wheat field, near Cheshire. Visited by a welcome group of ladies from the country, who supplied us abundantly with nice pies, cakes and apples.

July 23d. In camp; 24th, moved camp a mile to a cool grove; 25th, marched down the river 12 miles to Galliopolis; camped near town; 26th, in camp; 27th, marched to the river and sailed on boats bound to Cincinnati; sailed all day and all night. July 28th, arrived at Cincinnati at 4 p. m.; crossed to Covington; took quarters in the barracks; distance from Galliopolis, 500 miles. July 29th, joined the captors of Morgan. July 30th, whole command in camp; drew fresh horses and new clothing; shipped on filthy cattle cars for Lexington, Kentucky. Boys mad. Ran all night; beautiful weather.

August 1st. Reached Lexington at daylight. This is a beautiful town and was the home of that truly great statesman who so long and earnestly labored to ward off the clash of arms that now causes so much misery, and which his clear vision foresaw was inevitable unless opposing interests met in compromise. No American patriot can gaze upon the beautiful monument of the great Henry Clay, near the town, without feeling proud that he, too, was an American citizen. We took train to Nicholasville, then mounted and marched to camp "Dick Robinson;" and camped Sunday, August 2d. A detachment of 120 men of the 14th, under Lieutenant Colonel Jenkins and Captain Jenkins, was sent with Colonel Wolford's command, in pursuit of the rebel Colonel John S. Scott, who had made a raid into Kentucky. They started at 3 p. m., was gone several days and rejoined us; the enemy had retreated; having marched 70 miles. They found two rebel doctors who had been left to care for some wounded rebels. The main command, under Captain Sanford, marched August 2d to Dandridge, halted a while, then marched to Stanford, arrived at 9 p. m.; found the 112th Illinois and 2d Tennessee Cavalry. We camped a half mile from town; marched 15 miles.

August 3d. Election day; found plenty of blackberries, potatoes and fresh pork.

August 4th. In camp; smiths busy shoeing horses; afternoon marched 17 miles. Major Davidson, Captains Lupton and Dent returned to us.

August 5th. Breakfasted, then marched 3 miles; fed sheaf oats, marched to camp. Afternoon, marched 15 miles to Somerset; arrived at 6 p. m.; rained hard. Colonel Jenkins and detachment joined us.

August 6th. In camp. Colonel Capron has gone to Glasgow to bring up the detachment left there. An important move is anticipated.

August 7th. In camp.

August 8th. Moved camp a short distance to where a nice spring emerges from a cave.

August 9th. In camp.

August 10th. In camp.

August 11th. Marched toward Glasgow, passing over the ground where Zollicoffer was killed. Major Davidson in command. Camped at dark in a beautiful grove; marched 20 miles; heavy rains.

August 12th. Marched at 4 a. m.; passed through Sulphur Springs; reached Columbia at dark; camped 5 miles beyond; marched 36 miles.

August 13th. Marched at 4 a. m.; today we passed an old revolutionary soldier of more than a hundred winters. He stood by the roadside greeting us as we passed. He said he hated the tories of the revolution; but, if possible, he hated the traitors of the present day still more. Arrived at Glasgow at 5 p. m.; glad to meet the comrades from whom we had been separated for five weeks; distance marched, 30 miles.

The itinerary of those left at Glasgow. The withdrawal of our effective cavalry at the front left eastern and southern Kentucky exposed to rebel cavalry raids and guerrilla invasions. The few infantry could do nothing more than guard a few local points, as they could not follow cavalry. Many raiding parties were sent in. On page 705 General Judah says: "There is no doubt that Wheeler is at, or near Lebanon." Page 706, General Boyle says: "Dispatch from Lebanon says a rebel force is approaching that place." Page 734, General Boyle reports: "Wheeler and Breckenridge approaching." Page 828, July 31st, Burnside speaks of rebel Colonel Scott's retreat from Kentucky, and says: "He entered Kentucky to make a diversion in favor of Morgan." Page 829, General Hartsuff says, July 28th, that "a force of the enemy, 1,000 to 1,500 strong, is apparently approaching from Williamsburg and Somerset."

Frequent reports reached Glasgow of intended raids by Hamilton's guerrillas from the Cumberland, which kept Major Quigg's forces vigilant. The Major had succeeded Colonel Harney (page 735) in the command of all the forces at Glasgow. In consequence of many rumors of rebel invasion in eastern Kentucky, all the available cavalry at Glasgow marched under Major Quigg, July 27th, toward Lebanon at 5 a. m.; crossed Barren river; camped on bottom; marched 26 miles.

July 28th. Marched early; crossed Green river; camped near; march, 23 miles.

July 29th. Marched early, 11 miles to Lebanon; arrived 9 a. m.; found this beautiful town terribly marred by the fierce battle fought there by its handful of brave defenders against the cruel army of Morgan. The depot and many dwellings burned. Other buildings and fences and ornamental trees riddled with war missiles. We camped on a dry creek 3 miles N. W. of town; a poor camp and no water. In this camp until August 1st; then moved to a pleasant grove 2 miles N. E. of town; remained here until August 6th. Fair weather; nothing of note further than daily scouting and guarding polls of election on the 3d; and the arrival of our howitzers and some of the men from the Morgan raid.

August 7th. Marched early toward Glasgow, 18 miles; camped in a wood. Saw today many Union flags displayed; a sight seldom seen before the destruction of Morgan's army, which had been the terror of the Union people of Kentucky.

August 8th. Marched early, 18 miles; camped on Barren river.

August 9th. Marched early, 20 miles to Glasgow; arrived 3 p. m.; camped west of town, where we remained until August 13th.

This detachment, though not engaged, through the vigilance of its commander, rendered essential service in watching over the almost unprotected regions of southern and eastern Kentucky during the absence of nearly all the cavalry after Morgan. This ends one of the most important and active campaigns.

CHAPTER III.

CROSSING THE MOUNTAINS INTO EAST TENNESSEE.—CAPTURE OF KNOXVILLE.—CAPTURE OF CUMBERLAND GAP.

We now enter upon a far more interesting portion of our history. We were heartily tired of chasing cowardly guerrillas, who would never stand to fight; but like John Morgan they kept us constantly chasing after them. With their facilities for hiding in the mountains, or in disguising as citizens, or their *dernier resort,* taking the oath to be broken the next day; it was a most disgusting service to which we were glad to bid farewell.

But disagreeable as the service had been it had its compensation. A reference to the official reports shows that our regiment had earned in Kentucky a high reputation, and the effect that this reputation had on the *morale* of the regiment, was to establish a laudable pride to maintain this high standing, and to create a confidence in their ability which tended to make them invincible; for nothing tends more to make soldiers invincible than a firm belief that they are. The official records show that as early as the autumn of 1862 a movement into East Tennessee was contemplated. Events, however, demonstrated that this was but the outgrowth of that sanguine expectation that contemplated the conquest of the south as a mere "before breakfast" job. Bragg's invasion of Kentucky, though with Buell's kind consent, put an end for the time to this premature advance of the Army of the Ohio.

As soon as Burnside took command of the Army of the Ohio, Rosecrans being in command of the Army of the Cumberland, both of these commanders were vehemently and persistently urged to make the forward movement. Neither of these generals was furnished with sufficient mounted force; scarcely enough for occupancy of their present lines. An advance meant not only extended territory to protect, but greatly extended lines of transportation to protect, in order to supply the advanced armies;

and this, too, through regions the best adapted to the guerrilla warfare that would be practiced upon our lines of transportation. It was also an essential that no stronghold should be left in our rear and Vicksburg was yet in their hands. On page 193, part 2d, is correspondence between Rosecrans and Burnside. Rosecrans said: "Want to know if you can't take the line of the Cumberland, or put a strong force at Tompkinsville? * * * What can and will you do to enter East Tennessee?" March 30th, 1863, Burnside answered: "I shall occupy the line of the Cumberland as soon as possible, and hope to pass into East Tennessee."

Our first chapter shows that the first promise had been fulfilled; regarding the second, the situation was not yet ripe. Burnside called for his corps—the 9th—to be sent to him to protect Kentucky when he advanced with his present forces. The 9th Corps was sent, but immediately sent to Grant, at Vicksburg, where there was pressing necessity of reinforcements. The fall of Vicksburg, July 4th, relieved the 9th Corps to be sent to Kentucky, but now the Morgan raid had called Burnside's mounted force in pursuit, which postponed movement another month. Meantime Burnside began preparations anticipating a more speedy termination of these hindrances. Had an earlier advance been attempted there would have been a scarcity of local supplies; but now the new crops are matured and another difficulty is removed. The destruction of General Morgan's large and well equipped force of cavalry also rendered the time more propitious. We will now consider the situation as it then existed.

Rebel General Buckner, headquarters at Knoxville, East Tennessee, with an army, August 10th, 1863, total, 25,733 —15,000 of it cavalry, and having in his department 80 cannon. General Wheeler's cavalry nearby; total, 14,907, and Forrest cavalry force at Kingston, total, 6,701; besides Sam Jones' army (formerly Humphrey Marshall's) within supporting distance, strength varying from 5,000 to 15,000. To invade East Tennessee in the face of these opposing forces Burnside tells us (see page 548, serial 51): "Preparations were again made for a move into East Tennessee. It required much time and labor to effect an organization, as the troops were so worn and scattered.

By the 16th day of August we succeeded in organizing a force of about 15,000 men, which composed the 23d Corps, under the command of General Hartsuff."

The different divisions were located August 23d as follows: Infantry—White's at Columbia, Hascall's at Stanford, Carter's at Crab Orchard. Cavalry—Graham's at Glasgow, Wolford's at Somerset. General Samuel P. Carter commanded fourth division of cavalry. First brigade, Colonel Robert K. Bird, regiments, 112th Illinois Mounted Infantry; 8th Michigan Cavalry; 45th Ohio Mounted Infantry; 1st Tennessee Mounted Infantry; 15th Indiana Battery. Ours, the second brigade, commanded by Colonel John W. Foster; regiments, 14th Illinois Cavalry, Colonel Horace Capron; 5th Indiana Cavalry, Colonel Felix W. Graham; 65th Indiana Mounted Infantry, Lieutenant Colonel Thomas Johnson; 9th Ohio Cavalry, (four companies), Major Wm. D. Hamilton; 8th Tennessee Cavalry (four companies), Major John M. Sawyer; 1st Illinois Light Artillery, Battery M, Lieutenant John H. Colvin. Two Rodman guns, belonging to 5th Indiana, and four mountain howitzers, belonging to 14th Illinois.

The third brigade, commanded by General James M. Shackelford; regiments, 9th Michigan Cavalry, Colonel James L. David; 2d Ohio Cavalry, Colonel Geo. A. Purington; 7th Ohio Cavalry, Colonel Israel Garrard; 2d Tennessee Mounted Infantry, Major David A. Carpenter; 11th Michigan Battery, Captain Charles J. Thompson; 1st Tennessee Battery, Captain R. Clay Crawford, and an unattached cavalry brigade, commanded by Colonel Frank Wolford, containing 1st Kentucky Cavalry, Colonel Silas Adams; 11th Kentucky Cavalry (nine companies), Major Milton Graham; 12th Kentucky Cavalry, Colonel Eugene W. Crittenden; howitzer battery, Lieutenant Jessee S. Law; reserve artillery, Captain Andrew J. Hinkle; 2d Illinois Light Battery M, Captain John C. Phillips; 24th Indiana Battery, Lieutenant Henry W. Shafer; 19th Ohio Battery, Captain Joseph C. Shields; 1st Rhode Island Light Battery D, Captain Wm. W. Buckley.

August 20th orders were issued for all these troops to march on different routes through various gaps of the Cumberland range. August 18th, 6 a. m., that portion of our brigade at Glasgow marched under command of Colonel Graham, 20 miles to Ray's crossroads, and camped, awaiting the coming up of other portions of the brigade and trains.

Nineteenth and 20th in camp, preparing for an arduous march.

August 21st. Marched at 8 a. m. toward Mud camp, 12 miles; camped in a field near Marrowbone.

August 22d. Company "I" and two other companies of the 14th Illinois sent to cross the river at Celina, to scout the country and repair roads. About 1 p. m. brigade moved southward toward the Cumberland river; passed "Mud Camp," where the first battalion, under Major Davidson, was sent on scout toward Tompkinsville. The brigade crossed the river at a ford near "Mud Camp," about 4 p. m.; marched down the river; country very rough. Our road lay between a high range of hills on our left, and the river and a precipice on the right. One of the guns of the 5th fell over, but was recovered, with an injured carriage. A caisson was lost. Some wagons also went over the declivity. Camped about 11 p. m.; march, 16 miles.

Sunday, August 23d. Started late; halted several hours in a valley, then marched again; camped in a field four miles above Celina; march, 14 miles.

August 24th. Marched at 6 a. m., 14th in advance; took the road to Jamestown, Tennessee; entered a mountainous country. About 9 a. m. a force of the enemy was discovered; the 14th formed line of battle, with the howitzers in position and awaited an attack. The force proved to be a detachment which was captured by our vanguard; then resumed our march; halted at noon, fed straw; rained hard; crossed the Obee river, a small stream with steep banks, in descending which, one of the ambulances was thrown forward upon the horses, breaking the ambulance and severely injuring the driver and horses; marched 16 miles, and camped in a wood; fed corn stalks.

August 25th. Marched early; a heavy fog prevailed; our road very rough and winding round the sides of huge hills. We again crossed the Obee river, a beautiful little stream. But few inhabitants or improvements in these mountains, and these seem to be the property of rebels, so prejudiced against the old government as to refuse greenbacks, while they took with readiness the Confederate rags that were captured in Major Hamilton's trunk. With these the boys could purchase anything that their circumscribed potato patches produced. The former possessions of the few Union people who had inhabited these regions, were marked by the ruins of burned dwellings. Camped in a wood near an orchard which, with some hardtack, furnished our supper, while we fed our horses from a barn near. March, 18 miles. The first battalion joined us here. They had marched all night after leaving us; breakfasted in Tompkinsville the 23d, then marched through Sulphur Springs and camped 6 miles beyond; crossed the Cumberland river 10:30 a. m. the 24th; drove a band of rebels from there on double quick. A party of our forces intercepted them. The battalion then came up and captured them. The battalion then marched 5 miles, when Captain Sanford, with a small party, was sent out after a party of the enemy. Our band charged upon the enemy, wounding one and capturing two more; then rejoined the battalion in camp at night.

August 25th. Battalion marched at 5 a. m.; reached Livingston before noon; captured a few more rebels. A few of the boys got some drugged liquor, which made them very sick. Overtook the rear guard of brigade, Company "L," about 5 p. m.; soon after reached camp, having marched 22 miles.

August 26th. Brigade marched early; country so rough that in some of the defiles a small force of the enemy could have impeded our march. We found the roads in places blockaded with fallen trees and expected an attack, but no enemy appeared except small skulking parties. Some of our men who had strayed from the command were fired upon and the rebel skulkers were captured. We saw today a curiosity to Yankees—a hog with a bell on. We omitted to mention that the party that intercepted the rebel party on the 23d was Company "I," Company "K" and another company that marched by the way of Celina. They then joined the first battalion. They had encountered no other party of the enemy.

August 27th. Marched early; soon reached a more level country, the summit of the Cumberland range; the soil very thin, the timber a mixture of oak and pine. Passed through Jamestown, a miserably dilapidated group of old log huts, in the midst of a desolate country. The second division of infantry (White's) was camped here; having come in on another road. We camped in a field 7 miles from town; little to eat and nothing for our horses but cornstalks. Marched 17 miles.

A Captain Tinker, with a small band of Union men, hiding in the mountains by day, with no dwelling place but God's great wall tent—the sky—kept the enemy in constant dread; like Marion in the Carolinas, by vigorous and bold attacks at night.

August 28th. In camp on half rations. Our wagons were sent back after clothing and rations.

August 29th. Reveille at 2:30 a. m.; marched at 4:30. A large force said to be at Montgomery awaiting to give us battle. Marched rapidly; first 10 miles level; then entered a broken country, descending from the range. At 3 p. m. halted to feed from a cornfield, which rapidly disappeared; prepared a hasty dish of coffee; then mounted and on again. As we neared Montgomery an old lady very excitedly warned us *to be very careful* as 300 rebels with *a small cannon* was in Montgomery, all primed and waiting for us. Of course we were *very cautious* not to keep them waiting long. As we passed through the town we missed the main body of the enemy, encountering only a Dutchman and his frau, armed with *loaded "cider mugs."* Each of the boys had to take a shot, as rapidly as they could discharge and reload their pieces. This was all the battle we saw that day. Camped within a mile of town; march, 30 miles. A few of the members of our Tennessee regiments here found their families, who had suffered shameful persecution. One old gentleman had been cruelly shot down in the road that day, simply for holding Union sentiments. Such are the demons we have for foes. Rations scarce; no horse feed.

Sunday, August 30th. In camp near Emery river; send 3 miles for forage. Marched at 3 p. m. through Montgomery, and camp in a field near Flat creek. March, 6 miles. Burnside's whole force has come up. On page 566 of serial 51, is report of Orlando M. Poe, chief engineer of the Army of the Ohio. He recites the different routes on which the various commands marched, and says: "So accurately was the march made that after passing over 112 miles each (on different routes) the heads of the two infantry columns reached Montgomery at the same time. When the distance marched, the character of the country, and the condition of the roads are taken into account, this may well be considered a most remarkable feat in concentration. The march of the cavalry was equally good and well timed." "From Montgomery, the entire column, except one brigade (ours) was projected upon Kingston, having Loudon for an objective point. At the Indian tavern, 45 miles from Knoxville, and 8 miles from Montgomery, one brigade of cavalry (ours, under Colonel J. W. Foster), was detached, and by a rapid movement, succeeded in occupying Knoxville on September 1st."

August 31st. Burnside's infantry was passing all last night. Today 300 pack mules loaded with sugar, salt and coffee pass us; suggesting to us, "a good time coming." Our cavalry had fared hard on this trip; glad when they could get hardtack and apples, and often without anything. Our horses fared even worse. About 10 a. m. resume our march; soon after halt for General Burnside and staff to pass. We then moved on. The country is now much better. Halt at noon and fed in an orchard; plenty of corn for horses, and apples for ourselves. Rations scarce. Resume our march and camp after night at a gap 30 miles from Knoxville. Our regiment was rear guard and forced to camp on a side hill so steep as to suggest the necessity of anchors to hold us in position. No feed except hay, and no rations. March, 18 miles. Rumored that the rebels are fortifying a gap in our front.

September 1st. Cool night, but very pleasant morning, much like Indian summer. We seem to have emerged into a different zone. In the mountains we had much rain, hot days and very cool nights. In the morning was circulated and read a very strict order against individual foraging, with penalties as follows: "Drummed out of service," "branding on the cheek," "head shaved," "death." The order was well meant for the protection of loyal citizens, but to the cavalry, who was so much of the time out of reach of government rations, and without the means of carrying them, the order seemed not only harsh, but cruel,

MAJOR JAMES B. DENT.

and had all the penalties been stictly enforced, what a grand army of bald headed and branded patriots would have stepped to the music of the "Rogue's March;" only saved by this disgrace from the greater penalty "death." How harsh it now sounds even to repeat these facts. We had reveille at 1 a. m., and "boots and saddles" at 3 a. m.; many of the men got no breakfast; marched at 6 a. m.; our brigade alone taking the road to Knoxville. Twenty-five miles from Knoxville we passed through Winters gap and entered one of the most beautiful and romantic valleys. We now increased our speed through a country recently rich in production, but now desolated by war. The citizens all along this route were perfectly wild with delight; telling us that they had long prayed and longingly waited our advent. The ladies came to their doors, and many to the roadside welcoming us, some with shouts, some with songs, some with tears of joy, and all with uncontrollable emotions. Our march resembled a Roman grand triumphal march. General Pegram's brigade was retiring before us. They had been ordered to defend Winter's Gap and, in case of necessity, to fall back to Walkersford. Colonel Scott's brigade was at Campbellsville. These brigades were to have united to oppose our advance; they were now in inglorious flight. Fifteen miles from Knoxville we forded the Clinch river, a beautiful stream somewhat resembling the Miami at Dayton, Ohio. Five miles from Knoxville we came to the Knoxville and Cumberland Gap road. Our advance cut the telegraph running to Cumberland Gap. Rebel Colonel Scott's brigade had passed down to Knoxville several hours before. We now pressed forward with increased speed, expecting a strong fight at Knoxville, as it was General Buckner's headquarters, and in addition to the force previously there, two brigades from above had now passed down to them; and we were only one brigade. We were surprised when we reached the city to find the whole rebel force skedaddling like a lot of frightened rats. We could only give them a parting volley. Our speedy march saved the military stores for us, as they had been ordered to burn everything, and had already begun their work. We captured some prisoners; all the army stores, three locomotives, one large train of cars with a quantity of coffee and sugar, several empty trains and one large warehouse filled with bacon. Burnside, in report of campaign (page 548, serial 51), outlines the movement of his troops to Kingston and Loudon, and mentions the burning of the bridge at Loudon by the rebels. After the capture of Knoxville Colonel Foster manned a train and sent up the railroad to Morristown and Greenville, and near Jonesboro captured a lot of army supplies. We halted in the suburbs of the town in a pleasant grove about 6 p. m. Knoxville had two good earth forts to guard the approach on the north and west. It appeared strange to us that we had met with so little resistance. In an hour, "To horse" was sounded. We mounted and marched through the city; a beautiful one, much resembling our northern towns in beauty and regularity. We passed the dwelling of the famed Parson Brownlow—a humble dwelling, but brilliant in that it recalled the grandest patriot and hero of modern times. We also saw the gallows erected to hang him on, but such was the devoted love for this great man by the loyal people of East Tennessee, that, though all the Union men were driven from the country and the rebels had undisputed possession and they took him to this gallows three times with the avowed intention to hang him, the cowardly poltroons did not dare to do it. Without doubt they feared the attack of the broomstick brigade. Parson Brownlow printed his paper, the Knoxville Whig, long after the rebels occupied Knoxville, and in it scored the rebels without mercy until they destroyed his press. He kept the Union flag flying from the roof of his house long after. One day in his absence a squad of rebels went to his house to tear it down. To get at the flag they had to pass inside and up a stairway and out through a trap door in the roof. They passed in toward the stairway, but Brownlow's daughter, revolver in hand, met them and kindly informed them that the first man who took another step forward would be the first one dead. These braves slunk away from the flashing eyes of this excited heorine. As we passed through the city we were followed by a mass of the people swarming on the streets to welcome us with every demonstration of joy. Amongst the throng stood a tall, venerable figure with patriotism beaming in his eyes and flushing in his countenance. Casting his delighted gaze at us, then raising his eyes toward heaven, with devotion breathing in his tones he exclaimed: "Glory! GLORY! GLORY! the long-looked-for day has come at last! I have been enslaved, but now I am free!" This, as we afterward learned from Major Connelly, was Judge Patterson, son-in-law to President Johnson, and afterward United States Senator from Tennessee. Union flags were now displayed all over the city. We marched through and camped near a cornfield and near the fair grounds, on the Strawberry Plains road. Beautiful day and night.

Wednesday, September 2d. Reveille at sunrise. The following list of prices exhibits one phase of the evils of rebel rule: Tobacco, $6 a plug; a common article of ladies' shoes, $35 a pair; gentleman's boots, $100 a pair; common prints from $3 to $7 a yard; butter $4 a pound; flour, $15 a barrel; bacon, $1 a pound. Yet all this is a mere shadow of the sufferings of the loyal people. Tyranny and violence, the very extreme of barbarity, they were compelled to endure. Scouting parties brought in many prisoners, and also many conscripts who had fled to the mountains to hide from conscripting officers, who arrested all they could, and compelled them to bear arms against their beloved country.

September 3d. The beautiful weather continues. About 11 a. m. we were visited by a procession mostly ladies and children, with a few venerable men. They came from the country beyond Knoxville, bordering the Clinch river; marching with Union banners flying and with martial music. They brought with them abundant supplies of pies and cakes and other delicacies for their Yankee friends, who they were overjoyed to see. It was now evident that the oft repeated story of the loyalty of the people of East Tennessee had never been exaggerated. An audience was soon gathered, who listened to an eloquent speech by Lieutenant Colonel Jenkins, urging soldiers and citizens to mutual kindness and gentle deportment toward each other. He was replied to on the part of the citizens by Colonel Brown, a venerable and intelligent loyal citizen. He said he could but feebly express the joy of the citizens at witnessing the advent of their deliverers. He painted in burning words the tyranny, abuse and persecution they had endured at the hands of the rebels, then pointing to the proud old flag they bore, he said: "That is the flag that we trained under two years ago, but Governor Harris compelled us to hide it, but we have resurrected it; we hope never again to be buried in obscurity." He was followed by Captain Dent, of Company "C," 14th Illinois, who gave us a stirring and appropriate speech in his usual happy style. This closed the colloquial entertainment, which was followed by a culinary entertainment of the good things which our friends had brought; and after an exchange of reciprocal regards these welcome visitors returned to the city with martial music and the old flag waving. At 2 p. m., moved camp to a grove near a small creek and near the railroad, one mile N. E. of the city. Old rebel camps were near, well guarded by their vermin namesakes. Burnside arrived in the city today and addressed throngs of delighted citizens.

September 4th. Beautiful weather. The streets of the city crowded. There seems to be no end to the arrival of prisoners and conscripts. Our forces are busy in repairing railroad in both directions. Burnside realized that now we must again have possession of Cumberland Gap to open a route of communication with his base of supplies— the Ohio river. Anticipating this before he left Kentucky he had ordered Colonel De Courcey to organize a brigade at the proper time to approach the gap from the Kentucky side. After a few days of rest in camp he ordered an advance from Knoxville of a force of cavalry.

Colonel Graham, with the 65th Indiana, had been sent toward Sevierville to capture or drive out Thomas' legion of Indians. Colonel Foster, with a considerable force, was sent up to Greenville, and the rest of our brigade, including the 14th, was now temporarily under command of General Shackelford, who is now ordered to Cumberland Gap. We make some extracts from a published account by Major H. C. Connelly, who was in charge of General Shackelford's escort. He says: "The cavalry, with General Shackelford in command, left Knoxville to assist in capturing the Gap; approaching it from the south side. On the 6th of September, at Powell's river, on our way to the Gap, we had a heavy skirmish with the enemy and drove him until he took refuge behind his works in the gap. We had 2,000 men and two batteries. On the 7th, the Gap being invested, an unconditional surrender was demanded both by Shackelford on the south and by De Courcey on the north. General Frazer, who commanded the rebel forces, declined to surrender. On the 9th General Burnside came up with some reinforcements, having marched 60 miles in 50 hours. He cut the matter short by demanding an unconditional surrender."

The 14th came with Burnside. The following is from our original notes. This was one of the strongest inland fortresses in the world. When Burnside made his demand for surrender, our cavalry drawn up in column behind the cover of a wood, with troopers dismounted by the side of their steeds, and ready at a moment's warning to spring into their saddles, anxiously awaited the order to "Charge" up the mountain road, between the long lines of rifle pits occupied by rebel sharpshooters, and facing the fatal belching forth of the rebel batteries, charged with deadly missiles and trained with precision on the road over which our charging column must advance. Strange as it may seem, there were those who said they hoped the rebels would not surrender and spoil the sport. We confess that although our batteries were in position to support us, we were not of the number ambitious to risk but one chance in ten of reaching the rebel stronghold alive; but we were with those who, when the welcome news arrived of the surrender of this strong fortress, flung high in air our caps, with loud huzzahs that the terrible sacrifice was averted. This was a bloodless victory, but one of vast importance, as is evidenced by the preparation for the terrible sacrifice that would have been made to capture the place if it had not surrendered. The only hope in capturing by a charge was the capability of rushing victims over the deadly passage more rapidly than the enemy could mow them down. Though bloodless, it was none the less honorable to the brave soldiers who waited only the command to "charge," without flinching from duty though almost certain death or mangling awaited them. On page 599, serial 51, is a long list of ordnance stores captured. Twelve cannon, occupying as many strong rock forts, at different elevations, and each surrounded by strong rifle pits dug in the solid rock; 6 forts on the north descending road, and 6 on the south or Tennessee side, and all at such elevation that their shells were found thrown five miles to Powell's river bridge. This was their batteries, with magazine and headquarters dug out of the mountain in solid rock. Miles of rifle pits, equally strong, with full six months' provisions and ammunition, with nearly 2,500 men, were surrendered to Burnside. We have a plat of their fortifications drawn by Comrade Thomas Featherson, but want of space and facility prevent inserting it. On page 627, Rush Van Leer, rebel engineer officer, says: "Our position, I confess, was one of great strength. * * * Our defenses consisted of rifle pits and five batteries, aggregating 12 guns." There was much angry correspondence between several rebel officers relative to the surrender, but as it was no concern of ours, we do not include it; being well enough satisfied with our part of the arrangement.

The mountains here are about two thousand feet high, overtopping the gap, which, though high, is a sink in the mountains. This was Cumberland Gap which, with the forces, the war material, and the provisions, could well have maintained a siege of six or eight months. Nothing but a vigorous assault, with a loss of many times the number of the defenders could have captured it. We now went into camp just in the edge of *"the sacred soil of Virginia,"* about two miles from the Gap and in full view of it. This camp was near the corner of three states—Virginia, Tennessee and Kentucky. Since leaving Knoxville we have marched rapidly and fared hard, scarcely having an average of one good meal a day, and scarce of horse feed. In this camp we have no supper, and had no dinner and a scant breakfast. Our commissary was blamed with this deficiency and we believe was arrested.

September 10th. In camp; no breakfast until 10 p. m., then a small ration was issued. We get plenty of ripe peaches. Smiths are busy shoeing horses. Yesterday the 5th Indiana marched to reinforce Colonel Foster, who today we hear occupies Greeneville.

CHAPTER IV.

A BUSY PERIOD OF SERVICE.

September 11th. Reveille at 3:30 a. m.; drew rations and marched to Tazewell, 12 miles. Take the left-hand road to Morristown, 40 miles S. E. of Cumberland Gap, and 40 miles above Knoxville. From Tazewell the rest of the troops march on the Knoxville road. We halt at noon to feed; get plenty of good peaches. Crossed Clinch river at a very rough ford. Some of the horses stumbled over large rocks, giving their riders an unceremonious baptism which, judging from their conversation, did not effect much spiritual good. Marched two miles beyond and camped on a rough creek bottom, a very disagreeable camp; march, 23 miles.

September 12th. Reveille at 3 a. m.; march at 5 a. m. Arrived at the foot of Clinch mountain as day began to break. A heavy fog tinged with frost, curtained the landscape. This is the first indication of change from the charming weather we have had since entering East Tennessee. Our road over the mountain was rugged and serpentine and verged, in places, steep declivities. The scenes were highly romantic. Precipices and cliffs, ravines and running brooks, the varying foliage of many species of trees and shrubs, the charming songsters of the forest warbling their morning songs, all conspired to make us forget the toil of ascent. At the summit we paused to survey a lovely scene, over which Mountain Deities seemed to preside. We made the descent dismounted; so steep that a direct descent would have been impossible. A serpentine route, carefully selected and built up, rendered it barely possible to climb down the steep sides of Clinch mountain. On reaching the foot, a glance back at the precipitous sides of the towering mass of rocks and earth made us to doubt that we had climbed down its sides. At the foot of the range we passed some medical springs. We marched two miles and halted at Bean Station, a small collection of houses in Richland Valley, which in frontier life was an Indian trading post, and which, soon after this, became famous in the history of our regiment. Several parties were sent down the valley to procure horses and beef cattle, as an order had been published that our army, in a measure, must rely much on local supplies. A Mr. Joe Williams, long a terror to Union citizens, made an unwilling contribution of fine stock, and so did his neighbor, Mr. Johnson. After all the parties had returned to camp, we marched five miles and forded the Holston river. From this ford to Morristown is six miles. We reached M. before night, passed through and camped near. We found little corn and no rations. Here were several brigades of infantry. The citizens were nearly all loyal and very kind. Near here is the old and humble family mansion of that eccentric and able ex-Congressman, David Crocket. Day's march, 19 miles.

Sunday, September 13th. Very hard rain and wind last night, which completely drenched us, having no tents. Reveille at 1 a. m.; soon after marched breakfastless toward Greeneville, 33 miles off; very dark and raining hard; have difficulty in finding the road. After daylight, marched rapidly, having heard that the enemy have the 5th Indiana nearly surrounded. Pass through Russellville, a small town on the railroad six miles above Morristown. Blue Springs is 20 miles above Morristown; here we turned off the main road two miles and halted a while to guard a railroad bridge; then returned to main road, fed and dined; then marched and camped one mile from Greeneville at 8 p. m., having marched 35 miles; fine weather.

September 14th. Reveille at dawn; marched immediately, without breakfast, through Greeneville and camped one mile from town. Greeneville is a beautiful town of 1,500 inhabitants; surrounded by a rich and beautiful country; the inhabitants nearly all intensely loyal. This was the home of President Johnson. Soon "Boots and saddles" sounded and we again mounted and marched back through town and camped one mile south; found our trains; got breakfast and fed at 10 a. m.; then moved to first morning camp, having marched five miles.

September 15th Reveille at daylight; rumor that a

large force of the enemy is near. We are on half rations. Many citizens are flocking in to enlist under Uncle Sam. Company "C," under Lieutenant Porter sent on scout; they returned, having marched 24 miles; forage scarce.

September 16th. Reveille at sunrise; in camp having horses shod. At 8 p. m. marched up the railroad along with our Tennessee regiment; came to the 5th Indiana picket, which now rejoined us. Marched all night; very dark; rained hard.

September 17th. Morning; still on the march northward; passed Rheatown in the night, and a small village called "Full Branch." In the forenoon, halt to feed; get plenty of apples. Have left Greene county and entered S. E. corner of Sullivan county, of which Blountville is county seat. Kingsport on the Holston, near the Virginia line, is in Sullivan county. Bristol, on the Virginia & Tennessee Railroad, is partly in each state. Kingsport to Blountville, 18 miles. K. to Bristol, 25 miles. Blountville to Bristol, 10 miles. Zollicoffer on railroad 14 miles below Bristol, and east of Blountville 8 miles. Country broken and timbered; inhabitants nearly all rebels. We have outlined the situation in this section as it became the scene of very active service soon after. After breakfast, marched rapidly. When we neared Kingsport, two women stood by a house, near the road, and railed at us in a fearful manner; screaming like demons and calling us vile names and expressing the hope that their husbands in the rebel command near by would shoot every one of us. About 1 p. m. our advance came upon the enemy near Kingsport. They were on an island in the Holston river. A brisk skirmish ensued. The second battalion of the 14th, under Major Quigg, was thrown across the river to cut off their retreat. Discovering our movement they beat a hasty retreat on the Blountville road. It now became an exciting race between Quigg's battalion, with drawn sabers flashing in the sunlight, and the flying enemy, to reach first the intersection of the two roads. They say fear lends wings to a fugitive; this seemed so for they beat us sufficiently, notwithstanding that we spurred our horses apparently to their utmost, we reached the main road just as the last of the enemy's column passed, and falling in their rear pursued at the utmost speed; the rest of the 14th joining in the chase. Many of the rebels threw away their guns and other belongings. Occasionally the hoof of a charging steed would strike the hammer of a rebel musket and explode it. Strain our utmost, we could not overtake their main body; a few prisoners and their whole train, nine wagons, loaded with camp equipage, clothing and cooking utensils, were captured. For 12 miles on that warm September day it was a race between hope and fear, in which, though fear lost much, yet escaped. This was reported to be a rebel force of 1,700 cavalry, that had retired from near Cumberland Gap, but whether this, or General William's force, then in that vicinity, we did not learn. We halted from sheer exhaustion of our horses. Our brigade now came up, and we bivouacked near a small place called "Edons;" tied and fed, but did not unsaddle. We lay down on the damp ground supperless and blanketless. The weather turned cool at night and we suffered. Our casualties, several wounded and Lieutenant Horace Capron's horse killed. Loss of the enemy, 12 known to be killed, a few captured. Citizens on our route cheered us lustily. Our march night and day, over 60 miles; the last 12 miles at a charge. Our horses and ourselves had on this march, but one feed. Series 51, page 579. Itinerary of 23d A. C. says: September 17th. "Colonel Foster left Greeneville to meet the enemy." And September 18th, "Foster drove Carter's rebel command, after a severe fight, from the ford above Kingsport."

September 19th. Reveille 4 a. m.; no breakfast; marched at daylight to Blountville, 9 miles, about 9 a. m. In this town are three churches; but one Christian Union family. Near here our advance came on the enemy's pickets, skirmishing with them until we reached Bristol, when we charged upon their main force and drove them from the town, capturing and destroying a large amount of arms and ammunition, including some of the celebrated Henry rifles. We burned the depot, containing clothing, provisions and flour, saving only what we could then use. We destroyed much of the railroad track. Serial 51, page 579, September 19th, O. R. says: "Second brigade (ours) (4th division) drove the enemy, 700 strong, out of Bristol, cut the railroad, destroyed the bridge and a large amount of subsistence and stores and returned to Blountville."

Camped near Blountville; having heard that the enemy were approaching from Zollicoffer. A few who could carry flour had supper; most of the command were without. Marched 29 miles; day pleasant, night cold.

September 20th. Marched to Zollicoffer double quick and was soon engaged with the enemy in strong force at that place. Our line was formed: 5th on the right, 65th right center, Tennesseans left center, and 14th on the left. After a brisk fight of several hours, scouts reported a large force of the enemy marching to gain our rear, and cut us off. The 14th was sent back on double quick to meet the rebels. We were soon joined by the brigade. We had expected that Burnside would move up on the opposite side and entrap General Jones; he marched as far up as Carter Station, some miles below. This movement in falling back and subsequent similar movements, gave much dissatisfaction throughout the brigade, and brought out much criticism of those high in command. It was even hinted that some of our commanders were cowards. Indeed, we never understood these movements until the Government official reports fully explained them. Ever since we came into Eastern Tennessee Burnside had been constantly harassed by orders from General Hallack to move his main force to within supporting distance of Rosecrans. Burnside had as often explained that this would eventuate in the abandonment of upper East Tennessee with all its rich stores and loyal citizens, to rebel occupation and rule; that his force was now barely sufficient to occupy this department, and that with this force to occupy and guard a line 200 miles long, was an impossibility. At this time General Rosecrans had added his strong pleadings with urgent orders from Hallack, and Burnside was now making a strong feint towards these strongholds of the enemy, designing, under cover of these movements, to rapidly move most of his forces to Rosecrans' support. A small force of cavalry, including our brigade, was selected to remain and defend the territory the best they could. A large force of Burnside's infantry was now on the march to reinforce Rosecrans. In official reports (serial 51, page 617, Sept. 13th; 638, Sept. 14th; 655, Sept. 15th; 717 and 718, and 755 and 770 and 785 and 904), the reader may find full explanations. The great dread of the enemy that we would march up and destroy the salt works in Virginia aided materially in covering up the present movements. As to the strength at this time of Sam Jones' army at Zollicoffer, Colonel Foster and General Burnside estimated it at 6,000 at least. In serial 53, page 711, Sept 28th, General Sam Jones owns to having 5,000 actually present and offers to send troops to Richmond if desirable, as he had learned that Burnside had sent off a large portion of his force. Burnside, in serial 51, page 547, says: "A heavy force of the enemy under General Jones, was in the upper valley holding the points which I was directed to occupy." And on page 550: "Colonel Foster's brigade (ours) had been doing most excellent service in holding him in check." And again: "I could see no other may of extricating this portion of the command except by a demonstration of this kind (referring to our movements upon Zollicoffer). A cavalry brigade under Colonel Foster was sent around to threaten their rear, and on that night he (the enemy) evacuated his position, burning the bridge." After all our brigade had arrived, we marched 3 miles on the Carter Station road and camped in a meadow; fed hay, but got no supper except a small allowance of beef and mutton; had slim breakfast and no dinner. The enemy pursued us nearly to our camp, skirmishing briskly with our rear guard, Company "H," 14th, which narrowly escaped capture. Day's march, 19 miles.

September 21st. Reveille at 3 a. m. A small piece of meat and very small quantity of coffee for breakfast. March at sunrise, first on a cross road several miles, then on Jonesboro road. Jonesboro is 22 miles below Zollicoffer;crossed the Holston and Watauga rivers before noon; both nice streams. Passed a high rocky cliff on the top of which was a group of ladies, who waved their 'kerchiefs as signals of welcome. About noon, as we passed a dwelling a woman came out wringing her hands and weeping bitterly. About 15 minutes before our advance came up, a party of mounted rebels rode up to the house, and seizing her husband, a peaceable Union man, carried him a few rods from the house and shot him, and then skulked through the woods. This was only in keeping with their usual barbarity. We saw a rebel picket on another road a mile off. We soon left the Jonesboro road and marched toward Carter Station, where a brigade of our troops had engaged the enemy that day. We camped in a wood six miles from Jonesboro, and two miles from Johnson Station. We had one fourth of a meal for breakfast, no dinner, no supper; get corn for our horses in a field near by; march, 24 miles.

September 22d. Reveille at 3 a. m.; without breakfast we marched at sunrise back on yesterday's route; recross the Watauga and Holston. Our advance overtook the enemy's pickets, who fell back skirmishing; halted three miles from Blountville, fed and dined; but before completed, "To horse" sounded, and we hear musketry in front. We charged upon the enemy near Blountville, a raking fire is poured from a battery at our charging column, of the 14th, missing the column two or three feet. The remainder of the brigade was in line already engaged. The 14th, which had been rear gard, is now thrown into line to protect our battery. The enemy were strongly posted on the hills and had a number of batteries. The 65th, on our right wing, engaged the enemy fiercely; on their left the 5th Indiana were fighting near their guns. The Tennesseans on the left were also hotly engaged. Now came an order for the 14th Illinois to charge the enemy mounted, but this order was quickly followed by another for the 14th to dismount and form on the left of the Tennesseans, where the enemy were getting the advantage. The 14th were quickly in position, when the enemy finding themselves balked in that quarter, concentrated on our right and fiercely charged the 65th, for a time endangering that wing. Now comes an order for the second battalion of the 14th, under Major Quigg, to charge through the town mounted and break the rebel center. Many of the old wooden houses are in flames, set on fire by shells. Led by Major Quigg, the second battalion charge through the burning town, hoping to capture the enemy's batteries. Our line now presses forward vigorously and the whole rebel line is soon in full retreat toward Zollicoffer. We pursued them for two miles, then halted, establish a picket and build barricades; the second battalion of the 14th advance picket. Regarding this fight we quote from page 579, serial 51. Itinerary of 23d A.

C.: "Foster's (our brigade) engaged the enemy, 3,600, and routed them, capturing 70 prisoners and one piece of artillery at Blountville." The main command bivouacked near Blountville. The enemy were known to be in strong force near. We could hear the rumbling of wheels on the Bristol road to Zollicoffer, indicating heavy reinforcements sent to the enemy. Our advance, the second battalion, was without any rations and had no breakfast nor dinner. Our notes say 25 dead rebels were found and 200 captured. Our loss, 15 killed and 20 wounded. Marched 27 miles. Several young ladies were heard singing Union songs after the fight. On being questioned they said they had always been quiet and careful to avoid offending either side, but that the rebels came that day and murdered their father, and now they could not look upon rebels only with horror. Our force in this fight was about 1,400; little more than one third that of the enemy.

September 23d. Cold last night for the season. Early in the morningCompany "I," of the 14th, under Captain Hagaman, was sent up the Zollicoffer road to reconnoiter. They encountered the rebel pickets, charged upon and drove them until they met three rebel regiments. The remainder of the 14th pressed forward, and now began a lively skirmish, which lasted through the day; the whole brigade being engaged. The country was timbered and each side took shelter behind trees. Our men having short range guns, constantly sought a shorter range. The enemy, with long range guns, preferred a greater distance; thus they gave back while our men pressed them. At one time they made a longer stand. To illustrate the nature of the fight we relate an incident. A Yank and a reb, each behind his tree, were engaged in "shot about," when Yank's ammunition for his gun gave out; reb, seeing this, advanced upon Yank, calling upon him to surrender; but Yank, whipping out his Colts revolver, presented it and cried out: "You —— Reb, if you advance another step I will give you this." Reb had no desire for the gift presented "business end first," so he again treed. Trains were heard all day long on the railroad, indicating that reinforcements were being sent to Zollicoffer. We listened for the booming cannon to tell us that Burnside was engaging the enemy on the other side, but we did not then know of his plans, nor that our attack was a mere feint. In the evening couriers brought orders from Burnside, and at twilight we were ordered to build fires with rails; and then began a forward movement to the rear. The men retired sullenly, muttering imprecations on their officers; some even calling their commanders cowards. Meanwhile the enemy vigorously shelled our rail fires. No account of the loss this day is given on either side. The enemy followed us, skirmishing with our rear guard. In the afternoon a flag of truce came from the enemy, asking that a major and another rebel officer be permitted to visit their families in Blountville to secure new homes for their families; alleging that their dwellings were burned. Realizing that these families were among friends, as all were rebels, and not willing that spies, at this time, should be admitted, their request was not granted. We marched on the Jonesboro road; the night was cold. After crossing the Watauga river, two of our wagons tumbled over a declivity and were lost.

September 24th. About 3 a. m. halted in a wood, posted pickets, procured corn from a field and bivouacked, having had neither breakfast nor supper the previous day. For 48 hours many of the men have had nothing to eat. Reveille at sunrise; beautiful day; march at 7 a. m. towards Jonesboro; passed J. about 5 p. m.; camped in a field a half mile S. W. of town. Water, forage, wood and rations scarce. A few had supper, many had no breakfast, and all were without dinner. Day's march, 25 miles.

September 25th. Reveille at 4 a. m.; night clear and cool; morning pleasant. March at 5 p. m. through Leesburg. Afternoon through Rheatown and Greeneville, about sunset, where our Tennessee regiment was left as a garrison and never again with us. Camped late at night four miles beyond; plenty of feed, but no rations.

September 26th. Reveille at 3 a. m.

Sunday, September 27th. Reveille at 4 a. m.; march at sunrise. Weather beautiful; roads very dusty; pass New Market; country beautiful; cross Holston river and camp five miles from Knoxville; marched 30 miles. For the last two days have had less than half rations.

September 28th. Reveille at sunrise. Many of our horses were broken down, and we turn them over to the government corral, to be recruited up, receiving in exchange other horses previously broken down, but recruited up by good care and rest in the corrcl. Some of our *new* horses, as we called them, were not as serviceable as those we exchanged for them; two of them died on the road to our camp. At 10 a. m. brigade marched to Knoxville; passed through and camped in a grove S. W. of Fort Sanders; draw rations; smiths at work shoeing horses. March, 7 miles. Serial 51, page 579, Sept. 28th. Itinerary of 23d A. C., says: "Foster's brigade arrived at Knoxville, having marched 228 miles since the 17th instant."

September 29th. Reveille at early dawn; smiths busy night and day shoeing horses. We hear rumors of fighting at Loudon, 30 miles south of Knoxville. The itinerary of 23d A. C. says: "September 28th cavalry driven in at Loudon." This was Wolford's cavalry falling back from Philadelphia, where they were surprised by a large force of rebels and badly routed, losing their howitzer battery. General Burnside, in a report to President Lincoln, September 23d, says: "One of our brigades (ours) had a sharp fight at Blountville in which the enemy were beaten and dispersed." And again: "Our cavalry, under General Shackelford (who was now our chief of cavalry) has been continually in contact with the enemy, driving them all the time." And again: "Colonel Foster has been on the flank. He whipped the enemy very handsomely at Blountville and at Bristol."

September 30th. Reveille at 5 a. m. Under orders to move; rained hard last night and all day.

On October 1st had reveille at 4 a. m.; orders to march at 9 a. m. Fifth Indiana and one company of 14th march toward Loudon. Main command, with horses saddled, remain in camp ready until 6 p. m., then move on road to Loudon; raining hard. The night was darker than a stack of black cats in the shade of a beech tree; Egyptian darkness would have made a shadow in trying to shine through it; a darkness which might be felt, and was, by more than one luckless trooper who, guided only by the sound before him, cut across the corner where the road made a turn to the left, and found himself floundering in the mud and water of a deep ditch, into which his steed

CAPTAIN WM. A. LORD, COMPANY H.

plunged. Several teams also ditched their wagons. The column became divided and entangled, and halted until it was again untangled, then resumed the march until 2 a. m. of October 2d; halted, fed and laid down on the wet ground, tentless, wet and hungry. Morning clear and cold; hungry and wet, marched breakfastless through the small railroad towns "Conard" and "Lenoir" and through the valleys "Glàssy" and "Opossum." Reached the Tennessee river at Loudon at 11 a. m. The river here is deep and broad. The destroyed railroad bridge was a grand structure, one fourth of a mile long. We crossed on a pontoon bridge. Marched a mile south of town; halted to feed and breakfast. This town is surrounded by many hills; some of them fortified. Near here was the battleground where it was said Wolford, with two brigades, defeated the enemy much stronger than his force. We marched to Philadelphia, five miles below; camped in a bend of the Sweetwater creek. Plenty of good water and forage, but rations scarce. Colonel Capron is now in command of the brigade. Remained in this camp until October 5th, and get plenty of flour, bread, potatoes and meat. It turned cold on the 4th.

October 5th. Reveille at daylight; march at sunset back to Loudon; cross the river, march 12 miles beyond; camp near Lenoir Station 1 a. m. of October 6th; weather uncomfortably cold. Reveille at daylight; march at 7 a. m.; without breakfast or horse feed; halt at 10 a. m., fed and got breakfast, then march to Knoxville, 18 miles; arrived at 6 p. m.; camped on same ground; marched since previous evening, 36 miles. Get supper, but no horse feed.

October 7th. Reveille at daylight; breakfast, but no horse feed; marched toward Greeneville at 8 a.m., 12 miles, leave main road, halt and fed poor corn; go into camp. Sam Jones has sent General Ransom, with a strong rebel force to Greeneville. (See serial 53, page 720, and page 725.)

October 8th. Reveille before day; march at sunrise; cross "Flat creek," passed Blain's cross roads, halt to feed; camp in the evening four miles from Bean Station; plenty of forage; rations scarce. March, 26 miles.

October 9th. Reveille before daylight. We hear of

terrible atrocities committed by inhuman rebels in Greene county; good men tied to trees and shot as a mark; 300 houses burned; one peaceable Dunker, opposed to war, they hung up to make him tell where his money was hidden, and finally shot and horribly mangled him. Another peaceable man in the same neighborhood shot; all because they would not aid, or sympathize with the rebel cause. Many other atrocities were committed. We marched through Rogersville, where was a female seminary now running. Camped a mile north; plenty of corn, but little rations. Marched 27 miles.

October 10th. Reveille 4 a. m.; night cold; march at 8 a. m. back through Rogersville and on the Rheatown road. Fed hay at Williams' Mills, 19 miles from Rogersville; get hasty bite to eat, then mount and march slowly to within one mile of Rheatown, halt until 10 p. m. We were in the rear, or rather the front, of a large force of the enemy that Shackelford, with his cavalry and a body of infantry had badly whipped at Blue Springs, and were now driving them. We remained in the enemy's rear until 2 a. m. of October 11th, when for some unknown reason, which has never been satisfactorily explained, the 5th Indiana alone was left in this position and the rest of the brigade was moved back on the road we came, several miles. General Burnside says in a report (serial 51, page 551): "Colonel Foster's brigade was sent around to the rear of the enemy with instructions to establish himself in the rear of the enemy at a point near Rheatown, over which he (the enemy) would be obliged to retreat. It was not desirable to press the enemy until Colonel Foster had time to reach his position." Again: "Colonel Foster met with serious difficulties in the way of rough roads, so that he did not reach the point on the line of retreat to make the necessary preparations to check him." There was great dissatisfaction in the brigade at the failure to even attempt to check the enemy. As to the obstacles referred to they were all fanciful. We did not see them. On the 9th, with ordinary roads, we marched 27 miles; on the 10th, part of the day marched rapidly and the latter part slowly, and yet reached the ground in the forepart of the night; remained four hours without attempting to fortify, and then with three hours to spare, we moved out of their way, leaving one small regiment to meet the enemy. The whole movement is inexplicable and so different to the former course of the brigade and its commander, that we must pass it unexplained. In the evening Captain Dent, with 40 men, was sent to reconnoiter. He passed through Greeneville, which was occupied and patrolled by the enemy. He passed within half a mile of a large rebel force in camp. About daylight we hear cannonading, which tells that the spunky 5th have engaged the enemy. Our men held back in the rear were angry that they were not allowed to join the 5th. About 7 p. m. squads of the 5th reach camp and report their regiment all cut to pieces, and their battery and Colonel captured. There were loud imprecations in the brigade, that the 5th should have been left alone where the whole brigade desired to be, and should have been. The enemy have passed and now the 14th is ordered forward, but can now do nothing more than attack the retreating enemy to arrest their progress. Major Tompkins, with one battalion and one section of the battery, has the advance. The battery is placed in position and opens on the enemy with effect. A brigade of the enemy move upon our right as if to flank us. A battalion of the 14th is thrown upon that flank and the 65th Indiana is hurried forward on the right. Three hours we hold them in a warm fight. Colonel Capron has fears that they may attempt to turn our left, which is concealed by heavy timber. The writer was sent, with a portion of Company "I," 14th, to picket a road on our left; was joined soon after by a party under Lieutenants Boren, of "G," and Boeke, of "I," 14th, with orders for all under Lieutenant Boren to reconnoiter the enemy's right (our left); the united party numbered 40 men. A circuitous route was taken in order to reach their extreme right, and ascending a high ridge we saw below us a large body of dismounted rebel cavalry, and at the same time discovered by the course of the shells from our battery that we were in the rear of their right wing. Without a moment's hesitation our party dashed down among the enemy, delivering their fire and receiving a volley in return, which killed one horse, but before more injury could be inflicted on us, we were again on the ridge with two captured rebels, who informed us that there were in this body 1,700 cavalry holding their right wing; and that they were fearful of being attacked in the rear. This body of the enemy immediately mounted and fell back. We had no doubt that they supposed our party, which had attacked them so boldly, were the van guard of a large force in their rear. When we again reached our main command they were in pursuit of the retreating enemy, who made another stand and formed line on high ridges two miles in rear of their first position. Our brigade again pressed forward and engaged them in a lively skirmish, but they soon again retreated. Some of Shackelford's cavalry was now near, and the enemy moved rapidly toward Blountville. Our loss, except that of the 5th, was small. The 5th lost heavily, but did not lose their colonel nor their battery, as reported. The loss of the enemy we could not ascertain. General Ransom, who had been holding Greeneville, had effective present 5,885. General Williams was also present with a force doubtless as great. (See serial 56, page 613.) Prisoners gave their number from 6,000 to 10,000. In serial 53, page 274, is an account of the fight at Blue Springs and subsequent pursuit, and also a reference to our fight at Rheatown (or Henderson Station). We halted six miles from Rheatown and bivouacked; little forage; less rations; march yesterday and last night, 32 miles; march today, 10 miles; pleasant weather.

. October 12th. Reveille at dawn; all day in camp; plenty of forage, but only one fourth rations.

October 13th. Reveille before day; rained last night and this morning. Marched at 10 a. m. on Blountville road; camped at night between Holston and Watauga rivers; on half rations; day's march, 20 miles.

October 14th. Reveille at 3 a. m.; marched before day. One regiment was sent forward last night to get possession of Blountville, but were driven back. Today our advance skirmished with the enemy until we came within three miles of Blountville, where we found the enemy in strong position. Carter's brigade, which had come up, occupied the right and right center. The 14th on the extreme left, with 5th Indiana next and the 65th Indiana on the right. The rebel batteries, of which they had a number, opened fiercely. As soon as our batteries could secure a good position they poured in a well directed and incessant fire, and at the same time our whole line pressed forward, forcing the enemy back. They made another stand in the village, but in an hour they were driven from the town and were in rapid retreat towards Bristol. In this engagement all our troops fought gallantly. We now returned two miles on the Rheatown road and camped, having marched 18 miles. Plenty of corn, but no dinner or supper. We captured about 150 prisoners; beyond this there was no record of casualties on either side.

October 15th. Reveille at 4 a. m.; marched at sunrise through Blountville and on Bristol road. Companies "K" and "C," of the 14th, advance guard. Skirmished with the enemy to Bristol, then charged upon their main body and drove them from the town. A short distance beyond Bristol our advance was ambushed. A heavy volley from them killed Lieutenant Stein's horse (of Company "K"), another horse and one man of the advance was wounded. Company "I," of the 14th, now dismounted and advanced to their support, and the rebels were driven. The whole command followed closely the retreating enemy. Captains Dent, of "C," and Sanford, of "K," conducted the skirmishing with great credit. At one time their little band was charged upon by a large force and thrown into momentary confusion, from which the skill of their officers soon extricated them, when they rallied and drove the rebels in confusion. Lieutenant Stein, of Company "K," showed great courage and skill. Sergeants Balderston and Beckwith, of Company "C,".were sent forward to reconnoiter. They discovered a rebel party three times their own number, charged upon, and routed them. Six miles above Bristol the enemy made another stand, loth to relinquish any of "Virginia's sacred soil." Our artillery was planted and our lines formed for a charge, when they broke in confusion and we pursued for a short distance, then returned and camped on the battle ground. Day's march, 8 miles. Corn plenty, but short rations.

October 16th. Reveille at 4 a. m.; raining hard, night and day. Called in line at 9 a. m. Rumored that the enemy have been reinforced and intend driving us in turn. We waited their attack until 1 p. m., but no enemy appeared. Parties sent out destroyed three miles of railroad track, the railroad bridge, and all the cars and railroad property at Bristol, including the depot and all war supplies. After completing our work the command marched back through Bristol and camped after night in a wood four miles below; get some horse feed, but have no supper and had no dinner. Marched 10 miles. Captain Sanford, with Company "K," was sent out to get horses and returned with a few. We had been fighting General Ransom's division. Shackelford's report, October 16th, says: "We burned 5 bridges and destroyed railroad above Bristol; burned 28 box cars, 2 passenger cars, 3 locomotives, 6 gravel cars, and also destroyed the track at Bristol and part of the road below town. We have driven the enemy from East Tennessee." They left regretfully their strong military points and a country of rich supplies. October 14th General Jones reported that the counties of Jefferson and Greene, Cocke and Grainger, East Tennessee, could supply 100,000 barrels of flour, 1,500,000 pounds of pork. He also says to General Ransom (serial 53, page 749): "Order out the militia." Shackelford in one of his reports says: "We have fought for every inch of ground." Again: "Bristol, October 16th. We drove the enemy 10 miles above this place yesterday evening. Our advance still in pursuit, 10 miles up the Abingdon road. The railroad bridge and block house at Zollicoffer have been destroyed. We are destroying cars, locomotives and railroad tracks here, above and below."

October 17th. Reveille at 4 a. m.; marched at 9 a. m. The picket on the Bristol road had been fired into, but no other attack was made. Passed through Blountville and on the Zollicoffer road, through heavily timbered, unsettled country. When we reached Zollicoffer we found it to be a very strong position naturally, and it possessed some strong works, which could have resisted a heavy assault from this (Blountville) side. The town was insignificant. The Watauga river ran near, crossed by a dilapidated bridge. Marched a mile, tore up railroad track in many places for several miles. Marched 4 miles; camped after night; got corn, but no rations; no supper. March, 17 miles.

Sunday, October 18th. Reveille at 4 a. m.; march at 6.

Passed through Jonesboro; camped in a wood three miles southeast of town. Marched 19 miles.

October 19th. Reveille at sunrise. Get fresh beef and mutton without salt and one hardtack per man; forage scarce.

October 20th. Reveille at daylight. Horses saddled all day, but did not move. No bread; fresh beef without salt our entire fare.

October 21st. Reveille at daylight. Same fare as yesterday.

October 22d. Reveille at daylight. In camp until 3 p. m. Same fare. Then the effective men of the brigade marched toward Zollicoffer. Rumor of strong force of the enemy near. March 8 miles and camp. Plenty of corn; rations scarce.

October 23d. Very hard wind last night. March 4 miles to Holston river, cross and march to Zollicoffer. The enemy had fallen back to Bristol. Company "I" of 14th sent on scout; captured a rebel, Colonel Bottles, too badly wounded yesterday in a fight with 8th Tennessee union to be removed; returned to camp. Whole command countermarched and camped near previous camp ground. On page 688, serial 54, Shackelford speaks of a flag of truce, asking permission for Mrs. Bottles to visit her husband, who is said to be dying. She was admitted through our lines.

October 24th. Reveille at 5 a. m. Heavy drenching rain all last night. This hydropathic treatment does not prove effective in the cure of hunger. Marched to the Jonesboro camp; arrived at 11 a. m.. Usual starvation fare. Our trains, which were sent to Kentucky for clothing, returned empty. The men are very destitute of clothing, not having drawn any for many months, and when they left Kentucky in August they were ordered to leave everything not needed in that hot weather. Day's march, 11 miles. We are under orders to move.

Sunday, October 25th. Major Tompkins, with 130 men of the 14th, sent on scout to Elizabethtown, county site of Carter county, 20 miles distant. Rumors of rebel force approaching from that direction. He marched and returned 40 miles, discovering only about 30 rebels, who skedaddled. Weather fair, but hard fare.

October 26th. Reveille at daylight. In camp; same fare; weather cool.

October 27th. Reveille at daylight: Cold and raining. At 5 p. m. the second battalion, with detachment from the first and the third battalions of the 14th, under Major Quigg, march on double quick to Kingsport, 25 miles from Jonesboro, and halt within half a mile of rebel camp at that place, where are camped two rebel regiments. Our detachment number 150 men. We returned 12 miles, halt and feed at 4 a. m. of October 28th, having marched 40 miles. Breakfasted, then marched back 7 miles; establish pickets; remain until 10 a. m., then march to Greeneville and Jonesboro road 18 miles; then to Greeneville, 20 miles, where we arrived at 10 p. m., having marched since morning 45 miles, and since 5 p. m. of yesterday 85 miles. The main command remained in camp until 11 p. m. of the 27th, then formed line. The enemy reported approaching on three important roads. Remained in line on the Blountville road till morning. Marched 4 miles.

October 28th. March at 9 a. m. toward Greeneville Camped at 10 p. m. March 21 miles.

October 29th. Reveille at daylight. Major Quigg's command came in last night. Moved camp half a mile to a pleasant grove. Usual fare.

October 30th. Reveille at daylight. Hard wind.

October 31st. Reveille at 3 p. m. Mustered for pay. Religious service; sermon by Chaplain Chase. Inspection of arms and clothing. Page 607, serial 56, General Sam Jones' reports, October 30th: "My cavalry is on the Watauga and Holston (rivers) from Carter station to Kingsport. Infantry moving to the same lines." On page 613 he reports his effective strength for October: Cavalry, 3,026; infantry and artillery, 4,950; total, 7,976.

November 2d. Reveille at daylight. Weather pleasant. Captain Dent, with a party, was sent out after horses. In camp until an hour before sundown, when the effective force of the brigade marched southeast of Greeneville to capture a force of the enemy. They found the supposed enemy to be a newly recruited union command which had not yet drawn government clothing. Marched 8 miles through wilderness country and returned, reaching camp at 10 p. m., having marched 16 miles. Send far for forage. Our fare for some days has been flour without meat or salt, or anything else but water. We have had no sugar, coffee or tea for weeks. Flour and water for breakfast, changed to water and flour for supper; dinner we had none, because we could not ring in a change in the above rotation. The Alleghany, here called the Smoky range, is in sight. It appears to be near, though many miles distant. On this range is the state line between Tennessee and North Carolina.

November 3d. Reveille at daylight. Captain Dent returned with a few horses and was again sent out for more. We are under orders to move at daylight tomorrow.

November 4th. Reveille at 3 a. m. At sunrise move up the road toward Rheatown. At 10 a. m. we were thrown into battle line dismounted. A force of infantry and cavalry pass toward Greeneville. Colonel Graham reports rebel troops, two brigades of cavalry and one of infantry, with four days' rations, moving toward Tazewell (see serial 56, page 63). We now marched to within half a mile of Rheatown and camped. Forage and rations scarce. Day's march, 9 miles.

November 5th. Reveille at daylight. Remain in camp till 4 p. m., when "boots and saddles" and "to horse" are sounded. Formed column and marched at sundown toward Greeneville, passed through and bivouacked without unsaddling. We are four miles southwest of town; weather cold; marched 16 miles.

November 6th. Night cold and disagreeable. March at daylight. Passed through "Bull's Gap," where was camped a force of infantry, a part of General Wilcox's command. About 8 a. m., while on the march, we heard heavy cannonading in the direction of Rogersville, which lasted several hours. This proved to be an attack of the two rebel brigades of cavalry and one of infantry which Colonel Graham had reported as marching toward Tazewell. They had surprised Colonel Israel Garrard's brigade at Rogersville, composed of the 7th Ohio Cavalry, 2d Tennessee Cavalry and Phillips' battery. The brigade was badly cut to pieces, our estimated loss 500 old troops and 150 new recruits, four pieces of artillery and 36 wagons, the 7th Ohio lost 100 men, the battery 40 men; the remainder were Tennesseans. It was a most disgraceful surprise and rout. Horses lost, 600. (See serial 56, page 127.) On page 670 is Sam Jones' report. He says: "On the 6th our cavalry captured at Rogersville, Tennessee, 850 prisoners, 4 pieces of artillery, 2 stands of colors, 60 wagons and 1,000 animals." We camped at Morristown (a few miles above). Marched 30 miles.

November 7th. In camp. Rations more plenty.

Sunday, November 8th. Reveille at daylight. Captain Dent again sent out for horses. From this time until the 17th of November, in camp, with nothing of importance. Had brigade inspection; drew a small lot of clothing, not a tithe of what was needed. Weather cold, but have plenty of wood. This ends our railroad patroling, which for over two months has kept us busy, marching and fighting, sometimes day and night. We suffered much privation, marched nearly 1,000 miles, and fought many engagements, six of importance. Our principal route marched: From Loudon, 30 miles south of Knoxville, to Bristol, 60 miles northwest, or 90 miles of railroad patroled.

CHAPTER V.

RECORDS NEARLY ONE MONTH OF SEVERE EXPOSURE, PRIVATION AND PERIL, INCLUDING A SEVERE ENGAGEMENT AGAINST OVERWHELMING ODDS.

Our brigade was now commanded by Colonel Felix Graham. Colonel John W. Foster commanded our division, composed of our brigade and Colonel Garrard's brigade, which was not with us in the operations recorded in this chapter. General Bragg, having defeated General Rosecrans at Chattanooga, determined now to capture General Burnside's army, or drive it from East Tennessee. For this purpose he sent one of his very best commanders, Lieutenant General James Longstreet, with his veteran corps, to Knoxville. His army was composed of Hood's division, 4 brigades of 20 regiments; McLaw's division, 4 brigades of 20 regiments; Benning's brigade of 4 regiments; Buckner's division, 2 brigades of 9 regiments; Vaughn's brigade of 3 regiments; total infantry, 56 regiments. Estimating 400 men to the regiment (not an overestimate, when we remember that, unlike our practice, the enemy embodied all new recruits in the old organizations), they have 22,400 men. His cavalry was Wheeler's, soon after commanded by Major General William T. Martin; Martin's division; Morgan's brigade of 5 regiments; Morrison's brigade of 6 regiments; and Armstrong's division, Hume's brigade of 4 regiments; Tyler's brigade of 4 regiments; and Wharton's division, Harrison's brigade of 4 regiments, in all, 23 cavalry regiments, which by the same estimate would be 9,200 men. His artillery was Alexander's 6 batteries, and Leydon's 3 batteries, and attached to his cavalry, 3 batteries. His army proper being thus estimated, infantry, 22,400, added to cavalry, 9,200, makes a total of 31,600, with 12 batteries. See Longstreet's report of campaign, beginning page 455 of serial 54, in which report we find that he asked for and received the aid of General Ransom's army, of General Sam Jones' command; Corse's brigade, 3 regiments; Wharton's brigade (sharpshooters), 3 regiments; Jackson's brigade, 2 regiments of infantry; and of cavalry, Giltner's brigade, and Jones' brigade (called also Jones' division), and Jenkins' brigade, 3 regiments, with 6 batteries of artillery (see serial 54, pages 451 to 454. The report of Ransom's division for November, 1863 (see serial 56, page 770) was: Total for duty, 10,251, of which Jones' division of cavalry, officers and men, was 3,668 (leaving 6,583 as infantry). Adding Ransom's division to Longstreet's, we have 101 regiments, embracing infantry, 38,183, and cavalry, 12,868; grand total, 41,851, and 18 batteries.

Burnside's report shows present for duty at this time, of 23d A. C., 6,947; of 9th A. C. (lately arrived), 4,347. Wilcox's command at Tazewell, infantry, 2,752 (mostly six-months men). The cavalry force was 8,245. Burnsides' whole infantry force (exclusive of force at Cumberland Gap, 1,998), was 13,292, added to cavalry, made total, 21,537. Burnsides' forces were scattered in upper East Tennessee. Longstreet, with his command proper, was met at Loudon, on the Tennessee river, November 14th, by Burnsides' 9th army corps, and the passage of the river disputed, only with the expectation of delaying Longstreet's movements. Again, at Lenoir and at Campbell stations, Longstreet was resisted. With the expectation of being besieged in Knoxville, General Burnside ordered General Wilcox to take command of all outside forces and concentrate at some point between Knoxville and Cumberland Gap, and keep open a way of escape by that route for Burnside's forces in Knoxville, in case that move became necessary and practicable. The cutting of telegraphic communication to the Gap was to be the signal to Wilcox of his authority to act independent. Wilcox (on page 403, serial 54) says: "Night of November 16th telegraphic communication ceased." Wilcox concentrated his forces. He says (page 404): "Garrard's brigade was ordered to Evans' ford, Big Springs and Bean Station, to watch Ransom's forces, and Graham's brigade to Walker's ford. November 17th Longstreet's forces invested Knoxville, where Burnside, with 8,000 or 9,000 men, many of them convalescents, was penned up.

November 17th our brigade, encamped three miles above Morristown, under command of Colonel Felix W. Graham, received orders to join General Wilcox at Tazewell.

November 18th. Reveille at 3 a. m. March at sunrise. Crossed the Holston at 9 a. m. River high and ford rocky. Some of the horses stumbled, plunging horse and rider into the water. Marched to Bean Station, 12 miles. Camped in a field, a half mile southwest at 2 p. m.

November 19th. Reveille at 4 a. m. At noon the brigade, except the 65th, marched toward Knoxville. The trains, packhorses and ailing men, under Lieutenant Colonel D. P. Jenkins, with the 65th as train guards, crossed Clinch mountain to Tazewell. Our brigade marched down Richland Valley 12 miles to Rutledge, about 3 p. m., where we heard distinctly the siege guns at Knoxville, 30 miles off, signaling to us the uncertainty of the fate of the brave command there, as well as the uncertain fate of glorious East Tennessee. We marched to within one mile of Blain's cross roads and bivouacked, supperless, around fires, as it was cold. Marched 12 miles. A detachment from the 14th and the 5th, under Lieutenant Rowcliff, of Company "M," was sent toward Knoxville to reconnoiter the enemy's lines. They proceeded to within five miles of Knoxville, where they captured a vidette and learned that the city was completely invested.

November 20th. At daylight "to horse" was sounded. Formed line, but remained till 9 a. m., then marched toward Bean Station, 10 miles; crossed Clinch mountain at Powder Spring Gap, and camped near Clinch river. Marched 20 miles. Rations plenty. Heavy rains in the night thoroughly drenched the men and raised the river.

November 21st. Reveille at daylight. Crossed the river at 10 a. m., marched without breakfast to Tazewell, 10 miles, and camped in a wood one mile north of town at 3 p. m. Forage and rations scarce. We found our trains all right.

Sunday, November 22d. Reveille at 4 a. m. Hear nothing from Burnside. The road to the gap is lined with citizens going north. The Union people are alarmed at the prospect of again coming under rebel rule. The prospect to citizens and soldiers is gloomy. Transportation supplies cut off, local supplies in the country exhausted, with our main army cooped up in Knoxville by a superior force. We doubt if Valley Forge, with all its historic gloominess, exceeded in any respects, either in privations or despondency, the gloom that hung over beautiful East Tennesse from November 17th to December 2d, 1863. We were ordered to provide four days' rations, but where were they to come from, and whither were we bound? Dame Rumor said: "Across the mountains into Kentucky."

November 24th. Reveille at 4 a. m. Night clear and cold; ground frozen. Brigade marched . at 6 a. m. Crossed Powell river. Camped on a heavily timbered hill a half mile beyond and five miles southeast of Cumberland Gap. The 5th today burned one of their disabled ambulances. Marched 9 miles.

November 25th. Reveille at 4 a. m. Very cold last night, and the poorly clad soldiers suffered severely. Foragers go five miles and get little. Rations scarce. Details of recruiting officers made from the regiment today to go to Illinois to get recruits to fill our depleted ranks.

November 26th. Reveille 4 a. m. Night very cold. Draw small amount of clothing, not one-tenth of what was needed. Some of the men so destitute that they are compelled to sit up all night to keep fires going so they shall not freeze. We hear nothing from Burnside. Rations of men and horses reduced to one-fourth.

November 27th. Reveille at 4 a. m. Night very cold. We now begin an important movement. We give the report of our brigade commander, Graham, to our division commander, Foster. Beginning on page 426, serial 54, he says: "Sir—I have the honor to report that in accordance with orders I marched from camp near the bridge over Powell river, on main Cumberland Gap road, on 27th of November, 1863. My brigade consisted of the 14th Illinois Cavalry, Colonel Capron commanding; 5th Indiana Cavalry, Lieutenant Colonel Butler commanding; 65th Indiana Mounted Infantry, Captain Hodge commanding; Colvin's (Illinois) Battery, Captain Colvin commanding. Besides the four guns of Colvin's battery, there were four mountain howitzers attached to 14th Illinois Cavalry and two 8-inch rifled guns attached to 5th Indiana cavalry. My entire force numbered 10 field and staff officers, 47 company officers, and 1,031 non-commissioned officers and enlisted men, making an aggregate of 1,088. I moved by way of Tazewell, taking the straight creek road at that point to within four miles of Walker's ford, where I encamped for the night. On the morning of the 28th I crossed Clinch river and bivouacked at Brock's ford, four miles from Walker's ford, where my command fed. Toward night moved down the right hand road, recrossed Clinch river at Headham's ford and camped for the night near Headham's mill. On the morning of the 29th I moved down Clinch river to Onsley's ford, where I crossed and took the direct road to Maynardsville, where I camped for the night."

Captain Dent, with Company "C," was sent on the 27th on through Hogskin Valley and Gap, to a crossroads within three miles of Maynardsville, to scout and picket the road. The brigade got corn at the mill, but no rations. March 17 miles.

November 29th. Reveille at daylight. Very cold; freezing hard; the road a glare of ice. Camp one mile northeast of Maynardsville. March 14 miles. Captain Sanford, with his company "K," is sent with dispatches to General Granger, reported to be at Kingston with reinforcements for General Burnside. Captain Dent joined us here last evening. His vidette had been attacked, but the enemy were driven off. Heavy cannonading was heard at Knoxville.

November 30th. Very cold. A call was made for volunteers to cut their way through the rebel lines to Knoxville. All were eager to go, but on inspection few horses were found in condition for such service, some smooth shod, not able to go on the ice, many not shod at all. Resume Graham's report:

"November 30th I marched with all of my available force on the main road leading from Maynardsville to Knoxville. Sent a detachment of the 5th Indiana in advance to go to the enemy's picket and report back as soon as it was found. Proceeded 15 miles, when a courier reported a small rebel party on the road about four miles in our advance. I halted my command at this point and remained some time, awaiting further information. On learning that there was a force of rebels at Blain's Crossroads, I moved back to Maynardsville and camped, first throwing out a strong picket force and small patrol parties on all roads on the front and left."

Our record says: Within 16 miles of Knoxville we discovered a very large force of the enemy, said to be General William E. Jones' cavalry division of General Ransom's army. Having completed our reconnoisance, we returned to camp at Maynardsville, having marched 28 miles.

December 1st. Reveille at 4 a. m. Pickets at the gap, four miles below Maynardsville, on the Knoxville road, are attacked. Graham says: "They were speedily reinforced from the brigade. Two of the howitzers of the 14th, under Lieutenant H. C. Connelly, of Company "L" (14th), were also sent. More or less fighting took place during the day, both parties holding their ground. Scouting parties were sent out in considerable numbers." Our record says: About 1 p. m. Private Chase, of Company "D," 14th, returned from scout and reported a large force of the enemy's cavalry advancing from Blain's Crossroads. A scouting party of 40 men, under Captain Dent, was sent out, but they were driven back. About this time the picket on the Old Scott road, commanded by Lieutenant Horace Capron, of 14th, was advanced four or five miles. Sergeant Agnew, with 16 men, was sent to reconnoiter. They encountered a party of rebel troopers and charged upon them, routing them, and pursued them about a mile, and came upon the camp of the rebel General Jones' division of cavalry, when our boys "reversed motion." The enemy now advanced upon Lieutenant Capron, who fell back a short distance to a pass in the hills, where he held the enemy in check until reinforced as stated. They then fell back a short distance to a position more favorable for the use of artillery. Lieutenants Capron and Connelly rode forward to reconnoiter, when a sharp volley compelled them to retire. Skirmishing now became sharp until sundown. The enemy made several attempts to charge the post, but each time the skillful use of the two guns compelled them to retire. Graham says: "During the afternoon I had information as led me to believe that a considerable cavalry force of the enemy was approaching, and by 9 p. m. I became convinced that an attempt would be made to surround and capture my command." About dark Colonel Capron sent out Major Davidson, with several companies of the 14th, to find Captain Dent and his party, whose delay in returning caused uneasiness. He proceeded on the road to Blain's Crossroads, found Captain Dent and his command, then together they continued toward Blain's Crossroads, until they discovered a picket of the rebel General Armstrong. They returned to camp on another road, reaching camp at 11 p. m. We afterward learned through citizens that the enemy were confident that they had us in a pen from which we could not escape. So thoroughly did our scouts scour every road that every move of the enemy was known to us. Graham says: "I decided at once to move, but several of my scouting parties being several miles out, I could not get my force concentrated till near midnight, when, all being in, I moved quietly on the road to Walker's ford, leaving Company "M," of the 5th Indiana cavalry, at the point where the road from Blain's Crossroads comes in, with instructions for a part of it to patrol the road back to Maynardsville. Proceeding on to Brocks, I halted, that the men and horses might be fed. This was about 5 a. m. of December 2d. Rations were being issued as daylight appeared, and my picket in the rear, Lieutenant Miller and his company (of 14th) were vigorously attacked." The enemy's plan to capture our brigade was good. Armstrong's command was hurried to Blain's Crossroads, from which point a road led into the Walker's ford road in the rear of our camp at Maynardsville. This force was to and did reach the intersection of these roads just before day, when it was planned that General Jones' division and Morgan's division should come up from toward Knoxville and catch us in a fine trap. But for the effective manner in which Graham's scouts from the 14th and the 5th had thoroughly ascertained the plans and movements of the enemy, they would doubtless have succeeded. They too soon boasted of "taking the flying brigade (as they called us) in out of the wet." But as well try to catch a weasel asleep as to try to catch Colonel Graham napping, or the men and officers of the 14th and the 5th, either. The trains were hurried back to Walker's ford in charge of that skillful officer, Captain Dent, of the 14th. Lieutenant Miller, in command of rear picket posted at the intersection of the roads, found Armstrong's force on time, and skirmishing began as soon as the outlines of a foe was visible. As expected, our small picket force was compelled slowly to retire, before the enemy, Armstrong's force, falling into the Walker's ford road and pursuing. Company "B," of the 5th, and Company "A," of the 65th, the latter armed with the celebrated Henry rifle (16-shooters), were sent forward to reinforce Lieutenant Miller. They withstood the enemy until by sheer weight of the enemy's overwhelming numbers they were forced slowly back. General Jones' division now also came up, and Colonel Graham soon became aware that a strong force was being thrown around his left flank, by way of a road parallel to the Blain's Crossroads route. We resume Graham's report: "Although my command was tired, the men sleepy and hungry and the natural condition after a night's march somewhat irregular, yet all were under arms and in shape to repel the attack in the very shortest possible time." Graham became aware of an attempt to flank his command on his left. He says: "I immediately sent the 14th Illinois cavalry, under Colonel Capron, to the river, and down the road leading from Walker's ford to Rutledge, feeling confident that I could, with the rest of my command, keep the enemy in check and make good my retreat to and across the river. Two guns of Colvin's battery were sent to Walker's ford, with orders to cross and take position on the bank of the river, so as to command all the approaches to the ford. By half past seven my pickets had fallen back to Brock's house. The enemy advanced in such numbers as to compel them to give way at this time. My main force was in position, the 65th Indiana on the left of the line, a portion of the second and the third battalions of the 5th Indiana in the center, and one company of the 65th and one company of the 5th Indiana Cavalry on the right. The guns of the 5th were put in position in the rear of the center, on a rise of ground from which they did good service in keeping the enemy in check. Three companies of the 5th, under Major Wooley, and one section of Colvin's battery, under Captain Colvin, were placed in reserve. The firing had now become somewhat brisk, and the enemy not only showed his force, but made attempts to flank my position. I could only prevent his doing so by gradually falling back, which I did, to the point near Yeadon's house, where I brought my command into close order under cover of a fence and log house and barn. The enemy here made a charge in column, which was splendidly met by a portion of each regiment, and which proved decidedly disastrous to the enemy." The Henry rifles handled by picked marksmen, with which one company was armed, dealt death showers of well-directed lead into the charging column, at long range and at short range. Sixteen well-directed shots from each gun, as rapidly as the lever could be worked, and then reloaded for sixteen more shots in less than half the time required to load a muzzle-loader. Their comrades also did good execution. Riding over the field next day showed the carcasses of horses so thickly strewn over the valley as to indicate that their loss in men here must have been great, as we were not warring especially against horses.

Graham continues: "My artillery had now been retired, the formation of the ground on which it had to pass being unsuited to its use. The enemy, exasperated at this repulse, pushed on furiously, but the gallant officers and men of my command were not to be driven back so easily. On the contrary, they manfully contested every foot of ground, falling back slowly to a point about one mile from the river, where they were reinforced by the 116th and 118th Indiana Infantry regiments, under Colonel Jackson, commanding brigade. These regiments being in position, and my command being out of ammunition, I retired my force across the river, thus ending the fight, as far as the 5th Indiana and 65th Indiana Mounted Infantry were concerned."

Graham says, however, that Colvin's battery and the 14th Illinois Cavalry continued the fight longer. He highly praises the conduct of his officers and men, and speaks well of Colonel Jackson's men. Of the 14th Illinois Cavalry he says: "I respectfully refer you to the report of Colonel Capron, herewith attached, for an account of the part the 14th Illinois Cavalry took in repelling the attack and advance of the enemy. I am glad to state that the officers and men of the 14th Illinois Cavalry acted nobly their part. On their efforts depended much of the success of the day." Graham estimated the loss of the command with him at 53, and the loss of the enemy at very much more. He continues: "I now come to speak of the enemy, his designs and expectations. After hearing reports of citizens along the line of the enemy's march, I am confident that there were five brigades of cavalry and mounted infantry brought against my little force, the whole under command of Major General Martin. The design was to keep my force engaged at the gap, four miles below Maynardsville, until a portion of their forces could be moved from Blain's Crossroads into the road between me and Walker's ford, and at the same time a sufficient force had been sent around my front. At daylight on the morning of the 2d my entire command was to have been surrounded. The enemy moved on to a consummation of the object so devoutly wished for, only to find that he had surrounded a camp barren of everything save the fires my men had left in good order. In surrounding my camp he did, however, capture a portion of 'M' Company of 5th Indiana Cavalry, which had been left to patrol the road back to Maynardsville, and were not able to cut their way out. Finding themselves foiled in their first attempt, they next tried to cut my command off at Walker's ford, and that, too, proved a failure, and at the same time cost them a considerable loss in killed, wounded and prisoners."

In this closing language Graham refers to the movement of Jones' division down the blind road to Irwin's ford to get in Graham's rear, which the 14th Illinois Cavalry met and held in check. Colonel Graham's report was made soon after the fight, and only from such sources as one enemy in the field might be able to obtain regarding the movements of his foe, who kept his plans concealed. But to show how accurately he estimated, as well as to prove from undeniable sources the cunning plans and tremendous odds he had to meet, we now quote from the published reports of the rebel commanders themselves. Referring to Longstreet's report of campaign (serial 54, page 462), we find that Longstreet was preparing to abandon the siege of Knoxville and to move his army by way of Blain's Crossroads up toward Virginia. Serial 56, page 769, Longstreet to General W. E. Jones, November 30th: "Move your command out on Maynardsville road toward the river and scout in the vicinity and endeavor to annoy and distress the enemy as much as possible. You will probably find parties of the enemy on this road, which you will be able to capture." In serial 54, page 546, Major General Will T Martin reports: "By order of Lieutenant General Longstreet, I moved with part of my force toward Tazewell to meet a supposed advance of the enemy from that direction. Reaching the vicinity of Maynardsville in the afternoon of the 30th, I found General Jones' division skirmishing with the enemy. It was too late to attack. General Armstrong, with his division, was sent around to the right, to reach the rear of the enemy before daylight. The remainder of my force moved at daylight on Maynardsville, but the enemy had rapidly retreated soon after daylight, leaving a small picket, which was captured." General Martin had just spoken of Morgan's division rejoining him when he made this march, so that when he spoke of sending Armstrong's division to our rear and moving with the rest of his force upon our front, he meant Morgan's division, as Jones' division, near by and also engaged, belonged, not to General Martin's force, but to General Ransom's army, and had only just arrived. We thus have proved from the rebel reports not only their object to capture our brigade, but the precise plan to accomplish it as outlined by Colonel Graham in his report. Graham's information was obtained through the activity and intelligence of the scouts of the 14th Illinois Cavalry which were sent out on every road. In serial 54, page 453, is given Martin's command; Morgan's division; Morgan's brigade, 5 regiments; Morrison's brigade, 6 regiments; Armstrong's division; Hume's brigade, 4 regiments; Tyler's brigade, 4 regiments; total of these two divisions, 4 brigades, or 19 regiments. Wharton's division also belonged to Martin's command, but as it is not mentioned here we omit it. The numerical strength is not given here, but a month later, when its ranks were thinned (see page 889, serial 56, December 31st), Armstrong's division is 1,804 and Morgan's 2,190; total, 3,994, and doubtless at this time exceeding 4,000. Fortunately we have report of Jones' division, November 30th, just two days before. Effective present, officers and men, Jones' brigade, 2,046; Williams' (or Giltner's) brigade, 1,322; total Jones' division, 3,368; grand total employed to capture our brigade of only 1,088 was 7,362. These figures are taken from rebel sources. We now continue General Martin's report. He says: "Being joined by General Armstrong's division (that is, after our brigade had retired past the junction of the roads), his division was pushed toward Clinch river, while General Jones' command (3,368) was sent to the right to endeavor to effect a lodgment between the enemy and the river. A force of the enemy prevented his success." We will now show what force it was that prevented his success, and how they did it. Graham says in his report: "Finding themselves foiled in their first attempt, they next tried to cut my command off at Walker's ford, and that, too, proved a failure." Graham in the beginning of his report speaks of this attempt to flank him on his left, and says: "I immediately sent the 14th Illinois Cavalry, under Colonel Capron, to the river and down the road leading from Walker's ford to Rutledge." We now give Colonel Capron's report, found in serial 54, page 429, to Colonel Graham. He says: "Sir—I would respectfully report that on the morning of the 2d instant, being ordered to move down the right bank of Clinch river to the forks of the road five miles from Walker's ford, I moved my command, the 14th Illinois Cavalry, down the river two miles, until I came to a ford and road leading to Maynardsville, intersecting the main road from Maynardsville to Walker's ford, in the rear of the enemy at that time engaging the remainder of your brigade. Hesitating to proceed farther, I halted my regiment and awaited your orders, sending scouting parties on the Marnardsville and (on) the river roads (Company 'M' on Maynardsville road and Companies 'A,' under

Lieutenant H. Capron, and part of 'I,' under Lieutenant Kilbourne, on the river road). I had hardly received your orders to hold the Maynardsville road and river crossing before our advance (Company 'M') on the Maynardsville road was attacked by the enemy two miles from the main body. My regiment was then posted on the river crossing. I immediately sent the third battalion (under Major Tompkins), to reinforce the advance, which, after advancing one-half mile, engaged the enemy. Our forces taking position in the center of the road running through a narrow gorge, the rebel cavalry advancing in column down the road and charging our center, but were repulsed. The rebels then moved a column on our right and center, and were again repulsed at both points. They then deployed skirmishers on both our flanks on the hills, and again charged our right. The remainder of my regiment having been placed in position, the third battalion was ordered to the rear and reform, which they did, the rebels advancing on our line, attacking our whole line with skirmishers. Two companies were sent to the hills to dislodge their sharpshooters, who were annoying our lines, and a rapid and heavy firing was continued through our while line. At 1 p. m. the third battalion, with howitzers, were withdrawn to the left bank of the river, the first and second battalions still fighting the rebels, but compelled to gradually fall back, overpowered by superior numbers and flanked by sharpshooters. The third battalion was immediately deployed on the left bank of the river, and the howitzer battery placed in position. At this moment our position became critical, as their sharpshooters occupied the heights in good range of our position, but were fortunately held in check by our howitzers, until the fire of the rebels gradually slackened and our ammunition was nearly exhausted. The main part of my regiment was withdrawn to your command at Walker's ford, leaving two companies with the small amount of ammunition necessary to hold the ford, which they did until relieved by a regiment of infantry. The whole command fought with coolness and bravery, and our loss must have been much greater had not the natural position of the ground been greatly advantageous to us. Twenty-four officers and 300 men, with a loss of 18. The engagement commenced at 10 a. m., continuing until 3 p. m. From information obtained from prisoners, the force attacking us was General (W. E.) Jones' cavalry division, containing two brigades. I would also report the capture of 18 prisoners on the 2d and 3d instant." We had from our notes written a description of this battle, which, though couched in different language, was yet in substance the same as Colonel Capron's report. As the official report of commanding officers is properly esteemed better authority than the notes of any subordinate, for the reason that commanding officers have better and more sources of correct information relative to all military movements, and as Colonel Capron's report is a very correct outline of the fight, we will merely use the information in our notes to more fully explain the various movements and positions. Colonel Capron's statement: "Our loss must have been very much greater had not the natural position of the ground been greatly in our favor." Then he adds the number of our regiment officers and men,"324." Had he then known, as we now know, that Jones' division, which we there fought, numbered 3,368, or more than ten times our force, he would have realized that we must have great compensating advantages to have withstood such a host for even a short time, not to say five or six hours. Capron described our position in a road running down a narrow gorge between two ranges or ridges of high hills. This is correct, and we add that these high ridges began several miles back in moderate hills, which increased in height until near the river. Especially on our right, toward Walker's ford, they might be termed mountains, and all the way these ridges were covered with heavy timber. This itself gave a slight compensating advantage to our men in this, that it compelled the enemy, contrary to their choice, with long range guns, to seek a close range, as the woods prevented effective firing at a distance. Close range was what we desired, as our short range carbines could be loaded and fired much more rapidly than could their guns. Besides, each of our men possessed at least one large navy revolver with six loads, and this more nearly balanced the effectiveness of our forces. But the greatest element of strength with us, and without which we could not have long with-

CAPTAIN WM. R. SANFORD, COMPANY K.

stood their overwhelming numbers, was our howitzer battery, commanded by Lieutenant H. C. Connelly and manned by his company "L." This was placed on a slight elevation commanding the road between the ridges. When the enemy first struck our advance, Company "M," it was of necessity forced rapidly back by the enemy, who were pressing forward to get into the river road that led up to Walker's ford, where they expected to plant themselves in Graham's rear. When Company "M" was reinforced by Major Tompkins with the third battalion, they tied their horses in their rear, that every man could be in the line. This force succeeded in giving a momentary check, but it was only momentary. They saved their horses by hastily sending back a squad, who cut them loose and drove them to the river. Major Tompkins fell back fighting, having divided his command to the right and left of the road on the sides of the ridges. Our main command was similarly divided, leaving the road itself clear for the use of the battery. As Capron says, "The rebel column advanced down this road and charged our center," when they received from our battery a sweeping, destructive fire, and at the same time our lines on right and left poured into their charging column an enfilading fire, and their proud column was driven back in confusion. They next moved a force on the ridge on our right. To meet this movement Company "D," under Lieutenant Miller, was posted on the right, and when the enemy again attacked the center and the right, they succeeded no better in the center. But though Lieutenant Miller and his command fought manfully, they would have been overpowered but for the timely arrival of Captain Dent, who had been sent to Walker's ford with the trains. With his Company "C," and Company "G," he was hurried to the support of Lieutenant Miller, and took command. These three companies, by the most heroic efforts, aided by a few shells which Lieutenant Connelly found opoprtunity to send into the rebel columns on the hill, while he did not neglect their column advancing on the center. His quick eye saw where the enemy needed most attention, and there they received it. They were again repulsed. Meantime Captain Crandle, of Company "E," with several companies was posted on the left hand ridge, but as that was not in the direction of their objective point, Walker's ford, they did not make as much effort there. They now, however, attacked with skirmishers our whole lines, flanks and center, where, besides, the battery, was now posted Company "I," at first mounted, but soon after dismounting and sending their horses to the rear. While their skirmishers attacked our whole line, they fiercely charged our right with a heavy column. The battle there became terrific, our battery aiding much by shelling their advancing column. At this time the third battalion was temporarily thrown in the rear to reorganize. After this repulse there was a temporary lull, which augured mischief, so, at least, thought Captain Dent, when he sent Martin West and a companion over the crest of the right hand ridge to reconnoiter. These men soon returned with information that a body of the enemy on the other side of the ridge was advancing to flank our position. Two companies were immediately sent to head off this move. They were successful only in part, as several parties of sharpshooters had succeeded in passing our right and in gaining the heights on our right rear, from where they greatly annoyed our lines. The battle now raged in fury along the whole line. Seeing the inevitable necessity of falling back across the river, the third battalion and the battery were crossed over the river, taking position to aid the two other battalions to cross when compelled to. As Capron says, this was indeed a critical time. Compelled, in the face of an exultant enemy of ten times our number, and with their sharpshooters in our rear to mow us down, and in the face of this powerful force not only to retreat, but actually to retreat across an important river. Here again our battery saved us, not only by holding in check their heavy columns, eager to charge upon us and crush us, but their sharpshooters, perched upon their lofty elevation, poured down on the colume which was crossing a shower of bullets that sounded in the water like a heavy shower of hailstones. The two battalions were, however, in no haste to cross. One company at a time crossed and took position to repel a charge. Company "I," from the right, and Company "E," from the left, were the last to cross.

We will here mention an individual incident out of respect for one of the bravest and best comrades, as well as one of the most skillful gunners, who that day fought his last battle. Guy Niles, of Company "I," was one of the best gunners in the service. At Buffington Island he had charge of one section of our guns that did such admirable service. In this fight Guy was wounded in the foot, and as Company "I" was falling back the writer observed Guy limping slowly in the rear and hastened to his assistance and aided him to reach the horses. Guy crossed the river and rode up to the battery boys. He pointed to a large party of rebel sharpshooters collected in a recess of rocks on the overhanging cliff and engaged in the pleasant pastime of sending as many balls as they could at our crossing column, without danger to themselves. Guy said: "I believe those are the rascals that shot me, and I would like to give them one shot in return." The battery boys gladly consented. Guy alighted, measured the distance and elevation with his eye, cut the fuse accordingly, loaded the gun, sighted it and fired. More than one who knew Guy's skill watched that shell with interest as it sped on its journey, landing precisely in the nest and exploding just at it reached the recess. A better shot never could have been made, and we could easily believe citizens when the next day they told us that that one shot killed twenty rebels. But, alas, it was Guy's last shot. His foot grew much inflamed, and in spite of his protestations he was soon compelled to go to the Knoxville hospital, where he soon after took the smallpox and died. Peace to his memory.

An incident that occurred just as we were preparing to fall back doubtless had something to do in checking the enemy from crushing us, when we attempted the dangerous movement of retiring across the river in the face of such overwhelming odds. Major Davidson came riding down at a full speed on the opposite bank of the river, and in his stentorian voice called: "Hold your position, boys, for fifteen minutes, and you will be reinforced by 40,000 infantry." The only foundation for this was the fact that two regiments of infantry had already marched to Walker's ford, and one was marching for our ford. They came from Wilcox's forces at

Tazewell. As the enemy anticipated a column of reinforcements from Kentucky through the gap, under command of Major General John G. Foster, the ruse was sufficient to cool their ardor somewhat.

Two companies, "I" and "C," were left to guard the ford, which they had but little trouble to do, until the arrival about sunset of an infantry regiment to relieve us. The enemy had found themselves completely foiled in their attempt to cut off any of our forces at the river, and having no further object in pressing forward, they gradually retired. Companies "I" and "C" now marched to Walker's ford and rejoined their comrades. There were mutual congratulations between the comrades of the different regiments. Each felt proud of all their comrades and felt an increased faith in them, a condition essential to the best success of any military organization. We will now give the reports and official statements made by others of this affair. General Martin in his report bestows the highest praise on the 14th, where, speaking of sending General Jones' division to cut Graham off at Walker's ford, he says: "A force of the enemy prevented." Yes; 324 brave officers and men of the 14th Illinois Cavalry prevented Jones' division of cavalry, 3,368 strong. Our corps commander, General Wilcox, noticed this affair in several reports, from page 394 to 397, serial 54. We make short extracts: "Graham thinks Wheeler is present with his whole force, 6,000." Again: "They are pressing his left wing (14th Illinois Cavalry)." Again: "After quite a struggle to-day (December 2d) our troops remain in possession of Walker's ford." Again: "Colonel Graham's brigade have expended all their ammunition, and will require to be replenished by morning." Foster refers to the battle and says: "Three divisions of Wheeler's cavalry and Jones' division came out and drove Graham's brigade back from Maynardville to Walker's ford, on Clinch river.

After dark our brigade was withdrawn, leaving the infantry to guard the fords. Marched two miles and camped. Small rations and horse feed. Day's march, 10 miles.

December 3d. Reveille at 4 a. m. Weather cold. Marched at sunrise. The 14th was sent across at Walker's ford to reconnoiter. Marched 3 miles and camped. Day's march, 7 miles.

December 4th. Reveille at 4 a. m. At 2 a. m. Lieutenant Boeke, with a dozen men of Company "I," 14th, was sent with dispatches to General Granger at Kingston. At 4 p. m. regiment marched to a crossroads within three miles of Maynardville, where we found our first battalion on picket. Built strong barricades, then bivouacked. Marched 3 miles.

December 5th. Reveille at 4 a. m. At noon report came that the enemy were advancing. Formed line, but no enemy appeared. Then returned to camp in Hogskin valley. March, 6 miles.

December 6. Reveille at 5 a. m. At 9 a. m. march toward Knoxville. Passed through Hogskin gap; camped near it in a grove. Found our road blockaded. Working parties sent out to clear obstructions. We are almost entirely destitute of rations and horse feed. Marched at 2 p. m. through Bull's gap into Bull Run valley, then around by Emery's ford, into Hickory valley, where we rejoined the 5th and 65th, who had encountered and whipped a rebel command. We bivouacked after night in a heavy piece of timber. Marched 20 miles.

December 7th. Reveille at 2 p. m. Called out, formed line and remained till morning. At daylight Colvin's battery shelled the enemy's camp. The first battalion was advanced, but the rebels did not reply to their fire. The brigade moved up at 7 a. m. The rebels had retired. We followed through Emery's gap, into Emery's valley, skirmishing with his rear, until he took position in Powder Spring gap, in Clinch mountain. We sent forward skirmishers, who engaged them for a few hours. The roughness of surrounding mountains prevented a flank movement. The road was blockaded with fallen timber, and the enemy were intrenched behind rocks, fallen timber and barricades, and their batteries planted to sweep all possible approaches. Our forces withdrew, retiring to Emery's gap, fed and dined, then marched into Hickory valley. The 14th went on picket down the valley; marched 12 miles. Major-General John G. Foster, in serial 56, page 351, says of this affair: "I expected to join a brigade of infantry (with the cavalry), and drive the enemy from the summit of Clinch mountain, * * * but the troops were so weakened by the one-quarter rations that they have had for some months, that they did not get to the position in time. The cavalry had skirmished with the enemy all day." General Foster, in some of his reports, pictures the want of food and clothing with the troops as extreme. He says of his small force of cavalry: "They are splendid men, but almost destitute." He says, December 2d: "I have kept the small force under my command skirmishing with the enemy continually. Their forces being larger than mine, we have not been able to make much progress."

December 8th. Reveille at 5 a. m. At 9 a. m. marched down Bull Run valley. Reached Blaine's crossroads at noon, and joined General Shackelford, now in command of all of Burnside's cavalry. He had orders to pursue General Longstreet, who was compelled to raise the siege of Knoxville by heavy reinforcements from Grant's army. Longstreet is now retiring towards Virginia. The roads are one continued mud hole, and every succeeding command that passes over them leaves them worse. We moved up the valley two miles above Rutledge. Marched 20 miles. We now get no government rations and depend entirely upon the country, and the rebels have cleaned Richland Valley of everything except mud.

December 9th. Reveille at 5 a. m. March at 10 a. m. up the valley; camped in a wood on the right of the road, a half mile below Bean Station. March 15 miles.

December 10th. Reveille at 4:30 a. m. We have had only quarter rations for the last five days. Today we had general review, and a splendid speech by General Shackelford, in which he regretted the retirement of General Burnside from East Tennessee. Citizens and soldiers all regretted his withdrawal. Wm. G. Brownlow, in a petition to President Lincoln, said: "We beg you not to let East Tennessee be abandoned by our troops. Burnside, whether he holds or has been defeated, is a glorious moral and military hero, and deserves everlasting honor." General Foster says (page 281): "I arrived here (Knoxville) on the evening of the 11th, and received the command from General Burnside the 12th. General Parke was now above Blaine's crossroads, with about 10,000 infantry, being the number of the 9th corps, and the 23d corps, capable of marching and fighting. The cavalry were in front of Bean Station, harrassing the enemy. I find the commissariat of the department very destitute; there being only a very few days' supply of the most requisite parts of the rations, which are now, and have been for a long time, issued in half and quarter rations." In regard to mounted forces, after stating that for general purposes it was the most needed, he says (page 283) : "This kind of arms is much inferior in number to that of the enemy, and must be increased." Both General Shackelford and General Parke were ordered not to bring on an engagement, but if attacked, to fall back to Blaine's crossroads. The cavalry at Bean Station was 13 regiments, consisting of Graham's brigade, and Wolford's division; all cavalry and mounted infantry: 14th Illinois, 5th Indiana, 65th Indiana, Colvin's Battery, 4 guns ; 2 guns of the 5th ; 4 howitzers of 14th ; Wolford's command : 112th Illinois Mounted Infantry, 6th Indiana, 1st Kentucky, 11th Kentucky Mounted Infantry, 27th Kentucky Mounted Infantry, 8th Michigan, 9th Michigan, 2d Ohio, 7th Ohio, 45th Ohio Mounted Infantry. Many of the men were on detached service and foraging, so that with the thinning out by the disabilities of men and horses, the whole cavalry force at Bean Station did not exceed 2,500 or 3,000. Many of the men went long distances to get forage, in which occurred many little adventures and skirmishes. Lieutenant Payne, our regimental commissary, led a small party to a mill, and while engaged in securing meal, the mill was surrounded by a large party of the enemy, and our party, forage and all, was captured, except the Lieutenant, who escaped by slipping under the water-wheel.

December 11th. Reveille at daylight ; a detachment of 500 of Graham's brigade, under Colonel Graham, marched in the morning up the valley to reconnoiter. Near Mooresville, 8 miles above, we encountered a large force of cavalry and mounted infantry. This was Longstreet's mounted forces. We formed line, planted our batteries and drove them from their camp to the adjoining woods and hills beyond Mooresville. We briskly engaged the enemy for several hours, resulting in several killed and wounded on our side; their loss unknown. One small party of Company "I," 14th, under Lieutenant Kilbourne, misunderstanding orders, actually penetrated the rebel lines between two strong positions occupied by them, a half mile apart. Their capture or destruction would have been certain, but for the fear, on the part of the enemy. that this small party was the bait of a trap set for them. When our lines were withdrawn this party escaped by skillful maneuvering, as the enemy were too fearful of an ambuscade to press too closely. Having ascertained the force and position of the enemy, the brigade returned to camp at 8 p. m. Marched 16 miles.

December 12th. Reveille at 5 a. m.; in camp.

December 13th. Our whole command was called out and formed line about one mile above the station, to check an anticipated attack of the enemy; but he did not appear. Page 495, serial 54, shows this to have been rebel General Humphrey's brigade, sent to support Colonel Giltner's cavalry advance. They approached within three miles, and then returned.

CAPTAIN WM. H. GUY, COMPANY F.

CHAPTER VI.

BATTLE OF BEAN STATION.

In this description we shall frequently refer to the official reports, which, unless otherwise stated, will be found in serial 54, series 1, volume 31, part 1. We make extracts from General James Longstreet's report (page 462); he says: "As our position at Knoxville was somewhat complicated, I determined to abandon the siege and draw off in the direction of Virginia, with an idea that we might find an opportunity to strike that column of the enemy's forces reported to be advancing from Cumberland Gap. The orders to move in accordance to this view were issued December 2d. The column reached Rogersville December 9th." On page 463: "On the 12th (Dec.) I received information that a part of the reinforcements from Chattanooga had returned to that place, and that the enemy had a force consisting of three brigades of cavalry, and one of infantry at Bean Station; his main force being between Rutledge and Blaine's crossroads." Longstreet was well posted as to the position of our forces, though mistaken as to a brigade of infantry at Bean Station. There was no infantry there, and none within less than 20 miles in that direction. Three brigades, or 13 regiments of mounted men, was the whole force there. Longstreet says: "Orders were issued to the troops to be in readiness to march on the 14th (Dec.), with the hope of being able to surprise and capture the enemy's forces at Bean Station. Our main force to move down from Rogersville to Bean Station. General Martin, with four brigades of cavalry, was to move down the south side, and cross the Holston opposite Bean Station, or below; and General W. E. Jones, with two brigades of cavalry, was to pass down on the north side of Clinch mountain, and prevent the enemy's escape by Bean Station gap."

Longstreet's forces at this time exceeded 21,000 men, including General Ransom's force, which was with him.

It consisted of McLaw's division, of Kershaw's brigade, 6 regiments; Wofford's brigade, 6 regiments; Humphrey's brigade, 4 regiments; Bryan's brigade, 4 regiments; total McLaw's division, 4 brigades of 20 regiments; Hood's division, Jenkin's brigade, 6 regiments; Law's brigade, 5 regiments; Robertson's brigade, 4 regiments; Anderson's brigade, 5 regiments; Benning's brigade, 4 regiments; Hood's total, 5 brigades, of 24 regiments; Buckner's division, Johnson's brigade, 3 regiments; Gracie's brigade, 6 regiments; Buckner's total, 2 brigades, of 9 regiments; Ransom's infantry, Corses' brigade, 3 regiments; Wharton's brigade, 3 regiments; Jackson's brigade, 2 regiments; total Ransom's infantry, 3 brigades, of 8 regiments; total of Longstreet's infantry, 14 brigades of 61 regiments; General Martin's cavalry consisted of 3 divisions, of 5 brigades, of 22 regiments, and Ransom's cavalry, 3 brigades, of 14 regiments; total cavalry, 8 brigades, of 36 regiments; his artillery was Alexander's, 6 batteries, and in McLaw's division was 3 batteries, and in Ransom's division was 6 batteries, in all 15 batteries. A grand total in Longstreet's army, of 22 brigades, of 97 regiments and 15 batteries. The numerical strength of Ransom's, November 30th, was 5,873; and Longstreet's for December was 15,362, and on December 14th probably reached 16,000, or total, 21,873, with 15 batteries. This was terrible odds, in an attempt to capture 3 small brigades of only 13 regiments, of less than 3,000 men, with 10 pieces of cannon.

Immediately after the battle, the writer gave a description of it which was approved by the officers and men; but the most wonderful thing is that the published official reports of the enemy do not contradict it in anything, and in many things, even down to the minutia, their reports confirm it. Our space will not permit a full copy, but to our description will be added a fine description of a portion of it, by Major H. C. Connelly, and also portions of the reports of rebel officers, descriptive of the battle. The following is a portion of our description:

"Scouting parties sent out reported all quiet, and on the 14th (Dec.), not anticipating an attack, many detachments were out on scout duty and foraging, so that little, if any, over 2,500 men were present, and as we fought dismounted, deducting those that cared for the horses, we could not have had 2,500 in line of battle. Of our brigade, many were on other duty, and of the 14th, nearly two whole companies were gone to bear dispatches.

About 1 p. m. the bugles sounded "Boots and Saddles," "To horse," and "Assembly," in rapid succession, warning us that there was work for us. We marched double quick, and were formed in line near the position formed on the day before. Colonel Wolford, with his division, formed on the right of the road, facing up the valley, his left resting near the road, and his right extending out towards a range of hills in the direction of the Holston river. Our batteries were planted; Colvin's on an elevation to the right of the road, and on the left of Wolford's line. The two guns of the 5th Indiana were planted a little to the left of the road, on an eminence in advance of Wolford's line. The howitzer battery of the 14th Illinois, commanded by Lieutenant H. C. Connelly, and manned by his company, "L," of the 14th, was advanced 300 yards, and slightly to the left of the guns of the 5th. Our brigade, commanded by Colonel Graham, constituted the left wing, and was posted; the 65th, with its right resting near the howitzer battery, and its left extending out toward the Clinch range. The 5th Indiana was posted to the left, and in advance of the 65th; its left reaching to the foothills of the range. The 14th, the left of the brigade, and extreme left of the whole line, was advanced a half mile in front of Colvin's guns and Wolford's line, and in advance of the 5th, on the foothills with its left out towards the range. This arrangement of our brigade was designed to prevent flanking our left wing; a wise precaution, as the sequel showed. The ground occupied by the 14th, and on its front, was much broken, and grew more broken as the Clinch range was approached. The enemy first attacked our right. Soon Wolford was engaged with vastly superior numbers; the fury of the storm increased until the battle strife was terrible. Like a mighty torrent rolling down a mountain side, the enemy's dense double columns rolled towards our left. Soon their columns have reached to the front of our batteries. As soon as within range all of our batteries opened upon them. The roar of our larger guns, mingled with the intonations of our smaller but splendidly operated howitzers, almost drowned what before had seemed a terrible roar of Wolford's battling line. Now the enemy get into position 10 pieces of artillery, so arranged as to enfilade as well as giving a front fire, raking with round shot and shell our batteries and their supports, as well as the whole line within range. The conflict in this quarter now became terrible and grand. Again and again the rebel columns were formed for a charge upon our batteries. Great gaps were opened in their densely solid ranks, by the fierce and rapid discharges of our skillfully operated pieces. From an elevated and advanced position on the left of these operations, we witnessed the slaughter in their dense columns, by each discharge of our guns. Nothing daunted, and with a boldness worthy of a better cause, their broken columns were instantly re-formed, prepared again for a charge.

One column was seen to approach at a point where the nature of the ground might screen them until near enough to make a sudden dash, hoping thus to effect the capture of our guns. But, alas for human calculations; nature seldom makes valleys without occasional hills; so these sly Johnnies found that they must cross a rise of ground. No sooner did their forms appear in sight, than our gunners opened upon them a fire so fierce and withering that even Longstreet's veterans could not endure it. Still determined to persevere, they threw themselves prone upon the ground, crawling along like the living type of South Carolina's banner, until a more sheltered position was reached, when they ventured to rise once more. But as soon as their forms were exposed above the grass the same withering fire met them, melting their column so rapidly that southern chivalry could not stand, but gave up that attempt to take our guns. Meanwhile the enemy have planted additional batteries. Their guns, so superior to ours in number and in caliber, are worked with equal rapidity, though not with equal fatality, owing partly to the inferior skill of their gunners, but principally to the fact that their missiles did not find the dense mass of human forms to mangle and destroy as did ours; but instead, only a thin line of skirmishers, especially on the left, vainly striving with their attenuated line, to cover all the front of their powerful foe.

The enemy's fierce cannonading, though sending a continuous stream of cannon balls from enfilading positions, and raining down showers of shells and screaming railroad iron, which, by its screaming, sounded like the shout of a legion of demons, seemed to threaten annihilation, yet effecting but little. The rebel sharpshooters, of which they had a great number, were a special annoyance to our gunners. A few of these were brought down by the advance of the 14th. The writer, from an elevated and advanced position, was enabled to survey the battlefield in its successive developments, while fighting with us on the left had not yet opened in all its fierceness; but the enemy continued to extend his solid lines farther and still farther to our left.

At this moment an uninterruped view of the conflict could not fail to excite to the highest point of possibility, the minds of deeply interested spectators. Rapidly the eye surveyed the prospect, and the mind contemplated the probabilities of the awful conflict. Wolford was still engaged on the right. Terrible volleys and demoniac yells indicated the fierceness of the strife in that quarter; but alas! they also indicated by their changing direction, that his brave band was being forced back by the terrible odds against him. The enemy's batteries now increased the fury of their fire; shells flying like flakes of snow in a constant shower, while several of their guns, opening upon the left, made devil's music by their discharges of railroad iron, which, during its strange gyrations along its curved and fiery path, exhibited a novel appearance as of some fiery demon, on an errand of "misery to man," whilst its loud shrill screaming did but increase the fancy of its demon nature. The immensely dense mass of infantry which the enemy now brought in view as he extended his lines farther and still farther to our left, awakened intense anxiety as to our fate; a thin and scattered line of skirmishers of dismounted cavalry, armed with carbines and navy revolvers, inferior weapons against long range guns at a distance, or sharp pointed bayonets in close conflict; a mere skirmish line, without base or reserve. Can it be wondered at that the eye, moistened by pity at the threatened fate of our slender, but heroic band, was turned with frequency and expectation down the road, in anxious hope to discover the expected and now greatly

needed reinforcements of gallant blues from that quarter.
Intensity was increased as the perilous moments flew
rapidly by, but alas! no support appeared. To increase, if
possible, the height of that intensity, our howitzer battery
was now withdrawn from its position and hurried to the
support of Wolford's melting line. Alas! could we then
have known the truth, as now we record it, another pang
of anxiety would have been added. The battle on the left
had now begun with great fury. Pressing duty precluded
any further observation on the right. Fortunately we are
furnished with an account of subsequent operations on
the right, by Thomas Featherson, of Company "I," 14th,
and by Major H. C. Connelly, then a Lieutenant of Company "L," and in command of the howitzer battery; both
of whom were now sent to reinforce Wolford. As Featherson's description is incorporated in an article published
in the National Tribune, by Major Connelly, we make extracts. "It was a beautiful day; the sun shone warmly
and brightly. After a time the second line of battle came
in view. All the artillery we had, Colvin's battery, the
two guns of the 5th, and the howitzers, were loading and
firing with great rapidity. As the shells burst over the
heads of the advancing foe the line would drop to the
ground, rise, close up and advance in splendid order. It
was inspiring to see the enemy advance with solid front.
Our weak line of battle confronting so large a force with
intrepid daring, caused the enemy to hesitate. The rapidity with which they fired their artillery was enough to demoralize our command. They report that in this battle
they shot about 800 shot and shell. After a time my ammunition was expended, and I hurriedly went to the train
to get a supply. We quickly made the trip in the midst of
a most fearful cannonading, and securing a supply of ammunition returned in haste to the line of battle. We were
now directed to report to Colonel Wolford, who was being
strongly pressed on our right flank. We planted our guns
in position on the crest of a hill and opened our battery.
Immediately the sharpshooters directed their attention to
us, but we stood our ground until our ammunition was
exhausted. As we fired our last shot, we discovered the
rebels coming out of the woods and charging to take our
battery. We quickly limbered up and got out, and as we

were leaving the field a volley was fired into us. A horse ridden by a postilion was shot, and I directed the rider to dismount and cut him out. This work was done almost without stopping the gun, and we came off the field with our entire battery." Connelly continues: "Lieutenant W. L. Sanford, of Company "I," 14th Illinois Cavalry, was in a position to see what was going on that day. He wrote a description of the fight, a part of which we quote: "We will now follow our battery to the right, and witness the struggle there as depicted by Featherson, who, with a provost guard of 40 men, was sent to reinforce Wolford at this time. Featherson says: "Lieutenant Connelly, after reporting to the brave warrior, planted his little battery and again opened on the enemy with his spherical cased field shells, with telling effect. At length Colonel Wolford rode up and remarked that his command being out of ammunition, the whole line would be compelled to fall back. The Lieutenant remarked: "I have but few shells left and would like permission to plant them among the enemy." This request was granted, but the delay caused by carrying out the suggestion nearly proved fatal to Wolford's command and the battery. About the time the last shell was fired, the rebels emerged from the woods on the right, charging with fiendish fury and overwhelming force. His men being out of ammunition Wolford's whole line now fell back in good order, bringing off all the guns successfully. Whilst Lieutenant Connelly was engaged in expending his last shells Wolford's brave men, though out of ammunition and thus powerless, remained coolly and defiantly in their position, receiving the fierce fire of the foe without power to retaliate; whilst the little battery poured a constant shower of shells into their massed lines, with precision, and which exploded with regularity, scattering fragments of death dealing iron in their midst. The slaughter of their men at this point was terrible and kept in check their lines, until Connelly, too, was exhausted of ammunition, and the line compelled to fall back, as narrated. In Wolford's command was the 112th Illinois Mounted Infantry, as true and noble a band as ever kept step to the music of the Union, and commanded by the gallant Colonel, now Brigadier General Thomas J. Henderson."

Colvin's battery, and the guns of the 5th, all being out of ammunition, were compelled to retire. Now our whole line, from the road to the extreme right is all gone. The vacuum is rapidly filled by the fierce onrushing legions of the foe. Only our slender brigade is left to dispute the advance of Longstreet's army. Brigades are passing us on our right; they have possession of our morning camp. Heavy columns have passed us and are striving to move round our left. In our front a division has halted, and forms line with their lines far overlapping both of our flanks.

Now has gathered a cloud of war, so black and impenetrable, portending a storm so terrific as to require not bravery or heroism to stand and contemplate its awful probabilities, but instead those attributes termed *rashness, presumption;* a fearless defiance of earth and hell. The dense mass of the foe, with their many thousand bristling bayonets, advance upon the slender lines of the 14th, whose position far in advance of the line of the brigade, necessitates its retirement to that line. Every rod of ground is desperately contested as the 14th is forced slowly and sullenly back to the line of the 5th Indiana. While stubbornly contesting every hill until our assailants were near, we were ordered to concentrate on a church and hold it. Before the church was a hill which we held until the foe was close upon us, intending to rally on the church and hold it; but when we reached it we saw at a glance that it was far better suited to a prison than as a castle of defense, as it was located in a ravine with hills far overtopping it on every side. To halt here meant a sacrifice of our command. Captain Dent in command ordered "Forward." We had withstood the enemy until they were near. Now we have before us a rugged hill; it was a mountain then; it was bare of trees or protection of any kind. We have no alternative but to climb its steep sides before the fierce fire of the demons at our heels. Well does the writer remember the superhuman effort. Weak from a previous fit of sickness, his strength gave way; three times he grew faint from sheer exhaustion, but rebel bullets rattling all around were a strong persuader, a veritable stimulant, and called into action those latent powers so often described, but so seldom realized; staggering like an inebriate, the

brow of the hill was reached and the descent was more easy. We now reached the line of the 5th; an attempt was made to form a line to check the advance of the enemy. It was beginning to grow dusk. At one point a column approached, and uncertain as to our identity, they challenged with: "What command is that?" Our boys answered: "14th Illinois Cavalry," and then challenged the others: "What command is that?" The reply, "15th and ——, South Carolina," was rendered indistinct by the terrible volley poured into our ranks. Here it was that Geo. H. Mason, of Company "C," our regimental standard-bearer, was killed, falling with his face to the foe. Here some of our bravest men yielded up their lives, a sacrifice on the altar of our country. Lieutenant Kilbourne, of Company "I," was severely wounded and borne off the field. Our Adjutant, Lieutenant Chauncey Miller, was captured. He was engaged in directing the formation of our line, and observing this force and supposing them to belong to our brigade he rode forward to give command. As they had heard his commands to our men, they knew who he was and instantly fired a volley that killed his horse, and before he could extricate himself he was a prisoner in their hands, and was subsequently sent to those horrid prisons of the south, to eke out months of miserable existence in those dens, suggested, provided and controlled by the Spirit of Evil himself.

Orders now came to hold this line at all hazards, as stores at the station were not yet all removed. Our brigade line was now formed. On our right was a large force that had passed us and occupied our morning camp. On our left the enemy was endeavoring to throw brigades around to our rear. Only a thin line of skirmishers and the extreme ruggedness of the ground to prevent; but kind nature came to our relief, throwing the dark curtain of night over the bloody pictures of the battlefield, and confusing the plans of our enemies. We succeeded in holding this line until past midnight, when we retired from this hotly contested field.

Our commanding officer, General Shackelford, never reported this battle, doubtless because, with General Burnside, he had asked to be relieved, and his successor, General Sturgis, had already been appointed, but had not yet arrived to take command. We know no other reason for this failure and cannot surmise why no other officer except Colonel Wolford made any report, and his was a meager one. Fortunately that our record was kept, and fortunately, too, that in the official reports we have so many rebel reports from the commanding General down to Colonels and Majors. And fortunate, too, for our reputation as historians, in not a single instance do they contradict our record, but on the contrary, they confirm it not only in the main points, but even in much of the minor details. Of course, we can give only short extracts, but giving volume and page we challenge criticism of the correctness of our statements.

We have already given the preliminary of Longstreet's report. On page 463 (serial 54) he says: "The infantry column, however, reached Bean Station in good time and surprised the enemy completely. General W. E. Jones (with two brigades of cavalry) also got his position in good time, and captured a number of the enemy's wagons. (This was on the opposite side of Clinch mountain.) Brigadier General B. R. Johnson, commanding Buckner's division, advanced directly against the enemy and drove him steadily to the buildings at Bean Station, where he met with a strong resistance. General Kershaw, at the head of McLaw's division, was ordered in upon the right of Johnson to push forward and cut off the force that was occupying the (Bean Station) gap. Kershaw executed his orders literally, but we could not catch the enemy's cavalry; the enemy escaped to a strong position three miles below (page 464). This was the second time during the campaign, when the enemy was completely in our power, and we allowed him to escape." We suppose the first time was December 2d, at Walker's ford, where, as here, they attempted to capture our command, using an overwhelming force and as signally failed as here. McLaw's division, commanded by General Kershaw, which Longstreet says was thrown upon the right of Johnson, consisted of Kershaw's brigade, of 6 South Carolina regiments, and Wofford's brigade, 6 regiments; Humphrey's brigade, 4 regiments; Bryan's brigade, 4 regiments. A total of 4 brigades, or 20 regiments, who passed or formed in front of our one small regiment. Were we not justified in terming this a dark, portentous war cloud? We now go back to follow up the details of the battle as reported by the rebel officers who commanded. On page 531, Confederate General Bushrod R. Johnson says: "December 14th this (Buckner's) division moved on Bean Station at the head of the infantry. * * * About 3 miles east of Bean Station at 2 p. m. the cavalry encountered and drove back the enemy's pickets, and sharply engaged the reserve. As the skirmishers ascended to the top of the hill east of the station, the enemy's artillery opened from three points on the elevation west of the station. Two of these points were on the north side (the 5th Indiana guns and the howitzers of the 14th), and one (Colvin's battery), on the south side of the Knoxville road. Our skirmishers were now ordered to lie down until our artillery could be brought up. Taylor's battery, of 4 Napoleon guns, was now placed in position on the north side of the road. These batteries (Taylor's and others now brought up) opened mainly on the two batteries north of the road (the 5th and the 14th). Johnson's brigade was now advanced in line of battle with skirmishers in front, to the top of the hill east of the station, and on the left (south) of the Knoxville road, and became exposed to the fire of the federal battery on the south side of the road (Colvins), while skirmishing with the enemy's (dismounted) cavalry on an elevation just in its front (Wolford's line). Meantime McLaw's division (under Kershaw) was moved by the flank on to the ascent of the mountain on the north side of the road, intended to turn the enemy's left flank (our brigade). I ordered a section of Parker's battery to the left and front on the right of Johnson's brigade, where it opened on a well formed line of the enemy (Wolford's line), in its front and on the south side of the valley. The line of Gracie's brigade had been advanced and was exposed to the fire of the federals occupying the large hotel building at Bean Station, and firing through loopholes cut in the walls of the second and third stories. In this movement the 60th Alabama was exposed to the heavy fire of a line of federals west of the hotel (our brigade and our batteries), and it consequently halted, and the men attempted to cover themselves by lying down on the ground." This precisely corroborates our description regarding the rebels lying down, although they conceal the fact of their design to capture our batteries. They also seek to conceal the terrible destructiveness of the fire of our batteries, by attributing their losses to the fire of our men concealed in the brick hotel. This prevarication is made plain when we consider that two or three shots from any one of their guns, of which the chief of their artillery, Colonel Alexander, reports all his batteries (16 in number) as present, would have sent the material of that house flying in every direction like so many fragments of shells. It must be an obtuse mind that can not comprehend that the hotel under such conditions could not be held for a moment. Except this error, Johnson's description is a true one and corroborates our record. Again Johnson says: "The deliberate fire delivered with accuracy continually struck the men of the 60th Alabama regiment as they lay on the ground, and when that regiment subsequently arose to advance again, its line was marked out by the dead and wounded. Johnson's brigade was now moving in a handsome line down the western slope of the hill, east of the station and south of the road (as Connelly described it). In this movement it was exposed to the fire of the enemy's cavalry in line of battle (Wolford's line), and to a battery of artillery (Connelly's howitzers), and on passing the creek at the foot of the slope its line was enfiladed from the loopholes of the hotel in its prolongation to the right. This brigade sought, by lying down, the shelter afforded by the undulations of the ground, while the companies on the right fired on the hotel." That phantom hotel troubled them much, but it need not when they had on the field 16 batteries. (See our description "Nature seldom makes valleys without occasional hills"). Johnson continues: "The enemy's battery in front of Johnson's brigade (our howitzers), retired as soon as that brigade descended below its range." The cavalry retired a little from the brow of the hill, but maintained their line. Johnson in describing another advance, says: "In this advance Colonel Sanford (of the 60th Alabama), was knocked down by a shot, but afterward joined the regiment at the stable. I immediately requested General Jenkins to move one or two brigades by the flank through the woods on the slope of the mountains on the south side of the valley, with a view to turn the enemy's right flank." This was the force described as charging from the woods just as Wolford's men were retiring. Rebel General Jenkins reports moving on our right. His force was Jenkins' brigade, Anderson's brigade, and Benning's brigade, in all 15 regiments. On page 536 Johnson describes Jenkins' movement on our right, and Kershaw's movement on our left and adds: "The federal forces had resisted our attack persistently and gallantly, no doubt with a view to save their little camp equipage, trains, etc." On page 537 Johnson says, truthfully: "The enemy's forces are said to be three brigades of cavalry." Rebel Colonel Alexander, chief of artillery, on page 480, speaks of the movement of his battalion of artillery (23 guns) to Bean Station. In McLaw's division, which attacked our brigade of much less than 1,000 men, there was not less than 5,000 of the enemy. On page 524, Rebel Colonel Ball, commanding Bryan's brigade, acknowledges being present and supporting General Kershaw in passing our left flank. The advance of the 14th was the first attacked by Kershaw's brigade, composed of the following, all South Carolina regiments, viz.: the 2d, the 3d, the 7th, the 8th, the 15th, and the 3d South Carolina battalion, all infantry commands (see page 451). Major Wm. Wallace, C. S., commanding second S. C. of Kershaw's brigade, says (page 708): "December 14th we marched to Bean Station and took part in the skirmish at that place, and lost 22 men in the fight." Colonel James D. Vance, commanding 3d South Carolina, says (page 509): "My regiment belonged to Kershaw's brigade." And on page 511: "On the 14th (December) we returned as far as Bean Station, where in the afternoon the brigade, as well as other portions of the corps, became engaged with the enemy's mounted infantry." Portions of our forces were mounted infantry. He fails to report any loss. Captain E. J. Goggins, 7th South Carolina, on page 513 reports being present and engaged and lost 3 men. Captain Duncan McIntire, of the 8th South Carolina, on pages 514 and 515, says: "On the morning of December 14th, with the brigade, we came back to near Bean Station, and coming up with the enemy, the brigade was formed in line of battle; the 8th occupying second position, the 15th being on the right, and to the right of the main road, and rear of Captain Parker's battery. The brigade was moved by the right flank three-fourths of a mile." This brought them in front of the 14th Illinois, the extreme left of our brigade; the right of the brigade resting near the road. Captain McIntire continues: "The 15th, being fronted, was ordered to move forward; the 8th was fronted and moved forward. Here I received orders to advance on an eminence occupied by the enemy." The enemy was the advance of the 14th Illinois, the extreme advance of our brigade. The captain speaks of moving slowly at first; and driving him (the 14th) from the church (see page 515). This description identifies the enemy whom we fought, and confirms our record, which also details our retreat to, and abandonment of this church. As the captain says, the 8th occupied second place and the 15th the first place, it is evident that these two regiments were together and this makes plain what two were referred to when a short time afterward our boys challenged them and they answered "15th and —— South Carolina," meant 15th and 8th South Carolina. All these reports considered together prove that it was Kershaw's brigade of 6 South Carolina infantry regiments, that attacked the 14th Illinois in its advanced position. The captain continues: "After passing the church and advancing about 200 yards, we came upon the enemy under a heavy fire. Darkness prevented any farther advance." Thus is our record, made at the time and more than 30 years before the rebel reports were published, confirmed, not only in the general details and plans of operations, but even in much of the minor details, such as the enemy falling prostrate when advancing on our batteries, as well as in the terrible slaughter of their men at those points. Captain McIntire reports 22 men lost by his regiment. On page 517 is report of Captain S. H. Sheldon, commanding 15th South Carolina; he says: "On December 14th, accompanied by the rest of the brigade, the command marched in the direction of Bean Station. Finding the enemy at this place, measures were taken to attack and, if possible, capture him. We occupied the extreme right (of the brigade) and after the brigade had been put in position along the slope of the Clinch mountains, we advanced upon the enemy at a charge, and drove him back from his position. We were then moved farther to the right and advanced, capturing a few prisoners and killing and wounding a few. Night coming on soon after we were ordered to halt, stack arms and rest for the night; the regiment lost 7 men." On page 518 is report of Lieutenant Wm. C. Harris, adjutant of James S. C. battalion; he says: "December 14th retraced our steps to Bean Station; coming up with the enemy, made an attack on him, drove him from his position, losing 3 men." Some of their commands, like ours, reported no loss, although doubtless they did lose. The total reported loss of Kershaw's brigade was 56. The officers of our brigade made no report of the battle nor of losses, except a tabulated statement made on page 293, giving the losses in each command, aggregating 115 of the whole force. Either this is incorrect or Colonel Wolford's report of 130 for his division alone was far wrong. It is much more probable that our whole loss was not less than 175. As to the loss of the enemy, their loss must have been very much greater. General Johnson reported the loss of his division at 222. Considering the report of the destructiveness of our fire as made by his own officers, this report does not appear correct. Citizens informed us next day that they lost in killed 800, while the aggregate of their report gives total reported 278. If all their commands had reported it would have shown much more. General Shackelford commanded our forces in this battle. It was the last of his service in East Tennessee, as, like Burnside, at his own request he had been relieved, and his successor appointed, who had not yet arrived to take command. Shackelford's career as a commander was one of continued successes. Nor was this, his last, in any way inferior to all of his victories, for victory it surely was, in this, that it completely thwarted the enemy's design and so completely demoralized Longstreet's forces as to render them harmless the next day, when they possessed such superior advantages.

Colonel Graham, in command of our brigade, and Colonel Capron, in command of our regiment, each performed their duty with the same skill, courage and coolness that characterized all their service. Their coolness inspired their men to intrepid daring.

Captain Dent, in command of the advanced skirmishers of the 14th, which bore the brunt of the attack of McLaw's division, at first alone, exhibited the capability of a skillful commander. Every officer and every man was worthy of the highest honor; but what shall we say of the bold and skillful manner in which the men and officers of our battery performed their duties? Colvin was the same brave and skillful officer as usual; his battery did great execution. The guns of the 5th Indiana also were served effectively; but the howitzer guns of the 14th, occupying an advanced position and having a close range, were fired with such rapidity and skill and effectiveness, that it must be conceded that it was one of our principal elements of salvation on that hotly contested field. Lieutenant Connelly won such honors that day as advanced him immediately to a captaincy. The absence of Major David Quigg on other duty deprived us of the services of one of our bravest and most skillful officers. The major was absent attending a court martial. We were furnished the following account of an adventure that day, which was not related for publication, but it so well illustrates the heroism of that splendid officer that we publish it: He related in a private letter to a friend that being absent attending a court martial, he learned of the battle, and though compelled to pass within the range of the enemy's batteries to get to his command, he ran the fiery gauntlet, which he describes as the hottest place he was ever in, expecting, as he said, to have his head shot off.

Having completely checked the advance of the enemy at dusk, we held our lines until midnight, having extended our picket lines across the valley. We then fell back, but it was near 2 a. m. of December 15th before the last of our forces withdrew. We retired down the Richland valley four miles, to a position already occupied by General Hascall's division of the 23d Army Corps. They had already built a strong rail barricade across the road, and extending out on our right flank. This infantry force occupied this barricade. Our cavalry forces were thrown into line on the right of the infantry, Wolford's division first, and to their right was our brigade, the 14th extreme right, except the guns of the 5th, and of the 14th. The 14th fortunately occupied ground having many large rocks and large trees, which formed a fairly good protection. The enemy formed line across the valley nearly one mile in our ad-

vance. Strong skirmish lines were thrown forward and occupied temporary breastworks, perhaps 300 yards apart; the rebel skirmishers being about 80 rods from our line. The rebel skirmish line was strong, and our own was very light, so that our main line was engaged with the enemy, but not vigorously. Colvin's guns were posted on the road and opened on the enemy's distant line; but without eliciting a reply. Our battle flags were waved defiantly towards the enemy, as a signal that we dared them to attack, but, with the exception of a slight skirmish, we could not provoke an engagement.

In the afternoon the enemy succeeded in dragging in position several batteries on the high hills or mountains precisely on our right flank, so that their fire could rake our whole line. This fire became very annoying, and as our trees could protect us only on one side, and the enemy's fire came from front and flank, there was some dodging to avoid the enemy's fire from both directions. They again used both shells and railroad iron, which made much frightening noise, and would hurt where it struck; yet, barring its frightful noise, it was little feared. Our small batteries attempted to reply, but owing to the height of the hills, as well as the distance, our shots could not reach them, and our batteries were withdrawn, as they were exposed to damage without being useful. We will give extract from Rebel General Martin's report. On page 546, after detailing his movements of the previous day, in which he did not succeed in engaging us, he says. "Early next morning I was ordered to move on the enemy's flank, on the Knoxville road, 4 miles from Bean Station. This was done immediately, and a high hill gained, from which my artillery could enfilade the enemy's breastworks. With great labor the guns were placed in position, and rapidly and effectively served. My guns were in sight of, and within 500 yards of our infantry skirmishers, who, it was expected, would attack in front. With concert of action great damage could have been done the enemy this day. Colonel Giltner was on the side of Clinch mountain, on the enemy's left flank, and prepared to second any movement of our infantry. As no movement was made I held my position. My fire continued for one hour and a half, and the enemy began to retire, but was able to detach a large force to hold my men in check, as he was not pressed in front." That we were not more vigorously attacked on this day, was due to the fact that Longstreet's veterans had received such rough handling the day before that they had no appetite for fight.

True, on the 15th we had the aid of one small infantry division, but that was offset by the complete co-operation of all the enemy's cavalry on this day. Those who may think that we have drawn on our imagination for our description are invited to examine the reports of the rebel officers in the published reports. Why this battle has not received its proper notice in history is due to the fact that our commanding officer had been superseded, and perhaps did not think it incumbent on him to report, while his successor had not yet arrived, and could not therefore report. On page 468, under date of December 30th, General Longstreet gives vent to his disappointment in the following language:

"I regret to say that a combination of circumstances has so operated, during the campaign in East Tennessee, as to prevent the complete destruction of the enemy's forces in this part of the state. It is fair to infer that the fault is entirely with me, and I desire therefore that some other commander be tried."

This was a humiliating confession for one of the very best commanders in the southern army to make. The combination of circumstances alluded to was his defeat at Knoxville—a very unfortunate circumstance. Then his failure to capture our one little brigade with his whole cavalry force at Walker's ford was another hard circumstance, and now again at Bean Station, when he used his whole army of five divisions, he again attempted to capture our small force and failed. This again was an unlucky circumstance, and the whole such a combination of circumstances as plainly showed that not Longstreet, but the fact that Longstreet's veterans now found a class of American soldiers to oppose who differed materially from those he had previously encountered, was the real cause of his failure.

CHAPTER VII.

SERVICE UNDER BRIGADIER GENERAL SAMUEL D. STURGIS.

Important changes have been made in the army in East Tennessee. At his own request Major General Ambrose E. Burnside has been relieved of the command of the army in East Tennessee, and Major General John G. Foster took command December 11th, but made no changes in General Burnside's plans until after the battle of Bean Station. There had been much difference of opinion between General Halleck and General Burnside as to the best disposition to be made of General Burnside's forces. At length Assistant Secretary of War Charles A. Dana was sent to upper East Tennessee to investigate, and after a careful study of the situation and plans of Burnside, he perfectly approved of Burnside's course, and when General Grant took command of the army near Chattanooga he too approved of Burnside's course. After General Longstreet was sent by General Bragg to capture or drive out Burnside's forces, thus opening the way by weakening Bragg's army for the great victory over it soon after, and the final victory over Longstreet, perfectly demonstrated the wisdom of his plans. East Tennessee was now made safe. It was the opportune moment for him to surrender the command, as he had long desired to do because of failing health. General Shackelford had also asked to be relieved, and after the battle of Bean Station he, too, surrendered the command of the cavalry to Brigadier General Samuel D. Sturgis.

About this time Colonel Felix Graham also resigned, and Colonel Horace Capron was placed in command of our brigade—the second of the second division of the cavalry corps. The regiments of the brigade were commanded as follows: The 14th Illinois by Major F. M. Davidson, in the absence of Lieutenant Colonel D. P. Jenkins; the 5th Indiana Cavalry by Colonel Thomas H. Butler; the 65th Indiana by Captain Walter G. Hodge.

Other important changes were made in the composition of the army. Many of the former regiments had been sent home to veteranize, and not a few had returned to Kentucky. On the other hand, Major General Gordon Granger, with a part of the 4th corps (infantry) of General Sherman's forces had been retained. General Washington L. Elliott also came with his cavalry division. For the organization of General Foster's army at this time, see serial 56, page 559. Present for duty, 9th A. C., 4,875; 23d A. C., total, 7,672. (Hascall's division, 4,212.) Left wing forces (General Wilcox), 4,768; cavalry corps, 5,360; grand total Foster's army, 22,678. four companies of the 9th Ohio Cavalry were now joined to our brigade. This battalion was commanded by Major William D. Hamilton.

December 15th. We remained in line until after night, then fell back to near Rutledge, having marched 16 miles.

December 16th. Reveille at daylight. Drew a small amount of rations. Marched at 8 p. m. Martin's cavalry pursued and skirmished with our rear guard. At 1 p. m. a detachment composed of details from the various commands—about 500—was sent across the ridge southeast of our road toward the Holston river to reconnoiter, as it was rumored that the enemy designed to interpose a force to cut us off. The main command proceeded to Blaine's crossroads. The reconnoitering party crossed the ridge, but found no force of the enemy. Company "I," of the 14th, was sent to the river, where it was reported that the enemy were crossing. They learned that they designed crossing in a few hours. On returning they heard volleys a few hundred yards east of the road. On hastening to the spot they found two small parties of the gray and the blue engaged in a leaden argument concerning the right of possession of some supplies in an old mill. The blues won the case. We then rejoined the detachment, and with them marched to Blaine's crossroads, arriving at 9 p. m., and found there General Granger's infantry, and General Elliott's cavalry not far off. The 14th was sent up the valley on picket. Posted videttes, then bivouacked, with horses saddled. No supper; had no dinner, and a slim breakfast. March of regiment, 10 miles; march of detachment, 23 miles.

December 17th. Rained hard last night. At daylight "to horse" sounded. Marched up the valley a short distance, dismounted and advanced as skirmishers. Remained engaged with the enemy until 3 p. m.; were then retired behind the infantry and went into camp on the Maynardville road. When ordered to fall back the picket lines were ordered to leave the road and fall back along the foot of two high ranges of hills between which the road ran. When we reached our lines we found a masked battery posted to sweep the road. It was supposed that the enemy would make a cavalry dash to cut off our pickets retiring on foot, in which case the masked battery would sweep the road. This scheme was defeated by the obtuseness or contrariness of the commander of the detachment on the road, who disobeyed the order and retired on the road. Our camp was near a creek three miles from Blaine's crossroads. Fed our horses, but had no rations. Marched 5 miles. Rations in the evening one-quarter, and that what the boys called "dried beef"—that is, flesh of the living animals dried on the bones by poverty; not a smidgen of anything else, not even salt. What emphasized the hardship of this fare was an order issued at this time threatening the death penalty upon any soldier caught foraging without belonging to a detail of foragers acting under orders. The condition of the country and the interest of soldiers and citizens required that a proper disposition by proper authority should be made of the little that was left in the country. The infantry, who had a better opportunity of getting their share of the rations, had little to complain of, but the cavalry were so often separated from all chance of sharing in the rations gathered by details, that they were restive under the order, and with very good reason. Lest some who read these pages might think that we have somewhat colored the description of our hardships and privations, I will give some official information from the published reports, after giving statements from our own records for the past few days.

December 14th, some had a full breakfast, some a slim one; a few had an early dinner, most of the men had none, and no supper for any. December 15th, had one good meal. December 16th, most of the men had one meal; some had none. December 17th, the same fare.

December 18th, a half pound of flour each, with nothing else. For six days an average, perhaps, of one meal a day. Serial 54, page 281, two days after taking command, General Foster reported: "Commissariat very destitute; but few days' supply of the most requisite now and for a long time issued in quarter and half rations. Nearly all rations and all forage drawn from the surrounding country. Difficult to continue to supply our army this winter. Our mounted force is much less than that of the enemy, and only about 10,000 of the 9th and 23d army corps able to march. Question of supplies very serious. Difficult that I get quarter rations from day to day." And on the 19th he says: "Men suffering for want of shoes and clothing. The issue of bread and meal rarely equals quarter rations." On page 329 General Sturgis says: "No forage for horses." Serial 56, page 214, November 21st, General Wilcox reports: "Neither forage nor breadstuff for the command." Page 408, General Thomas J. Wood, December 14th, tells of the bad sanitary condition and want of tents and clothing, and then says: "The country can do little more in the way of affording supplies. The local stock of supplies is well nigh exhausted, even to the infliction of great want, perhaps starvation, on the inhabitants." Page 409, General Granger indorses this statement, saying: "The statements herein contained are substantially correct, and afford conclusive proof of the impossibility of further offensive operations until clothing, shelter, subsistence, forage and transportation are provided." Serial 56, page 464, December 21st, General Granger reports: "My forage trains for the two days last past found it impossible to procure a sufficient supply, and report a great scarcity in the surrounding country." Serial 56, page 457, December 20th, General Wilcox says: "I regret to report that this command will be crippled in its movements for want of bread. The troops are barely able to subsist from day to day."

We could make many more such extracts confirming our record of our privations in this campaign, but let this suffice.

December 18th. Reveille at daylight. Night cold. A

part of the regiment was paid today. Rations drawn—a half pound of flour to the man and nothing more.

December 19th. Reveille at daylight. Quite cold. Payment of the regiment completed. No rations until night, then quarter rations of beef without salt or anything else.

December 20th. Reveille at daylight. Weather cold and clear.

December 21st. Reveille at 5 a. m. Serial 54, page 330, General Parke ordered, December 21st: "Colonel Capron, commanding brigade, is directed to keep up communication with General Wilcox." Serial 56, page 462, December 21st, Colonel Foster to Colonel Capron, commanding second brigade, says: "Reports of scouts quite satisfactory. General Parke is anxious that you should be able to get a view from the heights of Clinch mountain in the vicinity of Powder Spring gap. * * * The general will expect you to keep 'Flat creek' and 'Bull Run valley' clear of the enemy and protect the communication between Tazewell and Maynardville, watching the country as far as Clinch river. You should watch Powder Spring gap closely; if it is not too strongly held you might be able to get possession of it."

December 21st. Brigade marched at 10 a. m. towards Cumberland gap; camped at Cedar ford, on Flat creek. Marched 5 miles. Our commissary has taken charge of a mill.

December 22d. Reveille at daylight. Ground frozen hard. The following order received from General Parke (see page 468): "Colonel Capron, commanding brigade of cavalry—I wish you to move a strong scout up to Powder Spring gap tomorrow morning, starting at 8 a. m. An infantry force will move up the valley, and I have no doubt you will be able to drive the rebels out without difficulty." Captain Ditzler, with Company "B," of the 14th, sent on scout, and Captain Dent, with 150 men, and Captain Map, of 65th Indiana, sent on scout to Powder Spring gap. They found it evacuated. They heard that 200 rebels had gone towards Maynardville. They marched to that place, but found no rebels. They returned to camp about 2 p. m., having marched 24 miles. Horse feed scarce; rations more plenty.

December 23d. Reveille at 3 a. m. Page 477 is the following order to Colonel Foster, division commander: "Move Colonel Capron's brigade on the Rutledge road, extending reconnoisance to Bean Station and beyond, also over to the river road and fords of the Holston above the mouth of Buffalo creek." Major Woolley, with a detachment of the brigade, took possession of Powder Spring gap. Got orders to move at daylight tomorrow.

December 24th. Reveille at 3:30 a. m. Marched at sunrise toward Blaine's crossroads and to the Holston river and crossed at Crawford's ford. Page 481, an order explains this change of movement. General Parke says: "I ordered Colonel Capron, instead of moving his brigade up the Rutledge road, to cross the river and join Sturgis at New Market. He is now on the way." We halted three miles from New Market, procured forage, got supper and prepared to camp at sunset, but "to horse" was sounded, and we moved on and encamped in a fine oak grove a mile from New Market at 10 p. m. Marched 25 miles.

December 25th. Reveille at 5 a. m. Plenty of corn and some rations. We are now a part of General Sturgis' corps of cavalry, which is concentrated near here.

December 26th. Reveille at 4 a. m. At daylight mounted and moved up Mossy Creek valley two miles and formed line of battle. Serial 54, page 628, December 26th, Sturgis reports: "This morning my line occupied a fine position above Mossy creek. It was my intention to attack the enemy, whose line was about three-fourths of a mile beyond. Heavy rains threatening to raise the river in my rear, I did not attack in force. Becoming more favorable about 11 a. m., our line of skirmishers was pushed forward and engaged the enemy. Our artillery opened and was replied to by the rebel batteries, but they were soon driven from their position." The readiness with which they fell back suggested the probability that the enemy was trying to draw him into a trap. He attempted to regain ground from which he had been driven. We charged upon their advance and drove them back. No advantages gained on either side. Skirmishing through the day. Our bands play "Yankee Doodle" and the rebel bands play "Dixie." Our bands strike up

"Dixie" just to show them that they cannot beat us in anything. Then they suddenly change to "We'll Rally 'Round the Flag, Boys," when their batteries and musketry, which was silent when "Dixie" was played, now opened up spitefully. In the evening we bivouacked near. Very little feed or rations. We find in *The National Tribune* some valuable articles published by Major H. C. Connelly, giving a good description of this campaign. Although in the main much the same as our own record, yet we find some information not embraced in our notes. This, with Major Connelly's permission, we incorporate, and as we are compelled to economize in space, no especial credit will be given for extracts used in connection with our record.

December 27th. "Boots and saddles," "to horse" and "assembly" at early dawn. No breakfast nor horse feed. We formed battle line immediately. Serial 54, page 629, is Sturgis' report, December 27th: "We attacked the enemy this afternoon at Mossy creek and drove him from every position back to within a short distance of 'Talbott's Station,' when, night coming on, we had to desist. Our troops went forward through the rain and mud in fine spirits. Martin's and Armstrong's divisions were both in our front." Our brigade went into camp near Talbott's Station, on the Morristown road. Still raining. We had little rations or horse feed.

December 28th. Reveille at daylight. "Boots and saddles" and "to horse" soon after. Plenty of horse feed. Serial 54, page 630, Sturgis reports: "The enemy not in sight this morning."

December 29th. Reveille at daylight. Formed line soon after near the road. No breakfast nor horse feed. Remained in line nearly two hours; then our division, with four regiments of Wolford's division and four mountain howitzers, were sent toward Dandridge. Colonel LaGrange's brigade and two 3-inch rifled guns moved to the point where the Mossy creek road to Dandridge crosses Bay mountain. Colonel Campbell, with the only remaining brigade of cavalry, was left to occupy the entire original line. Serial 54, page 648, Sturgis reports: "The reason for moving second division to Dandridge was the report from union sources that a considerable force of Longstreet's cavalry was there, apparently intending to flank us and get in our rear." Reaching the vicinity of Dandridge, scouts sent forward soon returned and reported no enemy there. We were then ordered to feed and get dinner, but before dinner was prepared we heard the ominous roar of battle thunder, which increased until it became terrific. We were soon mounted and went double quick on the road we came for several miles, when the shifting noise of battle warned us that our brave comrades were falling back, and well we knew that they were facing tremendous odds, perhaps Longstreet's whole force. To continue on this road would divide our force. We quickly crossed over to the New Market road and passed on with all possible speed, reaching New Market in the rear of our battle line. Colonel Campbell had just been reinforced by Colonel LaGrange's brigade, and our boys were just charging the enemy, in which we attempted to join, but the rebels now fell back so rapidly that we could take but little part more than to follow rapidly and keep them on the move. We were soon again in complete possession of our morning position. Longstreet had advanced most of his cavalry and one division of infantry and two batteries of artillery. Our loss was about 100 killed, wounded and missing. The enemy lost from 200 to 400. We buried on the field 20 of his dead. Citizens reported their loss very heavy. In this fight the 1st East Tennessee Cavalry, commanded by Lieutenant-Colonel Jim Brownlow, made a sabre charge which did honor to this dashing officer and his soldiers. General Sturgis' report, on page 648, serial 54, confirms our account. General Elliott also reports substantially the same, but estimates the rebel loss at 400. The attack was made about 9 a. m. by about 6,000 cavalry and one command—a brigade or division— of infantry. On page 647 Sturgis says: "We have checked the enemy completely, but our loss is severe. The engagement was general along the whole line, and the troops behaved with great credit to themselves and to their country. His whole force moved to our front last night, and today got badly whipped." Rebel General Martin's report admits the presence of the cavalry forces named, which in their last previous report gave the numbers as we state. The reinforcement by Lagrange's brigade checked the advance of the enemy and the rapid approach of our division caused them to waver, and when the two brigades charged them with determination their lines gave way at every point. General Foster acknowledges the services of our cavalry as follows (serial 56, page 509, December 27th) : "General Sturgis has been and is almost constantly engaged with the enemy's cavalry in front." And on page 519: "General Sturgis, with his own and Elliott's cavalry, have been almost constantly engaged with the enemy's cavalry for the past two days. I am glad to hear so good news from General Sturgis, who is performing his duties right gallantly." On page 646, serial 54, is report of General Foster concerning the engagement of the 29th, confirming our statements. Through this busy time of service the 14th Illinois Cavalry bore its full part and never failed in its full duty. We went into camp on the Morristown road, having marched 24 miles.

December 30th. Reveille at 5 a. m. Called out and formed line; had slight skirmishing; retired to camp. Slim rations; send far for forage.

December 31st. Reveille at 5 a. m. Rained much last night and to-day. Heavy cannonading in the direction of Bean Station. Fare as yesterday.

Friday, January 1st, 1864. Reveille at 4:30 a. m. Commenced freezing at midnight; cold increased until it was fearful—the coldest known for half a century. Tremendous icicles and sheets of ice formed where the water poured over a mill dam near by. Think of this, those of you who were in comfortable homes. We did not even have tents, but lay out on the cold ground, scarcely half clad, as we had not drawn clothing for six months. We could only keep from freezing by building large log fires and lying near them. Forage scarce and rations more scarce. Often foragers of the blue and the gray would meet in the same field. Sometimes the stronger would drive out the weaker, and sometimes they did not molest each other.

January 2d. Reveille at 4 a. m. Cold increasing. General Grant has arrived in Knoxville.

January 3d. Reveille at 4:30 a. m. Weather slightly

moderated. "Boots and saddles" at 5 a. m. Moved out and formed line, without breakfast. No enemy appeared. At 11 a. m. moved camp to a beautiful grove. Remained in camp with horses saddled. March 1 mile.

January 4th. Reveille 4 a. m. In camp. Rained all day.

January 5th. Reveille 5 a. m. In camp. Rained and snowed.

January 6th. Reveille 5 a. m. Quite cold. Rations and forage scarce.

January 7th. Reveille 4 a. m. A flag of truce came to-day from Longstreet with remonstrance against circulating President Lincoln's emancipation proclamation amongst the confederate troops. President Lincoln ought to have known that this would be displeasing to the rebels.

January 8th. Reveille 5 a. m. Send ten miles for forage.

January 9th. Reveille 5 a. m. In camp. Usual fare.
January 10th. Reveille 5 a. m. Weather very cold.
January 11th. Reveille 5 a. m. More moderate. Requisition made for clothing.

January 12th. Reveille 5 a. m. In camp.
January 13th. Reveille 5 a. m. Sleeted last night.
January 14th. Reveille at 4 a. m. "Boots and saddles" at dawn. Marched at sunrise toward Dandridge. This morning Colonel Capron, with one recruiting sergeant from each company of the 14th Illinois Cavalry,. started for Illinois to raise recruits for the regiment. Command reached Dandridge, on the French Broad river, about 2 p. m. Dandridge contained five churches and 1,200 inhabitants. Our advance skirmished lightly with parties of the rebels. Some of the boys captured a rebel flag in town. This place has been a kind of middle ground between the opposing armies, scouting parties from each side meeting almost daily in the streets, sometimes skirmishing, but often the weaker party would retire. Procured feed for our horses, but were soon ordered forward without feeding. Marched 2 miles. Ordered to camp in a grove, but "To horse" was sounded, and we moved back a half mile and camped in a grove about dark. Some of the men went for forage, some felled trees to make warm fires, some attended to cooking and other camp

duties, so that by each doing all he could we were able to lie down about 11 p. m. This is only a picture of the usual routine when in active service. About 3 p. m. we were thrown into line of battle, but no enemy appeared. Marched 14 miles.

January 15th. Reveille at 4 a. m. Ordered to draw 60 rounds of ammunition. In the evening were called into line.

January 16th. Reveille 5 a. m. "Boots and saddles" at daylight. "Assembly" at sunrise. The following clothing was issued: Four tents, four pairs of blankets and four pairs of boots to each company, where each man needed all these articles, and more, too! Our brigade and two other mounted brigades moved out six miles on the Bull gap road, where we encountered a strong picket of the enemy. They were driven, and we pursued a mile, where we encountered a strong force of the enemy in line. We engaged them for an hour and drove them from their position. We now heard the sound of battle all along our lines on our right. A mile farther we came to a stronger line of the enemy. Our brigade was dismounted and took position in a wood on the right of the road, the other brigades forming on our left. The enemy were in strong force in a wood 100 rods in our front. They also had possession of a grove on our left, midway between the opposing lines. The 9th Michigan Cavalry, being armed wth Spencer rifles, dismounted and drove the rebels from the grove in handsome style, routing them in confusion and taking possession of the grove. Meanwhile the skirmishers all along the line were warmly engaged. Off to the right the noise of battle increased. Now a rebel brigade of infantry approached from three different points to retake the grove. Knowing the valor and skill of that noble regiment, we watched with interest the result. The enemy were allowed to approach within easy range and to fix bayonet for a charge, but they then opened upon them such a continuous sheet of fiery balls that the charge was soon turned to a rout to the rear. We would soon have disposed of this force of the enemy, but now couriers arrive with orders for us to fall back, as our troops on the right had been driven back. We gave the enemy a few more volleys before retiring, then while moving back we planted our batteries at every advantageous position to prevent the enemy from advancing impolitely. The 14th was rear guard, and Captain Dent was in command of the rear of the regiment, which was hard pressed, compelling the 14th frequently to form line and check their too rapid advance. The enemy finally withdrew, and we retired to camp at 9 p. m., lying down about midnight. Marched 18 miles. Night chilly.

Sunday, January 17th. Reveille 5 a. m. Night cold. Send 20 miles for forage; had little rations or forage yesterday. At 2 p. m. the 14th, under Major Davidson, marched alone, passing through Dandridge and crossed the French Broad—a beautiful river—a mile below town. Here a working party were busy constructing a bridge of army wagons and plank, over which to pass our artillery and infantry. After crossing, the 14th moved up the river through a heavily timbered country, to get possession of Hay's ford, 10 miles above. It was rumored that the enemy designed throwing a force across at this ford to get in the rear of our forces. Our lines were heavily engaged as we passed up. Marched 8 miles to a crossroad leading to the ford; marched 1 mile toward the river; learned that the enemy had crossed in force. We formed line and waited an hour, expecting an attack, then marched back several miles, halted, put out pickets, fed and bivouacked about 11 p. m. Marched 22 miles.

January 18th. 1 a. m. couriers arrived with orders for us to move down the French Broad with haste, or we would be cut off by a large force of the enemy. We were ordered to cross the river far below and march to Strawberry plains. We secured a guide and struck a circuitous route from the river, and by long and rapid marching succeeded in circumventing their design. We halted at 8 a. m., procured feed, which we carried with us, and crossed the river at Evans' ford. Halted at Mossy creek road about 2 p. m. to feed and get dinner. It rained hard. We mounted and continued march to the plains. Our whole force was now moving toward Knoxville. We now learn that our forces about Bean Station have been defeated, thus compelling this line to fall back. We passed through Strawberry Plains and crossed the Holston river on a newly constructed bridge about 5 p. m. Marched 2 miles toward Blaine's crossroads, then countermarched and went on the Knoxville road 1 mile and camped in a fine grove about 7 p. m., and laid down on the cold, muddy ground late at night. Marched 32 miles.

January 19th. Reveille at daylight. Breakfastless, we marched toward Knoxville. The weather had moderated, and the passage of so many troops left the road in a horrid condition. We drew a small quantity of rations on the road. We reached Knoxville about 3 p. m. Halted and remained in column two or three hours, then marched to cross the river, then countermarched, passed back through town and camped in a grove two furlongs northwest of town, getting ready to lie down about midnight, without supper or horse feed. Marched 17 miles.

January 20th. Reveille 5 a. m. Night cold. Have little rations and no horse feed. At 11 a. m. marched through town; crossed the river on a pontoon; halted in a grove of oaks a mile from the city. Got dinner, but no horse feed. Toward evening ordered to unsaddle and camp. No feed and scant rations. Marched 2 miles.

January 21st. Reveille at 4 a. m. and again at dawn. In camp. Get a half dozen ears of corn for each horse, the first feed our horses have had since 2 p. m. of the 19th. We had thought our horses fared hard enough before. In consequence of such hard service our horses were so broken down that both the 5th Indiana Cavalry and the 65th Indiana Mounted Infantry were dismounted, and their best horses were given to the 14th Illinois Cavalry. The 5th were to be sent to Kentucky to be remounted, and the 65th were properly infantry. We were sorry to part with those noble regiments, with which we had stood shoulder to shoulder in many a hard-fought battle, until our perfect faith and trust in each others' valor had rendered our brigade well nigh invincible. At 1 p. m., with a division of mounted men, we marched toward Sevierville 1 mile, halted, formed battalion order, remained two hours, then marched over a rough, muddy road. About sunset turned off the main road a half mile and camped in a wood, having marched 11 miles. Sent several miles for forage and get little; most of the plantations had protection papers and guards. We had but three small feeds in four days, and we were thus compelled to take feed wherever found, guards or no guards.

January 22d. Reveille at daylight. Marched at 8 a. m. on to Pigeon river, where the regiment was divided into detachments and sent to guard many fords and crossings on the French Broad river; headquarters at a mill on Pigeon river, two miles from the "French Broad." Distance marched, 10 miles. Here we remained till the 26th, with nothing of note. Weather very fine. Reveille each day at 5 a. m.

January 26th. Reveille at daylight. Weather very fine. Report of the capture at Dandridge of two companies of the 9th Michigan Cavalry is confirmed. We get orders to be very vigilant, as our troops are withdrawn from some of the crossings above, and the enemy is reported to be advancing on Knoxville again. About 10 p. m. we moved out and posted strong pickets a short distance from camp.

January 27th. Weather beautiful. Moved off at sunrise to headquarters on Pigeon river and built rail barricades. Company "L," 14th, with one section of the 14th battery, and Companies "I" and "E" as supports, were sent with Colonel Wolford's brigade toward Sevierville. We engaged the enemy about 10 a. m. and fought him until nearly night, driving him continually, and beyond Fair Garden, killing and wounding many, capturing two pieces of artillery and 200 prisoners. While falling back the rebels murdered in cold blood nine Tennessee home guards, who, organized only to protect their homes from both sides, refused to fight on either side. They killed one man who had been crazy for 30 years. We marched 15 miles.

January 28th. Marched at 1 a. m. Passed through Sevierville, turned northeast toward Dandridge; passed through very fine country, then through heavy timber and sparse settlement. When we approached the river the 14th, except the three companies with Wolford, were sent to guard the ferry near Dandridge. They found a strong force of the enemy. Preparations were made to attack them, when imperative orders came to fall

FIRST LIEUTENANT LEWIS W. BOREN, Co

back. We had one of the 5th Indiana Rodman guns and were anxious to attack. Wolford's command marched to a point a few miles above and drove the enemy to the river, where they had strong breastworks in a heavy wood. They had a strong force. The ground was unfavorable for the use of artillery, and we attacked them vigorously with musketry and carbines. All fought well, but the 112th Illinois Mounted Infantry fought like tigers. Though our loss was heavy, and that of the enemy, protected by strong works, was comparatively light, yet our men reluctantly obeyed the order to fall back. About 5 p. m. the 14th, under Major Davidson, marched toward Sevierville until midnight, then bivouacked about four miles from Sevierville. Marched 31 miles. Got little forage. Toward day called into line and remained until daylight, January 29th, then marched about sunrise, without breakfast; passed through Sevierville; crossed east fork of Pigeon river. Four miles from town turned to the left; passed through a beautiful country. Four miles further crossed the middle fork of Pigeon river; turned into a field of corn and fed, then marched toward Marysville. Country very broken. At noon crossed the west fork of Pigeon river, halted and fed. Those who had rations got dinner; most of the men had none. Crossed a mountain; passed through a small cove; camped in a wood near a creek. Marched 25 miles.

January 30th. Reveille 4 a. m. Marched at 7 a. m. Crossed another rugged mountain, covered with laurel and other evergreens, so dense in growth and so interwoven in their branches as to make beautiful arbors. The ascent and descent were difficult. At its foot we entered Wier's cove. The Tuckaleeche—a tributary of Pigeon river—runs through this cove. The cove is two miles wide and four miles long. These coves are inhabited principally by union people, and are very productive. Were we mere tourists we might picture beautiful and romantic scenery, produced by contrast of rugged mountains with peaceful and smiling valleys and coves; but our task is to record rugged events and not scenes. We next enter upon one of the most rugged and dangerous services, and the selection of our regiment by the commander from a whole corps of excellent cavalry was a high tribute to their worth, and compensates in a measure for the disappointment of the promise that our regiment should be sent to Kentucky to be remounted and better armed.

CHAPTER VIII.

OUR INDIAN RAID—A PERILOUS AND ROMANTIC SERVICE.

Introductory to the account of this service, we give an extract from a report of General Samuel D. Sturgis, furnished to us by Major H. C. Connelly. General Sturgis said: "While in Tuckaleeche cove I received information that the force of Indians and whites commanded by the rebel Colonel Thomas, formerly United States Indian agent for the Cherokee nation, was near the forks of the Little Tennessee and Tuckasegee rivers, North Carolina, who had been a terror to the union people of East Tennessee and the borders of North Carolina, from the atrocities they were daily perpetrating. I ordered Major Davidson, with his regiment (the 14th Illinois Cavalry), to pursue this force and destroy them." This band reported as a part of the army of Sam Jones, and known as "Thomas' Legion." Their last previous reported number (see serial 56, page 644) was, November 6th, 399. In Eastern Tennesee and North Carolina many of the most barbarous atrocities were committed, and most of them by all or some portion of this band. They were a kind of independent "flying command," to whom was assigned the commission of deeds that cowardly rebels desired to have done but dared not perform. That our regiment was selected from a whole corps of the best of cavalry to march across the mountains in midwinter and punish this band of savages, was the very highest indorsement of our worth as a regiment, and what emphasizes the value set upon our worth is the fact that the number of our regiment present and capable of that kind of service must have been much less than that of this band. We have no means of knowing our exact numbers on this expedition. One month before, at Walker's ford, when every man that could be out of the hospital was with us, we numbered 324 men and officers. Two hard fights and much hard service had thinned our ranks, and now all the men and horses not capable of the severest duty are selected out and sent to Marysville, and it is hardly possible that we had on this expedition 250 men. Nor did we have any support of any kind, as has been falsely claimed by a certain captain of the 7th Ohio Cavalry. Scouts reported the present number of the band then in camp at 300. We are now ordered to cross a high range of mountains in midwinter, carrying with us rations and horse feed, over mountain paths fully 75 miles, through narrow passes, where a very few men well armed and ammunitioned could withstand a large army, and attack on grounds of their own choosing, and in supporting distance of other rebel forces, a wily band of savages, outnumbering us. The prospect would have been discouraging to any but true Yankee soldiers, in whom the greatest danger always inspires the greatest courage. The fact that this band sent no prisoners to Andersonville, nor discharged any except with the bullet or the tomahawk, and that a failure on our part warranted the advertisement of that failure to be seen on their tent poles in the scalps of every man of the 14th, was certainly sufficient to inspire any command of American soldiers with intrepid bravery.

Sunday, January 31st. Weather cloudy. At 7 a. m. started from camp in Tuckaleeche cove, march 1 mile, halt, form battalion. Here was selected out all the men and horses unfit for such severe service. These were sent to Marysville. The four caissons of our battery were filled with ammunition, and two of the guns, in charge of Company "L," and commanded by Captain H. C. Connelly, were taken with us. We now left the main command and marched on the left hand road, going nearly southwest. We crossed the cove to the foot of Cedar mountain. We were now following what appeared to be a blind path, having with us a competent guide. We found the ascent of Cedar mountain far more rugged than any other we had yet seen. The troopers dismounted, and then the horses with great difficulty made the ascent. We can hardly conceive it possible for the artillery horses to drag even our light cannon over such rugged ascents. Company "L" and their brave commander are worthy of the highest honor for safely conducting over the mountains these guns. It was not only an herculean task, but it required great care and skill to prevent their going over yawning precipices that verged our mountain path. It was a novel sight to look upward at our column, now turning to the right, winding round some bold cliff or yawning chasm, now winding to the left to avoid a similar obstruction, and now climbing what at a distance seemed almost perpendicular sides of the mountain. Far above us the column in its windings resembled the contortions of a mighty serpent in an effort to climb a giant tree. On, on we toiled, until it seemed that we could toil no longer. But everything except eternity and the tongue of a professional scold must have an end, and so had our ascent up Cedar mountain. From its summit we looked down into Kades' cove, to which we now, with less difficulty but not with less risk, descended, but not with less difficulty to the cannoneers, who were compelled to hold back the cannon from descending upon the horses. Kades' cove is three or four miles in each of its dimensions, and is 600 feet above Tuckaleeche cove. It possesses a rich soil, and we found here abundance of hay, oats and corn. Its inhabitants were said to be mostly rebel sympathizers. We crossed the cove and camped in a cedar grove near abundance of good water. Our march, 13 miles. The evening brought indications of rain, and the night a mighty wind, which moaned and roared through the mountain forests, caves and gorges, making weird music not well calculated to soothe to gentle slumber.

February 1st. Called early. Torrents of rain pouring down. Marched at 7 a. m. back on the route we came and to the foot of Chilhowee mountain, and began its ascent. This was not so steep as Cedar mountain, but the heavy rains had made the roads slippery, so that the ascent was no less difficult. We found the same tortuous windings, to avoid yawning chasms. Now descending a space and crossing on a ridge, then ascending another towering hill. One novel appearance presented in mountain climbing is the constant hope that the monster hill before you is the summit of the mountain, and when its top is reached that the traveler may gaze down beyond at rich valleys and pleasant coves. But, the top of this reached, and there looms up before us another mountain, opposing to our progress the same difficulties and presenting the same hopes of final triumph at its summit. Thus mountain after mountain successively rises before us, until by patient toil the last mountain obstacle is surmounted, a fair representation of the experiences of mortal life in every department. On this mountain we passed a couple of hunter's cabins, with pelts and hides of various wild animals, including hides of black bears, nailed upon walls. These were the only signs of habitations, and these at present seemed unoccupied. From the summit of this mountain we descended a space, then ascended another mountain. The clouds were now below us, looking dense and dark, as though still pouring torrents of rain, whilst the air with us was crisp and sharp and bracing. From the summit of this mountain, gazing to the left front, was seen rising far above all other mountains one of huge dimensions, looking like a giant among infants. It seemed to be bare of trees or shrubbery, and seemed to be but a stone's throw distant. But we were told that the nearest point was four miles distant. We were told that this is Bald mountain, the highest peak in the Alleghany range. Turning from this picture of extreme desolation, we gazed to our right downward to seemingly immeasurable depths, to feast the vision upon scenes of loveliness. Rich valleys and coves, doubtless filled with comfortable dwellings and homes, and every evidence of human prosperity and happiness. And what is *that* which appears like a silver cord running through the valley scene as far as vision can penetrate each way, not in a straight line, but in tortuous windings? That is not a silver vein, but a river, the Little Tennessee, which, rising in North Carolina, whose other waters all flow toward the Atlantic, but this wayward stream, so determined to pursue a different course, that even the rugged Alleghany range cannot bar its progress, but, breaking through all restraints, it forces its way through mountains of opposition, until it revels in the beautiful valleys of East Tennessee. But even here it loses none of its independence of character by pursuing the course of other streams to the gulf, but, passing slightly to the south, it again strikes westward, and then northward, seemingly determined to avoid the southern waters, until captured by the muddy waters of the Ohio, it loses both its independence and its purity, and is borne, a helpless captive, to the south. But we have no time for poetic musings; our present duty brooks not poetic sentiment. A short distance farther we passed the boundary between Tennessee and North Carolina, and soon after began the descent of the range by the same kind of winding, tortuous paths. We passed "Stony Point" and reached the river just before sunset, fatigued beyond expression and hoping that here we might camp. But no, duty—and, may we not add, our own safety—prompt a further advance. We marched along the narrow gorge which afforded a passage for the river, which in some places claimed the whole passageway, compelling us to turn to the left and climb rugged hills until again the river permitted a passage for us. Thus we marched for 14 miles, crossing Eagle creek, near where we found a level camping ground, where, late at night, extremely tired and hungry, with 30 miles' march over mountain road, we camp, with orders to be ready for an early march in the morning, not waiting for the bugle call, as our march must now be silent, unless we wish our scalps to grace the Indian tent poles.

February 2d. At 4 a. m. we were aroused silently. The weather was cold and crisp. We marched before sunrise on up the Tennessee river, which in places was a raging, seething, boiling mass of waters, in strange contrast with the beautiful calm flow of its pure and peaceful waters through the lovely vales of East Tennessee. Four miles above our camp we passed several log huts, the only inhabited domiciles on our route thus far. Thirteen miles farther we came to the junction of the Little Tennessee and the Tuckasegee rivers. We proceeded up the north bank of the Tuckasegee and crossed Forney creek, four miles above, and four miles farther crossed "No Land Creek." Though receding from the mountain range, we were not yet beyond its desolation. Three miles farther we came to another dwelling, where resided a prominent and staunch union man bearing the unpoetic name of "Make Garrett," who informed us that the camp of the Indian legion was only three miles above, on the north bank of the Tuckasegee river and at the mouth of Deep creek. He accompanied the information with the emphatic expression of hope that we would kill every one of the thieving, murderous band. We were now in the enemy's country, having passed many dangerous defiles, where an ambushed foe could have destroyed our whole band. So far, by great caution, we had succeeded. But final success, and even the preservation of our precious scalps, depended upon our taking the enemy by complete surprise. They have a picket one and .a quarter miles this side of their camp. Should a single man escape from that post or a single shot be heard in camp, our scheme is thwarted. The Indian camp is on a shelf of land on the bank of the river which is on our right, while on the left hand, back of the camp, is a hill which is covered with a dense thicket, which is filled with low, scrubby thorn bushes. The camp is in a growth of timber which extends westward some rods, covering the camp from view on the side of our approach until we approach to within a quarter of a mile. On the west of the thicket, the side of our approach, the ground is open—an old field. Should the Indians receive any notice of our approach they would fall back to the thicket, where, screened from view, Indian marksmen could have fine sport in a shooting match, which would not have left one of our exposed charging line alive. A better battle ground for Indian fighting Indian sagacity could not have selected. The key to the situation was the successful taking in of the Indian picket, and that too without the report of our own or the enemy's guns sufficiently loud to be heard in camp. We have no account of the plan of this feat, nor even the names of the men nor the name of the officer who led. Of this we are very sorry. This we know, that not a man of the six sentinels at the post escaped, or in any manner gave warning. It was a remarkable achievement. There yet remained great danger that they would receive a signal of our approach. We now pressed forward with speed and in perfect silence until near the point where we could be seen from the camp. We were guided over the mountains and perfectly informed of the whole situation in and around the camp by a good union man, Captain Bushfield, captain

FIRST LIEUT. AND ACTING ADJT. ISAAC H. ALLEN

of a company of union home guards. Through this man's information the plans were all laid.

The command was divided into two forces. A column was formed to charge into the camp, composed of Company "A," commanded by Lieutenant Horace Capron, to lead, and Company "I," under Captain Hagaman, to follow "A" and Company "C," commanded by Captain Dent, to follow "I," Major Davidson having command. Major Quigg was with and in command of that portion of his battalion that was in this column, "I" and "C;" the other force—the remainder of the regiment, under the command of their officers—was directed to charge upon the thicket on the west side. This was none less dangerous than was the charge into camp, as it would be made over open ground, and in case the Indians had received warning and had fallen back into the thicket, it was far more dangerous. But then, we need make no comparison of the danger, as every man in the command was equally doomed in case we failed of victory. The Indians sent no prisoners to Andersonville, nor paroled any, except with the bullet or the tomahawk. It was with us truly "victory or death." Every direction and order was given in whispered tones. Our only hope lay in our succeeding in making an overwhelming, demoralizing surprise. Everything in readiness, the order "Forward" is given in low tones. We now "column half right," which gave us a little longer concealment. We reach a point where concealment is no longer possible, when the voice of the leader rings out in thunder tones, *"Charge!"* Down upon the Indian camp, with drawn sabers flashing in the sunlight, like an avalanche tearing down the sides of a steep mountain, we burst upon the astonished view of the Indians, and such a shout was given, each man contributing the full volume of his tones, now the more emphatic that all the " phone" valves had been so long closed. We do not believe that the equal was ever heard from Indians or whites since the day the walls of Jericho tumbled to the shout of Israel's host. We had no need of the trumpets then used, for they could not have been heard. Such Indians as attempted to stay the impetuous charge were soon laid low. They fell back to the side of the hill in the brush, and for a time poured a hot fire into our ranks, which formed line, left faced and gave the Indians a volley or two that sent them into the denser thicket on the summit of the hill. Company "I," without tying their horses or leaving horse guards, rushed into the thicket after them, and were soon mixed up with the Indians in an old-fashioned frontier fight. Company "C" followed "I." The other companies, except "A" and "G," entering the thicket from different points, were all engaged. Companies "A" and "G" having dashed around to the east side of the thicket to cut off their retreat, were engaged with parties of Indians who tried to escape in that direction. Lieutenant Capron, observing a party of the enemy concealed by some rocks, gathered several of his men who had not scattered in the wild chase and charged down upon these Indians. They fired a volley at close range, and the lieutenant fell, mortally wounded, and one of his men, Fred Henderson, was killed. The Indians were completely surrounded, except on the north. The fight was hot and exciting while it lasted, but 30 minutes completely cleared the battle ground, leaving 60 of their dead on the field and 56 captives in our hands. The prisoners were cornered, and taken as a farmer would corner a calf. The Indians had been told by their officers that if the Yankees captured them they would hang them, so they would not surrender when called upon to halt. Indians seldom abandon their dead and wounded, and it is impossible to tell how many they carried off. While the Indian loss was heavy, our loss in numbers was light, but it comprehended some of the best men and officers in the regiment.

Lieutenant Horace Capron was one of the most bold and skillful line officers in the regiment, and as a man and comrade, he was beloved by all. Sergeant Mattenly Addis, one of the best soldiers of Company "I," fell at the head of his company in the charge into camp. It was then supposed that he was mortally wounded. Near where we entered the thicket Thomas Heath, of Company "I," was killed. We had no better man in the company. Joseph Ridley, of Company "K," a splendid soldier, was also killed in the thicket. Six or seven were wounded, but except the two named, we do not know their names, as the company record seldom noted the wounded. It is impossible to distinguish any of the command as more courageous that day than others, for there was not a man or officer in the command that did not do to his utmost, his duty. This might be expected of men who willingly would enter upon an undertaking so full of peril, as all from the first realized of that expedition. Besides at the time every man realized that it was with us, complete and overwhelming victory or death, and each far preferred to aid to his utmost to make it what it was, an overwhelming victory. The battery boys of Company "L," and their brave leader, who had toiled so hard to bring along the two guns of their battery, were not disappointed in an opportunity to do their part. No men in valor or in practical service exceeded them. The Indians who escaped doubtless long remembered the thunder tones of our "wheel guns," as they called them, and of which, "Indian-like," they were in mortal dread.

After the Indians were convinced by our kind treatment that they had been deceived by the rebels, they agreed to stand as hostages for the safe return of two of their number who were to return to their band to inform them of the deception that had been practiced. The result was that many Indian families came into our lines for protection. Colonel Thomas had told them that the north had rebelled against the old Jackson Government, and these Indians desired to be loyal to the old Government.

Subsequent events, however, demonstrated that though they were well treated and convinced that Colonel Thomas had deceived them, yet there rankled in the bosoms of their warriors a thirst for revenge for the severe punishment we had inflicted upon them. Colonel Thomas himself came near being captured. A party was sent across the river to a plantation where he had been quartered. He escaped capture by having just changed his quarters.

General Sturgis, in a report, says: "I am just in receipt of dispatches announcing the surprise of the Indians on the 2d of February near Quallatown. The enemy were 250 strong. Of these 22 Indians and 32 whites were captured, including some officers. It is reported that less than 50 escaped, the rest being either killed or wounded, so that this nest of Indians may be considered as entirely destroyed; nearly 200 of them having been killed. In this affair Lieutenant Capron, a gallant young officer of the 14th Illinois Cavalry, was seriously and perhaps mortally wounded while charging the enemy. This was an enterprise of great difficulty; through a rough mountainous country, destitute of supplies of any kind. Major Davidson is deserving of great credit for the manner in which he executed his instructions." This was a message sent before all the facts were known. The number of the enemy killed, as far as we could learn, were as we state. The following account was published in the Knoxville Whig, published by Parson Brownlow. It also contains the same error in regard to the killed of the enemy, though correct in other respects. We are indebted to Major Connelly, who obtained from Mrs. Brownlow a copy of the paper. The following was published in the issue of March 6th, 1864: "The following dispatch from General Grant refers to the recent expedition into North Carolina, conducted, as we are informed, by Major Davidson, of the 14th Illinois Cavalry. It was a brilliant affair. In justice to this gallant officer and his brave command, let it be remembered that this expedition was conducted in the midst of the winter, over the highest range of mountains east of the Mississippi river. But few expeditions during this war have been so successful, or conducted so skillfully." Then follows this report by General Grant: "Washington, D. C., February 9th, 1864. The following dispatch has been received here: 'Nashville, Tennessee, February 8th, 1864. Major General Hallack, General in Chief, says, General Foster telegraphs from Knoxville under date of yesterday, that an expedition sent against Thomas and his band of Indians and whites at Quallatown, has returned completely successful. They surprised the town, killed and wounded 215, took 50 prisoners and dispersed the remainder of the gang in the mountains. Our loss was two killed and six wounded." There were three killed, besides Lieutenant Capron, who died of his wounds.

We now performed the sad rites of burial for our noble dead comrades; and having no ambulances we pressed several heavy wagons, in one of which we placed our severest wounded, Lieutenant Capron and Sergeant Addis, both of whom were supposed to be mortally wounded. This was a rough means of conveyance, and over mountain rocks at that, but it was the best we then could do. We were now in the enemy's country with a considerable number of the savage band left to seek revenge, and with other rebel forces not far off, while we were cut off by many miles of mountain road, from any support of ours. Many mountain defiles to pass where a few well armed and ammunitioned men could have held us at bay, or what is worse, could have ambushed and destroyed us.

It was determined that our safest route to return would be a roundabout, more southerly course, by way of Murphy; with some expectation to capture some horses. We had been disappointed in capturing those of the band, as they had been sent for forage. To Captain Bushfield of the North Carolina Union Home Guards, who was our skillful guide, is due much of the honor of the plans upon which our success depended. The fight began about 2 p. m.; that, and the burial of our dead and the gathering and destroying all the military belongings of this band, gave us a busy afternoon employment, giving us barely time to cross the Tuckaseege river and march 4 miles to camp, reaching it after dark. We camped on the plantation of a notorious rebel woman, whose plantation furnished, under Yankee soldiers' requisition, a small quantity of rations and forage and some Lincoln rails for fuel, which, of course, belonged to the Lincoln government. They made a good fire, which was enjoyed that cold night.

We posted a strong picket to prevent an Indian surprise, and then lay down on the cold, damp ground late at night, having marched 30 miles, besides our busy afternoon work. We had no dinner, and very little for supper, as our hostess, Mrs. Hart, did not invite us to supper.

February 3d. Called early without bugle note. Marched at 8 a. m. without breakfast, south a few miles to the Little Tennessee, where scouts reported that on our proposed route, the built up mountain road, was all broken down, and impassable. We are now compelled to return by the way we came, risking that our forces were able to prevent the enemy from gaining possession of the passes on our road. We passed down the Tennessee river, crossed a deep creek, and then the Tuckaseege river, halting soon after at the dwelling of one Major Sellers, an officer in the Indian Legion. As that legion now had no use for him and we had, we kindly took him with us. He was a merchant, and as we did not wish to separate him from all his property, we took with us what we could of flour and corn and other useful articles, including a fine two-horse buggy and harness, which we borrowed to convey our wounded men in. We marched 22 miles and camped within 4 miles of our last encampment on our upward route. The wounded were well cared for by Surgeon Wilson in houses near our camp. We had some rations, thanks to Major Sellers' unwilling contribution, and we procured some straw for our horses.

February 4th. Reveille 4 a. m. Our Major Sellers left us last night without a pass, and without his buggy and harness and other traps. His conduct was singular. We think there was a pretty big nigger in the fence, as our other friends, the redskins, were quietly there yet. We now hear that Longstreet has possession of our pass, but we hasten on, hoping to find some way out. Eight miles west of Stony Point we leave the mountain path that we came on to conceal our movements. We pass down the valley of the Little Tennessee. Passed through Chestnut Wind, and soon after entered and camped in Chilhowee Valley near the Little Tennessee. Forage and rations scarce; march, 26 miles. Chilhowee is Indian for "fine deer."

February 5th. Reveille 4 a. m. Marched at 8 a. m. down the river and into Cittico Valley; a very fine country; crossed Nine Mile creek at "Bess' Merchant Mills," and soon after camped in a fine oak grove near "Wood's Schoolhouse," on the Marysville road; marched 18 miles.

This ends one of our most important services, one which doubtless equals any other achievement of an equal number of men in any war.

February 6th. Reveille 4 a. m.; raining in the valley, while the mountains are white with snow. Our wounded had been sent on to Knoxville, where Lieutenant Capron died today, as we afterward learned. His loss was deeply felt by comrades and by all who knew him. To the finest military traits he added all the qualities of a gentleman. His body was sent to his friends in Peoria, Illinois. It is a matter of wonder that any of our severely wounded could live to cross over on our mountain road. Our prisoners were also sent to Knoxville.

February 7th. Reveille 4 a. m. In camp.

February 8th. In camp; cold day; reveille 5 a. m.

February 9th, 5 a. m. The 65th Indiana joined us to-day.

February 10th. In camp.

February 11th. In camp.

February 12th. March at 9 a. m. with 65th Indiana; Major Davidson commanding brigade, Major Quigg commanding 14th Illinois. Marched 10 miles; camped on rough ground; rations and forage scarce.

February 13th. Reveille at daylight. In camp; little rations.

February 14th. Reveille at daylight. In camp; little rations; send far for forage.

February 15th. Reveille at daylight; rained all night and all day.

February 16th. Reveille 4 a. m. Marched at 8 a. m.; weather very cold; men suffer much. Halted in Maryville, a small town, the county site of Blount county. Marched after dark toward Knoxville, passed through Rockford, crossed Little river and camped in a wood 7 miles from Maryville. We were rear guard of a force of cavalry; we suffered much with cold; marched slowly, halted often. We bivouacked 11 p. m.; marched 25 miles.

February 17th. Reveille 5 a. m.; suffered with cold last night. Marched at 7 a. m.; reached river opposite Knoxville 1 p. m.; marched 12 miles. As Longstreet, at Strawberry Plains, is threatening the reinvestment of Knoxville, the military defenses of Knoxville have been greatly strengthened since the siege.

February 18th. Reveille at 5 a. m. At 7 a. m. the effective men of the brigade marched on scout to Maryville, then toward Sevierville and captured a small party of rebels, then returned to camp, 10 p. m.; marched 28 miles; weather cold.

February 19th. Reveille 5 a. m. In camp; no forage.

February 20th. Reveille at daylight; marched 8 a. m.; crossed the river and marched on Strawberry Plains road. Major Davidson sick, Major Quigg commanding brigade; Captain Dent commanding 14th. We were sent to reconnoiter Longstreet's forces, who are approaching toward Knoxville. About 8 miles out we came in view of a force of the enemy across the Holston. Two miles farther we saw a strong picket at a barn on an eminence near the road. Colonel Garrard, who commanded the division, came up and our line was formed, a portion mounted, while a portion dismounted and advanced as skirmishers. Our object is to draw out the enemy that we may judge of his force. A few companies were sent to the left to open a skirmish. Sergeant Beck, with Company "K," 14th, was ordered to charge upon the barn; this was handsomely done and the enemy driven. A strong force now appeared in line a half mile off; both infantry and cavalry. Several companies of rebel infantry were sent to retake the barn. Two other mounted companies of 14th are sent to reinforce Company "K," and they held the barn until our reconnoissance was completed, when our brigade remounted and returned to Knoxville. We passed through, and camped on our old ground near Fort Sanders; bivouacking about 9 p. m. without rations; marched 24 miles.

February 23d. Reveille at daylight; foragers sent to Louisville, 15 miles off; get plenty of forage and rations, having been almost without for several days.

February 24th. Reveille at 3 a. m.; had hard thunder storm last night. Marched at sunrise through Knoxville, and on Strawberry Plains road. We passed General Judah's division and moved on to the river, then turn to the left on Rutledge road, leaving the river to the right and Blaine's crossroads to the left, and camped near Stone's Mills on Richland creek. No forage; little rations; marched 25 miles.

February 25th. Reveille at daylight; marched at 9 a. m. up the river and camped in the woods near Messinger's mills on Buffalo creek; poor camp; fare as yesterday. Marched 10 miles.

February 26th. Reveille at daylight. At 10 a. m. Lieutenant Guy sent on scout with a small party of men. They discovered a force of the enemy, who fired upon them. The Lieutenant fell back for reinforcements. Companies "A," "G," "C" and "D," of 14th, under Captain Carrico, sent forward, but the enemy had disappeared. Our party pursued to Rutledge, but could not overtake them. They then returned to camp at 10 p. m., having marched 35 miles. A part of Companies "F" and "H," 14th, were sent to Strawberry Plains to act as scouts for the infantry, which was crossing the river at that place and moving toward Morristown.

February 27th. Reveille at daylight. Marched at 9 a. m. toward Knoxville, on main road, then on Rutledge road; came to the old Scott road. Country heavily timbered and not much improved. Passed a dilapidated building where an old lady was intently gazing upon us through her spectacles. She exclaimed: "Well, men! can you tell me how *many* have passed here today?" One of the boys promptly answered, 6,000 (there were about 1,600). "Well!" said the old lady, "I never thought there were so many people in the world." We passed the spot where it was said that one of our videttes, with a Henry rifle, had killed a rebel soldier 1,000 yards distant, that is more than a half mile. We camped after night two miles from Knoxville; marched 25 miles.

Sunday, February 28th. Reveille at daylight; rain.

February 29th. Reveille at daylight; raining; march at 7 a. m. toward Powell Valley; rains hard; roads very slippery. Crossed a high ridge; camped in a nice grove. Forage plenty; marched 8 miles; rained all day. Mustered for pay.

March 1st. Reveille at daylight; rain, rain, rain. Marched at 10 a. m.; roads heavy; reached Bull Run creek, so swollen by recent rains as to be impassable for trains; camped in a wood near; marched 5 miles; rained hard all day. This morning Major Davidson resumed command of the brigade and Major Quigg of the 14th.

March 2d. Reveille at daylight; cleared off. Marched at 11 a. m.; crossed the creek, yet deep, near Loy's crossroads, in Big Valley; roads terrible; weather beautiful; camp poor; marched 12 miles.

March 3d. Reveille at daylight; weather fine.

March 4th. Reveille at daylight; march at 8 a. m. toward Clinton, 5 miles; camped in a beautiful grove in "Big Valley" near Wallace's cross roads; fine springs of water near.

March 5th. Reveille at daylight, rained at night; rations and forage more plenty.

Sunday, March 6th. Reveille at daylight; fine weather.
March 7th. Reveille at daylight; rain.
March 8th. Reveille at 5 a. m.; rain. March at 7 a. m., reached Knoxville 4 p. m., passed through and camped on our old ground. Passed by a soldiers' cemetery containing 680 graves of our fallen heroes. The graves were tastefully arranged in circles. Marched 23 miles.

March 9th. Reveille at daylight. Marched at 11 a. m. toward Loudon, passed through Campbell Station and camped two miles beyond in a beautiful grove near a creek; weather warm and pleasant; marched 17 miles.

March 10th. Reveille at daylight; rained all night; marched after sunrise; reached the river at noon; were several hours in crossing on pontoon bridge; camped 3 miles south of Loudon in a grove of pines and oaks about 4 p. m.; marched 16 miles over muddy roads.

March 11th. Reveille at daylight; thunderstorm last night. Inspection of horses and arms. The horses of the 65th were all condemned, and also all of the 14th, except 75.

March 12th. Reveille at daylight; drew five days' rations last evening; marched at 8 a. m.; passed through Philadelphia and through Sweetwater Valley and camped in a grove. Lieutenant Colonel Jenkins now joined us and took command of the 14th. The 65th were not with us again. An order from General Granger, in whose command we now were, was read. It prohibited soldiers from foraging, or from buying of citizens, or from entering their premises. Heavy penalties were threatened and promises were made to keep us supplied with full rations. Since leaving Kentucky we have seen little of army rations. We had no trains nor pack horses and were obliged to carry rations and horse feed on the horses we rode. We often lost our cooking utensils. They were very valuable, consisting of a general purpose kettle made out of an oyster can with a wire bail attached. This was coffee pot, tea pot, soup pot combined. Our frying pan was one half of a canteen. Sometimes we got flour without anything else, not even salt. This we mixed with water and wound the dough around a stick, which we held near the fire till it baked, and this beat "no bread" vastly much. Sometimes we drew fresh beef without salt or a smidgen of anything else, and nothing to cook this in. To give us an appetite we lay down in mud or snow or on three-cornered rails to keep us out of mud; happy the three or four boys who together had two blankets; one to lie on and one to cover over. Sumptuous feasting times were these for Lincoln's hirelings, weren't they, Mr. Soldier-Hater and his brother Copperhead? For almost seven months we saw no tea, coffee or sugar, but a small part of the time. But this was good enough for Lincoln bummers, who, of course, only enlisted for $13 a month and chance to board at Andersonville thrown in. We were often a day and sometimes several days without anything to eat. We had marched this day 13 miles.

Sunday, March 13th. Reveille at daylight; marched before noon to Madisonville, the county site of Monroe county, which for three months now became the headquarters of our regiment. We camped on the west side of town in a grove. Weather fine; marched 8 miles.

CHAPTER IX.

AN ISLAND OF PEACEFUL REST, IN AN OCEAN OF STORMY
BILLOWS.

From the middle of March, 1864, for three months the 14th Illinois Cavalry was in clover. With the exception of one attack, which Providence prevented from annihilating the regiment, and a few other small scratches, just enough to keep our swords from rusting in their scabbards, we had peace and rest. Indeed we could scarcely realize that we were a constituent part of an army, and in the midst of a cruel war. Nestled in quiet, cozy camps, near beautiful streams, or in the valleys and coves of lovely East Tennessee, with mountain views in contrast with the most pleasant plains and valleys, bountifully watered by the purest, cool mountain streams; the eye gladdened by the most romantic and pleasant views; the ear saluted from morn to dewy eve with the celestial harmony of forest choirs; with every decoration that the floral kingdom could furnish in this sweet vernal season; and last, but not least, a full supply of Uncle Sam's bountiful rations. The whole combined was sufficient to completely enervate us and unfit us for stern war. Contrasted with our past six months' experience it was enough to turn our heads. Only one element was lacking to fill the measure of earthly bliss, the presence of loved ones and the enjoyment of social and religious influences and privileges; the first being in a measure compensated by the extreme hospitality and friendliness of the inhabitants; the loyal from choice, and the disloyal from policy. Nor were we entirely lacking in religious privileges, as the rural congregations that gathered for worship in rude church buildings, had at least the element of fervency to recommend them.

We were still in the 23d Army Corps, now commanded by Major General John M. Schofield, and belonged to General George H. Stoneman's cavalry division, nearly all of which went to Sherman's forces in the front quite early. Most of the cavalry had been sent to Kentucky to be remounted. Our raid into North Carolina had prevented our regiment from a remount, and as our horses needed recruiting up by rest and good care, we were ordered to this new duty to relieve infantry commands that were posted at these points. These infantry forces were then hurried to the front. Our regiment was now divided into detachments of from half a company to two companies at one point, and occupied a line of posts at fords and crossings of rivers, and passes over the mountains, reaching from Loudon, on the Tennessee river, to Charleston, on the Hiwassee river. These posts were, on an average, from two miles to five miles apart; the line in its winding course was 40 miles long, extending through the counties of Monroe, McMinn, and Bradley. Our regiment was commanded by Lieutenant-Colonel D. P. Jenkins, with headquarters at Madisonville.

Could we have gathered notes and descriptions of the locations and interesting incidents of each detachment during this service, the record would be a volume of interest to all. We have such descriptions from two companies, "I" and "C;" to give these without giving similar records of other companies would seem to give too great prominence to the companies of the original authors; and besides, a full account would increase our volume beyond our present means, so we can give but little of these descriptions.

Our last chapter left us at Madisonville, March 13th. From this point detachments were sent off to their various posts at different times. On March 17th the writer's company (I) was sent to guard the mountain pass of the Murphy pike, 16 miles southeast of Madisonville. This was an important road across the mountains. Lieutenant Boeke was detached as ordnance officer at headquarters. About the 25th of March we had a heavy fall of snow on the peach trees that were in full bloom; a strange blending of stern winter and gentle summer. Our duty at this post was the usual duty, the alternating of vigilant outpost duty, with the lazy quiet of camp life. One little incident, trifling of itself, yet, as we believe, closely interwoven with our chance destiny, occurred while here. The writer was then Orderly Sergeant. One morning in early April the captain ordered the writer to take command of the company during his short absence. While out instructing the advanced vidette, a *young* lady (of uncertain age), Miss Fry, who resided about half way to Madisonville, came out to the vidette and asked to be allowed to pass through to visit a sick relative on the mountains. We asked if she had obtained a pass from Madisonville, as was required. To this the lady replied, with winsome smiles: "You surely would not subject me to the inconvenience of going 8 miles and back for nothing, just to visit a sick relative, would you?" This was, ordinarily speaking, sound logic, embodied in a plea backed by the strongest promptings of gallantry, and the persuasive eloquence of the smiles of beauty. Much against the promptings of a gentler nature, we were obliged to answer: "In these times of cruel war, we are compelled, for the protection of our army, as well as for our own safety, to do many things contrary to the code of gallantry, and that closely verge upon the code of cruelty. We are under the strictest orders to pass no one through the lines, on any plea, unless they show a genuine pass from our headquarters, and this you must have known before you left home. I am sorry to refuse your apparently reasonable request, but as a military man, I must refuse it." Just at this time the captain came out to the post and inquired what was the racket. On being informed, he rebuked me for my hard-hearted refusal, and ordered the vidette to pass the lady through. The worst of it was the captain, as well as all our command, well knew that all of this family were notorious rebels, and the evil results of this flagrant disobedience of orders, will be commented upon in connection with an event in our history while on this post. After the fall of snow mentioned, which was 14 inches deep on a level, we had a continued spell of the finest weather.

April 10th, the writer in command of half of Company "I," was sent to occupy a small manufacturing place two miles above the Murphy pike, on a road that led up the valley of Tellico river. The place was called "Tellico Furnace." This small river was a mountain stream, and the road led over the mountains. The position was romantic. The river here leaves the mountains and enters the plains. On one side were mountains piled on mountains, until they seemed to touch the sky, while in the opposite direction lay spread out to our enchanted view, the verdant peaceful beauty of lovely plains, in strong contrast with the distorted, rugged, martial aspect of the mountains. Before the war the abundant iron ore on adjacent hills was here manufactured into pig iron. The neighbors were all Union people except old Colonel Johnson, who owned the furnace and all adjacent lands. His aged father was said to be a Union man, so indeed did the Colonel pretend to be, but his neighbors said he was a rebel recruiting officer and furnished large supplies in stock and horses to the rebel army. After leaving that post the old Colonel trumped up a claim of $10,000 against our government, for the very things that he had furnished to the rebels. He even wrote to me inquiring the amount of wood we had used of his, gathered ourselves from down waste timber on the mountains, not worth a cent to him, but which we paid him for as we used it, as we were under strict orders to pay for everything we received from citizens. Of course, I never replied. Our post was 3 miles from Citico, which was the head of our line N. W., and was occupied by Company "E." We had good quarters in the deserted cabins, and plenty of fuel by gathering it from the hills and paying for it. Our duty was light, requiring only a vigilant vidette, on which duty each man alternated.

On May 27th couriers came from Company "E," 3 miles N. W., notifying us that a band of Indians had attacked that post, and being repulsed had taken to the mountains. Every available man was sent from Company "I," as well as from all the companies that could be reached. These congregated at Citico, the post that had been attacked; but so much time had intervened that the Indians could not be found. If each post was left as destitute of men and arms as was that at Tellico Furnace, their only safety from an attack from Indians who might be lurking in the mountains adjacent, would have been that, in their extreme weakness they did not offer game enough to attract savages in quest of blood. Cautioned by this danger, we built a rude block house at Tellico, so situated as to well guard the narrow valley. Not long after this, Captain Hagaman, with the remainder of Company "I," removed from the Murphy pike to the post at Tellico,

where we remained enjoying a quiet camp life with fair
rations, until we started for Georgia in June; when Captain Hagaman, who had resigned, left us, and Lieutenant
Boeke assumed command, Lieutenant Kilbourne having
also returned from leave of absence, caused by his severe
wound.

The record of Company "C," is given by Martin West,
our former cohistorian. His description would
afford a most interesting account for general publication,
but our unfortunate necessity of condensing our work
compels us to omit some fine descriptions, that do not relate to war history. We would be glad to include more of
his poetic descriptions and quaint pictures of camp life in
this romantic service, but we are compelled greatly to
abridge. Company "C" was one of the last companies
sent from Madisonville. They first went to Bowman's
ford on the Little Tennessee, seven miles from Loudon.
Company "H" was then at Riley's ford, 3 miles below;
the 74th Illinois Infantry being at Davis' ford below.
Subsequently Company "C" guarded all these fords, Sergeant (afterward Lieutenant) Beckwith commanded at
Bowman's ford, assisted by Corporal De Mule. Corporals
Wisner and Breed, and afterward Sergeant Day, commanded at the ferry. Captain Dent's headquarters were
at Davis' ford. Company "H," when relieved from Riley's
ford, was sent to Major Davidson near Charleston, the
right of our line of posts. The river at our post was the
boundary between the counties of Monroe and Blount;
the citizens were mostly loyal, respectable and hospitable."
Comrade West gives a quaint description of a dance he
attended, which so perfectly describes characteristics of
mingled hospitality and rural simplicity, that we grieve
that our limited space forbids its record, as it does that of
many other fine descriptions. We must, however, give
one of his beautiful descriptions. He says: "The valley
along the river was romantic in the extreme. Although
there was no range of mountains, to afford a view of
mountains piled on mountains like huge ocean billows,
until vision failed to distinguish them from the blue ether
above, yet the round, sloping hills on each side of the river
covered with the stately pine and majestic oak, spreading
their bright green foliage to rustle in the gentle breeze;

while thousands of beautiful varigated flowers rendered the air balmy with their fragrant perfumes. The clusters of willows along the river's banks, ever bending to gaze upon their counterparts which the sun (Nature's daguerreon) placed in the liquid depths below; or stooping, while fanned by gentle zephyrs, to kiss some cherished spot upon its placid bosom. The large green meadows, covered with a beautiful mossy turf, softer than the gorgeous carpets of a Turkish harem; and the thick, umbrageous groves, acting as mediators between the scorching noonday sun and the fevered brow. All these, formed a beautiful blending and harmonious contrast to the lovely murmuring stream and the quiet homesteads resting along its banks."

The duty of Company "C," like that of the other companies was light; consisting of a vigilant guard against the entrance of the enemy through their posts, and a pursuit of such bands as had entered our lines through other passes or fords.

From Major Connelly and Lieutenant Wm. M. Moore we learn that Company "L," under Lieutenant Moore, was posted at Loudon, and served as couriers and scouts for General Granger. While there they pursued and fought various roving bands of the enemy as they showed up. They were kept actively employed. Lieutenant Moore was an active and skillful officer and of fine appearance and gentlemanly in bearing. Captain H. C. Connelly, of Company "L" (afterward Major), was never lacking in important service. At this time he served as Inspector General on the staff of General Strickland.

From brief and interesting notes of Captain Wm. R. Sanford, of Company "K," we copy: "In command of first battalion of 14th, left Madisonville March 14th, 1864; marched to Motley's ford on Little Tennessee river; arrived at noon; relieved 2d Indiana Cavalry, commanded by Captain Edwards. This force had been very slack in picket duty. Gave strict orders to prohibit citizens from coming into camp. Weather very fine till 21st and 22d, when we had a deep snow. Twenty-third moved to Niles ferry. March 25th Captain Crandle asks for a reinforcement of 50 men, which are sent to him; 27th temporarily relieved by 65th Indiana, so that we could go to Madisonville to be paid. Weather cloudy and rainy until

April. Scarce of corn and rations part of the time. Rumor that we will be attacked by a large force. Sent out pickets on Tellico river. April 18th. Much excitement about a female spy—a Mrs. Law. Captain Carrico reports to Captain Crandle. April 26th, moved camp to Dawson. April 27th, get orders for myself and Captain C. to go to headquarters and then to Charleston to General Hovey. Marched at noon. Company "B," under Lieutenant Beechey, goes with us.

April 29th, 7 a. m. Left Madisonville; marched to Athens, and 30th reached Charleston at noon."

We are informed that Company "F" was posted on the Murphy pike after Captain Hagaman removed. Of Company "H," we have only the record that they were posted first at Citico, and then sent (West says) to Major Davidson at Columbus. Company "G," we are informed, was at Dry creek a few miles below Murphy pike. Major Davidson and his command was on or near the Hiwassa river. These records are as we have succeeded in gathering; there may be, and probably are, errors in the records; if so, comrades must excuse them, as we have made every effort to get correct notes. Fortunately we have a good account of the only important military event that occurred during this period. It was written by a participant, but by accident his name is blotted from the record, so that we can not give it. The account agrees with other facts so that we can safely say it is correct, or as nearly so as any account given by any one man could well be. From the record we have, Companies "B" and "E," commanded by Captain Crandle, marched from Madisonville to a post on south side of Little Tennessee river, at the mouth of Citico creek, 16 miles from Madisonville. This post was near the mountains, with fine fertile valleys around. They sent out scouting parties daily, sometimes in the mountains, capturing prisoners occasionally, which aggregated 40. We give the following as reported to us, and we believe it to be correct:

"On the night of May 27th, 1864, one of General McCook's scouts reported to Captain Crandle that Thomas' Indian Legion had planned to surprise his post, and kill every man, and then sweep down the line of our mountain posts, taking each by surprise in detail. They had planned to attack that night. Company "B" had gone to another post and Captain Crandle had but 25 men at the post. This was originally the hunting grounds of the Indians, and they knew every mountain path. It is well known that Indians seek to attack an enemy from unexpected directions as well as at unexpected times. Videttes were posted on every road and path. The tents were left standing and everything arranged to give the appearance that all the men were sleeping in their tents. The horses saddled and tied in a thicket, and the company armed and prepared, secreted near their tents. The evening was fair and the stars shone brightly while we eagerly watched, each moment expecting the attack. Only those similarly situated can even guess the extreme anxiety with which we watched the moments pass into hours, and the hours move slowly by. Each man was a vigilant sentinel, with a brave heart, ready for the worst, but anxious that the painful suspense might soon end. Everything was calm and still. Only the slight noise made by falling drops of dew, which told that it was growing late at night. The moon rose in splendor, shedding a silver light over a lovely scene. About midnight a gun fired on a picket post signaled the time of danger near. It proved to be a false alarm. We had not much longer to wait. About 1 a. m. the Indian war whoop rang out loud and clear on the still night air; a sound to strike terror into the hearts of even brave men, but not a man faltered; with nerves steeled to sell their lives dearly if conquered, they waited their time. The picket was killed, and with savage yells the Indians rushed into the camp and fired into the tents, supposing that our men were sleeping there. Yelling like demons they seemed to gloat over a feast of blood, but no sooner were their guns emptied than Company "E" sprang from their concealment and poured a volley into the astonished band, at the same time giving them a yell that Indian throats could never equal. Faster than they came, they went to the mountains. Couriers were immediately sent to Tellico and on down the line of posts, and a detachment was gathered that hunted for Indians all that day, the 28th of May, but no Indians could be found. They sought a sweet revenge on the 14th for our complete surprise of them in open daylight, but Indian savagery and cunning could not, even at midnight hour, cope with the vigilance and bravery of the men of the 14th, and again were they vanquished, beaten at their own game of surprise. This band of over 200 Indians and whites was commanded by the notorious Captain Kirkland. They had planned a sweet revenge, intending to attack each detachment of the 14th in detail, but they were dull, compared to the vigilance of our men, and they were cowards before the undaunted courage of wide awake Yankees. We could not learn their loss, as Indians never leave their dead or wounded on the field. When they were thus outgeneraled they expected to be attacked and fled so precipitately that they left Comrade Harvey Bradley, whom they had taken prisoner. Private James Daily, a sentinel, was killed. One other sentinel was severely wounded. Not knowing how soon the attack would be renewed, Captain Crandle, with his brave boys, fell back to Motley's ford, where Company "D" was posted, and soon after moved to a post 4 miles west of Citico, where they remained till the march to Georgia began. At this last post they built a block house to protect against an Indian attack. This ends all we have been able to gather of the positions and the services of the various detachments during this period.

A band was organized at Madisonville about April 20th, 1864. The first organization was as follows: Leader, Lieutenant Moses G. Hascal (then Sergeant), Company "I;" Wm. H. Cross, also of "I;" C. H. Spiller and E. W. Bowman, of Company "C;" Lorenz Walter, chief bugler and Charles Newmeyer, of Company "B;" Frederick Gray, Company "G;" J. J. Russ, Company "E;" A. N. Scribner and J. H. Sterling, of Company "L;" J. R. Fallenwider, Company "M;" Henry Smith, Company "K." The officers of the regiment furnished most of the funds for purchasing instruments and parts of an outfit. The first instruments were nearly worthless and soon became entirely so; the second were poor, not what were paid for; but under the skillful teaching and management, notwithstanding their poor instruments, the band was made a success. The subsequent changes in the band were as follows: Frederick Gray was captured on Stoneman raid and never returned to the band; Charles Newmeyer was captured, paroled and returned to the band; E. M.

Bowman was discharged in August. The following were added: W. Beck, Sergeant Company "K;" George W. Price, Company "B;" Andrew McCormick, Company "C;" G. W. Wolf, Company "L." June 12th, 1865, Sergeant Hascal was promoted Lieutenant and returned to his company, and James W. Beck, of Company "K," was appointed leader. No further changes were made.

CHAPTER X.

FROM EAST TENNESSEE TO GEORGIA.

June 13th, 1864. Longstreet has abandoned East Tennessee, which is now under the control of the Union forces, except as disturbed by predatory excursions of rebel raiders, mountain bushwhackers, and small local forces of rebels in neighboring portions of western Virginia. Major-General John M. Schofield, now commanding 23d Army Corps, reports on page 509, serial 73, that his army is massing as rapidly as possible at the front under General Wm. T. Sherman. Major-General George H. Stoneman, to whom was assigned the duty of organizing a cavalry division in Kentucky out of such cavalry of the 23d Corps as had been sent there to be remounted, has gone to the front with such cavalry as have been remounted and equipped. As our Indian raid prevented our remount in Kentucky, we were assigned to the duty we are now leaving, for the purpose of resting our horses and recruiting them up as much as possible. Stoneman's division is the 6th, and belongs to Schofield's army. Company "I," under Lieutenant Boeke, from Tellico; Company "F," from Murphy pike; Company "G," from Dry creek, all marched to Athens, Tennessee, and camped on northern boundary at 4 p. m. June 13th; march to each, about 25 miles. Athens is a beautiful Union town of 1,500 population. At Madisonville today a man of Company "D" shot and killed a comrade; both were intoxicated.

June 14th. The other companies, except those in Major Davidson's command, joined us today. All then marched and camped 4 miles south of Athens, in a timbered lot adjoining a fine pasture lot. March from Madisonville, 20 miles.

June 15th. Reveille at daylight; marched at 7 a. m., passed through Riceville and to Charleston on the railroad and on the Hiwassa river. Crossed on pontoon bridge, camped about 1 p. m. on a rough piece of timber land.

Marched 12 miles. Major Davidson's command joins us here.

June 16th. Marched at 7 a. m.; reached Cleveland at noon, passed through and camped a mile south near beautiful springs of water. March, 13 miles.

June 17th. Reveille at daylight. About noon Colonel Capron with a detachment of recruits joined us today. As nearly as imperfect records show there were 298 recruits, which were proposed to be apportioned to the several companies in such proportion as to entitle each company to a full complement of commissioned officers. As the records show it the companies received as follows: "A," 25; "B," 23; "C," 18; "D," 34; "E," 26; "F," 38; "G," 35; "H," 18; "I," 28; "K," 28; "L," 19; "M," 6. We cannot vouch for the correctness of these estimates further than that this is as the records, which in some respects we know are incorrect, show these numbers. Colonel Capron also brought with him a band of about 200, called McLaughlin's Ohio squadron, commanded by Major Richard Rice. About noon "Boots and Saddles" sounded, Companies "I," and "D," under Major Davidson, were sent out to hunt a rebel force that were reported near. Moved rapidly S. E. 2 miles; struck the trail of a rebel mounted force, variously estimated by citizens from 600 to 30,000; a fair illustration of the ability of the average citizen, to estimate the number in a mounted force. We moved rapidly on their trail for 15 miles, and came upon the camp that they had just left, where, in supposed security, their horses had been turned out to pasture. We quickened our march, but they had taken alarm and escaped to the mountains. This band numbered about 400. They were returning from a raid into Kentucky and designed to plunder the Union people of Cleveland, had not *weighty arguments* changed their purpose. We returned to camp, having marched 30 miles.

June 18th. Reveille at daylight. Companies "A" and "K," under command of Captain Wm. R. Sanford, of "K," are sent on scout. They followed a force of several hundred rebel troopers a dozen miles, returned to camp; marched 25 miles.

Sunday, June 19th. Rained; drew new horses from a lot brought by Colonel Capron.

June 20th. Very warm. Command called out last night on a false alarm. Drew some new equipments and the Starr revolver, a worthless arm. Dress parade afternoon.

June 21st. Rain.

June 22d. Marched at 6 a. m.; weather very warm; camped 2 miles beyond the Georgia line; marched 15 miles.

June 23d. Morning pleasant; marched at 5 a. m. toward Dalton. At 11 a. m. turned toward "Spring place." The first battalion, with Companies "I" and "C," under Major Davidson, sent on scout to the left near to "Spring Place." Find no enemy, return; march 22 miles. Regiment marched to Costamaula river and camped. Marched 18 miles.

June 24th. Morning pleasant; Major Davidson, with Companies "A," "G," "D," "C," sent on scout. The detachment marched 50 miles, but met no force of the enemy.

June 25th. Reveille at 3 a. m.; very warm. March at 1 p. m. south 9 miles; camped in a wood 6 miles from Resaca. Rough camp.

Sunday, June 26th. Reveille 3 a. m.; pleasant. Marched at 6 a. m. toward Resaca; cross the Costanaula river; camped near at 1 p. m.; poor camp grounds; weather hot. March, 8 miles.

June 27th. Reveille at 3 a. m.; take 4 days' rations and 2 days' forage; march at 6 a. m. through Resaca—noted for bloody battles; camped 9 miles beyond. March, 20 miles.

June 28th. Reveille at 1 a. m.; march at 4 a. m. to Cartersville on the railroad 45 miles from Atlanta, and camped in a pleasant grove at 1 p. m. March, 20 miles.

June 29th. Reveille at 3 a. m.; march at 5; pass through Ackworth and through Altoona and Big Shanty, now the headquarters of General Sherman. Here we saw a large number of rebel prisoners about to be sent north to cool off. We passed through and camped in a grove 2 miles south at 4 p. m. March, 20 miles. Heavy cannonading at Kennesaw mountain, within sight. The rebels are strongly fortified there. They have been driven from Pine mountain, and Lost mountain, to Kennesaw. Heavy assaults were made on each others lines on the 27th, with great loss on each side. Sherman's infantry have pressed close to the foot of Kennesaw, and are protected by slight earthworks, thrown up by his soldiers with bayonets and tin plates—Sherman's patent fortifying tools. During the night each alternately charged the other. We plainly heard, not only the cannonading and musketry, but even the defiant yells of the charging lines, which raised an eager excitement with our men, who were anxious to join in the fray.

June 30th. Reveille at 3 a. m.; morning pleasant; marched at 5 a. m. back through Big Shanty; then moved toward the right wing of Sherman's army. McPherson's corps of infantry is on the right wing. We are now the third brigade of Stoneman's (6th) cavalry division and composed of 14th Illinois Cavalry, commanded by Lieutenant-Colonel D. P. Jenkins; the 8th Michigan Cavalry, Lieutenant-Colonel Elisha Mix commanding; the Ohio Squadron, Major Richard Rice commanding; Colonel Horace Capron commanding the brigade. Stoneman's division was composed of Colonel Israel Garrard's brigade, the first; Colonel Biddel's brigade, the second, commanded by Colonel Biddel, and sometimes by Colonel Thomas Butler, and Capron's brigade, the third, and an independent brigade, commanded by Colonel Alexander W. Holman, and part of the time by Lieutenant-Colonel Silas Adams. In Colonel Garrard's (1st) brigade were: 7th Ohio, Lieutenant-Colonel Geo. G. Miner; 9th Michigan, Colonel Geo. S. Acker, Company "D," of 7th Ohio was General Stoneman's escort. In Biddel's brigade (the 2d) were: 16th Illinois Cavalry, Captain Hiram Hanchett; 5th Indiana, Colonel Thomas H. Butler; 6th Indiana, Lieutenant-Colonel Courtland C. Matson; Adams' Independent brigade, 1st Kentucky, Lieutenant-Colonel Silas Adams; 11th Kentucky, Lieutenant-Colonel Archibald J. Alexander. For organization see page 114, serial 72. Number in Stoneman's division, 2803. The remainder of Sherman's cavalry belonged to the Cumberland Army, General Kenner Garrard's division, 4822; McCook's divisions, 2570; Kilpatrick's division, 1678, in May, and in June, Stoneman's was 2530, and in July 1803, and Garrard's 3699; McCook's, 1634; Kilpatrick's, 2366 (see page 116). The 24th Indiana Battery was assigned to Stoneman's division July 6th. We marched to join our division 15 miles S. E. of Big Shanty, and camped in a wood near Stoneman's headquarters. Had heavy rains; drew 5 days' ration. From Ackworth to Kennesaw we were scarcely out of sight of the evidences of one continued battlefield. Buildings, fences and trees riddled and shattered or leveled in ruins by every form of missile used in war; while the remains of earthworks and other forms of defense were scarcely ever out of sight. The service of our regiment in Georgia until the last of July is merged in the history of the 6th Cavalry division, or rather, in Capron's brigade of that division.

July 1st. Reveille at 2 a. m. Marched at 4 a. m. west 5 miles, halted at Powder Springs; here turn east, then south and march to Sweetwater creek, and camped; march 12 miles. Companies "I," "C" and "L," of 14th, sent to guard Miller's bridge on Sweetwater creek.

July 2d. Regiment in camp near the bridge at Sweetwater village. Very warm. Company "D," with 50 men of Ohio Squadron, sent on reconnoissance; skirmish with the enemy and capture some prisoners.

Sunday, July 3d. March at 9 a. m. toward the Chattahoochee river 3 miles; halted and built barricades of rails. On page 514, serial 73, Schofield says: "During 1st of July General Stoneman, supported by General McCook, crossed the Sweetwater creek with a portion of his cavalry, and moved down the south bank to gain, if possible, the crossing near Sweetwater factory, and threaten Chattahoochee and Campbelltown." This was Capron's brigade. And again he says: "The enemy having retreated from Kennesaw during the night of July 2d * * * General Stoneman was left to continue operations with General McPherson (on the right). The rebel lines having fallen back to the vicinity of the Chattahoochee river."

July 3d at 3 p. m. Major Quigg, with the second battalion of the 14th, was sent forward toward the river to reconnoiter. Moved S. E. 2 miles, Company "I," under Captain Boeke, in advance. Sergeant Puckett, in command of vanguard, discovered a strong post of the enemy and attacked it with vigor; but was compelled by overwhelming odds to fall back. Having uncovered the enemy on this road, Company "I" then fell back to the battalion. Another road diverging to the left led through woods.

It was desirous to reconnoiter this road. Sergeant Sanford selected a half dozen trusty men and advanced on this road until they ran into a strong post of 50 or 60 of the enemy, when they were compelled to fall back, having now learned the position of the enemy's pickets. It was now important to know the position of the enemy's main line. Selecting two of the bravest and most skillful men of Company "I," Sergeant Sanford proceeded cautiously on foot, and succeeded in passing the enemy's pickets and discovered the rebel main line a half mile in rear of their pickets. Skirmishers from the second battalion were thrown forward, the remainder of the 14th was also advanced farther to the left, and a vigorous skirmish ensued, lasting several hours. Company "C," farther to the left, threw forward a vanguard, commanded by Sergeant Jacob Balderston, charged the pickets of the enemy and drove them back upon a strongly barricaded post, and received a heavy volley poured into their ranks. Sergeant Aaron W. Scott, one of the best men of the company, was killed, and a number were wounded and captured, and many more received in their clothing and equipments enduring evidence of the *warm* attachment that the rebs had for them. The brave little band was forced reluctantly back, when they dismounted and sent their horses to the rear, and being joined by Companies "L" and "E," of the 14th, they advanced under the command of their proper officers. The remainder of the regiment, farther to the left, also advanced dismounted, and the enemy's outposts, all along our line, were driven back upon their main line. The 14th lay on their arms, holding the ground from which they had driven the enemy. March, 5 miles.

July 4th. The second battalion, under Major Quigg, skirmished until 6 a. m. when they were relieved and fell back to get breakfast, having eaten nothing since the morning before. They then rejoined the regiment, which advanced and drove the enemy toward the river. While dismounted and driving the enemy, one of their batteries got the range of our horses and shelled them vigorously. This compelled us to fall back to our horses and find a more secure place for them, when we again dismounted and advanced and built barricades and skirmished until 4 p. m.; when our brigade was concentrated and charged a rebel battery, driving it in confusion, and forcing back their whole line, when we bivouacked in the woods at dark. March, 5 miles. On page 45, serial 76, is Stoneman's order to Capron: "Strike the Sand Town and Marietta road and scout the country." This we did. In Sherman's report of campaign (page 69, serial 72), is this: "On the 4th of July we pushed a strong skirmish line down the main road capturing the entire line of the enemy's pits, and made a strong demonstration along the Nickajack creek, and about Turner's ferry. This had the desired effect, and the next morning the enemy was gone and the army moved to the Chattahoochee." Thus it is acknowledged that we bore a conspicuous part in driving the enemy to his last stand across the Chattahoochee river. On the evening of the 4th, heavy cannonading on our left indicated that our lines in that quarter had not been pushed forward as rapidly as in our front.

July 5th. Reveille at 3 a. m. Pleasant weather. Stoneman ordered Capron to try to drive everything across the river and then move his brigade down the banks to Baker's ferry. Stoneman did not then know that the rebels had crossed. Companies "D" and "C," of the 14th, were sent on scout to the river and found the enemy strongly posted across the river. A battery of the enemy opened so fiercely that our boys were compelled to seek shelter behind the hills. Lieutenant Balderston was sent with dispatches to Colonel Butler, of the 5th Indiana Cavalry, at Sand Town three miles below. His party captured a number of rebels. The regiment advanced slowly along the main road, halting occasionally to build barricades, and were joined by other cavalry and infantry with artillery. The enemy were in force across the river and had a fort on an elevation. Our batteries were planted and an artillery duel began. There was some skirmishing with muskets in which the cavalry, with carbines, could not join. A few comrades borrowed muskets and took a hand in. The writer was fortunate in having a Spencer rifle, but as he could not see how many rebels he winged, his conscience has never troubled him on that score.

July 6th. Reveille at 3 a. m. We moved down the river a mile; halted, dismounted and formed line in sight of rebel forts across the river. Two 24-pounder brass howitzers of Battery "M" 1st Illinois, took position on an eminence and shelled the rebel fort. They were answered by showers of rebel shells. The cavalry retired to camp. Weather hot; march, 2 miles. On page 60, Stoneman says to Sherman, July 5th: "I think, or at least hope, that during the past 7 days we have accomplished all that was expected of us. If not, it has not been for lack of effort to do so. We have worked day and night and covered a good deal of country."

On page 61 is Sherman's reply: "Dear Stoneman: I have your note, which is very satisfactory. I have heard of your general success from other quarters. I will instruct General Barry to give you a good four-gun battery if he can get one from some of the commands."

July 7th. Reveille at daylight; in camp. Forage scarce. Captain Carrico, of Company "D," appointed A. A. I. G. and ordered to report to Colonel Capron, commanding third brigade, 6th division. Captain Crandle and Lieutenant Thomas, with 50 men of the 14th, sent to Powder Springs, where they burn a large grist mill.

July 8th. Reveille at 3 a. m. March at 4 a. m. to Sweetwater bridge; crossed and camped; marched 4 miles; day hot. Company "I" again sent on picket at Miller's bridge. Two men of Company "I" capture six Confederate cavalrymen with their horses, arms and equipments.

July 9th. Reveille at daylight; heavy showers. At 8 p. m. moved out and formed column and called in all the pickets; remained in column several hours, then the regiment and each detachment returned to the positions they had just left.

July 11th. Reville at 3 a. m.; passed uncomfortable night, lying in rain and mud. We have had no tents for a long time. March at daylight S. E. 2 miles; halt, get breakfast and feed horses; then march through wilderness country to the Chattahoochee river opposite Campbellsville. The opposing forces are constantly skirmishing across the river. All our led horses and mules now sent back in charge of Lieutenant Huntoon.

July 12th. Reveille at daylight. We saddle horses and await orders. At 10 p. m. the division marched southward through thinly settled region 25 miles and camped.

July 13th. Reveille at 3 a. m. March early southward

to Moore's bridge on the Chattahoochee river, charge upon and capture the rebel guards, who belonged to rebel General Hume's command (see page 880). Stoneman says (page 133, serial 76): "By taking a roundabout way by unfrequented roads we succeeded in capturing or cutting off every scout the enemy had out, and drove them from the bridge before they had time to set fire to the straw and pine knots prepared for its conflagration. The bridge had been partially destroyed by tearing up the sleepers and planks, but we will have it replaced during the night. It is a covered structure, well built and 480 feet long. Newnan, on the railroad, is 10 miles from here, and I understand the road leads through dense woods. There is another bridge at Franklin, 25 miles below." The bridge was completed the morning of the 15th. But the enemy had now gathered a strong force, with a number of batteries posted in sheltered positions in the woods from which they opened upon us. Stoneman's report says: "On attempting to cross the bridge the enemy opened upon us with four pieces of artillery and made an attempt to retake the rifle pits at the water's edge. We deemed it inexpedient to attempt to cross." On page 880, Rebel General Armstrong says: "July 14th reached Moore's bridge at 4 a. m., where Hume's pickets had been driven in." He says: "They (the Yankees) have an excellent position and have made breastworks. It is a division of cavalry with artillery." A lively skirmish was kept up several hours and several feints of crossing were made, which met with a vigorous resistance. The bridge was then burned by our men. We then went into camp near by. Our men had been told that we were to cross the river and attack and destroy the railroad beyond, and they were loud in their grumbling when, shortly afterward, we again moved northward. They did not then know that these movements were maneuvers in a "game of war." A scouting party was sent down the river early in the day to go to Franklin and destroy all means of crossing the river that they could find. In one of Sherman's orders to Stoneman, he says: "Keep up the delusion of our crossing below Sand Town as long as possible, and I have reason to believe the enemy expect it. We have a nice game of war." On page 146 is an order from Sherman for

Stoneman to fall back to Turner's ferry and the Nickajack. Our casualties had been light. At dark the division moved northward; the men grumbling that they were not led across the river as they had been promised; they attributed this failure to the cowardice of their officers. They did not realize that this was one of the many instances in which our mysterious movements were tricks in "the nice game of war," as Sherman expressed it. We arrived at our camp of 12th instant and bivouacked about 2 p. m. of July 15th, without rations. Marched 20 miles.

Reveille at daylight (15th). About 8 a. m. several companies including "L," of 14th, under Lieutenant Moore, and "I," under Captain Boeke; were sent on different roads, southward to Carrollton, 30 miles below, to capture horses and mules. They succeeded in getting a fine lot of stock and getting safely into camp on the Sweetwater, though they came near running into a force of three rebel regiments at Vilarica. The writer, with five men of Company "I," was separated from the main command in searching for horses, and after scouring the country started at dusk to return to camp; by mistake took the road to Moore's bridge, but learned the mistake when near, and also learned that a strong rebel command had crossed that day and were now scattered all over the country. When our squad reached our morning camp the brigade was gone, and they could not learn where to; by great caution moving on by roads they traveled northward all night without meeting the enemy, though they passed within two hundred yards of a rebel camp without knowing it until next morning. Once they left the road and dismounted in a thicket to rest and while there a large rebel party passed on the road. Soon after they mounted and having been told that the brigade had fallen back to Vilarica they moved to within two miles, when they changed their course for Sand Town on the river. Conflicting reports of citizens were bewildering, but they determined to go to Sand Town, which they reached at sundown, just as "Boots and saddles" was blowing and in half an hour the whole command was marching northward and marched till 1 a. m. of July 17th, then bivouacked. In going to Sand Town we were diverted from the straight road by a false report as to where our brigade had gone and a short time afterward a large rebel party passed on that road, who would have met us had we continued on that road. If we had reached Sand Town an hour or two later we would again have been left to work our way as best we could, by the help of rebel citizens, whose contradictory statements seemed intentional to deceive the Yankees and confuse them. This adventure is given, not as having anything unusual, but as fairly illustrating the many unrecorded adventures of small parties of our men, who were sent out on various duties. Some of them being captured and some were never again heard from.

Our regimental record July 16th. Out of rations; marched at 4 p. m. Crossed Sweetwater bridge and within 7 miles of Marietta and camped with brigade train; no forage; heavy rains.

Sunday, July 17. Marched at 1 p. m. 4 miles and camped on an eminence in sight of Atlanta; forage and rations scarce. About 10 p. m. "Boots and saddles" aroused the sleeping troopers. Marched 2 miles down the river; dismounted and lay on our arms. The cause of the movement was a rumor that the enemy in force were recrossing the river.

July 19th. Go into camp on a rough piece of ground; water scarce; no forage.

July 20th. In camp. Lieutenant Allen, with Company "D," of 14th, sent to open a road to the river opposite the rebel fortifications below us. A small squad of the 14th sent out to get coal for the blacksmiths was captured today by prowling rebel parties on our side of the river.

July 21st. At 5 p. m. marched to Sweetwater bridge and camped in the woods at 10 p. m.; marched 5 miles.

July 22d. Companies "D" and "K," of 14th, under Captain Sanford sent on scout. "Boots and saddles," at 4 p. m.; marched toward Sand Town, camped near the river at 2 a. m., July 23d; march 7 miles. A pontoon train passed us at daylight, going to the river. The 14th was sent forward dismounted to protect the working party while laying it across the river. In several hours the work ceased and the boats were taken up and the 14th retired to camp. The cause of the change was an order from General Sherman to withdraw Stoneman's division to Decatur, near Atlanta, on the left wing, and the replacing our division with

General Rousseau's cavalry command to guard Turner's ferry. (See page 236, serial 76). The 14th marched back to Sweetwater bridge and at 9 p. m. marched toward Vining Station 12 miles; halt and lay on our arms till morning; having marched 19 miles; cool night. On page 75, of serial 72, Sherman explains the movement to be to prepare for a blow at the Macon railroad simultaneous with the movements of the Army of the Tennessee toward East Point. This closes this chapter, and is the end of our mounted service north of the Chattahoochee river.

CHAPTER XI.

STONEMAN RAID TO MACON, GEORGIA, IN JULY, 1864.

In this account we give the substance of our notes and the notes of Captain Sanford, Lieutenant Thomas and others, without crediting to them. Captain Wm. A. Lord, of Company "H," 14th Illinois Cavalry, who was then on General Stoneman's staff, has given a full and authentic account. We are sorry that limited space forbids giving this in full; quotations from this account will be given by preceding the quotations by "Captain Lord" in brackets Frequent quotations will be given from the official records Series 1, volume 38, part 2d, Atlanta Campaign, serial No. 73. General Stoneman's Report (page 914), is credited by (Stoneman) in parenthesis preceding the quotation. In like manner we credit each of the following: Colonel Horace Capron's Report (page 925); Lieutenant Colonel Robert W. Smith's report (page 915) Assistant Inspector General on Stoneman's staff; and Major Haviland Thompson's Report (page 919), Provost Marshal on Stoneman's staff. Quotations from General Sherman's Reports will be preceded by "Sherman" and the page where found in parenthesis. Quotations from General Sherman's reports will be from different serials, the number and page of which will be given. (Sherman's general report, serial 72, page 75.) "The next day (July 23d, '64), General Garrard returned from Covington," (having destroyed the rebel railroads and bridges). "I then addressed myself to the task of reaching the Macon road, over which of necessity came the stores and ammunition that maintained the rebel army in Atlanta. * * * About the same time General Rousseau had arrived from his expedition to Opelika, bringing me about 2,000 excellent cavalry * * * and ordering it to relieve General Stoneman at the river about Sand Town, I shifted General Stoneman to our left flank, and ordered all my cavalry to prepare for a blow at the Macon road simultaneous with

it of the Army of the Tennessee toward East
iccomplish this, I gave General Stoneman the
his own, and General Garrard's cavalry, mak-
:ive force of 5,000 men, and to General Mc-
his own and the new cavalry brought by Gen-
u, which was commanded by Colonel Harri-
3th Indiana Cavalry, in the aggregate about
;e two well appointed bodies were to move in
former by the left around Atlanta to Mc-
id the latter by the right on Fayetteville, and
night, viz.: July 28th, they were to meet on
)ad near Lovejoy's, and destroy it in the most
nner. I estimated this joint cavalry could
Vheeler's cavalry, and could otherwise accom-
, and I think so still." We have a few com-
ke upon General Sherman's estimate of the
cavalry as here referred to, being able to whip
:r's cavalry. First he says he gave Stoneman
General Garrard's cavalry and counted this
toneman's as 5,000, while not only our notes,
)fficial reports show that Garrard's force only
Stoneman to Flat Rock; even Sherman in the
shows this. This change of the former plan
.n with not exceeding 2,200 cavalry to join
McCook in whipping Wheeler. All we can
: reasons for this change of plan is found in
ts, (see serial 76, on page 251), communica-
oneman to Garrard, giving directions to pre-
novement as ordered by Sherman On page
ird's report to Sherman in which he says:
do not recognize General Stoneman, but wish
;ettled in some way." This was dated July
·al Sherman then ordered Garrard to oper-
ort to Stoneman in preventing Wheeler from
neman. By this change of plan not only was
ft with only 2,200 men to help McCook to
:r, but subsequent events show that Garrard
in his appointed task of preventing Wheeler
g Stoneman. Again future events show that
rman had been greatly mistaken in his esti-
,trength of Wheeler's forces. This is shown
s own reports and other official statistics, as

we shall prove hereafter. In the initial correspondence between Generals Sherman and Stoneman (page 75, serial 72), Sherman says: "At the moment almost of starting General Stoneman addressed me a letter asking permission, after fulfilling his orders and breaking the road, to be allowed, with his command proper, to proceed to Macon and Andersonville and release our prisoners of war confined at those points. There was something most captivating in the idea, and the execution was within the bounds of probable success." Sherman consented to the undertaking.

In serial 76, page 264, is Stoneman's letter referred to, in which he says: "I would like to try it and can vouch for my little command. * * * If we accomplish the desired object, it will compensate for the loss, as prisoners, of us all, and I shall feel compensated for almost any sacrifice." Sherman replied (see page 265): "I see many difficulties, but as you say even a chance of success will warrant the effort and I consent to it. * * * If you can bring back to the army any or all of those prisoners of war, it will be an achievement that will entitle you, and the men of your command, to the love and admiration of the whole country." On page 260 Sherman says: "This is probably more than he can accomplish, but it is worthy of a determined effort." The language of these communications indicate that the difficulties and danger of this perilous undertaking were well understood by the commanding officers and the anxiety of these commanders to release our suffering comrades from those prison hells was no greater than that of the rank and file; there was a frenzied desire to try it.

(Capron). "On the 26th (July) I received orders from General Stoneman to prepare my command with ten days' rations, and in light marching order to be ready to move on the morning of the 27th at 3 a. m."

On Sunday, 24th, we had marched early to the bridge across the Chattahoochee, crossed and camped two miles north of Decatur; marched 25 miles. Saw 1,000 rebel prisoners on their way north for the benefit of their health. Night cool.

July 25th. In camp until 3 p. m., then move to a camp 2 miles farther from Decatur.

July 26th. In camp near a mill 8 miles from Atlanta. Morning cool. All disabled men and horses, not able to go through fire and water, are sent with the teams back across the river, and all preparations are made for a perilous raid.

On Wednesday, July 27th, we left camp about 4 miles north of Decatur, at 3 a. m., passed through Decatur at daylight. Rumor said the enemy's cavalry in strong force was in our front. We formed line of battle, but on scouting well to our right and right front, found no enemy in force. The federal batteries along the line opened up fiercely to create a diversion from Stoneman's movements. We moved around Atlanta on the north and east, striking an eastward course. We soon noted a striking contrast between the country hitherto passed over and that portion in the rebel rear carefully husbanded for the supply of the rebel army. Astonishing abundance filled the country. In the afternoon we passed to the right of the romantic "Stone mountain," standing as a lone sentinel keeping watch over a surrounding lovely country. Marched all day and all night, except a short halt at 6 p. m. at Lithonia, 35 miles from our morning camp.

(Captain Lord) : "Stoneman was escorted by General Garrard's cavalry as far as the bridge across Yellow river, where he was to remain three days, if possible, to prevent the enemy from following in General Stoneman's rear."

Morning of July 28th. Passed through and halted near Covington two hours and breakfasted. It was designed that these movements should be secret from the enemy, but in this we were disappointed. On page 912, serial 76, Hood says. "Last night the enemy (Sherman) drew back his left and extended his right somewhat. A raid has started in the direction of Covington; our cavalry in pursuit." On page 913, he says, July 27th : "There is a raid moving towards Covington; considerable force, ten pieces of artillery, Wheeler in pursuit; destination unknown." On page 916 Hood says to Winder at Andersonville: "The raid toward Covington is stronger than at first reported; destination still unknown. We have a heavy force in pursuit." Our night's march was 18 miles, making 53 miles without feed or rations, for lack of time to feed from the abundance in the country. Crossed the Ulcofouhachee river at 9 a. m., then through Stearnville to within 3 miles of Monticello. We had gathered up large numbers of fine horses and mules and contrabands to lead them. General Wheeler said in one of his reports that his cavalry was superior to Sherman's cavalry. This was doubtless true so far as numbers were concerned. It was equally true so far as good horses were concerned, as here in their rear they had a great number of the best and freshest horses from which they not only kept their cavalrymen well mounted, while we were compelled to use our worn-out horses, but in addition they were able at any time to mount bodies of infantry when necessary to move speedily from one point to another, or to reinforce their cavalry when needed; but that they were *not* superior in fighting qualities was well demonstrated in many a sharp conflict, nor were they equal in enduring long and arduous service. Capron occupied Monticello and kept his men mounted. (Captain Lord says): General Stoneman took the main road via Covington, Monticello, Hillsboro and Clinton to Macon, and pushed forward as rapidly as possible, only stopping to feed just south of Covington. He sent Colonel Adams and his command (from Monticello) westward toward Mechanicsville to scout down the Ocmulgee river to rejoin his command before reaching Macon. He was to gain definite information as to crossings between the mouth of Yellow river and Macon, and to oppose any movement of the enemy on his flank, reporting as often as possible. Colonel Adams' failure to report as expected caused some delay in the movement of General Stoneman's command, and a loss of nearly six hours at one time. It was ascertained, however from this command that there were no bridges or fords between the points mentioned and it became apparent that the river must be crossed at Macon if at all."

(Major Tompkins, page 919) says: "On morning of 28th Colonel Adams, with his brigade, was sent to Mechanicsville on the Ocmulgee river to watch movements of the enemy and to communicate with the general at Monticello in the evening at dark. No communication from Colonel Adams at 12 o'clock (midnight); became impatient; sent party to communicate, and ordered his command to join main column on the road to Macon. At

Monticello in the evening, the general received the first information that there were no bridges over the Ocmulgee river. His information, on which his movements were based, was that there were three bridges north of Macon over this river. His plan was now changed to destroy the Savannah and Macon road."

The reports of these two staff officers of General Stoneman's staff, ought to satisfactorily settle the question of the failure of General Stoneman to join and co-operate with General McCook at Lovejoy Station the night of July 28th, 1864.

The question may be asked why General Stoneman did not himself report these reasons. It must be remembered that General Stoneman was captured, and made but one, and that a short report under the surveillance of the enemy, and that it would have been imprudent to have revealed to them plans of movement. All that we find in his report is the following:

(Stoneman, page 914): "In regard to the operations of my command from the time I left the army up to the time I turned back from near this place (Macon, where he was then in prison), I will only say now that I feel assured, when you know what was done, and why it was done, you will be satisfied with reasons and results."

Why General Stoneman, after his release, did not afterward explain was probably owing to the fact that Major Tompkins' report to General Schofield was a sufficient explanation. And so it would have been had this information ever reached General Sherman officially; but there is no record in the published reports that this information was ever reported to General Sherman; hence in his general report made up from reports and statistics before him, he says, relative to the ability of Stoneman's and McCook's commands to whip all of Wheeler's cavalry, "and I think so still." Sherman seems also to have forgotten that instead of General Garrard joining with Stoneman to help to whip Wheeler with a combined force of 5,000 men, that the changed plan relative to Garrard, left Stoneman with only 2,200. The same was true also of McCook's command; it was afterward planned that Rousseau should be a support to McCook.

When we reached Monticello a portion of Capron's brigade occupied the town and all remained mounted. It is proper here to give the commands that were in General Stoneman's division on this raid. The proper source of correct information upon this point is the report of General Stoneman's Inspector General, Colonel Robert W. Smith, found on page 915, serial 73. He says: "The force under General Stoneman consisted of three brigades, one composed of the mounted portions of the 5th and the 6th regiments of Indiana cavalry, commanded by Colonel James Biddle, amounting to about 700 men; another of the 1st and the 11th Kentucky cavalry, commanded by Colonel Silas Adams, numbering 550 men; the other brigade was composed of the 14th Illinois Cavalry, the 8th Michigan Cavalry and a part of the 1st Ohio Squadron (McLaughlin's), numbering 800 men, commanded by Colonel Horace Capron; a detachment of the 24th Indiana Battery, under command of Captain Hardy, with two 3-inch regulation guns and 54 men, in all about 2,104 officers and men, the General and seven members of his staff."

On page 923 is report of Colonel Israel Garrard, of the 7th Ohio Cavalry; this report shows that his command arrived too late to join this expedition under General Stoneman, though we are informed through other sources that one company of the 7th Ohio was body guard to General Stoneman. In official reports the number of Stoneman's command on this expedition is given at 2,100 men and never exceeding 2,200.

The exact number of the 14th on this raid we can not give. At the battle of Walker's ford, over seven months before, the number engaged were 324 officers and men. Several hard fights and much severe service must have reduced them materially. On the way to Georgia we were reinforced by perhaps 200 new recruits; subsequent service in Georgia and most of all, the close sifting from the command of every man and horse that, as the order read, "was not able to go through fire and water," the regiment doubtless numbered little more, if any, than 300 men; estimating the squadron at 100 men and the 14th and the 8th each 350 men, make up the number in the brigade.

(Capron): "At Stearnville Captain Samuel Wells, acting assistant adjutant-general on my staff, was detached by order of General Stoneman, with 80 men of the Ohio

Squadron, with instructions to destroy the bridge and a large flouring mill at Henderson's Mills, and the bridge and Newton cotton factory on the Ulcofouhachee river. The captain joined the command at 4 a. m. the 29th after accomplishing the object of the expedition."

At Monticello some prisoners were captured and six rebel pickets taken. From Monticello marched rapidly to Hillsboro, where we destroyed a large amount of rebel property, then marched to Clinton where, by General Stoneman's order, Major Davidson (of the 14th), with his battalion and company "H," of the 14th Illinois Cavalry, in all 125 men, was ordered to move to Gordon, the junction of the Etonton and Georgia railroad and, using his own discretion, to destroy all public property on either railroad, and do all damage he could to the enemy and bring his command out safely."

The division, except Adams' brigade, moved forward, passing through Clinton and on to within 10 miles of Macon. A picket, under command of Lieutenant Wm. M. Moore, of Company "L," 14th Illinois Cavalry, left at the forks of important roads, succeeded in capturing a number of prisoners and had an exciting little adventure in being mistaken for rebels and were attacked by a detachment of our own forces. No great injury was suffered on either side, the mistake being soon discovered.

Colonel Capron was now ordered to move with his command to the left, to strike the Georgia Central railroad and follow it up to Macon, destroying it as he went, as well as all other public property, and join Stoneman in front of the city. Within four miles of Macon we met the enemy in force and pressed forward, driving him rapidly before us. Capron's brigade moved on the railroad fighting back the enemy. This brigade alone ruined most of the railroad track for seven miles, destroying two passenger trains, one stock train, loaded with horses and hogs, three locomotives, burned one large machine shop, used for manufacturing gun carriages, and in conjunction with Biddle's brigade, burned a railroad bridge near the city. The following furnished by a comrade, is not authenticated by official reports, but we presume it to be correct:

One party, under Lieutenant Albert B. Capron, of Company "A," 14th Illinois Cavalry, while engaged in destroy-

ing the railroad, captured a train, and se(
approaching, loaded with Confedera
Lieutenant sprang upon an engine, stan
all fired up, and uncoupling it from its tr
lever, opened the valve, and sent the en;
speed to meet the incoming Johnnies; th
crash, but the amount of damage inflicte
as we moved with alacrity from that posi
Capron (since captain) never mentione
to us.

Capron's brigade now joined in the
city. Captain Lord, after alluding to ?
expedition and Colonel Capron's work
says: "With the balance of his con
pushed on to Macon. The enemy wer
small force north of Clinton, but offere(
opposition; they were steadily driven, ev
tection of Fort Hawkins, an old U. S.
the east side of the Ocmulgee river on
ing both the bridge crossing and the cit:
found to be fully garrisoned and streng
so as to make it invincible against attacl
was further ascertained that there was
Infantry in Macon; and that there w
crossing the river below Macon as far S
of the Oconee."

The Confederate reports show that t
Macon a force of 3,000 militia (see pag
report to General Wheeler, July 29th,
This also speaks of rebel infantry sent.
cavalry, 1,000 to 1,500, was seen to ente
fighting across the river for several ho
the river above and below to find some
place, General Stoneman received a m
him that General Wheeler, with a force
and mounted infantry, was coming d
Here then was a strong probability of
tween the upper and the nether millstc
the intention to proceed to Andersonvill(
then to strike south or southeast, to tl
Atlantic, but scouts sent to a bridge bel(
information that the bridge was held by a

ortified. Captain Lord's narrative says: "An attack was made on the fort and the ground held for several hours. It was then hoped that Colonel Adams' command moving on the road near the river would make a sharp attack on the other side of the fort, which might result in a withdrawal of the enemy's force across the river or in the capture of the fort. But after several hours of anxious waiting no attack was made by Adams, and it was presumed that he had met with opposition. About this time information came that there was an enemy in our rear and that a number of our men were captured in and near Clinton. To describe our situation at this time: An entrenched enemy of superior force in our front, holding the only crossing of the river available to join General McCook; the Oconee river 20 miles east of us impassable. To the south, the west and the east, the gates of progress barred. *We must go north* in the face of pursuers. With heavy heart General Stoneman ordered the movement to the rear. We reached Clinton at dark on the evening of July 30th, recaptured the place and liberated about 35 of our men who were confined in the town jail. Here we learned that we were pursued by Wheeler's cavalry, estimated at from 8,000 to 10,000 men."

(Tompkins says): "Scouts reporting a large force of rebel cavalry moving on the west side of the river towards Macon and that all the ferries were destroyed above and below; he withdrew his main forces with intention to move toward Milledgeville. Information soon came that the demonstration east had drawn the enemy in that direction, and that but a small force was on the Covington road. He desired to press hard on that road and reach Hillsboro if possible, at which point he could take choice of three roads at daylight. But the enemy were too strongly posted and he could not reach Hillsboro by two miles."

Smith, in his report, speaks of the intended movement southward, and that the movement actually began, when information obtained turned the movement northward. Smith also speaks of the design to move eastward and that he was at a loss to know why this route was not chosen. Though our notes give good description of the movements, preference is given to the reports of staff officers, as being more satisfactory because official. (Smith says): "The general ordered the column to advance north along our old route, and about 9 p. m. (30th) the advance began to skirmish with the enemy which was kept up, we advancing very slowly until about 1 o'clock, when the skirmishing became so heavy in our front as to prevent any farther advance. We had now got some six miles north of Clinton and a halt was ordered."

(Captain Lord says): "We continued to advance driving the enemy before us until nearly midnight, having gained six or eight miles, and developed the enemy in such force as to bar farther progress at night. The troops bivouacked, but skirmishing continued until daylight, when the battle was renewed. Our troops were disposed as follows: Colonel Capron's brigade, which led the advance during the night, now occupied the right; Colonel Biddle's brigade in reserve in the center; Colonel Adams on the left."

Our notes say: "We began to fall back about 3 p. m. July 30th, Capron's brigade in advance. Halted, formed line and rested an hour, near the forks of the Milledgeville road, then moved forward on the Clinton road."

Here is where Stoneman made his great mistake, caused by heeding unreliable information. We encountered the enemy's picket near Clinton, charged and drove them through the town, liberating 33 of our men, who had been captured on the way down. We captured the guards and burned the jail; day's march, 30 miles. We then moved forward on the Hillsboro road, driving the enemy before us wherever we found them. Some three miles from Clinton we found a strong advance guard of the enemy, charged and drove them half a mile, when we encountered a heavy force posted behind barricades. The 8th Michigan being in the advance, charged and drove them from their position. We continued to drive them until near Hillsboro, where we found their main force about 3:30 a. m., of July 31st. Capron had been attacked in front and on the left flank. Heavy skirmishing had been kept up all night. We now found them in strong force on ground of their own choosing and well fortified with strong log and rail defences, built in the form of a semicircle with points circling round our lines, and extending far out on each flank. At daybreak Capron's command had met a strong force behind defenses, charged and drove them back to this, their main position, from which Stoneman now resolved to drive them.

There seemed to Stoneman to be but two ways: one through the enemy's fortified lines with nearly five times his own force, with liberty to the survivors; the other through Andersonville prison, perhaps with final liberty to the few shattered frames that chanced to survive its cruelty. All chose death on the field rather than Andersonville. The nature of the ground as well as their strong defenses made it necessary to fight dismounted, which required one fourth of the men to hold and guard the horses in the rear, liable to attack and capture by a rebel force coming up in the rear. Our condition was perilous in the extreme. The rebel force at Macon exceeded ours in number, and many of the enemy were armed with long ranged rifles; whilst our guns were short range carbines and navy revolvers, effective weapons in a cavalry charge, but inferior in fighting dismounted. Besides the enemy had on the field, several batteries, whilst we had but one third of a battery (two guns). The situation, however, admitted of no delay, for when the pursuing enemy from Macon came up we would be enveloped by a force six times our number and having no place in our rear for our horses, and the ground unsuited to fighting mounted. Wheeler could not well have chosen a position giving him greater advantages. Could we have fought mounted at least the 14th and the 5th Indiana and the 8th Michigan would have faced great odds against us. Of the rest of our force we can only presume the same. Perhaps none in the service were better trained in the use of the saber than the 14th Illinois Cavalry. Our men were in poor condition for a fatiguing fight. Since the morning of the 27th, four days before, they had scarcely halted for rest. Only about two hours at Yellow river and a few hours the night before reaching Macon; and having eaten but little, as it was necessary to move with speed. Colonel Capron says: "At daybreak the 31st General Stoneman ordered me to advance with my brigade and drive the enemy from their position, which I did for one mile and a half, when I found them drawn up in line of battle in my front and on my left, with two pieces of artillery in position, which they opened on us as we advanced. General Stoneman now came up and formed his whole command in line of battle. Colonel Adams' brigade, and the 8th Michigan Cavalry of my brigade on the left, and the balance of my brigade on the right, with Biddle's brigade and one piece of artillery in reserve, the other piece of artillery taking position in the center."

Our notes say our artillery in the center, supported by a portion of the 14th Illinois, commanded by Major Quigg. Our notes say their strong log and rail defenses in the form of half circle encircled our front extending far out and overlapping our flanks. Colonel Smith says: "A line of battle was at once formed and the enemy strongly felt, which resulted in the development that the enemy was therein force upon ground of his own selection, with strong works and barricades, on an elevation in the road in our front, with his lines of battle extending out from this point in the shape of a V (inverted) completely covering and enfilading our right and left flanks. General Stoneman at once prepared his command for a vigorous attack upon the enemy, advancing himself with the skirmish line."

Tompkins describes the situation thus: "The enemy had now concentrated their forces in front, covering the roads. And being now between two rivers only about 20 miles apart, with an enemy in his front and rear, he decided that he must break their lines in the direction in which he must move out."

Our notes agree with Colonel Capron's description of the formation of the line. A lot of negroes, who had followed us were now strongly urged to escape while they could, as their fate would be severe if captured with us and unarmed they could not aid us. Some followed this advice, but many others chose to remain with their Yankee friends at the risk of any fate. Everything being ready, nerved with the energy of despair, our whole line moved impetuously forward and engaged the enemy, rapidly driving in their advance and pressing up to the enemy's works, when a destructive sheet of fire from their protected front and enfilading columns, with a murderous fire at close range from batteries in front and on the left, mowed down our men as they advanced. This caused Adams' brigade and the 8th Michigan to swing half round. The

14th and the Ohio Squadron, supported by Biddle's brigade, not only for a time held their position, but actually dislodged the enemy from a portion of his works, but the superior numbers of the enemy enabled them to maintain a heavy reserve to throw into their weaker points, and being heavily pressed with these overwhelming reinforcements to the enemy, and being unsupported by the left, our right was compelled to retire. Capron says: "Between 9 and 10 a. m., in compliance with General Stoneman's orders, the whole line moved forward and engaged the enemy. They met us in superior numbers and with a yell charged our lines; causing the left of the 8th Michigan cavalry to swing one fourth way round. The right of the regiment (with the 14th) holding its position. A mounted force of the enemy, coming up a road to the right and rear charged my extreme right, but were repulsed. I then ordered two companies of the 14th Illinois Cavalry to charge them, which they did, driving them two miles and a half, when they (the enemy) took position behind barricades. The enemy now rallied in strong force and drove my men back. I immediately brought up four companies of the same regiment, checked them, charged and drove them a second time to their barricades."

Captain Lord confirms the description of line formation and the results of first attack, and alluding to the attack on our right rear he says: "The 14th maintained its position and four companies, which were in line mounted, repelled a cavalry charge from a road leading from our right in very gallant style, taking almost a regiment of rebel cavalry prisoners, which in being sent to rear under guard, found themselves in their own lines."

The 14th and the Ohio Squadron reformed on their first line, and the whole line was rallied and reformed and thrown with all possible force upon the rebel center, and by superhuman effort again succeeded in gaining control of a portion of the rebel fortifications, but again were met by an overwhelming attack from their reserves as well as a murderous enfilading fire, in which their batteries did great execution. Again were our lines hurled back. Charge after charge was thus made, sometimes concentrated upon one point, and sometimes an advance of the whole line, but always meeting the same overwhelming force wherever a temporary advantage was gained. Our perilous situation inspired more than mortal courage. We *must* succeed in breaking their lines speedily. The enemy could well afford to wait; we could not, as the rebel force from Macon was hastening on our rear. Now couriers inform us that their advance had attacked our horse guards in the rear; they were repulsed, but soon the main body of the Macon force will have our horses. Another advance of the whole line was attempted; but now comes word that the enemy were capturing our horses, at the same time the whole rebel force in front, knowing their advantage, charge en masse with terrific yells. A cavalryman without a horse is like a fish out of water; little wonder that our feeble lines gave way, seeing the enemy closing in on our left wing, separating our right wing from our main body. A rush was made for our horses. Tompkins says: " Desperate efforts were made from sunrise of 31st until 12 o'clock to break their lines, but at every assault our lines were driven back except the right. (the 14th). We had now lost many valuable officers and men. The men were nearly out of ammunition, and fatigued almost beyond endurance." Smith says: "The enemy charged upon the left and were in turn temporarily checked, but still kept gaining ground upon us, and using his battery with wonderful effect and accuracy. The fight thus continued with doubtful results until about 2 p. m., when it became apparent that the enemy was being reinforced directly in our rear by the force that we had fought the day before at Macon. The fight thus became general all along the line, and from that time until the surrender, we lost heavily in killed and wounded; but the enemy suffered none the less." Continuing Capron's report after the mounted charge he says: "During this time (the mounted charge) the balance of the 14th Illinois and the Ohio Squadron held the enemy in check in my front. I then fell back a short distance from my original position, and held the ground until 12:30 p. m. I was then ordered to strengthen my lines and prepare to make a heavy charge dismounted. I brought every available man to the front, including my provost guard. At 1 p. m. General Stoneman ordered an advance, he holding one regiment of Colonel Adams' brigade in reserve. As we moved forward the enemy rose up in heavy force and with a yell charged our lines, cutting off my communication with General Stoneman. When nearly surrounded I was forced to fall back to the horses, which created some confusion among my men, as the enemy followed close upon us. So closely did the enemy press my command many of the men were unable to mount their horses; the enemy, capturing and mounting the horses, repeatedly charged my rear as I continued to retreat. I made every effort to communicate with General Stoneman, but my staff officers were cut off and unable to report. I have since learned from one of General Stoneman's staff officers (who escaped) that General Stoneman made a strong effort to communicate with me but was unable to do so. Lieutenant-Colonel E. Mix, of the 8th Michigan Cavalry, now came up and reported that General Stoneman had surrendered."

Tompkins says: "The proposition was made to move to the right and pass the enemy. He (Stoneman) said he could not move the whole command without being discovered. He could make no resistance when pursued; he would have the outside track, with an enemy fresh, to pursue. His men would be broken up in detachments and murdered as some had been on the 29th; he would not refuse any from going, nor order them. If the enemy assaulted and broke our lines, do the best we could, but as for him, he saw no other way for the lives of the men to be respected but for him to surrender, which he would do only as a last resort. By this means all the detachments that did leave had five hours the start." This description indicates a council of war which Colonel Smith more fully describes as follows: "About 4 p. m. General Stoneman, his staff and most of his brigade commanders held a consultation, and it was thought best to make a desperate effort to cut our way out to our right rear, as this seemed to be the weakest part of the enemy's lines. Just as the general had given his directions for this movement, and the respective officers were starting to their commands, the enemy opened a battery on our right and left flank and continued their fire from the one in front, followed by a general charge. Our lines gave way and fell back. I was ordered to a certain point to rally a line. Whilst doing this I became separated from the general. The line soon gave way again, the enemy then being within 50 yards, both in front and on the left flank I at that moment met Colonel Adams, who had just come from General Stoneman with permission to cut out if he could, stating, moreover, that the General was about to surrender, but that he desired all to get out who could, and he would remain in person and engage the enemy as long as possible, so as to give those making their escape as much start as possible. This we knew he did, for we could still hear cannonading when we were out some two or three miles from the battle field. I came out with Colonel Adams and his brigade. Colonel Capron had escaped a few minutes before with a part of the 14th Illinois Cavalry, 8th Michigan Cavalry and the 1st Ohio Squadron. Lieutenant-Colonel Matson came out with most of the 6th Indiana Cavalry, all striking out in a northeasterly direction. There thus escaped about 1,200 or 1,300 men, at least two-thirds of the command (perhaps three-fourths) that was left at the time the battle closed."

The following is from General Stoneman's report: "Without entering now into particulars, we were whipped, and this principally on account of the bad conduct of the Kentucky brigade in the attack during the morning, and, in fact, throughout the day." In Captain Lord's account we have the following: "While the council was in session the enemy began a heavy artillery fire, followed immediately by a general advance of their lines. Our left and center, Colonel Adams' brigade and the 8th Michigan, gave way. From General Stoneman's report it would seem that the Kentucky brigade did not do as directed. They certainly did not develop much resistance, as the heaviest fire of the enemy was directed on the center and right flank. The 14th maintained its position." And regarding the final escape he says: "These events broke up the formation of Capron's brigade, and a hasty rally of all available men was made, and companies formed without regard to regiments, and officers available placed over them. We were now cut off from General Stoneman and surrounded by the enemy. The column was put in motion along the woods about one-eighth of a mile from the road leading to our right rear.

Within a mile we encountered the enemy, the first line being on foot and behind barricades. A cavalry charge (led by Captain Lord) made an opening, but within a short distance we encountered a force of cavalry, who fought bravely and gave us a running fight several miles that cost us dearly in men. A recount showed nearly one-half missing. Our ranks, however, were hourly augmented by squads of our men who availed themselves of the opening made by our charges." Our notes in the main correspond to the above reports and accounts of officers relative to the movements at the last. Now word reaches us that the Macon force has nearly reached our horses. With victory in our front almost grasped, we are compelled to turn back to save our horses. The enemy had weakened their front, thus giving us the hope to break their center, but they had rushed heavy columns down our flanks and soon closed in, cutting Colonel Capron, with the 14th and the Ohio squadron, off from General Stoneman and the rest of his command. Our men now rushed for their horses with desperation Some were cut down in the act of mounting, while some of the horses were captured by rebel soldiers, who mounted them and turned them upon our forces. One of Capron's brigade officers succeeded in making his way from General Stoneman and notified Capron of Stoneman's proposition. It required no time to decide that this was the only way open, and as Capron was on the right wing and in the direction of the intended movement, it was only proper that he should lead the charge. Again mounted, our brave men were ready for the fray. Lieutenant-Colonel Jenkins had been in command of the 14th thus far, but now this portion of the brigade is reorganized and divided into detachments, with able leaders for each, thus Colonel Capron, Lieutenant-Colonel Jenkins, Major Quigg, Captain Sanford, Captain Lord, and Captain Mayo each have their separate detachment. With a yell and with sabers flashing, they dash down upon the enemy's left flank, led by as brave and skillful officers as ever drew sabers. The enemy fought fiercely, carbines, revolvers and musket reports of the contending forces mingled in a loud roar; while flashing sabers crossed blades in the sharp conflict; but nothing could long impede the force of a charging column of desperate men, each of whom preferred death on the battlefield to incarceration in Andersonville, that hell presided over by the demon Wirz. The enemy's strong lines are broken, and woods and underbrush, usually great impediments to the passage of mounted men, are dashed through by these maddened troopers, as though they were dashing over a plain.

Captain Lord says: "We now marched rapidly in a northeasterly direction, and struck an old road called the "Hog mountain road," which favored us, as it led through a wooded and hilly country and was not much traveled. Twenty-four hours put 50 or 60 miles between us and our disastrous battlefield."

Capron says of the retreat after he heard of Stoneman's intended surrender: "So closely did the enemy press my command, many of the men were unable to mount their horses, the enemy capturing and mounting them, repeatedly charged my rear as I continued to retreat. I determined to extricate what I could of my command, and if possible reach our lines. I moved rapidly on, struck the Etonton road, and moved toward Etonton, the enemy still pursuing and harrassing my rear, wounding and killing a number of my men."

A few miles out we were joined by other detachments who had escaped through the lines broken by us. The forces were now reorganized, many of the men had lost their arms in charging the rebel lines, many more had exhausted their ammunition; the command numbered about 300. We crossed Murder creek and moved toward Madison, leaving Etonton on our right; marched all night, bearing off to the left of Madison. About 6 p. m., while passing through a long, narrow lane, we were vigorously attacked in the rear by a strong detachment of the enemy. Many of the men who had no arms or ammunition were panic stricken. Major Quigg, taking Captains Sanford and Mayo and Lieutenant Balderston, collected the armed men of the command, threw themselves in the rear and fought the charging enemy back, and thus saved the command from utter rout. The enemy, however, continued to harrass us till night.

August 1st, in the morning, were joined by Major Davidson and his command. We now marched rapidly through Columbus and Rutledge Station, and joined Colonel Adams' brigade at Powder's farm, 7 miles from Rutledge. We made our first halt between Madison and Yellow river, having marched 60 miles since the evening of July 31st to the evening of August 1st. Lieutenant-Colonel Matson, with a detachment, joined us about the time that we joined Colonel Adams. The united commands moved towards Watkinsville, arriving there the morning of August 2d.

Capron says: "After consultation with Colonel Adams it was thought best to attempt to cross the Oconee river at Athens. Colonel Adams (whose men were armed) was to make a demonstration on the town, with the understanding that if he could not effect a crossing at the bridge, he was to send me a courier and guide and I was to join his command, and cross the river at a ford two and a half miles above the town. The courier reported after it was found impossible to cross the bridge, but the guide mistook the road and led me six miles away from the route agreed upon. After a delay of six hours in trying to communicate with Colonel Adams, we learned that a heavy body of cavalry and infantry was approaching on the right. As we were not in a condition to make resistance we were compelled to move toward "Hog mountain," on the left, thus separating from Colonel Adams, who continued a northern course. We moved to "Jug Tavern," 18 miles, where we halted, fed and again moved forward until we passed the Jeffersonville and Lawrenceville road. The men and animals were now so completely exhausted that rest was absolutely necessary. Many of the men had fallen asleep on their horses on the night's march, and fell out of ranks and were picked up by the rebels."

We had made long and rapid marches and were almost constantly in the saddle since the 31st, and indeed almost without rest since the morning of 27th of July, 7 days before.

Captain Lord says of the consultation with Colonel Adams: "Colonel Adams determined to attack that place (Athens) and cross the river, with a view of making a detour into the mountains of North Carolina if pursued. His view was not shared by Colonel Capron or the writer (Captain Lord), but his command being fully armed and having a supply of ammunition, was in shape to defend itself, while a large number of Capron's men were unarmed, and many who had arms had no ammunition, so a separation was not deemed prudent by Colonel Capron." Captain Lord confirms Capron's statement relative to the guide, and continues: "We continued the march after losing several hours of valuable time. The command marched as rapidly as possible until between 12 and 1 o'clock on the morning of August 3d, when the men, overcome by fatigue and want of sleep, were absolutely unable to move and fell asleep by the roadside without any order. Major Davidson's command (having their arms) was placed as rear guard, and Captain Lord was in command of the advance guard. Just before daylight we were attacked from the rear, and the negroes (who were sleeping between the rear guard and the main body) were panic stricken."

The advance picket of the rear guard was commanded by Lieutenant Isaac H. Allen, of Company "D." He informed the writer that when first attacked by the vanguard of the enemy, his men were all asleep, but rallied and drove back the attacking party, and again dropped to sleep and in this condition were charged upon by the main body of the enemy, who killed or captured all his men; he also was captured. The charging column of yelling rebels swept down through the mass of sleeping negroes, who suddenly wakened, to be cut down; those who escaped this fate rushed in mass before the relentless rebels into Capron's column of sleeping men, who, suddenly wakened from sound sleep by the howling negroes and yelling rebels, found themselves in a mingled mass of confused soldiers, panic-stricken negroes, and relentless yelling rebels, who were indiscriminately cutting down all that were not of their command. Had our men been well armed, it would have been impossible in that confused and excited mass to have formed line and made a successful resistance, but unarmed as they were, there was no resort but flight. Indeed, so rapid was the rebel charge that as each successive soldier was reached and wakened, he had only time to be cut down or to escape that fate by dodging into the fields or woods or by rapid flight on the road. Captain Lord's men, in the advance, formed line to resist the attack, but were soon thrown into confusion by the fleeing mass, many of whom met their doom in Mulberry river a short distance ahead, as the bridge gave way with its overload, precipitating all into the river and drowning many. Most of those who succeeded in escaping did so by dodging into the woods singly, or in small squads, afterward making their way as best they could through fields and woods by night, concealing themselves by day, and subsisting on green corn, unroasted, and roots and berries, avoiding main roads and slipping round rebel pickets. They were hunted by rebel soldiers, and by guerrillas, and rebel citizens with dogs, and many of the captured were murdered on the spot, and others taken to Andersonville had a worse fate than sudden death. Colonel Capron, Lieutenant-Colonel Jenkins, Captain Lord, and Captain Mayo were amongst the number of fugitives who came in on foot; some of them coatless and hatless, and one of the commanders without boots. Many were captured; Wirz was made to rejoice at the number of new victims brought to him for torture. What a sad ending was the fate of these noble men, who, to release from that southern hell their comrades who were rotting and dying by inches, were themselves doomed to the same horrid fate. But not all who fell into their hands were sent to that horrid prison; many were butchered as they were overtaken, and many more captured made their escape before reaching prison, for it was difficult to hold bold, skillful, resolute men who well knew what their fate would be once confined within those horrid walls. While our records show the names of those confined in southern prisons and those who died there, they do not show the names of the many who were captured and made their escape. Seldom did one military undertaking furnish as many and as exciting individual adventures as did this raid to Macon, Georgia. We have gathered a few sketches, which may be taken as only fair samples of many scores of which we have not been furnished narratives.

Andersonville—no, Andersonhell. Oh! the everlasting infamy that crowns that monument of secession with a halo glowing with the fires of the infernal regions. Fittingly execrated by all the world. Even Turkey and Spain would be ashamed of it. What in the world's history can compare to it? Many of our fugitive comrades fleeing on foot and unarmed from worse than the jaws of death, traveling through swamps and thorns and briers, that they might avoid their bloodthirsty, relentless pursuers. With nothing but berries and roots and occasionally raw green corn to eat, they were so emaeciated and foot-sore with hundreds of miles of tortuous paths traversed, that when they reached our lines they could scarcely stand; indeed some were prostrated for days. We will now give the operations of Major Davidson's command, which left the main command 7 miles north of Clinton, moved rapidly toward Milledgeville to make a feint on that place; turned suddenly toward Gordon; struck the railroad 7 miles east of Gordon, burned a bridge and all the trestlework, and cattle-guards; sent a small detachment under Sergeant Aganew, who cut the telegraph; then the command pressed forward to Gordon, the junction of the Etonton and Georgia Central railroad; captured the operator and the town; burned a large brick depot filled with army supplies; destroyed 11 locomotives and 11 trains of cars, of which 40 were passenger cars; 80 box cars filled with army stores, and 20 open cars loaded with machinery, belonging to railroad company; also one cotton factory. One account says, 150 freight and passenger cars, and 275 flat and box cars loaded with supplies; destroyed the telegraph office and instruments; tore up half a mile of railroad track; then moved down Central railroad track eastward to Emmet Station, 16 miles, burning all the cattle-guards on the road; destroying much of the road as we went. At Emmet burned a large depot filled with supplies, and tore up quarter of a mile of track, then moved 8 miles farther to Toomsboro, burned a large brick depot filled with supplies, a flouring mill and a saw mill, and some trains, and tore up railroad track, and burned a railroad bridge 300 feet long. Reached McIntyre Station at daylight July 30th; captured a party of Confederate soldiers, whom we paroled; destroyed the depot and a large amount of army supplies. We then moved toward the Oconee river, burning thousands of cords of wood, destroyed cattle-guards and burned a mile and a half of trestle work, halted near the river, built barricades. Lieutenant L. W. Boren, of Company "G," 14th Illinois, with Companies "A" and "G," marched to the river, drove the rebel guards, 150 men, with two pieces of artillery, from the bridge. Sergeant Aganew, with a squad, was sent forward, who soon had this, the finest bridge in the south, and having 700 yards of trestlework, all in flames. In 15 minutes the mighty bridge swayed and tumbled into the flood, a total wreck. Although the rebels had a duplicate bridge prepared, it took them one month to get it in place. Sergeant Aganew needed not to send a courier to the main command to notify them that he had succeeded, the heavy column of smoke sent up by such a mass of burning dry pine was a sufficient message. Lieutenant Boren and party now fell back to the main command, which moved back, and just as they entered the main road they discovered a large rebel force that had just passed down to guard the bridge (but now to mourn over its ashes). Our party struck in between the main force and its rear guard, and charging down on the latter, drove them in utter confusion, never stopping to gather up the arms and hats that strewed the road. They drove them several miles, capturing some, whom they paroled; and at the first favorable diverging road they dashed off in a direction to baffle pursuit if it were attempted. When within five miles of Milledgeville we turned abruptly to the right, reaching the Oconee river 12 miles from Milledgeville at 8 p. m. A small flatboat was discovered on the opposite side. It now grew very dark. Lieutenant Anderson, of Company "H," volunteered to swim the river and get the boat. Although a thunderstorm prevailed and it grew pitch dark, except as flashes of lightning revealed objects, the Lieutenant succeeded, and with the use of this boat, the whole command was safely across by 1 o'clock a. m. of July 31st. At daylight we passed around Milledgeville, driving in their pickets. They had here a large rebel force. We pushed rapidly up the river, destroying large banks of wood, traveling mostly on byroads; halted at noon to take a cornbread lunch, recrossed the Oconee river on a small flatboat at "Walker's ford," 27 miles above Milledgeville. Marched on the Sparta and Macon road near to Eatonton; then northwest on the Madison and Eatonton road, calling at a boot and shoe factory, where our command was thoroughly supplied with footgear. An order to burn the factory was withdrawn when it was learned that a church, a schoolhouse and some dwellings would be endangered. The night was dark and rainy, but we pushed on, halting at 2 a. m. of August 1st, and slept about three hours, the first sleep enjoyed since starting on this raid the 27th of July, five days before. Some of our men had been lost by dropping to sleep in their saddles and being left behind. At daylight marched three miles, halted, fed and breakfasted, then pressed forward toward Madison. About 10 a. m. we came up with Capron's fugitive command, and was thenceforward a part of that force and involved in its fate. The Major had designed to cross the railroad west of the circle, pass out west of Monroe and Lawrenceville, into our lines; but being better armed than Capron's men, we were called upon to protect their rear. An agreement was made for all to go out on Davidson's route, but for some reason this intended route was abandoned for the one toward Athens." This small command had been handled with consummate skill, and had accomplished an immense amount of work. They had marched and worked five days and nights, marched 200 miles, burned 5 large depots filled with army supplies, destroyed 13 engines, 15 trains of cars, numbering not less than 400 cars, most of them loaded with supplies, and destroyed and crippled fully five miles of railroad track and trestlework; burned the largest bridge in the south, and not less than 12 bridges of various sizes, nearly all the cattle-guards on their route; 2 large flouring mills, 2 saw mills, 3 manufactories, many banks of wood, and much other public property, including miles of telegraph wire, and one telegraph office and instruments.

There was destroyed by Stoneman's main command, principally by the 14th Illinois Cavalry, 2 depots, 8 engines, 6 trains of cars, not less than 90 cars, and 5 miles of railroad track crippled or destroyed, 2 factories, 2 grist mills, 2 saw mills, large amounts of military stores and 5 or 6 bridges. Making a total for Stoneman's command, 7 large depots, with stores, 10 miles of railroad track and trestlework, 18 engines and trains, principally loaded with army supplies and war material, about 600 cars; and this with 2,200 men, marching round the rebel army, having that army and one large unbridged river intervening between him and any support. McCook, with 4,000 men, with no intervening river, cut his way through to Lovejoy Station, destroyed some railroad and some other property, but scarcely worth mentioning compared with that destroyed by Stoneman's command, while he met with nearly equal disaster, losing a large part of his command, all his captured property and prisoners. Sherman seemed somewhat disappointed at the results of Stoneman's and McCook's raids, but never complained of either. He concluded that General Kilpatrick could succeed better, so he takes a more favorable opportunity, when Wheeler had left with a strong force, estimated at from 6,000 to 20,000, to raid our rear. Sherman says, August 16th, in a message to General Thomas: "I do think our cavalry should now break the Macon road good. * * * What say you to letting General Kilpatrick have two of General Garrard's brigades, to strike across to the Macon road and tear it up good." (See serial 76, page 525.) Again, same page: "If Wheeler took out 6,000 with him I don't believe 4,000 good cavalry remains to the enemy in our front." Sherman is sanguine of success and Kilpatrick replies that he is sure of success. With 4,500 good cavalry he makes the attempt, starting August 18th. He succeeds in reaching the railroad. See his report (serial 73, page 858): "Left Sand Town August 18th, with force of 4,500 men." Again: "We effectually destroyed 4 miles of railroad." He also succeeded in destroying some other property, but insignificant as compared to that destroyed by Stoneman with less than half the force and in the face of all of Wheeler's cavalry before he had gone, as Sherman thought, with the greater part of his effective cavalry. It is now well known that Wheeler had not less than 25,000 good cavalry. Sherman was again disappointed, but his eyes were opened as to the difficulty of capturing the Macon road. In serial 76, page 628, August 22d, he says to General Hallack, after enumerating Kilpatrick's work, 3 miles of road destroyed, 3 flags and 70 prisoners brought in, he says: "I expect I will have to swing across to that road in force to make the matter certain." This he did soon after, using his whole large army in a determined attempt to capture that road, and after days of hard fighting he succeeded. A number of our fugitive comrades, in making their way to our lines, learned the force of Wheeler's cavalry to be very large. On page 495, serial 76, is a report of a deserter from Hood, a Captain J. B. Jordan. He says Wheeler's command numbered 25,000. From Sherman's Memoirs, as published in the National Tribune, we give the following facts: Sherman had striven, with the cavalry divisions of Garrard, McCook and Stoneman, to destroy the communications of Hood, and had succeeded except upon the Atlanta and Macon Railroad, to which the enemy clung with such tenacity that although great damage had been done, it was soon repaired. Sherman says: "Luckily I learned just then (August 13th) that the enemy's cavalry under General Wheeler, had made a wide circuit around our left flank and had actually reached our railroad above Resaca and captured a drove of 1,000 beef cattle, and was strong enough to appear before Dalton and demand its surrender." Again: "I became fully convinced that Hood had sent *all* of his cavalry to raid upon our railroads." Sherman then sent Kilpatrick, in whom he had great confidence, giving him a strong cavalry force, to break up the Macon road about Jonesboro. Sherman says: "Kilpatrick got off the night of the 18th and returned the 22d (August) having made the complete circuit of Atlanta with these results: Destroyed three miles of railroad, captured a battery and destroyed three guns, bringing one in; captured three battle flags and 70 prisoners." Sherman again complained of the failure of General Garrard on the left. Sherman says, on the 23d the enemy were again using the Macon road and he says: "I became more than ever convinced that the cavalry could not or would not work hard enough to destroy a road properly, and therefore resolved to proceed with my original plan." This was to use his whole army to do what he had expected a few cavalry to do.

On pages 308 and 320, serial 76, Sherman several times alludes to Stoneman's venture in language indicating great concern for him, but not one word of blame. On page 526 Sherman uses language relative to General Garrard, plainly indicating an intended rebuke for his failure to more effectually support Stoneman in that movement.

Our scattered fugitive comrades were days in reaching our lines. No inspection or attempted reorganization was made until August 17th. We then had but 14 men mounted, and under command of Lieutenant L. W. Boren, of Company "G."

August 19th. Ordered to turn over all Government property and draw five days' rations. (Page 608, General Order No. 3), assigned Colonel Capron to the command of the first brigade, cavalry division, Army of the Ohio, composed of 14th Illinois Cavalry, 8th Michigan Cavalry, 5th Indiana Cavalry and 6th Indiana Cavalry. Nothing of note occurred until August 23d, when a party of foragers were attacked by guerrillas, one of the men wounded and five were captured.

August 24th. Very warm, especially in our camp, when Enfield rifles were issued to us and we were ordered to do infantry duty.

August 25th. Drew six days' rations, and under orders, marched on foot at 11 a. m. India rubber could not stretch as our marching column did that day, in its plodding toward Sweetwater bridge. At dusk the head of the column was halted and ordered to get supper, but the men were too tired to obey this agreeable order. It was 10 p. m. before the column was closed up, when it was again ordered to march; proceeded to the mouth of Nickojack creek on the Chattahoochee river, and went into camp on a bluff, having tramped 17 miles.

August 26th. Our column still closing up. On page 642 is shown that the nature of our service is the guarding of that point, and of army property sent there.

August 29th. Lieutenant Boren and his mounted squad is sent on scout. The order for arming us with rifles is found in serial 76, page 628. Lieutenant Colonel Jenkins is in hospital, and Captain Crandle, of Company "E," is in command of 14th.

August 31st. Mustered for pay and inspection. Lieutenant Boren and his party, now numbering 25 men, were sent across the river toward Atlanta to reconnoiter. Five miles out they were attacked and a skirmish ensued.

September 1st. Lieutenant Boren and party sent on scout to Powder Springs.

September 2d. Lieutenant Boren and party sent as a vanguard of a command of infantry, sent to reconnoiter toward Atlanta. In serial 73, pages 331 and 332, Captain Scott reports, favorably mentioning the efficient services of

Lieutenant Boren and party, who were the first Yankee troops to enter Atlanta, and to successfully aid in driving the last remnant of Hood's army from Atlanta. The infantry, numbering 900, were commanded by Colonel John Coburn. On page 782 of serial 76, is an official order of September 3d: "The bridge at Turner's ferry is to be taken up and the dismounted cavalry, under Colonel Capron, posted on the north side, are to hold the ford." This was our post and this our duty, for nearly two weeks, with nothing occurring out of the daily routine of camp life and picket duty.

September 8th. Procured some sweet potatoes to add to our half rations that we have *enjoyed* for some time past.

September 11th. Dress parade and inspection.

September 12th. Under orders to move.

September 13th. March at 8 a. m. up the river to railroad bridge, then file left on the railroad track to within one mile of Marietta; camped 4 p. m. Marched 17 miles in good spirits. It was wonderful how the marching qualities of our men were improved by the news that we are to go to Kentucky to be remounted and rearmed with sabers, revolvers and Spencer carbines. The men are happy.

September 14th. Engaged in turning over quartermaster property, then marched one mile to Marietta, and boarded a northern bound train, filling it so that many take the upper deck, as the boys called the roof of the cars. Any position is agreeable that promises a glimpse of God's country, and a renewal of real cavalry service. Train started at 4 p. m.; ran all night.

September 15th. An hour after sunrise reached Chattanooga, 125 miles from Marietta. Started again at 10 a. m., got breakfast at soldiers' home at Stephenson; ran all night.

September 16th. Reached Nashville at 2 p. m., 288 miles from Marietta.

September 17th. At sundown started for Louisville; ran all night, reached Louisville 1 a. m. September 18th; distant from Marietta, 471 miles. Embarked on cattle cars and started for Lexington about dark; passed Frankfort and reached Lexington about 3 a. m. of September 19th. A train behind ours was fired into by bushwhackers.

After sunrise we marched out and camped on a beautiful green lawn a mile from town. Remained in this camp until September 22d, then marched at 7:30 a. m., reached Nicholasville at 3 p. m. The 14th went into camp one mile N. W. of town; a beautiful camp ground. March 12 miles. Lieutenant-Colonel Jenkins, who has been in command of 14th, now went to Louisville, leaving Captain Thomas K. Jenkins, of Company "F," in command.

September 25th. Major Tompkins returned from captivity and took command of the 14th. The 5th Indiana went home to vote and we hear that the 14th, too, will be allowed to go. The only regiments now left in the brigade are the 14th Illinois, the 8th Michigan and the 16th Illinois.

September 29th and 30th. Captains Dent and Lupton and Lieutenant I. H. Allen returned from captivity. Lieutenant John A. Edwards, of Company "C," is appointed assistant acting commissary, Lieutenant Bruce Paine having left us.

October 11th. We hear that Captains Dent and Lupton, who had started home on leave of absence, were captured on the 10th by a guerrilla party between Lexington and Paris. We thus again lost the services of these valuable officers in one of our most important campaigns.

CHAPTER XII.

A ROMANTIC NARRATIVE AND TRUE.

This Chapter Constitutes a Part of the Georgia Service.

When the night attack was made upon Colonel Capron's sleeping command, on August 3d, 1864, those who were not killed or captured were soon scattered into small squads. Many of the fugitives were killed or captured afterward, and those who eventually reached our lines did so on foot, and with great difficulty and suffering; living on green corn and roots and berries. The varied individual adventures while making their way cautiously through the rebel lines and the rebel country, hunted by rebel soldiers and citizens with hounds, would make a volume of unequaled exciting interest could they all be gathered and published. The forced limits of our history will not admit the publishing of more than one of length, and we select one which embraces the characteristics of the others, and which in distance traveled far exceeds any other. It was furnished by comrade George W. Norris, of Company "G," 14th Illinois Cavalry. Comrade Lieutenant John S. Welch, of the same company, and who was with Norris in this adventure, also furnished an account. We publish Norris', as it is more complete in narrating everything, though agreeing in substance. He says of the early attack: "Colonel Capron posted pickets and ordered the men to lie down and sleep two hours, but not to unsaddle their horses. The men were all so worn with fatigue and loss of sleep that a surprise was easy. Just before daylight the rebs made the attack, shooting the men in their beds. Captain Wm. Perkins, of Company "G," was shot in the foot while asleep, and a great many others were shot in their beds. Our camp was a mile from the bridge over Mulberry creek. Corporal Wm. Roberts and myself were orderlies for Colonel Capron, and were sleeping together near the Colonel. We were awakened by the volleys and yells of the charging rebels. By the time I was fully awake I found that comrade Roberts and nearly all of our command were gone. I had no time to saddle my horse, and while the rebs called upon me to surrender, I sprang upon my horse barebacked, determined that they should not capture me as they had captured my brother, Sergeant Norris, on the trip down, while he was out trying to get a horse for a comrade. I dashed down the road after my comrades, and coming to where a line was formed, fell into line, like most of the others, without coat, hat or arms of any kind. This line was soon broken, and then every man for himself in a rushing mass down the road and on to the bridge, which broke down and precipitated all into the water in a mass, drowning some. Here I found comrade John S. Welch, who had just rescued a young soldier from drowning in the struggling mass. We ran to the bridge and springing across the gaps we succeeded in crossing. We then ran for a hiding place. We halted to wait for Corporal Smith to come up, but it was another man, and we hastened on and reached a hill covered with bushes, and concealed ourselves all day and saw the rebels pick up our men. At dark we left our concealment and moved toward our lines, and soon met six or eight of our comrades, mostly 5th Indiana boys, and Jesse Brown, Company "M," 14th. We decided that small squads were most likely to succeed, and taking Brown with us the others went a different course. After dark we came to a small log house and resolved to get something to eat. We were told that we could have something by waiting a short time. While waiting for the young lady to get supper, the old lady said: "Boys, was you uns in the fight at the creek this morning?" We told her we were. Then she inquired our command. We replied that we belonged to a Mississippi Confederate regiment. Then she asked why we had on blue clothes? We answered that we had captured some Yankees and exchanged clothes with them. She said "Oh! that was right." She didn't think the Yankees had any business down there." Supper was now ready and we ate heartily. The old lady was well pleased that we had whipped the Yankees, and *that* paid her for the supper. She said her son-in-law was in the Confederate army. We thanked them, bade them good-bye and started on our way. After traveling three nights and resting three days, we resolved to get horses. We slipped close to a large plantation house in the evening, and seeing some darkies we called to one of them, and he was badly frightened. We succeeded in quieting his fear, and told him we wanted him to bring us something to eat before dark. We inquired about his master's horses. He had told us that his master was in the Confederate army. He said they had plenty of mules and horses, but they were all away in a pasture except some mules in the stables. We cautioned him to say nothing about us and bring us something to eat after dark. A rebel wagon train of six or eight wagons, guarded by boys and very old men, now passed us. We might have captured the whole outfit, but we did not choose to be encumbered. In the evening we left our hiding place and went to the house, where we discovered two young ladies and one old lady and an old gentleman sitting on the porch. We told the old gentleman that we wanted some animals to ride. He told us we could not have any of his horses; but we had made up our minds to ride, and Comrade Brown and myself started for the barn, leaving Welch on guard. Soon we heard comrade Welch call to someone to "halt and surrender." We ran back and saw a large man dressed in a new suit of gray uniform, and mounted on a good horse. Comrade Welch had the horse by the bridle, and was commanding the man to dismount and surrender, which he did, and Welch disarmed him. We ran to the stables and saddled two mules and rejoined Welch. We now had a prisoner on our hands that we had no use for. He was a rebel enrolling officer picking up deserters and enrolling all he could find. His revolver was a prize for me, as I had none. A canteen of apple brandy we thought we could find use for. We ordered our prisoner to move along with us as fast as he could on foot. We planned what to do with him. If we let him go, he would soon have the whole country after us, and to take him along was a clog to our movements. After we had traveled four or five miles pretty lively, our prisoner sat down and said we might kill him or turn him loose, as he had heart disease and now had an attack, and could go no farther. We gave him some of his brandy and took a little ourselves to prevent catching his disease.

He then begged hard for us to turn him loose, promising faithfully that he would not follow us nor persuade others to follow. We saw that we could do no better than to turn him loose and trust to his word. We bade him good-night and hurried off, all three well mounted. Near morning we heard some persons coming the same road; it was quite dark. Comrade Welch ordered them to halt and surrender, and throw up their hands; they obeyed, when we found that we had captured a squad of our own men with one rebel prisoner. I had discovered that one had on one of our cavalry belts; after passing a few words this man said: "Aren't this comrade Norris?" I answered yes; and said: "You are Andy Waddell, of 14th Illinois Cavalry." One of the others was a 5th Indiana man, and the other was a Johnny. We asked what they would do with their prisoner. They did not know. We told them what we had done with ours, and they decided to do the same. He promised faithfully that he would not follow them nor get any others to follow, and we believe he kept his promise. He kept with us for several miles, when he bade us good-bye after we had all tested the apple brandy again. Our comrades captured his horse with the prisoner, who made no objection to their keeping it; so that the two comrades had one horse between them. We five kept together until we reached the forks of roads where we disagreed as to the proper route to take, when each squad went their chosen way. They went to the left, and we to the right. At daylight we came to a house, fed our horses and got breakfast. We told a white lie—that we were Confederate soldiers going to our commands. We paid for our breakfast. We traveled till noon without interruption; got dinner and feed; in afternoon, while quietly riding along we heard the tramp of horses and looking back saw 12 or 15 mounted men coming after us as fast as they could ride. We put our horses to their utmost speed, but they gained rapidly upon us. They were armed with rifles and shot guns. We sprang from our animals and ran for a steep hill covered with thick brush. We climbed as fast and as far as possible, but were soon surrounded, and now saw that their leader was the enrolling officer, come for his brandy. They demanded our surrender and opened fire on us, which was returned by Welch and Bowman.

My revolver refused to do service. Comrade Welch singled out the enrolling officer and fired. His gun fell from his hands and he reeled in his saddle. When he recovered his seat he turned his horse and rode away with his party, without even asking for his apple brandy. We hoped that comrade Welch had given him a pill that cured him of heart disease. One of the band, being near us, surrendered; but we informed him that we did not want him, and that he had better "git;" and he got.

We climbed the hill, keeping secreted by the bushes; traveling through the woods until we came to a small cabin occupied by two women and some children. We told them that we were Confederates going to our commands, and asked for something to eat. They promised supper if we would wait for it. One of them asked if we belonged to the command guarding the ford down at the river. We answered yes, and managed to keep her talking until we learned all we wished to know about this command. We ate our supper and paid for it, and went our way to join our command as soon as possible. We reached the river a mile above the rebel post. Lucky that we could all swim. We took a few rails from a fence and constructed a rude raft, took off our clothes and tied in a bundle with our arms in it. We pushed the raft ahead of us and swam to the other shore; then dressed, and it was now dark. We hastened on and traveled all that night and found a good hiding place not far from a farm house, where we remained all day, sleeping and resting until evening, when we started to the house to try to get something to eat. We knew the rebels were in the vicinity and watching for our fugitives. We got supper and moved on all night. In the morning we found that we were at the foot of the Blue Ridge with only a bridle path leading over the mountains. We hoped that once on the mountains we would be comparatively safe, at least not likely to meet more than our number. After reaching the top of the mountain we reversed our order of march; traveling by day and resting by night. We lived on huckleberries and blueberries, which were abundant. We gathered our hats full and sat under shade trees and ate them. The best of water we found in abundance for drinking and for bathing our swollen feet. We did finely. It took us two days and a night to cross, not meeting a person on the route. The first house we came to we told them we were Confederates. The next night we had a fine hiding place on a hill behind a field of corn in sight of a big plantation. We left our hiding place and entered the road that led to the house. We met a woman, God bless her, and may we meet her in heaven; few can realize what it is to meet a good friend under such circumstances. She looked sharply at us and bade us good evening; which salutation we returned; then she said: "Boys! who are you; and where are you going?" We told her we belonged to Colonel Young's (rebel) command, and that we were going to the farm house down the road to get something to eat. She said: "Boys, you haven't told me the truth who you are." We insisted that we were Confederates, but we could not make her believe it. She said she knew we were Yankee soldiers by our talk and by our clothing. We then admitted it; then she told us there was a company of rebel soldiers down at that house, feeding and getting supper, and that they were looking for us. I went with her a short distance to where we could see them feeding their horses. We went back and told my comrades that chances down there for our supper were not very good. This good woman then said that she was our friend, and that if we would hide till night and then come to her house a quarter of a mile from there she would have supper ready for us. She gave us a small basket of peaches. After dark we started out to find her house, but got bewildered and thought we would be without supper. At last we stumbled upon a small house. We knocked at the door and got the inquiry: "Who is there?" We answered: "Friends!" She answered: "Is that you, boys?" We answered: "Yes!" She then opened the door and bade us come in. Then we got supper. She told us that she had concluded that we were not coming. She said she was a Union woman and it did her good to have us eat with her. Her husband was in the Union army. After eating a hearty supper, we wanted to pay her, but she refused pay. It was unsafe to stay. She told us where to find a Union man who would pilot us out of that part of the country. She said about four miles on that road we would find a two story log house on the right hand side of the road; that was where he lived. We then bade her farewell, feeling that we were parting with a true friend. God bless her! She wished us good luck. With courage renewed we again marched on. In an hour we reached such a house as our lady friend had described. We knocked at the door repeatedly and finally received an answer from a woman, who inquired who we were, and what we wanted. We told her to open the door and see us. But this she refused to do for a long time. At last she opened the door and we went in. We told her and her daughter that we were Union soldiers and wanted to get to our lines, and that we had been directed by a Union woman four miles back to call and get her husband to pilot us to our lines. At first she said she had not seen her husband for three months, and did not know where he was. But we persisted in asking to see him. She then said: "Now, boys, are you Yankee soldiers?" We answered yes! She again asked: "Who told you that my husband was a Union soldier?" We again informed her. Then again and again she repeated her inquiry: "Boys, are you Union soldiers sure?" We said we were, and if she would get a Bible we would swear to it on its sacred pages that we were. After a long time she said she thought she heard cattle in their corn. She went out to see and was gone half an hour; then returned and said the cattle were not in their field, but she repeated her question: "Are you Yankee soldiers?" over and over again. We used every argument we could to persuade her. After another long talk she again thought she heard cattle in the corn, and she again went out and returned in a short time and said she had been out to see her husband, and that he had sent in word for one of us to come out to him unarmed. I was selected to go. The woman was to go with me, but said she had no shoes. I then pulled off my boots and gave to her, as mine were the smallest we had, and I put on comrade Welch's boots, and left my revolver. We went back of a field and down a hollow, then turned up a hill, following a narrow path. Suddenly two men rose up and called "halt." They questioned me as the woman had, and asked how we escaped from the Stoneman surrender. After I had recounted to them our perils and narrow escapes they appeared better satisfied. When we consider the great risk these good Union people run, in giving aid to the

Yankees, we do not wonder at their extreme caution; had the action of this family in our case been known to the rebels, every member of the family would have been sacrificed; fortunate, too, if they had not been tortured. But these good people braved everything that they might serve their Yankee friends, and their country. We now returned to the house, exchanged boots, and taking my revolver we three comrades went to the husband and his comrade. We had a short friendly talk, then went up the hill, where we found a lot of straw and some quilts, and our friends said: "You are all right now; we can pilot you into our lines without trouble and little danger." They told us to lie down and sleep and they would stand guard. We slept soundly until sunrise and wondered why we were not wakened earlier. They said we needed rest and would lie by that day and start in the evening. This suited us well, and when the ladies brought breakfast, dinner and supper, the first meals we had eaten for a long time, we were in paradise, compared to recent experiences. We were then ready to start, after the husband had kissed wife and daughter good-bye; and we, too, had heartily thanked them and bidden them farewell. We traveled about six miles until it grew dark, when our pilot halted us and told us that we must now cross a stream of water guarded by a squad of rebel soldiers; but that we could surprise and drive them from the ford. We said we were ready for the attempt, but his comrade weakened, and would not attempt. Our pilot said: "Do as you please, but I am going through with these men." He then commanded: "Draw your revolvers and be ready for action." We advanced and found that the enemy were gone. We undressed, waded the stream and marched on. At daylight our guide took us to the house of a friend for breakfast; we then traveled all that day, not halting till night; then staid with another friend of the pilot. Started early the next morning, came to a town where Union men were organizing a regiment, and our pilot was elected captain of a company. I forget the name of the town; it was 30 or 40 miles from Madisonville. There we parted with our pilot friend. I gave him my revolver, but he would not accept money. I am sorry that I have forgotten the name of that brave, good man. We started next morning through country we had been in before. We reached a mill that night where a lady friend of comrade Welch lived. We now concluded to rest among our friends a few days. Comrade Brown also had a lady friend two miles from there, whom he went to see. On the second day, as Welch and I were sitting down to dinner, a neighbor lady came running in to the house, wringing her hands and crying out: "Run, boys, run; Wheeler's cavalry is coming." We jumped up, and without finishing dinner, hurriedly bade them good-bye, and started for Knoxville without time to notify comrade Brown, who was captured, after all his efforts to escape. We were sorry to part with him. Through kind friends we escaped. Being acquainted through this country we got along very well. We came to where one of our boys had left a horse in a pasture. We stopped and got him. We filled a sack with straw for a saddle and made a rope bridle and got along nicely by riding and walking alternately. We came to a house where a big roan horse stood hitched at the gate, having on him a cavalry saddle and bridle, and on the porch sat a rebel cavalryman holding a baby Johnny. We rushed toward him, he seized his gun while the mother snatched her child and begged us for God's sake not to shoot, for we would kill her babe. The rebel soldier jumped from the porch and ran through the cornfield. We followed but a short distance, then returned. I mounted my own horse and Welch mounted the roan, and going on a few miles we overtook a refugee family moving. This man had a good saddle and bridle. We soon managed to exchange with him. That afternoon we reached Motley's ford, where we were once stationed. We supposed we were far ahead of Wheeler's cavalry, and stopped for the night. Started early next morning and traveled without molestation for a time. We came to a road and saw evidence that a large cavalry command had just passed. This we knew was a part of Wheeler's force. It was now evening. We came to a bend in the road and saw two rebel troopers mounted. They saw us and called to us to halt. We knew there was a large force near and did not choose to halt. They dashed down toward us and it was a race down the road. Coming to a lane with a closed gate, Comrade Welch sprang from his horse, opened the gate and closed it, when we had passed, mounted and we had a race down the lane. We came to a timbered lot and there the Johnnies gave up the race. We staid in the timber until dark; it rained hard. After wandering in the dark we came to a road near a house. We called and asked for supper. The good woman asked who we were and when answered, she said we could have supper, but it was not safe for us to stay in the house, as a large rebel command had been passing in detachments all the afternoon; but as it was raining and no rebels in sight she thought we might remain in a while and dry our clothes, while herself and daughter would get supper and watch. When we were seated the woman ran in and told us to go out the back door and wait till she called us; a cavalry force was passing. The lady soon came and called us, but we were scarcely seated by the fire when we were again warned and hastened out. The lady now came out, and in a low voice told us where to get feed for our horses and that supper would soon be ready. We fed our horses, which we tied in a thicket, and then went to our supper while our friends stood guard. They soon warned us again, but these all passed without halting, so we were permitted to finish supper. Our friends said if we would risk it we could have a good bed, but we did not want to run risks now that we were so near safety. They gave us some quilts and we went near to our horses and made down a bed. It rained as hard as I ever knew. At daylight we returned the good ladies' quilts, and as they insisted, we remained for breakfast. We then bade them good-bye. God bless them, they were friends. It was about 30 miles to Knoxville. Near evening we saw a Union soldier sitting near a house. We told him that Wheeler's command was marching on to Knoxville, and advised him to go with us, which he decided to do, but urged that we have supper first. After supper he bade his people good-bye, and we three journeyed on with two horses for three men, dividing time in riding. Toward midnight we were halted by a vidette. We told him we were friends. He ordered one forward with hands over head. Comrade Welch advanced. Soon the vidette called for the others to come up. We were glad to get within our lines again. We were sent back to the main post, where were a Lieutenant and Sergeant and ten men.

After gathering around us and hearing our story the Lieutenant advised us to stay with him till daylight. This we were glad to do. They divided grub with us and the hardtack and sowbelly eaten with our Union comrades was to us a feast indeed, after having been for 22 days afraid to eat or sleep for fear of being surprised and captured. Next morning, same fare, with good strong coffee. We felt O. K. and supposed our troubles were over. We proceeded toward the city and reported to an officer in command of the troops on south side of the river. He questioned us and we told him our whole story, and that Wheeler was coming with a large force, and that he was near. He seemed to be posted on this matter. I asked him for a pass to cross the river and he wrote and handed me a pass for us three. Before we reached the end of the bridge we heard the command "halt." We obeyed and a lieutenant and sergeant came up and said they wanted us. They had six soldiers with them, who surrounded us and we marched with them. We asked an explanation, but got none, until we had crossed into the city, when they told us that we were arrested as rebel spies. A large crowd of soldiers and citizens followed us and amongst them a grayheaded old sinner who declared he knew us, and that we were rebel spies. When we reached the commanding general's quarters we were subjected to the most rigid scrutiny. We related the whole history of our adventures and told them the command we belonged to, and our officers' names, and that we were often encamped in and around Knoxville. Though there was a large crowd around none seemed to know us or our command, except the old gray-headed sinner who insisted that he knew us and that we were rebel spies. We had forgotten the names of citizens we had known and the prospect was good for ending our adventures at the end of a rope. Finally I saw a citizen ride by whom I had known and so informed the general. The man was called in and declared that he had never seen me before. I asked, and was granted, the privilege of asking him some questions. I said: "Did you not have charge of the government corral at the depot and bought horses for the government about a year ago?" He answered, Yes! He then looked at me again and said to the general: "I know that man, and he belongs to an

Illinois regiment;" but he did not remember my name. I then reminded him of writing some vouchers for me for horses that I had sold to him. He then remembered that my name was Norris. The general now ordered the sentinel to disperse the crowd, and he questioned me about comrade Welch. I informed him that he was the orderly sergeant of my company, "G," of the 14th Illinois Cavalry. He was now satisfied and we had passed a trying ordeal; the danger of being hanged on the accusation of an old gray-haired sinner."

We omit a small portion of comrade Norris' narrative that relates only to personal reminiscence that is interesting, but we are crowded for space in our history, being limited to the number of pages, and must omit that which does not relate to real history. Suffice it to say comrades Norris and Welch succeeded, after some difficulty, in obtaining a furlough home—a merited boon for the faithful services they had rendered, the hardships endured, and the perils escaped and after the march of over 600 miles through rebel settlements and rebel armed forces. Theirs was a wonderful escape from perils and full of romance, and above all else, it was strictly true. They both rejoined their regiment and served faithfully to the muster out of the regiment July 31st, 1865. In distance traveled these comrades were far ahead of other fugitives, while their real privations were not so great as some, owing to the choice of a route that evaded the rebel lines.

CHAPTER XIII.

REMOUNTING, AND SERVICE UNDER GENERAL SCHOFIELD AND GENERAL THOMAS.

The history from the remounting in Kentucky to the destruction of Hood's army, is in two chapters. Chapter Thirteen extends to the falling back to Columbia.

Colonel Capron had been promised a speedy remount and a full rearming as cavalry, including Spencer carbines, and that his command should rejoin Sherman at Atlanta. Capron says in his memoirs that he immediately made the proper requisition for horses and for cavalry arms, including Spencer carbines as promised. He says the command was inspired with the hope, and deemed this promise to be a recognition of their valuable services in East Tennessee and in Georgia.

October 14th. Reveille at daylight; marched in high spirits to the depot at Nicholasville, boarded a train and started for Louisville at 4 p. m.; passed through Lexington, reached Louisville at daylight, October 15th. Marched to soldiers' home, got breakfast, then marched to suburbs of the city and camped. Traveled 103 miles. The following officers captured are yet in captivity: Captains Sanford, Perkins and Mayo, Majors Quigg and Davidson, and Adjutant Chauncey Miller.

Sunday, October 16th. Drew horses and horse equipments, but no cavalry arms. These were now promised to be given at Nashville, as we were now under orders to march to Pulaski, Tennessee, to aid in repelling Hood's invasion of Tennessee. In serial 93, page 566, General James H. Wilson, now chief of cavalry of this division, speaks of this order.

Capron says: "The order was peremptory, and I was compelled to march without arms, it being understood that our cavalry arms would be forwarded by rail to Nashville."

October 17th. Mounted and started at 1 p. m. for Nicholasville; disappointed in both promises, to go home, and to be armed as cavalry and to rejoin Sherman. The latter was the great disappointment.

October 18th. Reveille at 3 a. m. Marched at daylight. Passed through Boston, Simpsonville, Hardinsville, Bridgeport and Shelbyville, 36 miles. Camped within two miles of Frankfort.

October 19th. Marched through Frankfort at sunrise; reached camp near Nicholasville at sundown, having marched 45 miles. Found our tents standing as we had left them. Sherman and Hood were playing a sharp game of war. Each was closely watching the other while concealing his own intentions. Hood had marched to Sherman's rear, but whether only to cut Sherman's rear, or to strike for Nashville and the Ohio river was known only to himself and Beauregard, who was the rebel commander of that department. When Sherman had determined to cut loose from his communications and strike for the sea, he sent General Thomas to Nashville to gather up an army with which to oppose Hood's advance northward, if he attempted it, or to follow and harrass Hood should he attempt to follow Sherman. A portion of the 4th Corps, under General Stanley, was hurried to Pulaski on the railroad in the southern part of middle Tennessee.

Hood's report (page 659, serial 93), shows that he left Palmetto Station, Georgia.

General Beauregard in report on page 647 says, on 19th of October, Hood was at Gadsden on his way toward middle Tennessee, with intention to cross the Tennessee river at Gunter's landing. A conference with Hood was held and Beauregard approved his plan of crossing the river and striking for middle Tennessee, and earnestly urged an immediate movement on that route. Both generals deemed that Sherman could not provision his army in a march through Georgia to the sea, and that he would be compelled to fall back to Tennessee, if his communications were cut in his rear. Serial 93, page 663, gives strength of Hood's army 6th of November, 1864: Aggregate infantry, 87,016; cavalry, 5,148; artillery, 4,203; total, 96,367; and on December 10th, infantry, 77,631; cavalry, 5,148; artillery, 4,283; total, 86,982. Of course his effective present was much less. A note says: "Crossed Tennessee river November 21st, with 30,600." His army was composed of the following army corps: Lee's, Stewart's and Cheatham's infantry and Jackson's division of cavalry. On October 19th, at Gadsden, Hood was only 40 miles from Gunter's landing, where he designed to cross the river. At that time there was no force gathered to oppose him in a direct march to Nashville. Hood was a most impulsive commander, his tactics were sudden and unexpected movements. General Beauregard strongly urged this course. Why Hood did not follow his usual tactics where everything favored it, seems to have been due to the fact that Providence was guiding him to his fate; that this cruel war might be ended, and the right brought to triumph.

Major-General James H. Wilson is now chief of cavalry corps, military division of the Mississippi. See his report beginning page 654, serial 93. On page 556 he says: "General Croxton's brigade of the first division, having been recently remounted at Louisville, Colonel Capron's brigade of the sixth division, and the fifth division (commanded by General Edward Hatch, see page 575), while on the march to join Sherman, were halted by General Thomas, and directed to act in conjunction with the infantry forces assembling at Pulaski under General Stanley, to resist the march of Hood." Wilson in another report (see page 557), gives the strength of this cavalry on November 23d: "The fifth division (Hatch's) 2,500 men, Croxton's brigade, about 1,000, and Capron's, 800; in all about 4,300." This was the situation at this time, and these the reasons for the change of our field of operations. We remained in Nicholasville, busy in our preparation for our march, and with pleasant weather, until October 23d at 9 a. m., started on march for Nashville; halted at noon at camp Nelson to have horses shod, then marched a few miles and camped. March 10 miles. Through some blunder we had no rations.

October 24th. Reveille at 5 a. m. Marched at 8 a. m. through Camp Dick Robinson at noon, and on Lebanon and Glasgow road, camped. March, 32 miles.

October 25th. Reveille at 5 a. m. March at 7; pass through Lebanon and on Glasgow road 32 miles and camped.

October 26th. Reveille at 5, march at 7 a. m. 25 miles to Barren river and camp.

October 27th. Reveille at 5; march at 7 a. m.; pass through Glasgow, so long our headquarters while chasing guerrillas through Kentucky. The sight of this place recalls many memories of our first service. Marched 23 miles and camped; rained at night.

October 28th. Reveille at 5; march at 7 a. m.; 25 miles and camp.

October 29th. Reveille at 5; march at 7 a. m.; pass through Gallatin, a nice town; march 25 miles and camp.

October 30th. Reveille at 5; march at 8 a. m. to Nashville, a nice city; crossed Cumberland river on railroad bridge; passed through the city and camped 3 miles S. E., near Camp Smith. Marched 15 miles through fine, well improved country. Capron's Memoirs say: "No cavalry arms could be obtained. The emergency of the service demanding that we should at once take the field, and as no other weapons were attainable, Springfield muskets were issued to the command; a weapon with which these troops had no experience, and a more unsuitable weapon for the service before us could not be; confronted as we were to be, with one of the best organized and equipped forces in the Confederate service, with Forrest's famous cavalry as its advance guard. This had a most damaging effect. These men had been much encouraged to expect that they would be properly armed, and they actually refused to receive the muskets. Many broke them around the trees and an open mutiny was the result, taxing the officers heavily to quell." Capron further says: "General Thomas' unguarded remark, that they would do to shoot guerrillas with, was not calculated to lessen the excitement, and I have since thought that he could not then have anticipated the heavy task before him. For this command it proved to be the most trying ordeal that cavalry could be subjected to." Cavalry in making, or resisting a cavalry charge, might as well have been armed with clubs. The officers alone, down to orderly sergeants, were armed with sabers and revolvers.

October 31st. Reveille at daylight; marched at 11 a. m. back through Nashville, then south on Franklin pike 15 miles and camped. Marched 18 miles through fine country.

November 1st. Reveille at 5; march at 7 a. m.; pass through Franklin, a nice town on the Harpeth river, and through Spring Hill and camped. March 28 miles. Fine weather until today it rained hard.

November 2d. Reveille at 5; march at 8 a. m., through Columbia, a small town on Duck river and on the Nashville railroad. Marched on the Pulaski road 15 miles and camped in a wood. March, 25 miles; rained very hard last night and today.

November 3d. Reveille at 5; march at 8 a. m., to Pulaski, an antiquated town, unimportant except as a strategical military position, necessary to be held because it was a key to the occupation of the railroad over which supplies must come to our army. We camped in a rocky piece of woods, 3 miles S. E. of town. March, 18 miles; rained hard last night and today. We saw several divisions of the 4th Corps coming into Pulaski. Pulaski was selected as a base of operations for our rallying army, because of its advantages as an advanced post of observation in watching Hood's movements, and as a good point to begin opposition to Hood's advance toward Nashville, should he attempt it. Hood was now at Florence, having changed his route, as he says, on account of the better provisioning his army, and to await the coming of Forrest's cavalry force, as he did not deem Jackson's division of cavalry, about 5,000, as sufficient to make his advance with, yet it was more cavalry than we were able to get south of Columbia, and had Hood moved promptly as he had planned to do by way of Gunter's landing, he would then have found no cavalry to oppose him, and no other force of consequence. Hood was now at Florence, on the Tennessee river S. W. from Pulaski. His movements indicated an intention to advance upon Nashville. There were a number of wagon roads from Florence and vicinity northward toward Nashville; neither of them striking Pulaski, but all converging on Columbia, 30 miles in the rear of Pulaski. The most direct being by way of Lawrenceburg, 22 miles west of Pulaski, another by way of Waynesboro, over 50 miles west of Pulaski. Other roads parallel to these entered each of them at various points.

This formed a triangular tract of country to be watched by our cavalry that was more than 50 miles wide at the base, and converging to a point at Columbia. The infantry at Pulaski could do no more than guard well that point, leaving this immense belt of country to the west to be guarded by our small force of cavalry. Hatch and Croxton having been remounted before us, had arrived and had been sent forward toward the river to watch Hood's movements. We remained in our first camp until November 8th, having much rain and cold.

November 8th. Reveille at daylight; marched at 8 a. m. back through Pulaski and up the Athens pike eastward 2 miles, and camped in a wood. Marched 5 miles.

November 9th. Reveille at daylight; rained all night and all day. A detachment from the brigade, under Major Beers, of the 16th Illinois, was sent on scout. They returned, having scouted four days without discovering the enemy in force.

November 10th. Reveille at 5 a. m. Scouting parties of 50 or 60 have been sent out daily. Today a party of 60 men, under Lieutenant Anderson, of Company "H," and Lieutenant W. L. Sanford, of Company "I," 14th Illinois Cavalry, marched to within a few miles of Columbia, then turned on a byroad westward toward Campbellsville, halted within six miles of that place and bivouacked till morning. Were in the saddle by break of day, and at sunrise entered Campbellsville. Halted to warm at the burning ruins of a dwelling, fired in the night by some Tennessee soldiers, in retaliation for homes burned by some of the rebel inhabitants of that village. While warming, our vidette in our rear were fired upon by a party of guerrillas, who were approaching on the road we had just pasesd over. Lieutenant Anderson, with a part of the detachment, immediately dashed down the road to attack them, when they broke across the fields westward toward a wooded hill in the distance. Lieutenant Sanford, with the remainder of the detachment, gave pursuit across fences and through deep mud, pursuing the party for two miles, when they made their escape into a high rocky and wooded hill, so inaccessible to mounted men as to be impossible to charge mounted, and posting themselves behind rocks at considerable height, all attempt to capture them was abandoned.

As we were under orders to report immediately back to camp, we had no time for maneuvering to capture them. This adventure is given, not for any especial merits of its own, but rather as a sample of the many others occurring almost every day, and which were never reported. We hastened back to camp, where we reported about 4 p. m. of November 11th; having marched since the morning before 70 miles.

November 12th. Reveille at 2 a. m. At 4 a. m. a large detachment of our brigade, under Major Tompkins, marched westward to reconnoiter. It was reported by General Hatch that the enemy were moving toward Waynesboro. Halted and fed at 1 p. m., after having passed through Lawrenceburg, a dilapidated town on the direct road from Florence to Columbia, and 22 miles west of Pulaski. We then continued to march rapidly until sundown, when we halted within a mile of Waynesboro; having marched over 50 miles. We sent forward scouts, who soon returned with intelligence that a considerable force had been in Waynesboro, and that the enemy were moving that way. Lieutenants Anderson and Sanford were selected to take a battalion and hasten back to Pulaski with dispatches, and were instructed to hasten to pass through Lawrenceburg, as it was reported that a force of the enemy was moving rapidly on that road. This battalion marched double quick, reaching Pulaski at 1 a. m. of November 13th, having marched since 4 a. m. of the morning before, 100 miles in 21 hours, or a continuous march averaging 5 miles an hour, not deducting the halt, the last half being at the rate of 7 miles an hour for 7 hours. Major Tompkins camped his men between Waynesboro and Lawrenceburg, where he remained a number of days scouting between those two places. The rebel force at Waynesboro, was three rebel regiments under Colonel Rucker.

November 13th. In camp. General Schofield arrived at Pulaski today.

November 14th. General Schofield took command of all the forces at the front today. (See his report, page 909, serial 93.) He reports his infantry force at 18,000, with four brigades of cavalry (Hatch 2, Croxton 1, Capron 1, 4,300 in all); he estimates Hood's infantry at 40,000, and his cavalry at from 10,000 to 20,000, under Forrest, who had now joined him. Scouts and captured prisoners afterward gave Forrest's cavalry at 15,000.

General Schofield, on the 14th, ordered Capron with his brigade to move to Mt. Pleasant, with orders to camp as far in front of that place as he could find forage, and scout well toward Waynesboro. (See page 885.)

On the 15th Hatch reports (see page 899) : "I have not cavalry enough to close in on my right to the Tennessee river. If you could spare me Capron's brigade, think we could close them in so effectually not a forage party could get out of Florence without a fight for it."

On the same page is Schofield's prompt reply: "Yesterday I sent Colonel Capron with his brigade to Mt. Pleasant, with orders to scout toward Waynesboro, and have now sent him your dispatch, with orders to communicate with you, and act under your orders when your forces meet."

As Hatch was on the left of Waynesboro, to form a line between Hatch and the river as he suggested, it was necessary for Capron to advance as far as Waynesboro. In obedience to the first order, we marched at 9 a. m. on the 14th, on the Columbia pike 17 miles, then turned nearly west a few miles and camped. March, 20 miles.

November 15th. Reveille at 3 a. m.; rained; march at 7 a. m. northwesterly, through rough country, 12 miles to Mt. Pleasant. Camped at 3 p. m. Whole march through rain and mud.

November 16th. Rainy night. A detachment of the 14th, under Captain Connelly, of Company "L," was sent on scout toward Waynesboro.

November 17th. We are now ordered to Waynesboro, 40 miles in advance of this point, toward the river, to watch the movements of Forrest and Hood. March at 8 a. m.; passed through Henryville, a small town, and through a wilderness country. Camped on a rough piece of ground, water inconvenient; march, 27 miles.

November 18th. At 1 a. m. our camp was alarmed and command called out. One of our ambulances approaching our rear picket was challenged and failed to respond; was fired upon and a sick man was wounded. The command was ordered to bivouack. At 8 a. m. November

18th, when within a few miles of Waynesboro, our advance, under Lieutenant Boren, of Company "G," 14th, encountered a rebel scouting party and charged upon them, killing, wounding and capturing a number of them, and having one man wounded. Our party pursued the rebels through and beyond Waynesboro. We camped in the town about 3 p. m., having marched 21 miles. Rainy day.

On page 936 Capron reports from Waynesboro, November 18th: "I occupied this place this evening with a loss of one killed, one mortally, and one severely wounded; and captured two of Forrest's scouts. Major Beers joined us from a scout today."

On the 19th it rained.

November 20th. Lieutenant Allen, Company "D," 14th, with 50 men, sent on scout toward Florence. They drove a party of rebels many miles, when the rebel party was so strongly reinforced that they in turn retreated. In this camp we suffered much for lack of rations and horse feed. On page 937 Capron reports: "I can hear nothing of General Hatch. Forage very scarce; none on the road to Mt. Pleasant, and none on Lawrenceburg and Mt. Pleasant road. I have four days' rations for the command, and my only base of supplies is either Columbia via Mt. Pleasant, 56 miles, or Pulaski via Lawrenceburg, 52 miles distant. A rebel force, under Colonel Biffle, is 15 miles west. Another at Linden, 28 miles north." On page 965, November 20th, Capron reports: "Impossible to procure forage for stock or rations for the men, either beyond, or to the rear of this place. I have sent out scouts on every road to obtain intelligence, and gather supplies. The country in every direction is destitute of everything for man or beast. The roads impassable for teams. It is impossible to advance my main force. I can obtain forage a few days longer at this place, but no rations of consequence. I can hear nothing of General Hatch. My scouts will penetrate farther today in hopes of finding him."

On same page to General Wilson, Capron alludes to the inefficient arms of his men, and adds: "We are in an isolated position, 55 miles from supplies in any direction. The country around us is completely swept of everything, and the roads are next to impassable. I was ordered to advance to this position, and if possible open communication with General Hatch. Yesterday my scouts entered Clifton, and penetrated within 3 miles of West Point, and 20 miles out on Florence road. I am at a loss to know what to do, in the absence of any further instructions from any source. I have reported regularly to General Schofield at Pulaski, but up to this time (November 20th) my couriers have not returned. I shall be able to eke out our subsistence for a day or two longer, by gathering in, for 20 miles around, everything eatable for man or beast. The impassable roads, incessant rains, heavy scouting, and the necessity for bringing in their forage on the horses on which they ride, our horses are fast being made unserviceable and useless."

On page 964, November 20th, Colonel Strickland, at Columbia, said to Capron: "The enclosed dispatch is from General Schofield, and he instructs me to say to you, to watch and delay Forrest's movements, and try and unite with General Hatch; who will move between Forrest and the railroad." The following is the enclosed dispatch from Schofield: "I have just received your note of 18th. You seem to have entirely misunderstood your instructions, and I expect to hear of the capture of your brigade. Move back at once toward Mount Pleasant as far as the intersection of the Lawrenceburg and Waynesboro roads, on the latter road. General Hatch reports Forrest advancing toward Lawrenceburg yesterday noon. Perhaps you may get this in time." This message indicates the great peril to which Capron's brigade was exposed, so great that General Schofield despaired of Capron being able to prevent his capture; but his declaration that Capron had misunderstood his instructions in going to Waynesboro, seems strange when those instructions were to comply with General Hatch's request, to form on his right a line extending to the river in order to pen Hood's foragers in Florence. The language "keep in the presence of the enemy;" a thing impossible to do unless he went to where the enemy were. Any one acquainted with the country, with the position of Waynesboro and the relative position of the contending forces, who would carefully study Schofield's instructions to Capron, must conclude that nothing short of Capron's advance to Waynesboro, would be obedience to those instructions. Even Schofield's present instructions through Colonel Strickland say: "Watch and delay Forrest's movements and try and unite with General Hatch." How Schofield expected Capron to unite with General Hatch, when he says in the same dispatch: "Who (Hatch) will move between Forrest and the railroad," thus placing Forrest between the commands of Capron and Hatch, is hard to understand. Capron could only do this by abandoning the Waynesboro road, which even the present dispatch commanded Capron to operate on, and "delay Forrest's movements." Viewed in any light, Schofield's language considered in connection with his instructions, sounds very strangely.

On page 963, November 20th, Schofield said to Hatch: "I ordered Capron to feel for the enemy from Mount Pleasant, and to open communication with you, *and he has wandered off to Waynesboro.* I am trying to get him back."

One thing was plainly demonstrated by subsequent events, that if Capron really misunderstood instructions, his *wandering off to Waynesboro* was the most fortunate misunderstanding of instructions that a military man ever made. Nothing short of this ever could have saved Schofield's army. We will here quote from official records, showing the situation. Schofield, with all his infantry, is at Pulaski on the railroad. The next important post on the railroad is Columbia, 30 miles in rear of Pulaski. Hood and Forrest are at Florence on the Tennessee river. Hood's object is known to be to reach Nashville, and if possible to destroy Schofield's army. To do this if he could reach Columbia with a sufficient force before Schofield could reach that point, he could cut off and destroy Schofield's army when no other force would interfere with his seizure of Nashville, nor with his march to the Ohio river. The most direct road to Columbia from Florence is via Lawrenceburg, near where General Hatch, with his division, 2,500, and General Croxton, with his brigade, 1,000, are posted to watch and oppose Forrest's advance. The incessant rains had rendered all the roads so nearly impassable, as to cause both General Thomas and General Schofield to believe that Hood could not possibly advance. There was another route for Hood's forces to Columbia via Waynesboro and Mount Pleasant. This route was longer, bending round in the direction of Savannah. Of course Hood's intended movements were unknown to Schofield, and when convinced that his army was moving, it was doubtless Schofield's expectations that Hood would move via the Lawrenceburg road, and that he would doubtless attempt, either to attack him at Pulaski, or strike the railroad in his rear. This is indicated by his disposition of his troops. His infantry force is all held at Pulaski, while his main body of his slender force of cavalry, Hatch's 2,500 and Croxton's 1,000, making 3,500, are all operating near Lawrenceburg, 22 miles west of Pulaski, and Hatch is ordered with this force to keep between the enemy and the railroad. The only force placed on the Waynesboro road was Capron's slender force of 800 men, insufficiently armed and posted more than 50 miles from the main force, and 30 miles from any support; even if Hatch could be deemed a support so distant and with the enemy's forces moving between them.

In serial 93, page 669, begins itinerary of Hood's movements, which shows that he had planned to outgeneral Schofield by pushing his army rapidly by an unexpected route, and seize Columbia and the railroad in Schofield's rear, and capture or disperse Schofield's army, little exceeding one-third the strength of his own. This itinerary shows that Hood personally, with the whole of Cheatham's corps, moved from the start on the Waynesboro road, and that Stewart's corps moved first by the Lawrenceburg road, and passed into the Waynesboro road not far from Henryville, perhaps 20 miles S. W. of Mount Pleasant. Lee's corps moved first on a road between the Lawrenceburg and Waynesboro road, and entered the Waynesboro and Mount Pleasant road 12 miles south of Henryville, so that from Henryville to Columbia not only Hood personally, but his whole force of infantry, 40,000 or 50,000 strong, is on that road, where only our brigade of but 800 unsupported are between the impetuous Hood and his expected victory.

On page 751 begins General Forrest's report, which shows that he ordered Chalmer's division of his cavalry forward on the Waynesboro road via Henryville and Mt. Pleasant. The report also shows that he was personally present with this division. He sent Generals Buford's and Jackson's divisions on the military road to Lawrenceburg, and thence toward Pulaski. Hood was surely outgeneraling Schofield in pushing forward and concentrating his army on this unexpected route, while he sends some of his cavalry to make a feint on Pulaski, and to keep the main body of our cavalry from succoring our weak force on the route of Hood's triumphal march, the only impediment to Hood's advance. Instead of playing a card to oppose Hood's sharp game, Schofield plays a card in his favor, by ordering all the rest of his cavalry to isolate themselves from all possible opposition to Hood's advance, by ordering Hatch to move between the advancing cavalry and the railroad. Such was the perilous situation, and such the task assigned to our handful of men, insufficiently armed. Had Schofield designed to effect the destruction of our brigade he could scarcely have planned it better.

We have received a number of communications from comrades describing in part our operations in falling back to Columbia, all of them good, and we are sorry that we cannot give them all in full, but our limited space forbids. In the main operations, our notes and the official reports are given; in detachment service we rely on comrades.

On the afternoon of November 21st Capron prepared to fall back, and none too soon, as the enemy's cavalry were in detachments all through that country. Captain H. C. Connelly of Company "L," 14th Illinois, was sent in command of the advance guard, charged with ascertaining whether Forrest was in force in our rear. He moved out about dark, it was sleeting and the roads were a glare of ice.

November 22d. Reveille at 3:30 a. m. Marched before daylight. Capron had received a second dispatch to watch and delay Forrest's movements, in which Hatch said: "Hold on where you are until pressed back, scout well your right flank, endeavor to learn if the enemy are moving round your right toward Nashville. I will keep your left well scouted." (See page 989.) On this promise of Hatch to keep him informed of the enemy's movements on his left, Capron was led into what came near to being a fatal movement. Captain Connelly, with Lieutenant A.

B. Capron, were ordered to scour well the country on the right toward the river.

Hatch was at Lexington on the 20th, when he sent the above dispatch, but when Capron began to move back Hatch was at Lawrenceburg, 25 miles away. A force of the enemy's cavalry followed us, annoying our rear guard and threatening an attack. Lieutenant Boren of Company "G," with a strong detachment, was sent to the left to endeavor to communicate with General Hatch; he had proceeded a few miles when he encountered a rebel brigade which was moving round our left. The lieutenant's party was vigorously attacked, and were scattered in confusion. When the first fugitives reached our lines it was thought that the lieutenant and most of his party were lost, but they were not made of material so pliable. Lieutenant Boren and most of his men came in hours after, having cut their way around the rebel force. We passed through Henryville and went into camp in a wood four miles from Henryville, and within a mile of the point where the Lawrenceburg road intersected the Waynesboro road; having marched 18 miles.

About 2 p. m. our rear picket was attacked, but held the enemy until reinforced. The command was called out and built barricades. Scouting parties sent out reported the enemy to be attempting to flank us. Lieutenant Sanford, sent out on the left rear with a foraging party, narrowly escaped capture. Strong detachments under able commanders were sent to the various points that gave a chance for the enemy to flank us. These detachments were vigorously attacked; the enemy sometimes concentrating their force at some one point, again attacking all the points at the same time. They were successfully repulsed at all points. Our men were learning to use their infantry guns to good effect in a dismounted fight.

Capron says in his memoirs, relative to Lieutenant Boren: "I became satisfied that Hood's army was advancing upon us in force, and I determined that notwithstanding Hatch's assurances that he would protect my left and keep open our communications, I would have a thorough reconnoissance made of the country between me and Lawrenceburg. Before daylight I sent out a strong party (under Lieutenant Boren) bearing a message to

General Hatch. They had been out probably one and a half hours, when two of their number came into camp under a full run, without their caps. They had run into a brigade of Forrest's cavalry; the ballance of the party were either killed or captured." Fortunately it was not so bad as that. Capron continues: "Our situation was critical; the emergency demanded prompt action to secure my command from being captured. The first thing to be attended to was to bring in our scouts; the one on my right, commanded by my son, Albert B. Capron of Company "A," 14th, might have found it important under my instructions to scout to the Tennessee river, 20 miles distant. The next in importance was to arrange my command to hold this position, for these parties to fall back upon. Two miles in my rear was found a more suitable position, with a straight, open road for a small force left in the first barricade to fall back upon, if forced to retreat hurriedly. Two squadrons under the command of Major (then captain) Connelly of the 14th, were left in the first barricade, with instructions to hold them until our scouts came in if possible; or, if forced out, to fall back upon our second position. With the balance of my command I proceeded to erect a second line of barricades; leaving open a space sufficient for the force left at the front to pass freely through if driven back. It was approaching night when all was in readiness. The troops were dismounted and placed behind the defences, with strict caution not to mistake a rapidly approaching body of our men for the enemy. In momentary expectation that something important would transpire, I waited the result at the opening in the line of our barricades. By my side was Major Buck and my Adjutant General, Captain Wells, both of the 8th Michigan cavalry, with a small sustaining force." Colonel Capron's choice of this position was a good one, both for the advantages of the ground and because it was a mile in the rear of the entrance of the Lawrenceburg road, as some of Forrest's forces were known to be on that road, from which they could have gotten in our rear had we remained at our first position.

Colonel Capron is mistaken in saying that Major Connelly was left in command of our first position when the main body fell back. The following is the account by

Major Connelly: "With a portion of the 14th and the 16th Illinois cavalry, I scouted to our right front. Captain Smith, a brave and capable officer of the 8th Michigan, held the enemy in check (at the first barricade) until my return from the scout on the evening of the 23d. Captain Hanchett of the 16th, who was acting assistant Adjutant-General to Colonel Capron, directed me to take a position and aid Captain Smith in holding Forrest, and so remain in that position until he returned. He left, to communicate with Colonel Capron, and was never again seen in our lines. Forrest by this time had gotten between our command (the rear guard) and the main command, and was quietly picking up our men; moving between our forces." Forrest, with a force, had come in by the Lawrenceburg road, which was between the rear guard and the main command. Connelly further says: "Hearing nothing from Captain Hanchett, I directed Lieutenant Moore of my Company "L" of 14th to take ten men and see if he could open communication with the brigade." The following is Lieutenant Moore's account. He says: "I was in command of the rear picket or skirmish line from the day before, and toward evening I received orders to draw in the pickets, as it was then thought we were surrounded; or that old General Forrest was between us and our brigade. After relieving the pickets, Captain Connelly ordered me to take ten men and try and open communication with Colonel Capron. It was late in the evening when I got the ten men selected; Joe Murry was the only one from my company. After riding some distance there filed into the road ahead of us to the right, perhaps one hundred yards off, a band of about 150 cavalry, going at a gallop. They looked like rebels. This made things look a little interesting, but we continued going all the same; slacking up a little to let those fellows keep a little in advance, and just at this time Captain Hanchett and his orderly came up with us, and wanted to pass to the front. I told him of the cavalry that had just filed into the road, and that I thought they were rebels. He thought not, and said if I would lend him one of my guns, that he and his orderly would ride on ahead and risk the chances of being caught. We gave him a gun, and they galloped away. We kept him in sight all the while. He was not more than 100 yards in advance. Presently we saw him ride up to the cavalry ahead of us, and disappear; and not a gun was fired. And when we came up to them they were in line on the right hand side of the road. Some of them were dismounted and in more or less confusion. Some had blue overcoats on, and others had gray blankets tied around their shoulders; so that it was difficult to tell in the dark which side they belonged to. At this time our horses were doing their best, as we all saw the tight place we were in, as they had more than ten men to our one. When we came to the head of the column, I spoke, and the officer in command replied with one shot at short range with his revolver, and to this day I can see the flash of that shot in my face, but the bullet missed me, and struck a little fellow on my right, Joseph Murry of my company. The bullet struck him two or three inches above the right ear. He dropped forward on his horse's neck. I reached down and caught him by the cape of his overcoat, and kept him from falling off, until he came to. I finally got him straightened up, all covered with blood. This was the only shot fired by them, and we came out with the loss of two guns.

We found out afterward that it was General Forrest and his escort, who were quietly picking up our men and horses, and taking them back to the rear, and I am certain that Captain Hanchett was captured by these men, for I saw him ride into their ranks, and I am also sure that I was the last one of our men that spoke to him. He never came back. We could not report back to Captain Connelly, and the only alternative was to ride through, which we did. I have often wanted to hear from those ten men that were with me, but knew none of them except Joe Murry. Those were the times to try men's grit, and "the-stand-up-to-be-shot-at" qualities of the soldiers of 1861 to 1865, who are now, in some quarters, called "coffee coolers" and "paupers," and other offensive names. But let me say right here, that I would not exchange my experience of three years in the service in the army for the whole southern confederacy, with all their northern sympathizers to boot, "don't you forget it." Good for you, comrade Moore, for though you have but repeated the many-times uttered sentiment of truly patriotic comrades, yet there is

in the heart-stirring ring of those sentiments so much of
the patriotic fire of truly loyal Americanism which under-
lies the safety of our country and its beloved institutions,
it would ever be new, though repeated ten thousand times.
Without doubt comrade Moore can congratulate himself
on having received a military salute from the greatest cavalry chieftain of the Southern confederacy, *The Hero of
Fort Pillow*. But we doubt somewhat whether poor Joe
Murry very highly appreciated the salutation. Pressing
duty just at that time prevented a return of the complement. On page 75, serial 93, begins Forrest's report of
campaign, in which he says: "My command consisted of
three divisions, Chalmers', Buford's and Jackson's. I
ordered Chalmers to advance via West Point, Kelly's
forge, Henryville, and Mount Pleasant. Brigadier-Generals Buford and Jackson were ordered to move up the
military road to Lawrenceburg, and thence southeastward
in the direction of Lawrenceburg." Relative to Henryville, he says: "At Henryville Chalmers developed the
enemy's cavalry and captured forty-five prisoners. At
Fouche's springs the enemy made another stand. I
ordered Chalmers to throw forward Rucker's brigade and
to keep up a slight skirmish with the enemy until I could
gain his rear. I ordered Lieutenant-Colonel Kelly to
move by the left flank and join me in rear of the enemy.
Taking my escort with me, I moved rapidly to the rear.
Lieutenant-Colonel Kelly being prevented from joining
me as I expected, I made the charge upon the enemy with
my escort alone, producing a perfect stampede, capturing
about 50 prisoners, 20 horses and 1 ambulance. It was
now near night, and I placed my escort in ambush. Colonel Rucker pressed upon the enemy, and as they rushed
into the ambuscade my escort fired into them, producing
the wildest confusion." Regarding Forrest's statement
that he fell in our rear, there is no doubt that this was his
plan, and that he moved to our right and on the Lawrenceburg road with his escort with that intent, sending Lieutenant-Colonel Kelly by his left, our right, to join him in
our rear. But Capron's timely falling back with his main
command, and posting strong detachments on our flanks,
not only prevented Lieutenant-Colonel Kelly from joining
in our rear as Forrest says, but although Forrest reached

the Lawrenceburg road and entered the Waynesboro road as Lieutenant Moore saw him do, though Forrest may have thought he was in the rear of our main command, he certainly knew better soon after, as our accounts show, and the only reason that he could have in not reporting his after repulse when, in following up Lieutenant Moore's party he charged upon our main command and was repulsed, is this, that the full report would have spoiled his fine, boastful account. Relative to his placing his men in ambush, if there was anything more in this line than the shameful violation of the recognized rules of modern warfare, by concealing the identity of his men in the uniform of union men, it will be found in the truthful account of Captain Connelly, of the heroic charge made by our rear guard through the lines of Forrest's veterans. We will now give Colonel Capron's account of Forrest's attack. He says: "Just as darkness was settling upon us, and it became too obscure to distinguish troops by their dress at any distance, a column of dust raised by a rapidly approaching cavalry force appeared advancing from the direction of our first position. Orders were repeated to withhold the command to fire until assured that this was not a part of our own men. In an instant of time a force of Forrest's cavalry charged in upon us, and delivered their fire directly in the faces of our men. They had flanked our first position, as it was conjectured they would. Their fire was promptly returned, and a rapid interchange followed. In the midst of the noise and confusion of the battle a shout and firing were heard in the rear of this attacking force, and in the next moment their line was rent asunder, and our men from the front dashed into our lines. It appeared that the scouts had been brought in, and were mounted for a leisurely retreat to our second position. The uproar and firing were heard and their precarious position fully realized. In an instant the resolution was formed to make the attempt to cut their way through the attacking forces. The columns were immediately put in motion, headed by Major (then captain) Connelly, and Lieutenant Capron of the 14th Illinois cavalry, and Captain Smith of the 8th Michigan cavalry, with the result as stated. Our casualties were: Major Buck, severely wounded; Captain Wells, mistaking the attacking force for our men, dashed out through the gap to meet and guide them through, and was captured; Sergeant-Major (now lieutenant) Allen, with 15 men, was captured, and others wounded; Captain Hanchett, assistant Adjutant-General, captured; Lieutenant Boren, with 25 men out on scout, cut off, but subsequently reported having lost several of his men and most of his horses." Captain Wells and Lieutenant Allen both escaped soon after.

We now give the account of the charge of the rear guard, as related by participants. Captain Connelly says: "Hearing nothing from Lieutenant Moore, I requested Captain Hattery of the 16th Illinois cavalry to take 25 men and see what was wrong in our rear. He had gone but a few hundred yards when the enemy poured a volley into his ranks. This was the signal for active work with us. Captain Smith, being the ranking officer, took the advance. When he struck the enemy with the head of his column they fired a volley into his band. The captain and a few others cut their way through. The main part of his command came back pell-mell, throwing my column into confusion. By this time it was dark. I saw the importance of promptly charging out and calling upon comrades to follow, the whole column followed. The men set up a terrific yell, and, dashing on to the rebel lines, fired their Springfield guns. The confederate line broke and ran like sheep, and we brought out safely every man we had with us."

This bold charge of Captain Connelly, through the select of Forrest's famous command, his body guard, was loudly applauded by our command. General Forrest's claim that at Henryville they captured 45 prisoners, and that he captured at Fouche's springs 50 prisoners, may be correct, nor is it a wonderful result, when we remember that scouting parties were liable to be cut off while coming in, and we know that detachments on our flanks fighting on foot, had their horses captured, and in moving on foot portions of these detachments were cut off and captured.

General Chalmers in his report, see page 763, says: "On the 23d Rucker's brigade met Capron's brigade near Henryville and captured 45 prisoners." He also says that Forrest soon after captured 20 prisoners. Though these rebel commanders do not agree in the number captured

by Forrest, it would not be strange, considering Forrest's
method of clothing his men in union uniform, and riding
between our forces as he did, he possibly succeeded in
picking up that number of unsuspecting men, who, because of being deceived by a trick that no honorable military officer would be guilty of, these unsuspecting men had
no chance of defending themselves. But regarding Forrest's boastful charge as he pictures it, the reports of Colonel Capron and Captain Connelly agree in showing, while
there was a confusion and rout, it was in Forrest's ranks,
instead of in the Union lines. Forrest forgot to mention
his brave exploit in shooting the boy, poor Joe Murry,
when there were but ten men to face one hundred and fifty.
These reports show that Capron's small brigade faced
Chalmer's division of Forrest's command, with both Chalmers and Forrest present. They also disprove the claims
of some of General Hatch's men, that Forrest pursued
Hatch's command. On the Lawrenceburg road General
Hatch, with 3,500, was attacked by Buford's and Jackson's
divisions of Forrest's cavalry, perhaps 10,000. This was
fearful odds to meet, but nothing to compare with the
task imposed upon Capron's 800, compelled to combat
5,000 of Forrest's famous cavalry, with the whole force of
Hood's infantry, headed by himself, now making a determined effort to destroy Schofield's army by capturing
Columbia, and thus getting in Schofield's rear, a feat that
he most surely would have accomplished had not Capron
"wandered off to Waynesboro," where he was not only
able to keep Schofield thoroughly informed of Hood's
unexpected movements on the Waynesboro road, but by
the most heroic and skillful conduct, he was able to fight
back this immense host, until a division of Schofield's infantry, sent forward by Schofield because of information
furnished by Capron, succeeded in throwing themselves
upon the Waynesboro road, until our worn out and shattered brigade could reach them, when their united forces
could barely, with superhuman effort, hold Hood's advance in check, until Schofield, hours after, could bring up
his main force. Hood did not have the "walk away" he
anticipated, merely because he found a tough customer in
his way, who should undoubtedly be pardoned for misunderstanding the orders of his superior; if indeed, he

did misunderstand them. It was surely a very fortunate mistake.

Information now reached us at Fouche's springs that General Hatch's force had been cut to pieces. This only added to the before almost hopelessness of our situation. An order now came to Capron that he *must* check Hood's advance, if it sacrificed his whole command. Up to this point we had been favored with woods and hills, which prevented the enemy from easily flanking us. But we are now approaching a more open country, having many parallel roads, with crossroads to reach them. Capron had repeatedly notified General Schofield of his precarious situation, and of the impossibility of preventing Hood's advance when the more open country was reached. To these dispatches repeatedly came the promise of re-enforcements, and orders similar to the foregoing, but no re-enforcements ever came. It appeared to us that General Schofield was slow in beginning his movements back, and if possible still slower in executing the movement. Capron adopted the plan of holding every favorable point as long as possible, and for this purpose kept a portion of his brigade in the rear, to build barricades at favorable points, whilst detachments of resolute men defended the flanks as well as the rear. From Fouche's springs we continued falling back from one fortified position to another through the night, as Forrest's eager forces pressed vigorously, and sought to flank us on parallel roads. Thus the battle continued all night. Capron realized that if he succeeded in holding all of Forrest's force in check for any length of time, it would only give opportunity for Hood to throw forward portions of his infantry on parallel roads to cut off Schofield, or capture Columbia. Ours was a task such as was seldom expected of so small a force, and therefore Schofield, realizing this, accompanied his orders to hold the enemy with, "If it sacrifices every man of your command." But of what avail would be the sacrifice of the command, if it did not accomplish the desired end, the holding of Hood until Schofield could reach Columbia by way of the Pulaski road? It was evident that Capron must not only retard Hood's advance on this road, but it was as important that he must not permit any portion of Hood's forces to beat him into Columbia on any parallel road.

Our flanks were well scouted to keep us informed of any such attempts. We reached Mount Pleasant early in the morning. Here were some army stores that were destroyed, to prevent their falling into the enemy's hands Schofield issued an order for Capron to hold this place, but it was not received in time, and had it been, the delay consequent would have permitted rebel forces to have flanked us by parallel roads on either side through that open country, and Columbia would have been captured, and also our brigade. We fell back a mile or two, fortified and held one position after another; retiring only when the movements of rebel forces on either of our flanks, through that open country compelled us. When within six miles of Columbia, a position was reached apparently more favorable. It was determined to make a more decided stand. The writer, with his company, was with the rear guard which was commanded by that resolute officer, Major Beers of the 16th Illinois cavalry. While at this position the enemy's columns were seen between our position and the Pulaski road, marching on a parallel road, until the head of a long column was in advance of our position. Scouts reported them also passing us on our right flank in like manner. We sent five different couriers to Colonel Capron, notifying him of this fact, and only received in reply a denial of the statement, and an imperative order to hold our position at all hazards. This conduct of our commander always seemed strange to us, until we found the following explanation by Captain Connelly. He says: "Our situation was critical, our left was entirely unprotected. We received no communication from General Hatch, who seemed to have all he could do to take care of himself. On the morning of the 24th I was with the rear guard under Major Beers. We were strongly pressed, but fell back with deliberation. Colonel Capron had his little army in line of battle when I came up. I rode up to him and asked him if he intended to make a stand there. He replied that Generals Schofield and Wilson were raining dispatches on him, insisting that he must resist the enemy's advance if it destroyed his command. That the infantry had not yet reached Columbia, and that the 5th Iowa cavalry would be with us soon. I called his attention to the confederate lines moving on both our flanks, evidently intending to form a junction, and capture us. I said to Colonel Capron: "If we remain here we will be surrounded by an overwhelming force in a few minutes and captured." To this the captain might have added, even if they do not see fit to capture us, their columns pressing forward on parallel roads will soon be ahead of us, and capture Columbia and cut off Schofield. Connelly says: "Colonel Capron gave the order to fall back." Capron's memoirs describing the operations from Fouche's springs says: "Precautions were taken against a night attack. Major Beers, with a battalion of picked men, was sent to the rear to select a position, and to construct barricades. During the night of the 23d the enemy having been beaten off, ceased to annoy us about midnight, but it was fully known that a heavy force was concentrating for the capture of my force in the morning. I therefore quietly withdrew from this line of barricades, under cover of night, passing through Major Beer's position and instructing him to join me at the proper time at our next position. I selected as good a position as possible and threw up defences, dismounted my command, and placed them behind them. Hourly couriers were sent to Generals Wilson and Schofield notifying them of our desperate condition, and the determined and resolute advance of the enemy." He then speaks of an order to hold his position, and a promise that the 5th Iowa would be sent to him. He then says that immediately after he received an order to hold Mount Pleasant at all hazards. This would have been impossible and useless. There were no defenses there, and no material to construct them of; besides, the whole country was open, admitting the enemy to pass freely on either flank. Capron adds that his force at that time was reduced by deaths, disabilities, captures, and on detached duties, to not more than six hundred men, and of the horses, not one really fit for the service. Ammunition nearly exhausted, and bread none. He says: "With this small force I was left to face what was probably one of the most thoroughly equipped forces of the war; advancing full of confidence and enthusiasm, many of them actually in sight of their homes and their families. Instructions were rained upon me to check, to hold at all hazards, the advancing foe. At 7 a. m., still no appearance of the promised support. The advance of Hood's army now in sight, pressing forward with evident intent to capture my command. From an elevated position I could plainly see, with my field glass, their movements. Forrest's cavalry was developing their forces on both my flanks, while artillery was visible, approaching in the distance."

Relative to our last position described by Captain Connelly, Capron continues: "There was now no time left for further deliberation. The simple question was, whether by sacrificing my command, I should gain more time for Schofield, than I would by withdrawing them, and trusting to chance to be able to still oppose their advance. The question of our capture was reduced to a certainty if we remained. I resolved to draw off my command with as little show of intention to retire as possible. Leaving a small force behind the barricades to keep up appearances of still further opposing them, the column was drawn out under orders to "walk march." Our retreat was protected from view of the enemy by the formation of the land and some timber, in which were placed small detachments partially withdrawn, to deceive the enemy as far as possible in regard to our intentions, and to mislead them in regard to our strength. The column was fairly in motion with no apparent excitement, more than a consciousness on the part of the men of the critical situation, and their utter helplessness when mounted and encumbered by the clumsy Springfield rifle. Every cavalryman can easily understand that. I had congratulated myself on a successful movement, when suddenly my rear guard was overwhelmed, and driven in upon us, with Forrest's command sabering them at their discretion."

As our men below the rank of orderly sergeants possessed no cavalry arms of any kind, it was utterly impossible to resist an impetuous cavalry charge. With their muskets empty and no time to reload, they were as really disarmed as if holding in their hands only clubs. To have attempted to fight on foot, would not only result in being surrounded by an overwhelming force and captured, but would have permitted the flanking columns of the enemy to have pressed on into Columbia unopposed. Nothing could be done by the rear guard unarmed but to mount and get out of the way. Those who possessed cavalry arms, the officers and orderly sergeants, threw themselves in the rear, and did the best they could to keep back the furiously charging rebel cavalry. To maintain an orderly rapid retreat under the circumstances was beyond the power of any officers. Anything short of a rapid retreat, would have permitted the enemy to enter Columbia ahead of them. To dismount and form line, even had they possessed plenty of ammunition, which they did not, would have given only a temporary check at best, with the chances of forces of the enemy beating us into Columbia, and when again compelled to move, the same results would have followed. It would have been vastly different had we possessed cavalry arms, for even the few who did possess them did excellent service. Not a few of the more impetuous Johnnies were made to bite the dust. General Chalmers in his report (see page 763), speaking of this affair: "I regret to say that in this pursuit Lieutenant-Colonel Dawson, commanding 15th Tennessee Cavalry, was killed while gallantly leading his regiment in a charge. He had discharged all the loads from his revolver, and was endeavoring to wrest one of the enemy's flags from its bearer, when he was shot."

The writer, with a number of others, saw him go down. As Captain Connelly describes it: "It was a wild ride." A portion of the way was through a lane, in which there was a perfect jam of running horses, and ever and anon as a trooper came to some obstruction, a fallen tree, a large stump, or a ditch, that could not be passed around by reason of the jam, the steed, in attempting to clear the obstruction, would go down, to be trampled to death or to be captured, horse and rider.

Disorderly as was this hasty retreat, we sincerely believe, that under the same circumstances, General Sheridan himself could have done no better, as the following description, authenticated by the official reports, will show: When at Henryville, Colonel Capron had sent forward a courier of Company "K" with a message to Columbia, to give information of the situation, and to ask for the much needed aid. When he reached Columbia no possible aid could be sent from there, and mounting a fresh horse, he dashed down the Pulaski road until he met General

Schofield, with his main command. General Schofiel‹ at once dispatched a message to Brigadier General Jaco D. Cox, commanding a division of infantry, ordering hir to move rapidly to Columbia.

Capron's memoirs speak of a temporary check of th enemy, at a wooded ravine, and then adds: "Not a ma had come out from Columbia to our support, and all wa given up as lost, when at the very last moment of time, th head of a column of infantry was seen approaching acros a field from the direction of Pulaski. They were on th double quick."

It proved to be General Cox's division of the 23d Arm Corps of Schofield's army. In serial 93, page 400, is Gen eral Cox's report. He says: "November 24th, at 4 a. m received orders to move at once with my division to Colum bia, and to cover that place during the concentration c the army there; the enemy being reported to be pushin our cavalry rapidly back on the Mount Pleasant and Co lumbia pike. The division was immediately put in mc tion, Reilly's brigade in advance, followed by Henderson' and Casement's brigade bringing up the rear, covering th train. At a point two miles from Columbia, I determine to take a crossroad, intersecting the Mount Pleasant pik one mile and a half from Columbia, and marching the hea of the column rapidly, reached the last named turnpike jus as the cavalry brigade, commanded by Colonel Capror reached the same point in hasty retreat, before a ver superior force of the enemy's cavalry, under Forrest, wh had been pressing them hard for several miles. This wa at 7 a. m. I ordered Reilly's brigade into position on th right, (west) of the turnpike; throwing forward the 100t Ohio Volunteers to the bank of the Bigby creek, to suppor a strong line of skirmishers, and check the enemy's ad vance, during the formation of the division. Henderson' brigade was put in position on the left of the turnpike. Again: "Capron's cavalry, by my order, rallied at th rear, and then took position on Reilly's right, coverin; that flank of the whole line."

By the aid of this wooded creek, which was then deep Cox's division and Capron's brigade were able to chec the enemy's advance for three hours, until at 10 a. m. th head of the column of the 4th corps reached Columbia, an formed on the left, and thus was Columbia and Schofield's army saved, by the most heroic efforts of Capron's brigade, in fighting back the enemy's main force on the Waynesboro road; and when no longer they could, in the open country, prevent the enemy from reaching Columbia before them without they rapidly fell back, they performed this movement successfully, though necessarily in some confusion. Though some critics, who know nothing of such service, have criticised this movement of Capron's brigade as a "disorderly panic," yet not one of our commanders speak of it in other than respectful terms, nor do even the rebel commanders, in their reports, speak of it in boastful terms; they do not even claim it as a victory. The fact was, it was to them a shameful defeat, inasmuch as it defeated the sanguine expectation of Hood to reach Columbia by the Waynesboro road, on which only so small a force opposed him.

General Schofield, in his report (see page 341), says: "My advance (General Cox's division) reached that place (Columbia), on the morning of the 24th, just in time to beat back a large rebel force, which was driving in General Capron's cavalry from Mount Pleasant."

General D. S. Stanley (page 112, report), referring to these movements says: "It was believed that the enemy could make but little speed, and the evacuation of Pulaski was made the afternoon of the 23d. The corps (4th) marched to Lynnville that night. During the night it was learned that the enemy had made good use of his time, notwithstanding the bad roads, and that Colonel Capron's brigade had been driven out of Mount Pleasant, it was believed, by an infantry force. General Cox's division was ten miles nearer Columbia, and marched at the same time as ourselves; he arrived in time to save Capron's brigade of cavalry from annihilation, and perhaps the town of Columbia from capture."

Although General Hatch had under his command 3,500 cavalry, well armed, a force nearly five times as great as Capron possessed, and had but two of Forrest's divisions to face, and no infantry, while we had less than one-fourth as many and had to face half as much cavalry, and all of Hood's infantry in their rear; yet they do not boast of any victory over us, while on page 768, rebel General Ross reports the attack made by his command and General Armstrong, on General Hatch's command, and describes it as a famous victory for the rebels. General Hatch makes no report of the affair. The enemy were vastly his superior in numbers, but in much less proportion than to us, yet we succeeded in reaching and saving Columbia, while General Hatch was cut off, and could not reach Columbia until long after.

On page 1026 is an order from General Wilson to General Johnson, November 24th, 2 p. m.: "Please send a squadron under a good active officer, out on the Lynnville pike, with orders to go till he passes the rear of Water's brigade, or to the neighborhood of the Campbellsville road, and endeavor to find General Hatch. He was, at 9 p. m. last night, four miles beyond Campbellsville, on the road toward Lawrenceburg, and trying to reach the military road, passing through Campbellsville this morning."

At Campbellsville is where General Ross says he defeated General Hatch.

Colonel Capron, in his memoirs, speaks of having received from General Johnson the above order. Relative to General Schofield's estimate of the services of our brigade in that campaign Major H. C. Connelly relates a conversation which he held with the General at Rock Island in the year 1889, in which General Schofield said: "When I wrote my first dispatch at Pulaski, and started it by courier to Waynesboro, I had no doubt that Capron's brigade was captured." Connelly then spoke of being at headquarters when the dispatch was received and in a few minutes moved out with the advance guard, to cover the roads and prevent the enemy from flanking us. Prompt action, after receiving the order, saved the brigade. Referring especially to the morning of the 24th of November, General Schofield said: "Your command did great service in holding Hood back until General Cox had formed his lines; your good work saved the army from disaster." And with much emphasis he said: "Major! every man in your command that morning was a hero."

We will close this chapter with an account of the sad fate of that highly esteemed and valuable officer, Captain Hanchett; captured, as narrated, by Forrest's cowardly minions, who dared not meet on equal grounds even a foe vastly inferior in numbers, but concealed their bodies under the uniform of friends. Major Connelly says (and the records confirm it) : Captain Hanchett was confined in the rebel prison at Cahaba, Alabama. Here he organized a company of about 50, who planned their escape. They succeeded in getting out, but after being pursued two days, he was recaptured.

Dr. Eddy, in his "Patriotism of Illinois," says: "A sad fate awaited Captain Hanchett. He was enclosed in a wooden box eight feet square, with one aperture through which his food was passed. Here he remained until the rebels heard that General Wilson was coming, and deemed it best to shift their quarters. Poor Hanchett, after over a month of such confinement, was reduced to too feeble a state to move, and they blew out his brains when they left."

The same account is found in the Illinois adjutant general's report. Comrades, let us not refrain the sympathizing tear, for the sad fate of one of our bravest and best comrades. Peace to his memory.

CHAPTER XIV.

DEFENSE OF COLUMBIA AND DUCK RIVER.—RETREAT TO FRANKLIN.—BATTLE OF FRANKLIN.—RETREAT TO NASHVILLE.—SIEGE OF NASHVILLE.—BATTLE OF NASHVILLE.—REPULSE, PURSUIT AND FINAL DESTRUCTION OF HOOD'S ARMY.

November 24th, evening. Drew small quantity of hard bread and bacon, having had little to eat since leaving Waynesboro. We passed through Columbia, crossed Duck river on the bridge, and camped a mile from town at 4 p. m. Capron's memoirs say: "So great was the exigencies of the service at the time of our arrival at Columbia, on the morning of November 24th, 1864, from that terrible retreat of 56 miles before Hood's advancing army from Waynesboro, that not one moment was allowed for the reorganization of the command. Time was not even given for the worn-out horses to be shod. From that time to the afternoon of the 26th no less than 25 orders were received, calling for details of men." We have only room to note the purport of several of them. One was for a detachment to search for General Hatch's command, as stated in previous chapter. Also a detachment to bear a message to the command at Hamilton's ford below Columbia. The command of 50 men there posted, was a detachment from Capron's brigade, commanded by Lieutenant I. H. Allen, of Company "D," 14th Illinois Cavalry. To send out all these details, scattered the brigade now reduced to less than 600 men. On the 24th Brigadier General R. M. Johnson assumed command of the 6th division of cavalry, to which Capron's brigade belonged. (See page 1026.) General Johnson's report (see page 597), shows that on the 24th of November the 5th Iowa Cavalry (armed with sabers and Spencer carbines), 500 strong and commanded by Major J. Morris Young, were temporarily added to Capron's brigade, and General Croxton's brigade was also temporarily added to Johnson's (6th) division.

November 25th. In camp; send our dismounted men to Columbia, to be sent to Nashville, to be remounted as soon as General Thomas could gather horses, which was slow work. Hood attacked the front this morning, but gained no advantage. Johnson's division was called out; marched down the river several miles, dismounted, remained several hours, remounted, countermarched to Columbia and Franklin pike, then on that pike north a few miles to Shelbyville road, then eastward (up the river) on Shelbyville road 7 miles and camped. Road rough and muddy; rained much. Marched 14 miles. Pickets have been sent to various crossings of Duck river above Columbia.

On the 26th Capron receives orders to prepare at once to move his brigade to the crossing of Duck river, by the Lewisburg and Franklin pike, and to find the whereabouts of the battalion sent out last night, and send a strong party to support it. This movement extended into the very dark and rainy night, over very rough and muddy roads, resulting in men dropped from the ranks, horses crippled, guns capsized, and wagons and ambulances overturned and wrecked. On this march Colonel Capron received an order from General Johnson to call in his pickets from the river above Columbia, and to have the fords from Lewisburg pike, down to Huey's mills, well watched and guarded, and was promised that Lieutenant Allen's party of 50 men, below Columbia, should be returned to his brigade. This order instructed, not only to guard well the crossings from Lewisburg pike down to where the pickets of Croxton's brigade began above Huey's mills, but to spare no pains to learn the condition of all crossings of the river on his beat, and watch carefully and report promptly every movement of the enemy. A dispatch from General Schofield to General Wilson, asserted that there was no doubt that Hood was working eastward (up the river), with a view to crossing the river above Columbia, and that all of Forrest's cavalry were in the advance. And again, November 27th, 4:10 p. m., this order: "Send a strong party on the Lewisburg road, with orders to satisfy you of the movements of the enemy in that direction."

Capron says: "It is perhaps needless to say that these and all other orders were promptly executed, and their results, with all other gathered information, were promptly sent to headquarters. It was ascertained that from Huey's mills up to the Lewisburg pike there were no less than six passable fords. Indeed for 15 or 20 miles above Columbia, there were many good fords, and many more possible crossings, some of them having mere bridle paths leading to them, yet possible of crossing by cavalry unencumbered by anything on wheels.

The two most practicable crossings for a large force, were the one at the crossing of the Lewisburg pike, and one a mile and a quarter below the pike. There was also a bridge at Shelbyville, a number of miles above the pike.

Sunday, November 27th. Had rainy night. Marched afternoon and night up the Shelbyville road, which ran on the north side of the river parallel to its general course, but owing to bends in the river, sometimes close to it, and at other points, miles from it. This road was a poor one, rough and rocky in many places, and passing through much land that was uncleared forest. We camped near the Lewisburg pike. Marched 7 miles. Lieutenant Allen of the 14th, with his command, has been relieved from duty at the ford below Columbia, and assigned to duty as a courier line between Columbia and Franklin (see page 1095).

November 28th. Reveille at daylight; march up the Shelbyville road two miles to its crossing of the Lewisburg pike, which is about one mile and a quarter north of the river crossing by the Lewisburg pike. Colonel Capron established his headquarters at the crossing of these two roads, retaining as headquarter guards a few companies of the 7th Ohio Cavalry, who, under their Colonel, Israel Garrard, had just joined him. The remainder of Capron's brigade was posted as follows: At the crossing of the river was posted Major Beers, with his regiment, the 16th Illinois Cavalry, and a portion of the 8th Michigan Cavalry; and at the ford next below was posted Major Young, with his regiment, the 5th Iowa Cavalry, and a portion of the 14th Illinois Cavalry, under Captain H. C. Connelly. The remainder of the 14th Illinois Cavalry, commanded by Captain Thomas K. Jenkins, was divided into detachments and posted at various crossings lower down. Just above the crossing of the pike the river makes a great bend to the northward, until it approaches near to the Shelbyville road, over a half mile above (east of) headquarters. Along this bend of the river were many shallow places, and a company of the 7th Ohio Cavalry was posted along the banks on this bend to watch, guard and report. Near where the river approached nearest to the Shelbyville road on that road, was a grove of timber with thick underbrush, while the land below that, including headquarters, was all open land. Above this grove was timber and brush for nearly a mile, and then an occasional small clearing, with two dwelling houses a mile above the grove, both being between the road and the river. In this grove on the road, was established a picket post, guarded by a company of the 5th Iowa. As soon as headquarters were fixed, Colonel Capron ordered the writer (Lieutenant W. L. Sanford) to select 25 picked men from his company, "I," and from Company "C," and relieve the Iowa company at the picket post in the grove, east of headquarters, and hold the post against any attack that might be made, and to scout well and regularly the road above the post. The importance of this post will be understood when it is known that this post now was the extreme left of Schofield's whole army, as Capron's brigade was the left flank command; and above this post the river could be forded in many places, besides the bridge crossing at Shelbyville above. And it was now well known that Forrest's cavalry was pressing eastward to find a crossing. The men selected by the writer to guard this all-important post were, from Company "I," the following: Lieutenant Wm. H. Puckett, Sergeant David Clare, Sergeant Thomas Featherson, Wm. B. Clair, Ed. Patterson, Wm. E. McCready, David E. Rice, Richard Fouke, Thomas Perrine, James Fair, Benjamin F. Puckett, George Klassy, Wm. C. Hibbs, George Burger, and Hobart Martin; and from Company "C" the following: John Bresner, Simeon Graves, John Weller, Thomas K. Moore, Andrew McCormick, Thomas J. Patterson, Robert Russell, Wm. B. Shields, Patrick Tway, and Wm. Wayman. This small band of men performed a service that day that entitles them to a bright page in history. The infantry were all posted near Columbia. Cox's division holding the fords just above and near to Columbia. Hatch's division had just been reinforced by a number of cavalry regiments. Three of his regiments were sent below Columbia; the rest of his division was assigned the river, from the position of Cox's division, up to near Huey's mills, where General Croxton's brigade, now temporarily assigned to Johnson's division, was posted. It was now well known that Forrest was seeking an opportunity to cross the river and fall in the rear of Schofield's army. All the cavalry were ordered to keep a close watch, and resist any attempt of the enemy to cross. Our brigade on the river bank was engaged almost constantly from the middle of the forenoon until night, with a strong cavalry force that strove hard to effect a crossing. Schofield had moved his forces from Columbia to the north bank of the river, on the night of November 27th (see pages 1086, 1088 and 1106); but this was all unknown to us. There were various estimates of the distance from our position on the Lewisburg pike to Columbia, but probably the most correct was 7 miles from the pike to Huey's mills, and 7 miles from that point to Columbia, or 14 miles from our position to Columbia.

Capron says: "I immediately commenced what I considered the most judicious disposition of my troops to meet the requirements of my instructions, which comprehended not only the careful guarding of all these crossings, but the scouring of the country opposite my front. Also to watch and report any movement of the enemy."

Lieutenant Patten, 8th Michigan Cavalry, sent by Capron with 15 men to scout on Shelbyville road three miles south of the river, found a heavy force of rebel cavalry (see page 1087). Schofield reported Hood moving eastward with design of crossing. Capron says: "My force being too much scattered for any concentrated opposition to so imposing a force, I dispatched a courier with full explanation of the condition of affairs in my front, and asked for reinforcements. On the morning of 28th Colonel Israel Garrard, of 7th Ohio Cavalry, reported with his regiment to me. Colonel Garrard being the senior officer, I proposed to him to take command. This he declined to do, as his orders were to support me. My disposition of troops was explained to him, which he approved." Capron says: "One company of the 7th Ohio was strung along the bank of the river from the crossing of the pike up to my headquarters. To the balance of the 7th Ohio, under Colonel Garrard, was assigned the protection of our headquarters and of our rear." There were rumors of parties of the enemy's cavalry prowling the country north of the river. The concentration of the enemy upon our front, both at the ford crossing and the one below, guarded by Major Young's command, became more apparent as the day progressed. At 2:30 p. m. Major Young dispatched to Colonel Capron: "The enemy have appeared on my front across the river in force equal to a brigade at least. A report this moment received of a heavy column moving up the river, marching by fours, bugles blowing." Shortly after this, Capron dispatched to General Wilson that a force sent across the river (referred to before) had been driven in, closely followed by the enemy, who charged spiritedly upon Major Young's position, and were handsomely repulsed. This report General Wilson sent to Schofield carelessly worded so as to read: "Colonel Capron reports at 11:20 a. m. his force driven back from south side of the river, by a heavy force of the enemy (see page 1111)). He is now fighting them across the river." And General Schofield in reporting to General Thomas, repeats the error in still more deceptive language. He says: "The enemy was crossing in force a short distance this side of the Lewisburg pike at noon today, and had driven our cavalry back across the river and the pike, at the same time." (See page 1107).

General Stanley also makes the same error, and that it was an error we need only quote from General Forrest's report (see page 753): "At 11 o'clock at night, I received a dispatch from General Buford (who commanded the division which we fought across the river that day), informing me that the enemy had made such a stubborn resistance to his crossing that he could not join the command until the morning of the 29th."

The truth is that none of Capron's brigade, except scouting detachments sent out, were across on the south side of the river that day, and as to our stubborn resistance to Buford's division that day, not only did the enemy acknowledge it, but Generals Johnson and Wilson and Schofield all acknowledge it in reports, as we shall show in proper time. At 3:30 Capron reported: "There is a heavy force of infantry and cavalry pressing us at the crossing of the Lewisburg pike. They are massing on our left, probably too strong for us. Will hold them if possible."

On page 1122, General Wilson to General Johnson: "Direct Colonel Harrison to hold the crossings of Duck river in his front, as long as possible, and be ready to support him with Croxton's and Garrard's brigades. You had better move Croxton's at once, who will assume command until you arrive. Keep me fully advised." This order reveals another error. It appears that Colonel Harrison had been ordered to take command of Capron's brigade, which he did a day or two after, when Colonel Capron left, but on the 28th of November he did *not*, but Genereral Wilson supposed he had. This order to Johnson was not obeyed, either by Johnson in taking command, or in the sending of Croxton's brigade. Johnson's report shows, that though he received this order shortly after 1 p. m., and he did move, and it took him until after dark to reach Rally hill, a number of miles in our rear. So far from supporting Capron in any manner, though both Generals Johnson and Wilson knew that the enemy crossed the river below us in strong force soon after noon, neither one of them ever notified Colonel Capron of this movement of the enemy, but left his command to be annihilated, and hurriedly retreated with their own commands, without making any resistance of consequence. The official reports abundantly prove what we here declare.

General Johnson had asked Colonel Capron to send a detachment to guard a crossing ten miles below him. Colonel Capron replied that he could not possibly spare the men, and that the point was near General Hatch's position. At 3:40 p. m. Capron sent to headquarters the information reported by Major Young, that "the enemy are engaging me across the river at Hardison's ford, and also at Morris' ford, a short distance below the Lewisburg pike, by at least a brigade. He also shows a column moving up." Capron also reported (see page 1124): "4:20 p. m. Large columns of infantry can be seen on the opposite side of the river, moving toward Shelbyville. Heavy skirmishing still continues in my front." Again: "Just at this time the firing upon Major Young's position slackened to some extent, and increasing upon Major Beers, I

FIRST LIEUTENANT Wm. H. PUCKETT, Company I

ordered forward a company of the 5th Iowa, which had been held in reserve. It was Buford's division of Forrest's cavalry that now confronted us." Again Capron's memoirs say: "Up to this time nothing had been heard from General Hatch's command on our right toward Columbia, but rumors were rife that some disaster had befallen them, and they had been driven back, but as no heavy firing had been heard in that direction, these rumors were not heeded, as it was believed that the crossing of Hood's main army would have met such a vigorous resistance from General Hatch, and the other commands below, as would have made itself known without the aid of couriers."

In order to the better understanding of the very perilous position of our command at this time, we will now examine the position and movements of the various forces of Schofield's army at this time, as well as the movements of Hood's army as shown by the official reports, all of which movements, except what occurred in our immediate presence, were unknown to Colonel Capron or to any of his command. Schofield withdrew his whole force at Columbia to the north bank of the river, during the night of 27th (see Schofield's report, page 341). General Cox reports his making resistance to the crossing of the river at his position just above Columbia (see page 402). General Hatch made no report that we know of, and being then under the direct command of General Wilson, all his movements were controlled by General Wilson, the cavalry corps commander. His report (see pages 557 and 558), shows the positions of Hatch, Croxton and Capron's commands, as we have given them; and says that at noon, the pickets near Huey's mills gave notice of the concentration of rebel forces near there, with evident design of crossing, but his report says nothing about any preparation to resist this crossing, nor is there in all the official reports any account of any such resistance having been made, nor even any statement that Colonel Capron, above that point was notified of the crossing of the enemy, though Wilson says: "The pickets at Huey's mills were soon driven in and the rebels immediately began crossing. At 2 p. m. I sent a dispatch to Major General Schofield, notifying him of the enemy's movements, informing him that I should endeavor to concentrate my force at Hurt's crossroads." This point was six or seven miles in the rear of Capron's position. Wilson adds: "Colonel T. J. Harrison, 8th Indiana Cavalry, had already been sent by General Johnson to the brigade at the Lewisburg crossing, with orders to hold the enemy as long as possible at the river." Again: "Colonel Harrison, however, had not reached his brigade, but having been posted by Colonel Capron, it held on as long as possible." The only recorded attempt of General Wilson to aid Capron's command was his order to Johnson to reinforce Capron's (or Harrison's) brigade, as before related. General Johnson in his report (see pages 597 and 598), is thus referred to, and described: "Croxton established a strong picket at Huey's mill, which lay directly south of his camp. On the morning of that day it became apparent, from the reports of my pickets, that the enemy were making preparations to force the passage of the river at Huey's mills, at the Lewisburg pike, and at many intermediate fords. At 1 p. m. of this day, under orders from General Wilson, I moved with Croxton's brigade for Hurt's house on the Lewisburg pike, at the same time sending word to Colonel Harrison, whom I then supposed to be in command of my first brigade (Capron's), to fall back to that point. The head of my column reached the Lewisburg turnpike just after nightfall."

The official records do not show a report such as General Johnson here describes, but they *do* show an order from General Wilson (see page 1122), sent at 1:10 p. m., and received at 2:10 p. m., to reinforce Capron's brigade immediately with Croxton's brigade, and to go himself and take command. Relative to the order from Johnson to Capron referred to above, Capron in his memoirs speaks of receiving this order after 7 p. m., long after he had fallen back, and states that it was dated after 3 p. m. As to any explanations of the inefficient management of the cavalry forces under Generals Wilson and Johnson, on the 28th day of November, 1864, when the cavalry were under such explicit orders to oppose the crossing of the river by any portion of Hood's army, and when the safety of our army so much depended upon the heroic resistance by our cavalry, I am thankful that I am not appointed to defend the course of our cavalry commanders, for I can find no justification of their course, in any of the official records, not even in their own reports. Having given the relative positions of Schofield's various forces, showing the extreme peril to which our brigade was exposed by the withdrawal of all our forces on our right, and the equal exposure on our unprotected left, all of which, except the left flank exposure, we were then entirely ignorant of, we will describe the operations on the north side of the river in rotation as they occurred. We, at the picket post on the Shelbyville road above Capron's headquarters, were in position to know positively of the rotation of the important events in relation to fighting on the north side of the river, being the first command attacked, and being in position to plainly see all the succeeding events as they occurred in our rear, until dusk. The ground between our post and headquarters, and in the front of headquarters to the river, being open ground, and as our observations are perfectly corroborated by the official reports of the rebel commanders, we have no hesitancy in saying, that as far as we describe our observations, we positively *know*, that we are correct. We have said that our post was in a concealed position in a grove, and that a timbered tract lay above the post. Near our post there were two tracks, probably five rods apart, the farthest north being an old, and now, unused track. Both of these tracks were defended by strong rail barricades. Just to the north of the old track lay a mass of high rocks, covering several acres; impassable except through a narrow and winding cow path, which led through it. As stated, we were ordered to reconnoiter the road above regularly, and as we were entirely unprotected on the left, and the enemy were known to be moving in strong force in that direction, the importance of this order, which was faithfully executed, can easily be seen. Both myself and Lieutenant Puckett, whom I consulted, were convinced that our army would soon be compelled to fall back, and were apprehensive, from various causes, that the army below us was moving, and knowing that the wings of an army, in such movements, were very liable to disaster, we were awake to the necessity for great caution and prompt action when needed. About 4 p. m. a squad of our foragers came dashing through our post, saying that they had been pursued on the

Shelbyville road above us, by about 40 rebel cavalry. This was the first positive information that we had that any of Forrest's cavalry were on our side of the river. Colonel Capron was immediately informed, and soon a force of 50 men of the 7th Ohio Cavalry, passed through our post, and up the Shelbyville road to reconnoiter. Consulting with Lieutenant Puckett, we both deemed it prudent to be personally better informed of the true situation above, and leaving the post in command of a faithful and vigilant officer, Sergeant David S. Clare, of Company "I," we mounted our horses and proceeded up the road some distance in rear of the 7th Ohio detachment, making it an especial point to examine carefully for roads or any passages that led to the river by which the enemy might cross the river, and into the Shelbyville road.

About a mile above our post were two dwellings not far apart, both being between our road and the river with lanes from these dwellings to our road, and perhaps roads from the dwellings to the river and across. Intending to investigate more thoroughly on our return, we passed above, about a mile, and then returned, and when within a hundred yards of one of these lanes two troopers with blue overcoats rode out of the lane, and passed toward our post. I supposed them to be some of our foragers; but Lieutenant Puckett declared that they were rebels. This seemed improbable to me, not alone from the blue overcoats they wore, but mainly for the readiness with which they went toward our post.. They kept about the same distance ahead, and began acting suspiciously; at one time turning in their saddles and preparing to fire upon us. As I then had on a faded officer's blouse, something the color of a rebel coat, I supposed that they mistook us for rebels and called upon them not to fire. They then continued on, but still acted strangely, until they finally wheeled and fired, and then dashed down the road. But we determined whether friends or foes, we would give them a chase, and drawing our revolvers, we pursued at breakneck speed down that rocky road. All doubts regarding their identity was solved when within a half mile of our post, they suddenly dashed into the woods at the point where the two tracks came together. Not only did we now *know* that they were rebels, but we also knew that a force of them were in those woods; doubtless intending the capture of our post. With these impressions we were not inclined to lessen our speed down the road, as the danger of the capture of our post was imminent, and the thoughts of imprisonment in Andersonville—a fate more dreaded than death on the battlefield—was as much a factor in the impulse of our movement as was the duty of warning and protecting our post. We had passed but a short distance beyond the point where these troopers had left our road, when we were fired upon from seemingly every tree and rock, until we neared our picket post. How many shots were fired at us we could only imagine, as we did not stop to count noses, having just then more important business on hand. We then supposed that we had run the gauntlet of a rebel battalion, and deemed ourselves fortunate that with singing bullets before us and behind us as we swiftly passed them, that neither ourselves nor our horses had received a scratch, and no injury except a slight retarding of the flow of blood to our faces, which our comrades declared were as pale as our mother's dish cloths. We never knew whether this compliment was intended for ourselves, or for our mother's dish cloths, and indeed we had no time to ask. Our comrades having heard the firing above the post, had no doubt of either the death or capture of their lieutenants, but the brave Sergeant Clare had his men in position and ready for the charge the enemy immediately made on the post, by dashing down the old track. A ready and well aimed volley from the boys at the post killed their leader, a Captain Wharton, of the 3d Texas Cavalry, as papers in his pockets showed. There is no doubt but many of their number were wounded, for they were driven back in disorder, and there were a number of our command who were crack marksmen. Captain Wharton was immediately brought in, still breathing mechanically, but unconscious. Surgeon Wilson was summoned, but nothing could be done. Colonel Capron sent up a company of the 7th Ohio Cavalry to strengthen the post, as we anticipated another attack from above. The following is the rebel account of this attack, which corroborates our statement that it was the first attack on the north side:

Brigadier-General Lawrence S. Ross, C. S. Army, commanding one of General Hood's brigades of Forrest's

ed forward the enemy rose up in heavy force and a yell charged our lines, cutting off my communica- with General Stoneman. When nearly surrounded s forced to fall back to the horses, which created some usion among my men, as the enemy followed close 1 us. So closely did the enemy press my command y of the men were unable to mount their horses; the ıy, capturing and mounting the horses, repeatedly ged my rear as I continued to retreat. I made every t to communicate with General Stoneman, but my officers were cut off and unable to report. I have ² learned from one of General Stoneman's staff officers o escaped) that General Stoneman made a strong t to communicate with me but was unable to do so. tenant-Colonel E. Mix, of the 8th Michigan Cavalry, came up and reported that General Stoneman had ₂ndered."
ompkins says: "The proposition was made to move ıe right and pass the enemy. He (Stoneman) said ould not move the whole command without being dis- red. He could make no resistance when pursued; he ld have the outside track, with an enemy fresh, to ue. His men would be broken up in detachments and dered as some had been on the 29th; he would not se any from going, nor order them. If the enemy ılted and broke our lines, do the best we could, but ir him, he saw no other way for the lives of the men to ₂spected but for him to surrender, which he would do as a last resort. By this means all the detachments that eave had five hours the start." This description indi- ₃ a council of war which Colonel Smith more fully ribes as follows: "About 4 p. m. General Stoneman, taff and most of his brigade commanders held a con- tion, and it was thought best to make a desperate t to cut our way out to our right rear, as this seemed ₃ the weakest part of the enemy's lines. Just as the ral had given his directions for this movement, and respective officers were starting to their commands, memy opened a battery on our right and left flank and inued their fire from the one in front, followed by meral charge. Our lines gave way and fell back. ıs ordered to a certain point to rally a line. Whilst

cavalry, in his report says (on page 769, serial 93) : Af[ter] recounting his previous movements, he speaks of cro[ss]ing the river on the morning of November 28th, and mo[v]ing on to the Shelbyville road, and says: "When near t[he] Lewisburg and Franklin pike again encountered t[he] federal cavalry. A spirited engagement ensued, beg[un] by the 3d Texas regiment, which, being dispatched to [at]tack a train of wagons moving in direction of Frankl[in] succeeded in reaching the pike, but was there met by [a] superior force of Yankees and driven back."

As Captain Wharton, whom we killed, belonged to t[he] 3d Texas, and as his force *did* make the first attack a[nd] was driven back, as General Ross describes, we have co[n]clusive proof that the 3d Texas Cavalry cut us off and a[t]tacked our post, and that this was the first attack north [of] the river; but if any doubts remained they were remov[ed] by the perfect agreement of what we soon after saw wi[th] the continued account of General Ross. Although [we] were still expecting another attack from above, immed[i]ately after the arrival of the Ohio company spoken of a[nd] before they had dismounted, we heard in the rear of Ca[p]ron's headquarters, on the pike toward Franklin, first [a] light volley, then a second much heavier, then loud a[nd] continued reports of fire arms as if in a fierce engagemen[t] which was soon followed by the sweeping in of a mass [of] gray coats, as if the whole southern confederacy were co[n]centrating at our headquarters and moving toward t[he] river. To us it appeared that not only were Colonel Capr[on] and headquarters captured, but doubtless our whole br[i]gade, and we even feared that all of Schofield's army w[as] gone. The following is General Ross' continued accoun[t.] "Seeing this (the repulse of the 3d Texas), I had Colon[el] Hawkins to bring up his regiment—the Legion—to t[he] assistance of the 3d, and ordered a charge, which was mad[e] in gallant style and resulted in forcing the Yankees fro[m] the field in confusion, and with the loss of several priso[n]ers and the colors of the 7th Ohio Cavalry." This was t[he] attack on headquarters that we saw and have describe[d.] General Ross continues: "In the meanwhile Colon[el] Wharton, with the 6th Texas, charged into the pike to t[he] right of where the 3d and the Legion were engaged, ca[p]turing an entire company of the 7th Ohio Cavalry, thre[e] stands of colors, several wagons loaded with ordnance, and a considerable number of horses, with their equipments."

A considerable portion of this account we know to be correct, as it was closely connected with our observations and movements. When the attack was made on headquarters I was in consultation with the lieutenant in command of the company of the 7th Ohio, sent up to reinforce us, as to the best disposition of his company to aid in defense of the post against another expected attack from above. While so engaged we heard the clash of arms in rear of headquarters, and without waiting for a word of consultation further, the lieutenant wheeled his company and dashed toward headquarters, with apparent design of cutting through the enemy's lines. As long as our picket post served a purpose as such, it was our duty to remain, and when soon after it was no longer useful as a picket post as the enemy in strong force were in our rear, still, though surrounded, we were so well concealed that our safest course was to remain where we were, in the hope that the movements of the enemy might open up a better opportunity for our escape, as the enemy were now all around us. At this moment occurred the movement just described by General Ross; the pursuit of this company of the 7th Ohio, which came dashing back upon our post with a whole regiment in pursuit. Concealment was now no longer possible, and ordering my men to mount I pointed out the path through the mass of rocks, the only avenue that seemed unguarded, and we dashed into the woods, just as it was growing dusk. The pursuing rebels were so close behind us, and our passage through the mass of rocks so slow, that two of our horses were killed, and several more were wounded, and four of our men were captured, and with them our company flag, which was doubtless one of those described as captured by General Ross. Without doubt the company described by Ross as captured was the company sent to reinforce us. Two of our men who were captured, William E. McCready and Hobart Martin, escaped soon after, and Wm. Clair and Ed. Patterson were taken to Columbia and escaped from them in less than two weeks after. As to my command, after entering the woods and passing the enemy's lines, we did not dare approach the Franklin pike, as we knew that the enemy were in possession of our headquarters and the pike in the rear, we could not tell how far; and we had no doubt that our brigade was captured and we feared that Schofield's whole army was cut off. There seemed no chance for us, but to strive to reach Franklin, 22 miles in the rear, and to do this we must keep off from the pike, striking through the woods, and on byroads parallel to the pike. Pursuing parties of the enemy were thrown off the track by our calling at houses as we passed, and asking the course taken by the Yankees whom we said we had whipped at the river. We pressed guides, generally boys, each of whom guided us as far as they knew, until we were half way to Franklin, when for want of any road or path we were compelled to go on the pike, reaching Franklin at 1 a. m. of November 29th. Here we heard that Schofield was pressing back toward Franklin; and early in the morning we retraced our steps to find our brigade if it were not captured.

We will now describe the operations of the rest of Capron's command, beginning with Capron's report as made in his memoirs. He says: "Later in the day, perhaps at 4:30 p. m., amidst the greatest excitement, and in momentary expectations of a more vigorous effort of the enemy to force his way across the river, Lieutenant Miller, of the 14th cavalry, rode up to me and reported that, returning from a scout on our right rear, in the direction of Columbia, he had run upon a force of the enemy's cavalry, and had ascertained that Hood had effected the crossing of Duck river, and that General Schofield had actually abandoned his hold upon Columbia during the previous night, followed up closely by Hood's army, and that fighting was then progressing seven miles in our rear; that Hatch and the other commands along the river between us and Columbia, had been forced back; and General Wilson could not be heard from." This report of Lieutenant Miller is corroborated by the reports of Wilson and Johnson, and was the last official report made to Colonel Capron by any officers of his brigade, as Colonel Harrison assumed command of the brigade immediately, as had been previously arranged, and Colonel Capron returned home. We have no remembrance of seeing him again, and we never reported to him the operations of this day, and we believe no other officers reported to him, so that his further account of these movements, as described in his memoirs, must have been mainly given from his own personal observation, hastily made at a time of great excitement, and little wonder if some mistakes were made.

Up to the time of the attack upon headquarters, Capron's account of all these movements is perfectly corroborated by the official reports, but in his subsequent account, he makes a few errors, owing to his want of information that would have corrected them. Referring to Lieutenant Miller's report, he truthfully says: "This, of course, confirmed all the previous rumors of the day, reaching us through resident citizens, and was the first reliable information I had received of the evacuation of Columbia by General Schofield, or of the retiring of General Hatch's command from our right. It was not in that direction we were expecting the enemy; our attention at the time being fully taken up with him in front. It was soon ascertained that we had been left without a word of caution even, deep down in a bend of that river, confronted by one of Hood's best divisions, which had been successfully kept from crossing a man, up to this time, then close upon the night; with Forrest's cavalry shoved in between us and the balance of General Wilson's command, as far in our rear as Rally hill; in fact completely abandoned by General Wilson; cut off and surrounded."

Colonel Capron's account here given is perfectly confirmed by the official reports of our commanders. He further says: "In this critical condition of affairs, with night approaching, I deemed it prudent to confer with Colonel Garrard. I at once dispatched a messenger requesting to see him without delay at the front. I made known to him the condition of affairs; showed him my instructions, which were to prevent, at all hazards, the crossing of Duck river on my front by the enemy. In the absence of any official order to retire, it was thought both by Colonel Garrard and myself, that although the safety of my whole command would be imperiled by remaining, to withdraw from our position and allow the heavy force already concentrated here to cross and fall upon Schofield's rear and flank, at that moment engaged with the enemy, would prove most disastrous to our army. It was therefore determined to hold our position until forced from it, or until darkness would allow us to retire unobserved by the enemy. Shortly after this interview Colonel Garrard having had no more than time to reach his command, a courier was observed approaching me upon a full run, bearing the intelligence that our pickets had been driven in on the Columbia road, and that the enemy were closing in upon us from every direction. I at once ordered up a company of the 5th Iowa cavalry which had been held in reserve, and directed them to follow me. On reaching my headquarters I found Colonel Garrard hotly engaged with a force of Forrest's cavalry. It was then in the dusk of the evening, and the flash of the weapons of the contending forces seemed to encircle the camp." This was the attack upon headquarters which we and General Ross have described as occurring immediately after the attack upon our picket post. The sun was just setting, and we could plainly see the gleam of saber flashes. Capron continues: "Not one moment was to be lost in dispatching couriers to the various commands along the river bank, notifying them to fall back upon headquarters, hoping at that moment of time to be able to hold that as a rallying point. Just at this stage of the excitement our ambulances, which had been started back on the Franklin pike at the first alarm, came down the turnpike on a full run, having been intercepted near Rally hill. The charge of Colonel Garrard, having forced back the enemy, opened the way for another trial, in which they were successful in slipping out safely." Now follows a description in which Capron was wholly misinformed in relation to the command named. He says: "Immediately upon this a confused mass of our pickets from our left up the river were driven in upon us. Not one drew rein, but charged past us, overthrowing everything in their way, and with them out went every man with the exception of myself, staff officers, and a few orderlies." We absolutely and positively assert that not a man from our picket post went in any manner to headquarters at that time, nor did any leave our post except as we have described, after Capron's headquarters was in the hands of the enemy, and it would have been folly then to have gone there, yet our post is the one referred to. That Colonel Capron really saw such a disorderly retreat is true without doubt, but if it was not the company of the 7th

Ohio cavalry that came to reinforce us, then it might have been the company guarding at the bend of the river, and if neither of these, all we positively know about it is, that it was none of our picket post, and this we could prove by every man of that number who is now living. The following we think are now living: Lieutenant William H. Pucket, Nora, Ill.; William E. McCready, Mount Morris. Ill.; David S. Clare, Ogden City, Utah. Capron continues: "The force coming down the river on our left probably crossed the river at Shelbyville, and, charging down along the pike and river bank, followed up our retreating pickets, until they struck the company of the 7th Ohio, when they held up long enough to capture the entire company." Colonel Capron evidently here attempted to describe what he could not possibly see from his position, and he got his description badly tangled up. The force that came down from the left was the 3d Texas, and they did not cross at Shelbyville, as Ross' report shows. They evidently swam the river, as Captain Wharton's condition showed, and as to following the pickets down in the direction described by Capron, was impossible. "Charging down along the pike and river bank," as Capron describes, could only be done by charging along the pike from Capron's headquarters along the banks of the bend of the river, for in every other part of the river its course was from east to west, while the direction of the pike was north and south. We spend time in making these corrections, for any reflections unjustly cast upon that brave party of men makes us perfectly indignant; although we believe our Colonel made these errors through ignorance of the facts, being unadvised by any official reports, and the movements entirely beyond the power of his personal observations. General Ross says of the later operations: "It was now after night and very dark. The enemy had disappeared from our front in the direction of Franklin, but before establishing camp it was thought prudent to ascertain if any force had been cut off and yet remained between us and the river. Colonel Hawkins was therefore ordered up the pike with his regiment to reconnoiter, and had proceeded but a short distance before he was met by a brigade of federal cavalry. An exciting fight ensued, lasting about half an hour, when the enemy, having much the larger force, succeeded in passing by us, receiving, as he did so, a severe fire into his flanks."

On page 604, serial 93, begins the report of Major J. Morris Young, commanding 5th Iowa cavalry, describing the movements of Capron's brigade, after Capron himself had been cut off, as he himself has described. Major Young says: "I have the honor to report the following action of my regiment and others temporarily under my command during the evening and night of November 28th, 1864. The 5th Iowa, under my command, was disposed by order of Colonel Capron commanding the first brigade of the sixth division, cavalry command, in different positions on the north side of Duck river, above and below the crossing of the turnpike, running from Franklin to Lewisburg, to guard the fords and prevent the enemy from crossing to this side, which was successfully performed in my command and front. At 5 p. m. my patrols and pickets reported the enemy in force, and Colonel Capron, commanding the brigade gone. Hastily withdrawing my regiment, except Company "A," which was posted four miles above, with the enemy between us, I formed the 5th Iowa in charging column on the pike, and was in the act of giving the command "Forward" when the other regiments of the brigade, consisting of the 8th Michigan, 14th and 16th Illinois, came in successively, much to my surprise, for I had supposed them gone out with Colonel Capron, and (they) reported the enemy closing in from every direction. I made the following disposition of my forces as hastily as possible. The 8th Michigan in line dismounted to the left of, and perpendicular to the head of the 5th Iowa column; the 16th Illinois, disposed in like manner on the right; the led horses of both regiments to follow up at a safe distance in their respective rears. The 14th Illinois was placed (mounted) in column of fours, to the left and rear of the 8th Michigan, and parallel to the 5th Iowa, which was in column on the pike. The left was most exposed to a countercharge of the enemy, who were known to be in heavy force on that flank. As soon as the enemy's fire was drawn, the dismounted men were to immediately fall back, mount and follow out the 5th Iowa cavalry, which was to go through with sabers. In fifteen minutes these dispositions being completed, the command was given "Forward." In fifteen minutes more we struck the enemy in line, barricaded and posted in the outhouses and buildings just evacuated by Colonel Capron. We received their fire, and instantly sounded the "charge," riding them down and scattering them in all directions. At 10 p. m. I reported the brigade entire to Major-General Wilson. In this charge, which was most gallantly executed, reflecting great credit on all the troops engaged, I do not think our entire loss out of fifteen hundred brought through safe, was more than thirty killed, wounded, and missing. Having been superseded immediately by Colonel Capron, who had preceded me some two hours, I have no means of ascertaining definitely our loss. The injury inflicted on the enemy must have been considerable. The groans and the cries of the wounded as we rode, cut or shot them down, could be heard distinctly above the noise and din of the charge. Permit me to add in closing, the fact of the growing confidence amongst our troops, that good cavalry never can be captured." This is doubtless an accurate report of these operations, except in the estimate of the force brought through. We do not know the strength of the 7th Ohio present that day, but as they went out with Colonel Capron they were not a part of the force brought through by Major Young. We have before shown that the official reports show the strength of the 5th Iowa when it joined Capron's brigade three days before was five hundred. Capron's brigade two weeks before was eight hundred, but when we reached Columbia on the retreat was reduced to six hundred or less. At least two companies of the 14th, and one of the 5th Iowa, were on detached duty, so that Major Young's force that charged through could not have exceeded one thousand. On page 1182 is shown report of November 30th, which confirms our estimate.

Major Young was a gallant and skillful officer. and deserves great credit, and his command that night showed the greatest gallantry and implicit faith in their commander, and perfect obedience to orders. His report is brief, precise, and truthful, as is shown by official reports and by accounts of associate officers and other comrades.

We make a few extracts from communications published in the National Tribune by Major H. C. Connelly and Lieutenant William M. Moore of Company "L," 14th Illinois Cavalry, concerning this affair. Connelly, after describing the situation as recorded, says: "The left (where the 14th was posted) was the most exposed (Major Young also says so). When all was ready, it now being dark, the command moved off. The shrill notes of the bugle sounded the charge; the enemy was attacked and cut to pieces at all points. I shall always remember the groans and moans of the wounded and dying. With the 14th, I was on the left flank. In the charge some hitch or break occurred in the 5th Iowa column. An officer of the 8th Michigan sang out: "Why don't the 5th Iowa advance? If it is not going to advance let it make room for those who will." The 5th, however, moved off, when the whole brigade came up to the work gallantly and charged out successfully. The confederates broke and fled precipitately, taking cover in a ravine on our left flank; they poured a terrible volley at us. In the darkness their aim was inaccurate; they fired too high, and we escaped, what, to us of the 14th, might have been a fearful slaughter. But few of our men were wounded. From the terrific noise made by their officers in trying to rally their men, it seemed as though the Confederates had two to our one. In leading and conducting this charge Major Young showed fine generalship."

Colonel Capron in his memoirs calls this "a gallant charge," and speaks in high praise of the officers and men.

Lieutenant Moore, referring to Connelly's published report says: "I was in command of Company 'L,' 14th Illinois, and I believe Captain Connelly of my company (since major) was in command of a battalion. Some one reported that Captain Jenkins, commanding the 14th, was shot. Captain Connelly rode along the regiment encouraging the men to do their duty. When the bugle sounded the 'charge' he was in the thickest of the fight at the head of the regiment. Courage like he exhibited deserves to be recognized."

General Johnson, on page 598, says: "The 5th Iowa and the greater part of the 14th and 16th Illinois cavalry, from whom Colonel Capron had been cut off by the enemy, came into camp, having charged through the superior force of the enemy, which had interposed itself between them and the rest of the command." General Wilson also speaks of this affair, page 558. A close study of all the Union and Confederate reports, with a full understanding of the relative positions and forces of the two opposing armies on the night of November 28th, 1864, lends to the following statements and premises of Colonel Capron in his memoirs, not only a strong probability, but almost a certainty. He says: "There is little doubt that General Schofield's fears, expressed in his general report, of the enemy endeavoring to reach Spring Hill in advance of him, and thus cut off his retreat, or strike him in the flank at Duck river, or both, as he had already forced his cavalry between General Wilson and his command, and cut off all communication between them, might have been fully realized had this brigade withdrawn all opposition to Buford's division at the crossing of Duck river (as all the rest of Wilson's cavalry did) when Hatch and Croxton withdrew from our right, as there would have been ample time for him to have joined his force with Forrest's command already in position, and accomplished exactly what General Schofield feared." See General Schofield's report of campaign, page 341, in which he says: "Wilson reported to him that the enemy's cavalry had forced a crossing at Huey's mill, 5 miles above Columbia, from which a road leads into the Franklin pike at Spring Hill." The crossing by the enemy was about 1 p. m., November 28th; this is what both Wilson and Johnson report. Forrest says (page 752) that he crossed with part of a regiment on the morning of the 28th; Chalmers' division also crossed, but at 11 o'clock at night he received a dispatch from General Buford (whom we kept from crossing) informing him that the enemy had made such a stubborn resistance to his crossing that he could not join the command until the morning of the 29th. Nor is this all. Brigadier-General Lawrence S. Ross, commanding a brigade of Jackson's division, says that his command crossed on the morning of 28th, and Jackson's division fell in our rear as recorded. We not only prevented Buford from crossing, but detained Jackson's division as well. Forrest says (page 753) : "I ordered Jackson's division to move along the Lewisburg pike toward Franklin until he developed the enemy." This shows the presence of Jackson's whole division in our rear. Again he says: "After waiting a short time for my troops to close up, I moved rapidly toward Spring Hill." This referred to Chalmers' division, of which just before he said: "Brigadier-General Armstrong notified me that he had struck the enemy, when I ordered him not to press too vigorously until I reached his flank with Chalmers' division." This shows that Forrest, with Chalmers' division, after waiting many hours for his other two divisions to join him, pressed on to the Franklin pike. The hours he had to wait would have enabled him to have reached Spring Hill on the night of the 28th, if not before. Both Schofield and Stanley in their reports say that Stanley, with two divisions, was on the morning of the 29th pushed forward to Spring Hill, where he arrived at 11:30 a. m. (see page 113), where the enemy's cavalry was then collecting. Hood says (page 652), after speaking of Forrest's crossing: "Early on the morning of the 29th, with Stewart's and Cheatham's corps, and Johnson's division of Lee's corps (nearly his whole infantry force) the troops moved in light marching order. * * * My object being to turn the enemy's flank by marching rapidly on roads parallel to the Columbia and Franklin pike, at or near Spring Hill, and to cut off that portion of the enemy at or near Columbia." Again: "The cavalry became engaged near Spring Hill about midday." With Hood marching rapidly with nearly his whole force on a road parallel to the Franklin pike, on which General Schofield was moving, and nearly abreast of Schofield, so near at least that the advance of his infantry joined with Chalmers' division of cavalry in the battle at Spring Hill, it is not difficult to surmise what would have been the result had Forrest's *whole* force of cavalry reached Spring Hill hours before, as they might easily have done had not our brigade held Buford's at bay at the crossing of Lewisburg pike, at the same time also detaining Jackson's division in their vain attempt to capture our brigade. We will now give other proofs that we fought these divisions at that point until the night of the 28th.

General Wilson, in his report (see page 145) says: "The cavalry (rebel) began crossing about noon at Davis ford,

LIEUTENANT WM. M. MOORE
COMPANY L, 14TH ILLINOIS CAVALRY

near Huey's mill, but could not get over at Hardison's on the pike till Capron and Garrard's brigades were struck in flank and rear by the rebels at Rally Hill." General Johnson (on page 598) says the same thing, and highly praises the charge made by our brigade that night, when surrounded at the post they had defended all day. Colonel Capron in his memoirs quotes from a history by General Cox as follows: "General Cox in his history of the Nashville campaign (page 72) was led into some errors when describing the occurrences on Duck river. He says: 'The National cavalry were broken into smaller detachments, part of them well out toward Shelbyville (that was correct). The nearest to the infantry being part of Capron's brigade at Rally Hill on the Lewisburg pike, where a branch turnpike turns off to Spring Hill.' Instead of this being the nearest to the infantry it was the farthest from it, with all the rest of the cavalry between those points. But again: 'The resistance made to Buford was so vigorous that he could not get over the river, but Jackson and Chalmers forced a crossing after a sharp skirmish, and Forrest himself does not seem to have found any resistance. He was confronted by Hatch and Croxton.'" He speaks of turning Chalmers and Jacksons divisions to the east (toward Capron's position). This would all have been correct had he stated that it was Capron's brigade that made such a vigorous resistance to Buford.

November 29th. All the cavalry fell back slowly on the Lewisburg pike, covering Schofield's right flank. Afternoon our division was sent forward, crossing the Harpeth river, two miles east of Franklin at Hugh's ford, and camped, having marched 17 miles.

November 30th. Reveille at 2 a. m. We were early in line and built barricades. Colonel Capron has now left, and was never again with us. He finally received his well-earned promotion to Brigadier-General. Colonel Thomas Harrison of the 8th Indiana cavalry is now in command of the brigade. Schofield's infantry reached Franklin, formed line, and built hastily-constructed defenses. Such disposition of the cavalry was made as would serve to prevent the flanking of Schofield, should Hood attempt to continue that movement. The disposition of cavalry was: The 5th Iowa with some other cavalry on the right, and on the left in the following rotation: Next to the infantry, first Croxton, next Hatch, and at the danger point, in case of attempted flank movement, was again placed on the extreme left Harrison's (our) brigade. Hood says in his report (see page 653), that he learned from dispatches to Schofield, captured at Spring Hill, that Schofield was instructed to hold Franklin until Thomas could fortify Nashville. So Hood determined to abandon the slower process of the flanking movement, as hitherto practiced, and concentrate his forces, and by a sudden and determined attack on Schofield's center, he hoped to crush the Union forces at Franklin, and capture all of Thomas' forces south of the Harpeth river. Forrest was ordered to attack our left, and Hood says: "If successful he was to cross the river and attack and destroy our trains, and our broken columns." Why he made no more vigorous and determined effort to attack our cavalry must have been due to the fact that he had learned throughout this campaign, in which, up to this time the fighting had nearly all been done by the cavalry, that our cavalry was entitled to proper respect; at least his efforts were feeble, and a few charges which were easily resisted and their cavalry finally forced back, comprehended the cavalry fighting. But it was different with the infantry, who, through this campaign, with the exception of a little fighting at Columbia and at Spring Hill, had enjoyed a play spell, with only an occasional tremor, lest our cavalry would not be able to prevent their being flanked by Hood; for now, by the change in Hood's tactics, they were given sufficient fighting to satisfy the most ardent desire for glory and for gore in one campaign. Such was Hood's determined effort to break Schofield's center that column after column, led by their generals in person, was dashed with fury upon his center. As each advancing column was driven back another fresh column was sent forward, charging, if possible, with increased fury. Pat Cleaburne, their best general, though a perfect gentleman in peace, was inspired in this battle with the spirit of a fury. Not satisfied with the failure of his own column, he threw himself at the head of other advancing columns, until cut down in his frenzied efforts to break our lines. The loss to Hood of the following disproportion of general officers, attests the desperate efforts of Hood: Killed, Major-General P. R. Cleaburne; Brigadier-Generals Gist, John Adams, Strahl and Granbury, and wounded, Major-General Brown; Brigadier-Generals Carter, Manigault, Quarless, Cockrell. and Scott, and Brigadier-General Gordon, captured. Twelve (some reports say thirteen) general officers lost on one side is such a disproportion to the numbers engaged as few if any battles of the world can show. Indeed few battles of the war can compare in severity with the battle of Franklin November 30th, 1864. The cavalry had before won a high reputation, and now the infantry at their first real opportunity, show equal valor. Perhaps no army, and certainly none of the war of the rebellion, is entitled to greater honor than the little army led in that campaign by Major-General John M. Schofield. Schofield's hastily constructed defenses were a feeble protection, much of the hardest fighting was done with bayonet and clubbed muskets over the breastworks; large masses of the rebel columns breaking through, but never again to fight in the rebel cause. The desperateness of the rebel efforts is attested by their loss, which was: Captured, 702; disabled, 3,800; buried on the field, 1,750; aggregate, 6,252. The Union loss was: Killed, 189; wounded, 1,033; missing, 1,104; aggregate, 2,326. The Confederates, of course, claimed the victory, as they held the ground, but it was such a victory as they would not care to repeat, for a few such victories would soon destroy a much larger army than Hood commanded. We believe that the battle of Nashville was more than half fought at Franklin. After that discouragement many deserted from their ranks, and even General Hood in his after movements indicated little more intention than to go through the motions of besieging Thomas at Nashville. Not but what there was some desperate fighting done at Nashville, for even a cowardly dog will fight when he cannot help it. The fighting began about 3:30 p. m. and lasted until after dark, skirmishing continuing until 10 o'clock at night. Under cover of darkness Schofield retired across the Harpeth river and began his retreat to Nashville, disposing his cavalry on the rear and flanks of the infantry. December 1st our brigade moved early toward the Murphy pike. We sent out parties to gather in horses and cattle. Our rear guard was attacked, but the enemy were easily repulsed; their cavalry seemed to entertain a wholesome fear of blue coats when they themselves did not wear the blue. We camped after night within 5 miles of Nashville, having marched 20 miles. We were called into line at 10 p. m. and built barricades, remained a few hours, then leaving a strong rear guard, we returned to camp about 2 a. m. of December 2d. It rained last night. We marched at 3 a. m., December 2d, to the suburbs of Nashville, fed and breakfasted. Afternoon marched through the city, crossed the Cumberland river and camped in Edgefield, having marched 9 miles.

December 3d. Reveille at daylight; slight skirmishing across the river.

Sunday, December 4th. Reveille at daylight; quietly in camp. How sweet to rest under the protecting care of Hood, who, while he generously besieged Thomas at Nashville, where he was receiving full supplies for his men; Hood, with a self-sacrificing spirit, is content to camp under God's great wall tent, the sky, and fare on "corn in the ear," sparingly doled out to his men, as our men who escaped from captivity reported. We "fared sumptuously every day" upon rations obtained from our rear, while re-inforcements were constantly being gathered to Thomas' army. There were many desertions from Hood's army. Rebeldom had staked all on the boastful promises of Hood, while many a defeat of his cavalry, and the unwelcome victory at Franklin, had convinced many of his men that the cause of secession was hopeless. This was all known to all of Thomas' men, who could see through a ladder; some, however, were despondent at being constantly driven back, and the country at large were in a tremor of excitement, in which even General Grant participated. Our men began now to take heart. They saw that the edict had gone forth to Hood: "Thus far and no farther shalt thou come, and here shalt thy proud cohorts be stayed." While with the people across the Ohio, the old adage: " 'Tis distance lends enchantment to the view," seemed to be reversed in this case. The level-headed Grant, perhaps the only time in his military career, exhibited signs of being "panic stricken." His messages to General Thomas exhibited undue alarm. In serial 94, page 70, Grant says, December 6th: "Attack Hood at once and wait no longer for a remount of your cavalry. There is great danger of delay, resulting in a campaign back to the Ohio river." On page 84, December 7th, Grant said to Stanton: "You probably saw my order to Thomas to attack. If he does not do it immediately I would recommend superseding him by Schofield, leaving Thomas subordinate." Page 97, December 8th, he says to Thomas: "It looks to me evident the enemy are trying to cross the Cumberland river, and are scattered. Why not attack at once? By all means avoid the contingency of a foot race, to see which, you or Hood, can beat to the Ohio river." To these urgent appeals Thomas, who knew that every day was strengthening his army and weakening Hood's, and that there was not the least danger of a foot race to the Ohio river, always replied that as soon as he could remount six thousand cavalry to cover his flanks he would move out against Hood. He made every exertion to obtain horses, but so many of his cavalry had been dismounted, and so few horses could be secured, that the work was slow, and as long as every day added strength to us, while it weakened Hood, he saw no cause for worry. On page 114 Grant says to Stanton: "Please telegraph orders relieving him (Thomas) at once and placing General Schofield in command." This was December 9th. On the same page (114), Thomas said to Halleck, December 9th: "I regret that General Grant should feel dissatisfaction at my delay in attacking the enemy. I feel conscious that I have done everything in my power to prepare, and that the troops could not have been gotten ready before this, and if he should order me to be relieved, I will submit without a murmur. A terrible storm of freezing rain has come on, which will make it impossible to attack until it breaks." On page 115 he repeats the same to Grant. General Thomas proved himself to be perfectly submissive to his superior, and though deemed slow in his movements, he always knew his own business. The order to relieve him was actually signed by the secretary as recorded on page 114. On page 115 is this reply of Grant to Thomas, December 9th: "Receiving your dispatch of 2 p. m. from Halleck, before I did the one to me, I telegraphed to suspend the order relieving you until we should hear further. I most sincerely hope that there will be no necessity to repeat it, and that the facts will show that you have been right all the time." Such was the unselfishness of Grant, ever ready to yield honor wherever due, without regard to self-desires.

December 5th. In camp and on picket.

December 6th. With a prospect of being soon remounted, we are now furnished with sabers and carbines In serial 93, page 598, General Johnson says: "In spite of the proverbial inefficiency of the ordnance department, Colonel Harrison, by untiring efforts, succeeded in procuring for all of his regiments Burnsides' carbines for the 14th and 16th Illinois regiments, and revolvers for the 8th Michigan regiment. In the matter of horses we were not quite so fortunate." It would have been wiser in Colonel Harrison and General Johnson to have expended their "untiring efforts" in first preparing their commands for the use of cavalry arms, or at least to have awaited for their remount before again placing them in the predicament of being supplied with arms entirely unsuited to their service.

December 7th and 8th. In camp; nothing of note.

December 9th. Turned very cold last night; sleeting and snowing today.

December 10th. Very cold.

December 11th, Sunday. Severely cold; snow and sleet. On page 151, serial 94, December 11th, is an order from General Wilson to General Johnson, and from Johnson to Colonel Harrison, to take instant measures to mount partly mounted regiments, by taking the horses of other partly mounted regiments, so that as far as this distribution of horses would go, there might be some fully mounted regiments. This order was a necessity under the circumstances, but it did not fit in well with the premature "untiring efforts" of Johnson and Harrison in furnishing cavalry arms to regiments, to whom they proved to be a nuisance. On the same page and date Johnson says: "I have had the 8th Michigan and 14th Illinois dismounted, and with their horses fully mounted the 16th Illinois and the 7th Ohio. These arrangements will leave about 750 mounted men in the first (now assigned to Harrison) brigade. In the second (Biddel's brigade, to which we were now assigned) the 5th Iowa alone is mounted, about

590 men." This arrangement was very unsatisfactory to the men, as well it might be with the bungling arrangement in just having them armed as cavalry. But we do not suppose that any preference in regard to the dismounting was given. We suppose that those regiments who were nearest fully mounted, were chosen as the ones to be fully mounted, and for that reason the 5th Iowa and 7th Ohio, which had seen the least service in this hard campaign, were mounted. The order in effect really honored the 8th Michigan and the 14th Illinois, for their severe service, which had so nearly dismounted them. The 16th Illinois were few in number, and so could be fully mounted with less horses. The sixth Indiana cavalry, Colonel James Biddel's own regiment, also dismounted, was also assigned to his brigade, but during the battle of Nashville the 8th Michigan, having nothing but revolvers, were left in the defenses at Nashville.

December 12th. Though the earth was covered with a glare of ice that made walking difficult, we marched at 9 a. m., crossed the bridge, passed through the city, and camped near Fort Negley, southwest of the city. Marched 4 miles. It was quite cold and we "toted" Lincoln rails quite a distance over icy hills, to build fires for cooking.

December 13th. Reveille at daylight; remains cold.

December 14th. Reveille at daylight; rain and fog, and ice all gone.

December 15th. Reveille at 3 a. m. We were called into line at 5 a. m. Now is to begin the grand struggle. The following formation and movements of Thomas' lines are found in his report (see serial 93, page 37): Major-General Steedman to make a sharp attack on the enemy's right, to attract attention. Then Major-General A. J. Smith, with a part of the army of the Tennessee, formed on and near the Hardin pike, to make a vigorous assault on the enemy's left; Major-General Wilson, with his cavalry to support General Smith's right, sending Johnson's division of his cavalry on the Charlotte pike to clear that road of the enemy, and observe in the direction of "Bell's Landing," to protect our right rear, until the enemy's position is fairly turned, when it will rejoin the main force. Brigadier-General T. J. Wood, with the fourth corps, on the Hillsborough pike, to support Smith's left. As the roads upon which these commands on the right advanced diverged greatly, Major-General Schofield, who, with the 23d corps, remained in the defenses, was to march out, and form on the right of Smith, to fill the gap between Smith and Wilson caused by the divergence of the roads. Two gunboats on the Cumberland were to aid Johnson on the Charlotte pike. The formation of our troops was partly concealed from the enemy by the broken nature of the ground, but more by a dense fog which providentially hung over the landscape until late in the morning. Johnson's division was much hindered in getting their position on the pike by McArthur's division of infantry, which was thrown across our road. When this obstruction was cleared we moved rapidly, but had not gone far until we found that our sabers, swinging around our legs, was a great impediment to our advancing on foot, and most of the men unbuckled them from their sides and threw them in a pile by the roadside. Others, however, said: "What right have we, without orders, to disarm ourselves in time of battle?" and so they retained their sabers. How our men longed to be mounted, that they might charge forward into the midst of the fight. Our division was pressed forward as rapidly as possible, for our dismounted men, unused to foot service, and greatly impeded by the mud, which was now deep. General Knipe's seventh and Hatch's fifth divisions, were the first of the cavalry to strike the enemy on the right of Smith, and drove them back rapidly, capturing a number of prisoners and a redoubt of four guns, McArthur's infantry aiding in this capture, the dismounted cavalry vieing with the infantry in the charge. The sixth cavalry division pressed forward on the pike and encountered the old enemy of our brigade, General Chalmers' division of Forrest's cavalry. To our division was assigned Battery "I" of the 4th United States artillery, Lieutenant Frank G. Smith commanding. The dismounted regiments, 14th Illinois and 6th Indiana cavalry were used as supports to the battery. Four miles from the city we struck Chalmers' division posted in strong position on the heights beyond Richland creek. General Johnson's account of this affair strongly convicts him of want of generalship. He says that he first ordered Biddel's brigade of dismounted men (the

FIRST SERGEANT GEO. W. NORRIS, Company G.

14th Illinois and the 6th Indiana) to lead the advance and charge their stronghold, after which he acknowledges his mistake in the following language: "But the movements of the dismounted cavalry were so slow, owing I suppose partly to their being unused to maneuvering as infantry, partly to the difficulty in crossing the creek, and partly to their sabers, which the commanding officer of the 14th Illinois cavalry had, with a singular shortsightedness, permitted his men to bring with them, that I finally ordered Harrison (with the mounted brigade) to pass the dismounted brigade, and attack the enemy with all possible energy." Just the thing that an able commander would have ordered in the first place, for while the impediments named by Johnson were a good excuse for the failure of the dismounted men to perform impossibilities, they were no excuse for General Johnson, who knew, or should have known, of all these impediments, and the last one mentioned, though he blames the commander of the 14th with it. General Johnson, through Colonel Harrison, was directly to blame, for, had they not "by untiring efforts" procured and distributed these sabers? Nor did his responsibility stop here, for it was his especial province to see that all his men were appropriately armed for this especial conflict, and he had ample time before the battle to find out that these men had not been mounted, so that sabers would not be a nuisance instead of a good weapon, and the commander of a regiment dared not take the responsibility without the orders of his superior, to change or discard the weapons with which he had been supplied, not knowing but what, for his men, some, to him unforseen emergency, might demand the use of these weapons. Some of the men, however, showed better judgment than their commanders, by taking upon themselves the responsibility to discard these nuisances. Relative to the first engagement, Colonel Biddel, our brigade commander, says (see page 606): "Four miles from the city we were met by the enemy in force; with artillery posted on the west side of —— creek. Here the brigade was deployed, covering the road and closely supporting the first (Harrison's) brigade. The battery attached to this division took position on the east side of the creek; the second brigade (14th Illinois and 6th Indiana) was brought up to support

the battery. The enemy being dislodged from his po[s]-
tion, the brigade moved forward about four miles, whe[n]
the enemy again made a stand." This account so far
it goes accords with our notes, neither of which say an[y]-
thing about any order for the dismounted of our briga[de]
to take the advance as described by Johnson, and bo[th]
agree in stating that we were used as support to our ba[t]-
tery, and our notes ascribe to the skillful use of the batte[ry]
the success in driving the enemy. Our notes say th[at]
Company "I" and one other company of the 14th were d[e]-
ployed on the right, to prevent an attempted movement
flank us in that direction. We well remember the atte[n]-
tion we received from the enemy's battery in this mov[e]-
ment. They were vigorously shelled by one of the en[e]-
my's batteries, while their other batteries poured a consta[nt]
stream of shells at the remainder of the line, especially
our battery. Lieutenant Smith gave them their own, wi[th]
compound interest, not in the number of shots fired, but
their telling effect. This artillery duel lasted an hour [or]
more. Our dismounted cavalry patiently taking their fi[re]
without power to return it. Harrison's mounted briga[de]
was then thrown forward on the left to attempt the ca[p]-
ture of their artillery. A charge led by that intrepid of[fi]-
cer, Major Beers of the 16th Illinois, would have succeed[ed]
but for the intervention of a stone wall, which so impeded his charging column that the enemy were enabl[ed]
to save their battery. The enemy fell back, making fo[ur]
more stands where the formation of the ground permitte[d]
The 14th and 6th were used as battery supports, and t[he]
first brigade was deployed dismounted on our left, b[ut]
on each occasion the planting of our battery and a sho[rt]
exercise of skillful gunnery soon drove them. Thus w[e]
pursued them all day, our division capturing 50 horse[s,]
some prisoners, and a battery of six guns. Late in t[he]
afternoon the enemy took a strong position on a woode[d]
ridge beyond a little creek that emptied into the Cumbe[r]-
land opposite "Bell's Landing," his left resting on the rive[r]
where they had a battery planted to control the river, the
lines dismounted and behind strong barricades, extendin[g]
from the river across the pike and far to our left. Harr[i]-
son's brigade made an untimely though impetuous charg[e]
and were roughly handled, losing one company of the 7th

Ohio captured. The 6th Indiana were retained as battery guard, while the 14th was deployed on the left in line. Between the contending forces lay an open field, with an even and gradual descent until the creek was reached; beyond this the ascent was rapid, and the ridge covered with brush and timber. There the enemy's lines were formed, and their batteries planted. The 14th, under orders, advanced in line as infantry down this inclined plain in the face of a furious fire of conical percussion shells, fired direct. Infantry never, under similar circumstances, preserved a better line, though at the flash of every gun they dropped to the ground, quickly springing up and dressing the line and advancing as before. With eagerness they awaited the expected order to charge and capture the rebel battery. They marched to the foot of the inclination and to within three hundred yards of the enemy, and were halted just as the enemy were abandoning the position of their guns. Why our men were withheld from their anticipated charge was never clearly known to us, unless the following plan of General Johnson explains it. He says that he here formed the plan of uniting with Croxton's brigade (on our left) and by swinging round the enemy's right, double them up and force them to the river, thus cutting them off from Hood's army, and by the aid of the two gunboats he hoped to be able to capture this force of cavalry. This plan failed in execution because of the lengthening of our lines caused by the divergence of the roads upon which both armies moved. This divergence separated Johnson and Croxton's commands, so that the needed co-operation could not be had. Johnson says in his report that he considered his division too weak unaided to perform that work. Doubtless it was, to carry out the plan as formulated, but we always *have* believed that a direct vigorous attack by his division, which. impatient for the order, aided as they now were by the gunboats on the river which sent into the masses of the enemy their monster shells that cut off trees that happened in their way, would at least have routed them from their positions and captured their batteries. We have no record of such movements of our dismounted cavalry as General Johnson describes, in which he says he ordered these dismounted men to attack the stronghold of the enemy, and continuing, says: "Their movements were so slow, owing as he thought, partly to the fact of their being unused to maneuvering on foot, and partly to the difficulty of crossing the creek, and partly to their sabers, which, hanging around their legs, impeded their movements." Now these reasons were all sufficient to explain slow movements, but not sufficient to excuse himself as the commander of the division, either to have permitted his men to go into battle on foot with such impediments, neither did it excuse him from the folly of pressing forward men in that condition to do a work requiring a speedy charge, when he had present a well mounted and well equipped command, so much better suited to the work. This is an attempt to throw the blame upon the commander of the regiment (Captain Jenkins), when he himself, with Colonel Harrison, "by untiring energy," procured and distributed these same weapons, and afterward dismounted them and left them in that condition. Captain Jenkins had no option but to fight with the weapons provided by his superior officers "with untiring efforts." Neither our notes nor the report of our brigade commander, Colonel Biddel, alludes to this affair, hence we doubt its correctness. Johnson's division now bivouacked in line, throwing out a strong picket line to prevent a night surprise. We had driven Chalmers' division of cavalry much further than Hood's infantry were driven. We were eight miles from the city, while our infantry bivouacked within five miles of Nashville. General Thomas, in his report (see page 39, serial 93), says: "The total result of the day's operation (the 15th) was the capture of sixteen pieces of artillery and 1,200 prisoners, besides several hundred stand of small arms, and about forty wagons. The enemy had been forced back at all points with heavy loss; our casualties were unusually light. The behavior of the troops was unsurpassed for steadiness and alacrity in every movement, and the original plan of battle, with few alterations, strictly adhered to."

December 16th. Daylight disclosed the fact that the enemy were gone from our front. They had moved across to the Hillsboro pike. Colonel Biddel says (page 601): "At break of day the following morning (the 16th) the brigade moved from the Charlotte pike to the Hardin pike."

Our notes say: "We marched down the Charlotte pike a mile, then following the enemy's trail we diverged by a dirt road to the left, crossing the Hardin pike at the brick church nine miles from Nashville. From there, following the valley of the Little Harpeth, reached the Hillsboro pike about 2 p. m., where, posted on a ridge north of Murry's house, we found the enemy in some force, and with artillery, which they opened on us. The first rounds, however, from Lieutenant Smith's guns silenced them, and on our advancing they retired, exchanging only a few shots with our skirmishers. Their main force retired by the road east, toward the Franklin pike, and a few down the Hillsboro pike, toward the Harpeth river." So rapidly was Hood's left wing doubled up on his main body by the rapid and vigorous movements of our cavalry, that even Johnson's mounted men could scarce move fast enough to engage in a healthy bout with the rebels, and so deep was the interminable mud that Biddel's dismounted men could only get a skirmish out of them by striking across the country to head them off and lay for them. There was little fighting in this quarter, for the enemy avoided us. The early and rapid advance of our cavalry had driven Hood's left wing to the rear of his main body, and we hoped to cut off his retreat, but by concentrating his main forces on the Franklin pike, he was enabled to move on that road. Thomas in his report of the 16th speaks of vigorous assaults of his infantry, but the enemy made but feeble resistance. He speaks of the movements of Wilson's cavalry by which they gained the enemy's rear and cut off their retreat by the Granny White pike. He says of the two days' operations, 4,462 prisoners captured, including 287 officers, of all grades, from major-general; 53 pieces of artillery and thousands of small arms. Brigadier-General E. W. Rucker, one of their best cavalry officers, was captured. The enemy abandoned all his dead and wounded on the field. Johnson's division of cavalry was sent to the Harpeth river." On the 15th and 16th besides fighting we had tramped on foot through deep mud 18 miles. On both nights it had rained hard.

December 17th. Moved out an hour before day. Marched through mud ankle deep—knee deep, increasing mud 10 miles, to Hillsdale pike and camped on Harpeth river, 5 miles west of Franklin; rained through the day. Since leaving camp near Nashville in the early morning of 15th, we had little to eat. While plodding on foot through deep mud we could not "tote" rations and we had no trains.

Sunday, December 18th. Rained hard nearly all last night. Marched at 11 a. m. to Franklin and Nashville pike, and camped on a creek a mile north of Franklin. Here we saw a large force of captured Johnnies on their way to *take Nashville*. Day's march, 8 miles.

December 19th. Reveille at 4 a. m.; hard rain at night. Marched at 10 a. m. through Franklin. Roads much obstructed with teams and troops. Marched down the Carterville pike 4 miles, and camped in a field; day's march, 5 miles.

December 20th. Turned very cold last night. We are under orders to march back to Nashville, as we are now useless in the pursuit, the retreat of the enemy being so rapid that none but mounted men can keep in sight. This ends all our fighting in the service. This campaign ended in the entire destruction of Hood's magnificent army, but a small proportion reaching the south bank of the Tennessee river. General Thomas says in his report, page 46: "There was captured from the enemy during the various actions recited, 13,189 prisoners, including 7 general officers and nearly 1,000 other officers of all grades. Seventy-two pieces of serviceable artillery and 2,000 deserters, to whom the oath was administered. Our own loss will not exceed 10,000 killed, wounded, and missing." General Thomas was the lion of the day, as "nothing succeeds like success." He had demonstrated to General Grant and the country *that he was right,* and all rejoiced. We marched 21 miles and camped; thawed through the day and rained at night; camped within 5 miles of Nashville. We are promised to be remounted.

December 21st. Reveille at daylight; rained and snowed last night; cold today. Marched at 9 a. m.; passed through Nashville; crossed the river and moved up the Gallatin pike; camped between the pike and the railroad 3 miles from Nashville; marched 9 miles; cold and snow in the evening. Our fare was extremely hard since the

14th, as we could have no trains with us. This ends this chapter and closes our fighting period.

* * * * *

The following, received too late for its proper place in the chapter, is too important to be omitted, as it gives the most correct estimate of Hood's force. It is from the National Tribune, contributed by William E. Doyle, Stevensburg, Va., and describes the battle of Franklin. He says: "The main portion of the battle was one terrible rush of the entire rebel army to overwhelm the inferior numbers opposed to them. It was like the flank attack on Sherman on the preceding 22d of July. Hood believed in these reckless charges of masses of men to overwhelm the enemy, but failed against the western troops, who reduced his troops from 85,000 at the beginning of the campaign to about 40,000 at Franklin. Of this number not 20,000 escaped from the battles of Franklin and Nashville, and Hood's army was no more in January, 1865. Hood's intention was to crush the Union forces at Franklin and capture all of Thomas' army south of the Harpeth river, and for this purpose generals led their commands to the charge; on foot and in the merciless slaughter five of them were killed, viz.: Major-General Pat Cleaburne. Brigadier-Generals John Adams, O. F. Strahl, S. R. Gist, and H. B. Granberry. This exceeds any battle of the war in this particular, as we lost no generals. The charges at Atlanta and at Franklin each far exceeded the charge of Pickett's division at Gettysburg, and the loss of the rebels was very much heavier on each occasion. There were not many of Forrest's losing regiments there; they were all fighters though, and credit for fighting should go where the enemy's loss is the heaviest."

Note.—Hood's nominal force was 96,000, and not less than 50,000 present. Schofield's infantry was 18,000 present.

CHAPTER XV.

SYNOPSIS OF SERVICE—NARRATIVES OF COMRADES—BIOGRAPHIES OF OFFICERS—ROLLS OF ENLISTED MEN.

The regiment remained in camp at Edgefield, near to Nashville, until early April, and was then ordered to Pulaski, where they remained until ordered to Nashville to be mustered out, which was done July 31st, 1865. Their period of encampment at Edgefield and at Pulaski was without incident worthy of note, more than the ordinary occurrences of quiet camp life, except the promotions and resignations of officers, and the return to us from captivity of our officers and men who had not previously rejoined us, and these incidents are recorded in the biographies of officers and the rolls of the men. The regiment had been promised to be remounted and sent on active duty, but the rapidity with which the armies of the Confederacy melted away after our complete destruction of their southern army under Hood, rendered it unnecessary to remount the dismounted regiments. Of the proud army under Hood, who, for the whole summer had resisted three armies combined under our great leader, William T. Sherman, and who crossed the Tennessee river in November with an infantry force of over 60,000 effective men, reinforced by General Forrest's famous Confederate cavalry, fully 15,000 strong, there remained to recross the Tennessee river in their retreat perhaps not exceeding 10,000 men. They had stranded on the "Rock of Chickamauga" and had gone to pieces, leaving in our hands over 70 pieces of serviceable artillery, with untold numbers of small arms and all manner of military equipments. Now at the termination of our active military service we can, with creditable pride, recount in brief synopsis some of the great achievements of the grand old 14th Illinois cavalry. First: To the cry so often heard contemptuously uttered, "Who ever saw a dead cavalryman?" We answer that in one single expedition covering a period of little more than

SERGEANT JONATHAN H. MELVEN, Company E.

one week, our regiment lost a larger per cent of its number than ninety-nine hundredths of the infantry regiments in the service through their whole term. Our loss in battle, compared to three amongst the best infantry regiments in this state, the 34th, 75th, and 92d, of killed, ours compared to the highest loss of the others was 34 per cent greater, and to the next two, it was nearly three times as great, and compared to the loss of the three regiments combined, their total loss in killed exceeded the loss of our single regiment only about 60 per cent. Our loss in killed was about one-third more than the combined loss of two of those regiments. The total death loss was 23 per cent more than the highest, and 73 per cent higher than either of the others. This, too, be it remembered, covered a period of less than three years of service, whilst of the compared regiments all were full three years, and one was about four years in service. A proof of the wonderful activity of the 14th in service is found in the fact that, without estimating the movements by detachments, which, with them, as was general with the mounted forces, constituted a very large portion of their service; the movements of the regiment in body, through a period of about two years of its active duty, covered a distance of over ten thousand miles, or over thirteen miles a day for every day, Sundays included, for seven hundred and thirty-two consecutive days. This includes, of course, the distances we were transported by railroad and by boat. Our initial service in Kentucky ranked high, as is proved by the official reports, while in the great pursuit of Morgan by our brigade we were the very first in line to prevent his entrance into Kentucky, and our regiment was among those who made the final pursuit and capture. In the very important and severe service in East Tennessee no regiment in that grand army exceeded in activity or important service rendered, the record of "the bloody 14th." Indeed so signal was the reputation of the regiment that it was selected from a whole corps of excellent cavalry by its commander for one of the most perilous and difficult military ventures of the civil war, the punishment of a band of Indians, exceeding in number our force, and the complete success of the undertaking demonstrated the wisdom of the choice, and called out the especial praise of the great commander, Grant. Our service in Georgia was merged in the history of Capron's brigade and in Stoneman's division, all of which in reputation, stood high.

The march around the great rebel army and attack upon Macon, Ga., in a region swarming with rebel cavalry, and completely cut off from all support, marks the heroism and endurance of the command, and the unfortunate termination of that expedition ought not to dim the lustre of the heroic adventure to release our suffering prisoners, while it ought forever to close the mouths of those who contemptuously cry out, "Who ever saw a dead cavalryman?" Our single regiment alone, reduced to little if any more than three hundred men, lost by death in that one expedition 98 men. How, out of the ruins of the regiments of our brigade, each of which suffered such losses and discouragements, it was possible to reorganize so efficient a force as our brigade proved to be in their last campaign in middle Tennessee, is simply a matter of astonishment. Disorganized and discouraged as they had been, and sent into that campaign crippled in efficiency as they were, by the inappropriate arms furnished them, they not only ranked equal at all times with the best of that most heroic body of Union cavalry that faced such tremendous odds, but on two occasions was Schofield's army saved from capture or destruction by the superior skill and valor of Capron's brigade alone.

We will now give the few individual narratives and adventures that have been furnished by comrades. These are not given as superior in interest, but rather as fair samples of the hundreds of unrecorded adventures and services.

We first give the narrative of Sergeant J. Harvey Melven of Company "E," the comrade who, on the evening before the muster out of the regiment, gave them such a rousing speech. We omit from the communication some portions that have appeared in the body of the history. Comrade Melven says: "I was after Morgan from start to finish, and never dropped out from June 25th until July 26th (when he was captured), thirty-one days, and nights, too. When General Morgan stopped and displayed his feeling of satisfaction as to the distance he had traveled, our regiment was under the command of Major Davidson (afterward colonel). He had us count off by fours, and we fell short one of having seven sets. The Major ordered us to dismount, and, turning to me, he said: "Sergeant Melven, take charge of these men and be ready to move at a moment's notice." He then rode over the hill to where Morgan was making terms of surrender, but no sooner had the Major left than at least 20 of our number were sound asleep, with that hot July sun pouring its rays square into their upturned faces. Several ladies and small children from a farm house near by came to us, and wept bitterly to see those poor men sleeping while the sun was roasting their faces. We who were standing to keep awake told them that we only wished that we could join them in their sweet sleep. Soon Major D., with several other officers of the regiment, who had taken an early flank movement on Morgan, and helped to corner him no doubt, came and told us to mount and return to Salineville for rest that night in as good order and as soon as possible. We mounted and slept our last horseback nap of that campaign. Before passing I must say: "God bless the noble, loyal people of Ohio, who for weeks fed us on either side of the streets as we marched through their towns." Should I live 100 years I shall never forget the cheering words they gave us, nor that delicious apple butter, together with tons of other good things.

After taking part in all the East Tennessee campaign with our regiment, from the capture of Knoxville to our stop at Philadelphia, on October 6th, 1863, I went on detached service with General Julius White, commanding the second division, 23d A. C., was in the battle of Huff's ferry (when Longstreet crossed the Tennessee river) and in the fights at Lenoir and Campbell station, and in the siege of Knoxville. On February 4th, 1864, I left East Tennessee for Kentucky, and at Paris, Ky., met about 200 recruits for our regiment from dear old Illinois. We soon moved to Nicholasville, Ky., where Colonel Capron commanded the post, and I assisted in drilling the recruits until June 3d, when we took up our march for the old regiment, joining it at Cleveland, Tenn., June 17th, 1864.

The Georgia campaign, which began soon after our uniting with the regiment at Cleveland, all survivors well remember.

When "boots and saddles" sounded early on the morning of July 27th, I thought of the campaign that ended in Ohio one year from the day before, how we had let raider prisoners retain their booty at Buffington Island unmolested, and wondered how it would be with us who might fall into the hands of the enemy, and that we were starting into the very jaws of death. Oh, how true I guessed!

In the charge at Sunshine church, about 10 o'clock on that fatal Sunday, July 31st, I received a slight wound in my right hand, and after having Dr. Wilkins dress it, I returned and assisted in guarding eleven prisoners captured in the repulse of the charge made on our right, in which I received the wound. One of them said only a few moments before our front was swept, that we were liable to be exterminated if we attempted a stubborn resistance, for they outnumbered us ten to one. In the stampede that followed Orderly Sergeant Duval of Company "E" and myself, seeing our horses failing, dismounted and took to the swamps, traveled by night through alligator and moccasin marshes, and slept in the brush in day time until the Friday following, without seeing another human face or speaking above a whisper since the Sunday before. We were joined by two of the 1st Kentucky Cavalry, whose term of service had expired the day General Stoneman surrendered. They insisted on our traveling in day time with them, which we consented to do, but in less than six hours we came in contact with a squad of rebel cavalry and one of the Kentucky boys fell into their hands. Three of us escaped, and while hid in the brush about 5 that p. m. two more stragglers came upon us, one of them being Dear Old Orderly Sergeant Philbrook of Company "F," the other was John Spiker of the Ohio cavalry squadron; they opened up some corn dodger and boiled pork, which had been given them by negroes, and we relished it more than blackberry, elderberry, and green corn diet of the past six days. When dark came we passed so close to a rebel picket that we heard them not only snore, but breathe. They were camped not more than 40 rods from our hiding place. In the afternoon of the day following we had just finished the delicious dodger and pork and were resting in a quiet thicket when a small white boy and a large negro boy, with two blood hounds, came on to us unexpectedly to all of us, even the dogs. Of course they escaped and we started north with a rush. Within less than an hour they or their dogs, with a squad of men, were making the welkin ring with their howls and yells, but when so near that we could hear the sniffle of the hounds the artillery of heaven broke loose and within 3 minutes the rain poured and the chase ended for that evening. On the day following, while asleep in our only blanket, about 1 o'clock we were startled by the shout: "Here they are; surrender boys and we will treat you well." There were four of them with guns and leading their horses, following four bloodhounds that were still tracking us as quietly as a cat stealing upon its prey. We were searched for arms, then for money, but they failed to find either on me, for I had no arms, and my $9 was in the wristbands of my old army shirt. At the first cry of our captors the remaining Kentucky man plunged into a dense thicket just below us on the hill side and was not noticed by the enemy.

Of us four who were captured there I am the only one who ever returned. We were taken from place to place, and turned over from one command to another for several days. At General Wheeler's headquarters at Covington, Ga., a rebel made a one-sided trade with me in pantaloons, giving me a pair of thin cotton ones that were soon in tatters. We were cast into a dismal old jail at that place for three days, then taken to Augusta, where we spent one day in a much finer jail. From there we were taken to Macon, where we spent from Saturday evening to Monday noon. From there we were sent to that court of death, Andersonville, which more able pens than mine have attempted to describe, so I will not try to picture it. We were moved from there to Savannah, where, on the day of my arrival, I was sunstruck. From there we were taken to Millen or Camp Lawton, thence to Blackshear, where we remained only two days. From there we were taken to Florence, S. C., via Savannah. We were locked in box cars and sidetracked at Charleston one night, and for want of room we had to pile on top of each other when lying down, and as I chanced to be the lower man, I found the skin had left my left hip before daylight came. I was

only at Florence one week when I was paroled on my 22d birthday. On leaving Millen I was lucky enough to be placed in a stock car, where cattle had been shipped a short time before, and I made my supper that evening on the scattered corn in that car, relishing it as I now do good bread. Twenty-seven of my company were captured. The time (total) of our captivity was nine months, 9 of the 27 died in prison, and of the 18 who lived to get out, only 3 of us survive. J. HARVEY MELVEN,
"Late Sergeant Company 'E,' 14th Illinois Cav."

The following narrative was furnished by Captain William R. Sanford of Company "K," one of our bold and skillful line officers. He says: "When our brigade, under Colonel Graham, was sent, about the last of November, 1863, from near Cumberland gap to Maynardsville, General Granger was expected at Kingston with a force to reinforce General Burnside in Knoxville. Sunday, November 29th, 1863, I was called to headquarters and ordered to pick 20 men from the 14th to carry dispatches to Major-General Granger, then supposed to be at or near Kingston. I selected my men and made all preparations and left camp at 8 p. m. We captured three horses and ran in a rebel picket. They made quick time at the crack of our carbines, followed by our saber charge. We got their horses. Four miles farther we struck the river, and had some difficulty in crossing, not knowing the ford. A picket was on the opposite side, we could not decide whether Union or Confederate; sent forward scouts, who reported all right. November 30th, reached Clinton at 3 a. m. Left 7 men at Clinton to get their horses shod; cold and hungry; found here the 2d Tennessee Cavalry, and was well treated by officers and men. Arrived at Kingston at dark; report to Colonel Bird's headquarters. General Granger had not arrived; feed and rations scarce. December 1st spent in getting horses shod. Corporal Lowrey and John Hall return to our command with dispatches from General Grant. December 2d, started at 6 a. m. for our command; captured eleven rebels and their horses. Camped 5 miles west of Clinton at the house of a rebel named Johnson, having marched 40 miles; had a very cold night. December 3d, moved at daylight; passed through Jacksborough and Fincastle; met Lieutenant-Colonel Davis, 1st Tennessee Cavalry, who expected to be attacked, having mistaken us for rebels. We supposed them to be our enemy, but mutually discovered our mistake before making an attack. Here we turned over our prisoners; camped at the house of a southern lady, whose husband is in jail at Richmond. December 4th, moved at daylight; left Cumberland gap road 10 miles from the gap, and struck across to Tazewell, where we arrived about 8 p. m. quite tired. December 5th, reported to our division commander, Colonel Foster, and learned that the 14th had a hard fight at Walker's ford. We found our regiment 4 miles from Walker's ford; they had given us up as captured. Corporal Lowrey and John Hall, who had served as scouts on our right and left to warn us of approaching danger; came in about two days after. This was but one of many raids that I made at the head of Company 'K,' 14th Illinois Cavalry, and I must add that no better company of men ever served on such duty; always true to their officers and knowing no fear when duty called."

Immediately succeeding the return of Captain Sanford's party, Captain Francis Boeke (then first-lieutenant of Company "I") was sent to bear dispatches to General Granger at Kingston. No report of operations has been made and as they reported success of their assigned duty, this is all we can give, though doubtless they had much the same experience as Company "K."

Sometime in January, 1864, while Longstreet occupied the country around Morristown, and the 14th was posted on fords and crossings of the French Broad river, Cassius C. Beemis of Company "I," 14th, crossed the river in a boat with several companions for a lark. A party of rebels surprised them and captured Beemis, the others escaped. Beemis was taken to Morristown and kept a number of weeks. Finally an order was issued to send all their prisoners to Richmond. That night the force of chain guards around the prisoners was doubled. Beemis had no friends in Richmond that he desired to see, and though the chance to escape was slim the irrepressible Beemis determined to try it. The prisoners were kept on a hill with many clusters of bushes. Beemis lay perfectly quiet, feigning sleep, but closely watching the nearest sentinel, and when the sentinel was in a favorable position he would roll gently over in the direction of some bushes. It was not very dark, yet he succeeded in reaching the bushes without discovery, and from there rolled slowly and quietly to the bottom of the hill, where the bushes were thicker. He cautiously worked his way completely out of sight, when he ran like a whitehead. Beemis was a great forager and knew all the Union families of that region, and by their aid he succeeded in working his way through the rebel lines and reached us in safety then at Knoxville. Beemis was one of the bravest men in the regiment, indeed he seemed to know no fear when duty called. Poor fellow, he was captured on the Stoneman raid and put in the Andersonville pen. But to pen Beemis long was a difficult task. With two others he succeeded in getting out, and with great skill they baffled the hounds and pursuing men, and succeeded in working their way far into North Carolina. One morning they discovered that a party of men with a pack of hounds was in pursuit. They separated, each taking a different route. Finally two, Mark Butterfield and we believe James McNichols, were captured. They heard the hounds baying and a volley of musketry in the direction that Beemis had gone; and when the parties all met again Butterfield asked where Beemis was. The only answer was: "You may be glad you are not where Beemis is." The thought of men being torn to pieces by bloodhounds, urged on by human beings, is too horrible to contemplate, yet in the case of Beemis we can form no other conclusion. To forgive such an unwarranted barbarity is a difficult task for the average Christian.

While our brigade lay near Bean Station and just before the great battle there, Lt. Payne, our commissary, crossed the Holston river and entered a mill for forage. While engaged in collecting it a strong party of the enemy surrounded the mill and captured the whole party except the lieutenant, who, somehow, slipped under the water wheel and escaped. He did not propose to give his enemies Payne.

Lieutenant Putnam Beckwith of Company "C," 14th Illinois, led the only squad that escaped from the Stoneman disaster mounted. He says: "On the morning of

JOSEPH M. THOMPSON, Company L.

the surprise, August 3d, 1864, I was awakened by George Weisner of my company, 'C;' he cried out, 'The rebs are coming.' I sprang up, saddled, and mounted the quickest I ever did in my life. The rebels were charging through the camp. I put spurs to old Gray and got out of that lane as fast as I knew how. I struck off on a byroad, as the main road was crowded with a rushing mass of our men. Quite a number took the byroad. We found a ford across the river. I had a squad of nine men with me representing each regiment in our brigade. Myself and two others from the 14th, one was Colonel Jenkins' orderly, the other a boy 18 years old. One sergeant and two men from the 8th Michigan, two men of the 5th Indiana, and two of the 11th Kentucky. I lost my hat charging through the timber. We rode up to a dwelling, where there were two rebel soldiers, who surrendered to us, and I paroled them. I ordered them to get me a hat; they brought me an old plantation hat without a band. I turned it inside out to make it stay on my head. Soon after we held a consultation about how we should proceed, and in what direction. The Michigan sergeant and I differed as to the direction; the sun was not visible. I told them which direction I was going and the boys of our regiment said they would follow me, and all of the others, except the sergeant, decided to go with us, and after starting the sergeant also came along and we traveled northwest toward the Chattahoochee river, keeping off the main roads most of the time. Sometime in the first day out we rode up to a house to get something to eat; there were three or four young ladies but no men at the house. They were much frightened, and said they had nothing about the house to eat. I answered that we were Confederates with Yankee clothing on, for the purpose of picking up Yankees; they then brought us apple pie. We moved as rapidly as we could through the day and at night tied our horses together and went a hundred rods or more away to sleep in the brush, so that if the rebels discovered our horses we might have the chance of escaping on foot. When we reached the Chattahoochee river we were a glad set of boys; the Michigan sergeant had insisted all the time that we were going south. We had captured quite a number of rebel soldiers, one and two and sometimes three together. Whenever we encountered a squad we charged up to them and I ordered them to throw up their hands. On the evening of the second day we overtook a soldier belonging to Company 'M,' 14th Illinois. I had him to mount behind one of the boys, and a short time after we captured a rebel cavalryman and his horse. This man informed us that a mile down the river was a battalion of rebel cavalry guarding a ford. I ordered him to guide us past this force and told him that if he run us into this force that he would pay the penalty. We came to a plantation half a mile from the ford, where we saw a nice black horse in the barn yard. I halted and ordered the extra man to dismount and get her, when a couple of young ladies appeared and protested loudly against our taking the horse, and assured us that we would soon be captured. I said: 'Not much, for there are ten thousand of our troops near by.' Just then four or five rebel soldiers appeared at the door, ran down, but did not interfere with us, nor we with them, as we could not bother with them. They belonged to the force at the ford and did not seem to have their arms. We got the horse and lit out on double quick, with the guide riding by my side. He took us by safely. We passed within half a mile of the ford, where the rebel battalion was guarding. The next day we got within ten or fifteen miles of a bridge on the river, guarded by a Union infantry regiment. I ascertained that there was a rebel command patroling the road twice a day down to our pickets. I determined to find out where that patrol was. I left the boys and crawled out to the road to watch for them and find out whether they were between us and our force, or whether they were back of us. I did not have long to wait. A Johnny came along, I halted him and invited him to an interview, and found out that the road was clear of rebel cavalry from there to our lines. He had on one of our soldier caps; I invited him to trade for my plantation hat. We traded. I suppose that he thought that I played him a Yankee trick, but if I could find him I would give him five dollars for that old hat. I went back to my squad and we took the main road and soon reached our lines. We were terribly hungry and relished the food our friends gave us in great abundance. We were very tired and rest over night was truly refresh-

ing, as we were in safety and feared no night surprise as we slept. The next day we reached Marietta, Ga. More obedient and braver men than our squad of ten men I never met. These were the only men that came through all the way from the Stoneman disaster mounted. I was then orderly sergeant of Company 'C,' 14th Illinois Cavalry.
"LIEUTENANT PUTNAM BECKWITH."

Upon our earnest request of Captain William H. Guy to furnish some account of his individual adventure or service for publication, he replied: "I can bring to mind no incident of the war at this time which would be of interest to the readers of the history without it would be the little raid I made to Mulberry gap, Tennessee, under the direction of General Foster, who was at that time commanding at Bean Station. At 4 o'clock in the evening (day not given) I was ordered to report at headquarters with 45 picked men of the (14th) regiment. My orders were to go to Mulberry gap, 18 miles distant, to occupy the same, and hold it until further orders. We arrived at the gap sometime before daylight and found it occupied by a full regiment of Alabama cavalry. They were camped in line across the valley, and looked like a very formidable body of troops to attack with 45 men, but we charged them dismounted, and after a half hour of severe fighting they were demoralized and panic-stricken in the extreme. We occupied the gap and held it as ordered." He says: "I have no dates to give other than the year 1864."

Note.—It was doubtless in January, 1864, at the time that Sturgis' cavalry corps was across the Holston river. General Foster commanded all the forces, and then had a force at Bean Station. Captain Guy also says: "I was captured at Sunshine Church, Georgia, July 31, 1864, on Stoneman raid, and was in prison at Charleston, S. C., about 4 months."

Comrade J. M. Thompson's (of Company "L") recollections of the night surprise August 3d, 1864: "They ran in on us and I mounted my horse after they had passed me. We went over a fence and struck a lane and I saw no more of our boys for a long time. I finally left my horse and went on foot and fell in with four of Company 'I' boys in about a week. We struck the Chattahoochee river, embarked on some small boats. Bushwhackers overtook us and demanded us to surrender, but we could not understand their language and they fired on us. I supposed all were killed but me and I jumped into the river and my comrades all followed and we used our little boats as breastworks until we could land. One man was shot in the back and went down, another in the hip, and we carried him until we came to a house and left him. We then struck out again without shoes, coat, or hat or any commissaries and that afternoon they overtook us again, and almost captured the whole outfit. They were mounted and found the house, where we were having some bread baked, and we had to run 80 rods to get to the woods and the rebs after us, shooting as fast as they could, but we reached the woods, losing one man, a darky, who was going through with us. That night we almost died with cold, having nothing but shirts and pants, forced to lay all night in the rain without any shelter. We piled together and 'spooned,' when we got so cold on one side that we could stand it no longer we all turned together. But what is the use to attempt a description of our trials and sufferings, as none but those who suffered them can appreciate, and they know all about them without being told.

"J. M. THOMPSON,
"Company 'L,' 14th Illinois Cavalry."

In an after communication comrade Thompson says that they lay concealed in a thicket within a mile of a rebel town for four days without a morsel to eat and not daring to leave their concealment. Their feet became so sore traveling barefoot and penetrating thickets that they were obliged to tear off their underclothing to wrap their wounded feet. Oh! what a chapter of horrors it would be could all the unwritten records of all the sufferings of the fugitives from the Stoneman raid be published. It would be second to nothing except to the history of that hell upon earth, "Andersonville."

BIOGRAPHIES OF OFFICERS—FIELD AND STAFF.

We are compelled to brevity in our biographies, but will give, in condensed form, important events of civil and military life, as far as furnished to us. Such officers as have not furnished their biographies, we will give the record as found in the Adjutant-General's report. We will also give the rank as given in this report, whether mustered or not, in the highest office to which commissioned, as it often happened that no mustering officer could be reached, and it would be unjust to good officers to record even the implication that they were unworthy of the rank to which commissioned.

BIOGRAPHIES—FIELD AND STAFF.

General Horace Capron, born August 31st, 1804, in Attleboro, Mass., died at Washington, D. C., on Washington's birthday, in 1885, caused by exposure at the dedication of the Washington monument the day before, when he commanded the cavalry that took part in the ceremony. His father, Seth Capron, was an aid to General Washington. It is said that General Capron was actively engaged in the United States cavalry service before our Civil War. In civil life he was noted for capability and success in agricultural lines, so much so that at the close of the civil war he was appointed commissioner of agriculture, in which capacity he so won renown that he was selected by the government of Japan as the head of agricultural interests in that country, and by his success in that position he merited and received the approbation and esteem of the Emperor of Japan. He was ordered by the Governor of Illinois in the summer of 1862 to raise a cavalry regiment to be numbered the 18th, to be rendezvoused at Peoria, Ill. Two other regiments, the 15th, Colonel Hamilton, and the 14th, Colonel Jenkins, were also authorized. Unforeseen difficulties rendered it necessary to consolidate the three germs into one, the 14th, of which General Capron was commissioned colonel. He served with high honor until his resignation, January 23d, 1865, and was brevetted brigadier-general March 13th, 1865. He commanded brigades during much of his service, and showed great generalship. From November 30th, 1864, he was absent from his command, but missed no important service except the battles of Nashville and Franklin and the Indian fight. The important service rendered by Capron's brigade in the last campaign in Tennessee, has never received its proper acknowledgment in history. There is no denying the fact that it twice saved Schofield's army.

Colonel Francis M. Davidson, born in Jonesboro, Union County, Illinois, in 1832; enlisted as private early in the war; was commissioned captain in the 60th regiment, Illinois infantry; served till July 3d, 1862; resigned to join cavalry; was mustered in January 7th, 1863, as first Major in 14th Illinois Cavalry. Served in that rank, though frequently in command of the regiment, and sometimes of the brigade, through the campaigns in Kentucky, East Tennessee, and in Georgia, until captured August 3d, 1864, when the command was surprised in the night. He was not exchanged in time for further active service, but was commissioned colonel of 14th, January 23d, 1865, and was mustered out with regiment. As a cavalry raider Davidson had no superior in the Union army.

Lieutenant-Colonel David P. Jenkins, born August 25th, 1823, at Mount Pleasant, Jefferson County, Ohio; educated in common school and Quaker seminary; graduated in law school, Cincinnati, Ohio, in 1845; admitted to practice in Supreme Court of Ohio, and has practiced law until within the last six years. July 1st, 1861, he was commissioned 1st major in the 1st Illinois Cavalry; was captured at siege of Lexington, Missouri, and exchanged in November and assigned to duty under General Grant at Cairo, Ill. In March, 1862, he was ordered to New Madrid, and participated in the battle at that place. Was next sent to the Ozark mountains to guard supply trains of General Curtis. Resigned June 14th, 1862. In September, 1862, he was authorized to raise a cavalry regiment, to be numbered the 14th Illinois. Unforeseen difficulties hindered the filling up of several cavalry regiments at that time, resulting in the consolidation of three germs of regiments into one regiment, numbered the 14th, of which Horace Capron was commissioned colonel and David P. Jenkins lieutenant-colonel. Served in that capacity, often in command of the regiment and sometimes of the brigade, through the campaigns in Kentucky, Tennessee, and Georgia; commanded the regiment through the ill-fated Stoneman raid, and escaped on foot to our lines from the disaster of August 3d, 1864. Resigned May 3d, 1865.

GEORGE W. SANFORD, Company M, 3rd Ill. Infantry.
Son of Lieut. W. L. Sanford, Co. L, 14th Ill. Cavalry.

Lieutenant-Colonel David Quigg, born in Litchfield, N. H., December 17th, 1834; graduated from Dartmouth college June, 1855; admitted to the bar at Bloomington, Ill., in the autumn of 1857; mustered into service as 2d lieutenant, Company "L," 4th regiment, Illinois Cavalry, September, 1861; served as battalion adjutant; resigned August, 1862; aided in recruiting and organizing 14th Illinois Cavalry; commissioned major of second battalion. In the Kentucky campaign commanded detachments that did much important duty. Commanded the forces left at Glasgow, Ky., during the Morgan raid in July and August, 1863. In the campaign in East Tennessee was with the regiment in all its hard service; sometimes in command of the regiment, and several times in command of the brigade. Was present and participated in the Indian raid into North Carolina and commanded a portion of his battalion in that fight. He also served with ability in the Georgia campaign until captured on the fatal 3d of August, 1864. He was imprisoned at Charleston, S. C., and was not exchanged until after the battle of Nashville, so that we were deprived of his valuable service through our last campaign. He was commissioned lieutenant-colonel June 10th, 1865, and was mustered out with the regiment. Colonel Quigg was a model gentleman as well as a superb soldier; equally fitted to lead an impetuous cavalry charge or to command in a prolonged fight requiring coolness and courage. He has been for many years one of the prominent lawyers in Chicago.

Major Haviland Tompkins mustered in as major of the third battalion of the 14th Illinois Cavalry February 6th, 1863; served with ability through the campaigns in Kentucky, East Tennessee, and Georgia, and also in the Middle Tennessee campaign under Generals Schofield and Thomas; often in command of the regiment. Resigned May 13th, 1865. Was on General George Stoneman's staff in Stoneman raid.

Major James Benoni Dent was born on Dent's run, near Morgantown, W. Va. His father's father and grandfather were officers in the patriot army of the Revolution. He is closely related by blood to Generals George H. Thomas, Wade Hampton and James Longstreet. When young his father moved to Magnolia, Ill. He was employed in a wholesale boot and shoe house in Chicago, and was sent to Galena to work in a branch establishment, where he became acquainted with General Grant. When the war broke out, on the first call he raised a company for the service, but it was not then accepted. When he ascertained that a cavalry regiment was being raised, with several of his neighbors he went 50 miles to Bloomington and joined a company being raised by Captain (afterward General) John McNulta, and was mustered in as 2d lieutenant, Company "A," 1st Illinois Cavalry, and served with the regiment until it was mustered out in the fall of 1862. Soon after he joined the 14th Illinois Cavalry, and was mustered as captain of Company "C," and in that capacity was in all the hardships, skirmishes, battles and raids in which the regiment was engaged, and was more often in command of detachments sent on important duty than any other line officer in the regiment. Just before the Stoneman raid, while going to Marietta, Ga., with only an orderly, he was waylaid and captured and sent to Charleston prison, and was exchanged in October, 1864, and rejoined his regiment at Nicholasville, Ky. He obtained leave of absence and started for home, and near Paris, Ky., his train was captured by a guerrilla band, and Dent was again taken to a rebel prison, so that through some of our most important service we were deprived of this one of our most valued officers. Captain Dent was one of our most skillful and heroic officers. He rejoined the regiment at Pulaski in the spring of 1865, and was mustered as major April 21, 1865, and was mustered out with the regiment. Major Dent was kind and affable to his men and a model gentleman.

Of Major Thomas K. Jenkins we can only give the data found in the adjutant-general's report. He enlisted at Vandalia, Ill., was mustered as captain of Company "F," 14th Illinois Cavalry, January 7th, 1863; promoted major May 31st, 1865, and was mustered out with the regiment. Captain Jenkins, being senior captain, was often in command of the regiment in the last campaign.

Major Henry C. Connelly, born December 22d, 1831, in Petersburg, Pa. His home was at Rock Island, Ill., when

(1891)
WASHINGTON L. SANFORD and NANCY J. SANFORD

he joined the 14th Illinois Cavalry, and went into camp about September 15th, 1862, and served most of the time as regimental adjutant till the first and the second battalions were mustered, when, January 7th, 1863, he was mustered as 2d lieutenant of Company "L." He was in the Celina fight, and next morning, with Lieutenant O'Neil, the afterward famous Fenian leader, he crossed the Cumberland river in a skiff to reconnoiter. He was in the pursuit of Colonel Hamilton, and was at the head of his company during the entire Morgan raid, and was present at the capture. He was through the East Tennessee campaign under Burnside, commanding for a time General Shackelford's escort. At Walker's ford, Bean Station, Mossy Creek, Dandridge, and Fair Garden, he had charge of the Howitzer battery. On the Cherokee Indian raid into North Carolina he took with him two guns, returning with them successfully. After exhausting all the mules in drawing the guns and caissons, the horses of soldiers were used to bring these into our lines. It required skill to get the guns over the great mountains, and by yawning precipices and through deep ravines. January 31st, 1864, he was commissioned captain of Company "L." In February, 1864, at his own request, he was relieved from commanding the battery, and was detailed as a staff officer at brigade headquarters, acting as assistant adjutant-general and afterward as assistant inspector-general on General Strickland's staff.

Learning of the Stoneman cavalry raid around Atlanta in July, 1864, he secured permission to join it, but arrived at headquarters too late. He was with the rear guard from the Tennessee river to Columbia, Tenn., when Hood advanced with his great army in the fall of 1864. On the night of November 23d, Forrest, having surrounded his command, he led the charge in person, a surgeon of the 8th Michigan and a sergeant of the 14th riding by his side. Forrest's line of battle was broken and scattered and the rear guard saved from capture. In the National Tribune we find the following from Lieutenant Moore of Company "L." He says: "In the night charge at Duck river, November 28th, 1864, I was in command of Company "L," and Major (then Captain) Connelly was at the head of the second battalion of the 14th Illinois. Some one reported that Captain Jenkins, commanding the regiment, was shot. Major Connelly rode along the regimental line to the head of the regiment, encouraging the men to do their duty. When the bugle sounded the 'charge' he was in the thickest of the fight, leading the regiment. At the battle of Nashville we were advancing in an open field (on foot) in the face of a heavy artillery fire. Major Connelly was with the second battalion, riding directly in my rear. The artillery fire was very heavy, and to escape shells we often dropped to the ground, then arising and moving forward. Amid all this iron hail we saw Connelly coolly sitting on his horse, but his men, seeing him thus exposed, insisted on his dismounting. He was so absorbed in the progress and the prospect of capturing the rebel battery that he gave no thought to his own danger." The officers of his regiment having elected him Major over several captains who held older commissions June 22d, 1865, General Oglesby sent him his commission July 4th, 1865. The war being over and Major Connelly having resigned, he was relieved from duty and departed for his northern home at Rock Island, Illinois, where he has been active in developing the resources of that thriving city. He has held important positions as a citizen and is a successful lawyer.

Major Chauncey Miller was born at Harford, Pa., October, 1838; was appointed post adjutant at the camp of organization at Springfield, Illinois, April 17th, 1861, taking rank as 2d lieutenant. Enlisted in 19th Illinois Infantry June 17th, 1861; was promoted to 1st lieutenant and adjutant August 21st, 1861; resigned in August, 1862; was commissioned adjutant in 14th Illinois Cavalry September 21st, 1863; was captured at battle of Bean Station December 14th, 1863; exchanged March 13th, 1865, and was mustered out with regiment. Adjutant Miller was a fine, capable officer. Elected Major July 18th, 1865.

Adjutant Henry W. Carpenter; mustered January 7th, 1863; resigned May 19th, 1863.

Adjutant James Thompson, born at Fort Bradley, Sault Saint Marie, Michigan, May 2d, 1833. His father was a major in the 5th U. S. Infantry, and his grandfather was a major in the patriot army of the Revolution. He was appointed 2d lieutenant Company "D," 10th U. S. Infantry, June 22d, 1854, by the President, and served till August, 1859, then resigned and went into telegraph corps May 8th, 1861; was appointed 2d lieutenant and assistant operator; was captured by Jackson's cavalry and exchanged, and rejoined his corps; served a year, when the corps was mustered out. The members were retained as civilians. October 26th, 1862, enlisted as private in Company "D," 14th Illinois Cavalry; was appointed duty sergeant, then orderly sergeant June, 1863; promoted sergeant major, and July 11th, 1865 appointed adjutant; was mustered out with regiment.

Quartermaster Samuel F. True enlisted December 3d, 1862. Mustered out with regiment.

Surgeon Preston H. Bailhache, born in Columbus, Ohio, February 22d, 1835. Went to Alton, Illinois, in 1838. Commenced practice of medicine 1857. Appointed post surgeon at Camp Yates April 17th, 1861; commissioned assistant surgeon 19th Illinois Infantry July, 1861. Commissioned surgeon 14th Illinois Cavalry February 14th, 1863. Was captured on Stoneman raid July 31st, 1864; exchanged September 3d, 1864. Served with the regiment and on detached duty until mustered out with the regiment.

First Assistant Surgeon George A. Wilson, mustered January 7th, 1863. Served with regiment till surrender of General Stoneman July 31st, 1864. Was soon exchanged; rejoined and served with regiment until resigned April 7th, 1865.

Second Assistant Surgeon John Ivory Wilkins, born in Dublin, Ireland, in 1829; educated at Trinity College; then as physician at a college of surgeons. Commenced practice at Galway, Ireland, in 1850. Emigrated to United States in 1852. Enlisted in Company "H," 86th Illinois Infantry; was transferred by promotion to second assistant surgeon 14th Illinois Cavalry in February, 1863. Was captured July 31st, 1864, at the battle of Sunshine Church, Georgia; was confined in Sunshine, Macon and Libby prisons; exchanged, rejoined regiment in March, 1865. Mustered out with regiment.

Chaplain Samuel Chase, D. D., mustered February 16th, 1863. Resigned March 2d, 1865.

Commissary—Bruce C. Payne, mustered February 6th, 1863. Dismissed April 22d, 1865.

Commissary Alba N. Scribner, mustered June 20th, 1865. Mustered out with regiment.

Sergeant Major Henry C. Carrico, enlisted as private in Campany "C," 14th Illinois Cavalry, mustered January 7th, 1863; promoted sergeant major; promoted 2d lieutenant Company "D;" promoted Captain Company "D;" resigned July 4th, 1865. Captain Carrico was an active and able officer, frequently serving as staff officer in brigade.

Isaac Hollingsworth Allen, born in Harford county, Maryland, February 11th, 1816. Died at his home in Mount Morris, Illinois, May 18th, 1886. Comrade Allen was one of the pioneers of Ogle county, Illinois, having immigrated in 1852. He first enlisted in Company "K," 69th Illinois Infantry June 4th, 1862; commissioned 2d lieutenant June 14th, 1862; mustered out October 6th, 1862; enlisted in Company "I," 14th Illinois Cavalry October 13th, 1862; mustered as orderly sergeant January 7th, 1863; promoted sergeant major; served as acting adjutant; promoted 2d lieutenant Company "D" June 7th, 1863; promoted 1st lieutenant July 18th, 1864. Comrade Allen was naturally a military man, always prompt and obedient, and doubtless the best drilled man in the regiment at its organization, and did most of the early drilling of the regiment. He was present with the regiment in all its active service until captured on the Stoneman raid, August 3d, 1864, being at that time in command of the picket that was first attacked that night. He and his men had been in Major Davidson's detachment and were, from July 27th to August 3d, with scarcely any sleep, and when attacked his men were asleep from utter exhaustion, and all were killed or captured. He was imprisoned at Charleston, S. C., and with other captives was placed under the fire of the U. S. bombarding fleet (the rebels said), as a retaliation. When exchanged he rejoined his regiment and served with great credit through the last campaign, and was mustered out with the regiment. After the war he was given a clerical position in the surgeon general's office of the war department at Washington, D. C., in which service he was stricken down by disease and died. Comrade Allen had many warm friends, and was buried with the honors of war at Washington, D. C., by his comrades of Post No. 5, at Washington. Comrade Allen never received the official acknowledgment that his eminent ability and valuable services merited.

Sergeant Major James L. Thompson, enlisted in Company "D," 14th Regiment Illinois Cavalry, October 26th, 1862. Mustered as 1st duty sergeant January 7th, 1863; was then promoted to sergeant major, and was commissioned adjutant; and mustered out with regiment.

Quartermaster Sergeant Charles West, enlisted in Company "A," 14th Illinois Cavalry, September 12th, 1862; was appointed quartermaster sergeant; then promoted 1st lieutenant Company "B" October 17th, 1864; and mustered out with the regiment.

Quartermaster Sergeant Sylvester A. Huntoon, enlisted in Company "C," 14th Illinois Cavalry, November 25th, 1862; promoted regimental quartermaster sergeant. Mustered out with regiment.

Commissary Sergeant Abna N. Scribner, enlisted in Company "L," October 13th, 1862; promoted regimental commissary sergeant, then promoted regimental commissary June 16th, 1865. Mustered out with regiment.

Commissary Sergeant Caius S. Norris, enlisted in Company "G," 14th Regiment Illinois Cavalry, August 15th, 1862; promoted regimental commissary. Mustered out with regiment.

Commissary Sergeant Seth C. Abell, enlisted in Company "C" September 18th, 1862; promoted commissary sergeant; promoted regimental commissary sergeant; and mustered out with regiment.

Commissary Sergeant Claude B. Hamilton, enlisted in Company "L" February 2d, 1863; promoted regimental commissary sergeant, and mustered out with regiment.

Hospital Steward George A. Sumner, enlisted in Company "L" October 26th, 1862; promoted hospital steward. Discharged July 25th, 1863, for promotion.

Hospital Steward Samuel A. Dow, enlisted in Company "A" September 13th, 1862; promoted hospital steward; discharged June 10th, 1864, for promotion to assistant surgeon 17th Illinois Cavalry.

Hospital Steward Jacob T. Gilmore, enlisted in company "L" October 11th, 1862; promoted hospital steward; mustered out with regiment.

Hospital Steward Frederick W. Livingston, enlisted in Company "A" September 13th, 1862; promoted hospital steward; mustered out with regiment.

Saddler Sergeant John B. Reed, enlisted in Company "M" September 15th, 1862; promoted saddler sergeant; mustered out with regiment.

Chief Bugler Henry S. Walker, enlisted in Company "A" October 1st, 1862; promoted chief bugler. Mustered out with regiment.

Chief Bugler Christian Newmeyer, enlisted in Company "L" November 28th, 1862; promoted chief bugler. Mustered out with regiment.

Veterinary Surgeon Alonzo H. Sanborn, enlisted in Company "K" October 16th, 1862; promoted veterinary surgeon. Discharged April 13th, 1865.

BIOGRAPHIES OF LINE OFFICERS BY COMPANIES.

A.

Captain Marvin S. Carr, mustered January 7th, 1863. Resigned February 10th, 1864.

Captain John S. Henderson, mustered as 2d lieutenant Company "A" January 7th, 1863; promoted captain February 10th, 1864. Resigned June 27th, 1865.

Captain Albert B. Capron, born at Laurel factory, Prince George county, Maryland, June 12th, 1844. With his father, General Capron, he moved to Illinois, where he enlisted in Company "B," 33d Illinois Infantry, August 20th, 1861; was regimental color bearer; was transferred by promotion to 1st lieutenant Company "A," 14th Regiment Illinois Cavalry, March 5th, 1864. In his military service, he says he participated in 23 general battles, besides many skirmishes, and had two horses shot under him, and was wounded three times, and was captured three times, the last time at the night surprise August 3d, 1864; was exchanged and joined regiment with Captain Dent in October, 1864, and commanded Company "A" through the Hood campaign. Was promoted captain July 11th, 1865; and mustered out with regiment. After the war he was employed by his father as purchasing agent for the Japanese government. For more than 20 years he has been a member of the Chicago Board of Trade, and carries on a general grain commission business.

First Lieutenant Horace Capron, born at Laurel factory, Maryland, October 26th, 1842; brought up to farming; emigated to McHenry county, Illinois, 1852; moved to Peoria county, where he enlisted in Company "G," 8th Illinois Cavalry, August, 1861, as a private; was promoted corporal, then 1st sergeant, and received a bronze medal for capturing a rebel flag. The medal had this inscription: "The Congress to 1st Sergeant Horace Capron, Jr., Company "G," 8th Illinois Cavalry, for gallant conduct at Chickahoming and Ashland, June, 1862." He was discharged for promotion November 17th, 1862, and was mustered as 1st lieutenant Company "A," 14th Regiment Illinois Cavalry, January 7th, 1863. He was always with his company, and often in command. He had a horse shot under him in a brisk fight in upper East Tennessee. He led Company "A" in the Indian fight February 2d, 1864, near Quallatown, N. C., and in a gallant charge upon a party of the Indians, was mortally wounded. With other wounded, he was transported over the mountains, at first in a heavy lumber wagon, which was exchanged for a carriage, in which he was taken to Knoxville, Tennessee, where he died February 6th, 1864. His remains were sent to his Illinois home, and buried with the honors of war. In his death the regiment lost one of its finest line officers, who gave great promise of high distinction in the cavalry service. He was highly esteemed by all who knew him, and especially by his company comrades.

First Lieutenant Richard S. Stephenson, enlisted in Company "A," 14th Illinois Cavalry, September 13th, 1862; was promoted to 1st sergeant, then to 2d lieutenant March 5th, 1864; then to 1st lieutenant July 14th, 1865; and was mustered out with the regiment. He was wounded at the battle of Bean Station.

Second Lieutenant Henry Seymour, enlisted in Company "A" at Galesburg, Illinois, October 15th, 1862; was promoted sergeant, then 2d lieutenant July 14th, 1865; and was mustered out with the regiment.

B.

Captain Paul Distler, mustered as captain Company "B" January 7th, 1863. Resigned October 16th, 1864.

Captain Henry H. Mayo, went with the regiment as sutler. He so gallantly fought in every engagement that he was commissioned 1st lieutenant in Company "B" April 22d, 1864. He fought gallantly in the battle of Sunshine church, and though wounded he was of great service in the charge through the rebel lines, and in the retreat. Captain Mayo was an excellent officer. He was commissioned captain October 17th, 1864, and was mustered out with the regiment.

First Lieutenant Henry Heineke, mustered as 1st lieutenant Company "B" January 7th, 1863, and resigned April 22d, 1864.

Second Lieutenant Philip Link, mustered as 2d lieutenant Company "B" January 7th, 1863, and mustered out October 8th, 1863.

Second Lieutenant Wm. R. Huntoon, born in Woodstock, Windsor county, New York, September 3d, 1818; removed to Illinois; enlisted in Company "C," 14th Illinois Cavalry, September 18th, 1862; was appointed sergeant, then promoted 2d lieutenant Company "B" June 22d, 1864; was captured July 31st, 1864; was exchanged and rejoined the regiment October 8th, 1864; and was mustered out with regiment.

C.

Captain James B. Dent; promoted; see field officers.

Captain Jacob M. Balderston, was born in Ohio. He enlisted in Company "A," 1st Illinois Cavalry, in July, 1861. He was captured at Lexington, Mo., September, 1861, and was exchanged and discharged July 14th, 1862. He enlisted in Company "C," 14th Illinois Cavalry, September 8th, 1862; was appointed quartermaster sergeant, then promoted 1st lieutenant July 3d, 1864—the day that he, at the head of a part of his company, charged upon a much greater force of the enemy near the Chattahoochee river, Georgia. He was severely wounded August 3d, 1864, when Capron's brigade was surprised, but he escaped. He was again captured at Nashville, but escaped by knocking down his guard and taking his seven shot

(1902)
FIRST LIEUTENANT WASHINGTON L. SANFORD
Company I, 14th Illinois Cavalry

Spencer rifle and rejoined his command after 12 days of captivity. He was commissioned captain of Company "C" April 21st, 1865; and was mustered out with his regiment. He is now a successful lawyer of Wichita, Kansas. He has served as county attorney and as judge of county court.

First Lieutenant John A. Edwards, enlisted in Company "C," 14th Illinois Cavalry, at Bloomington, Illinois, September 8th, 1862; was appointed 1st sergeant, then commissioned 2d lieutenant April 21st, 1865; and was mustered out with the regiment.

Second Lieutenant Harry M. Evans, mustered with regiment as 2d lieutenant in Company "C," and resigned October 5th, 1863.

Second Lieutenant Putnam Beckwith, born in Magnolia, Putnam county, Illinois, November 27th, 1842; was raised a farmer. Enlisted in Company "A," 1st Illinois Cavalry, July 3d, 1861; was twice wounded and was captured at the battle of Lexington, Mo., September, 1861; was again wounded on picket in southwest Missouri in May, 1862; was discharged July 14th, 1862. Enlisted in Company "C," 14th Illinois Cavalry, September 6th, 1862; was promoted to corporal, then to sergeant, then to quartermaster sergeant, then to 1st sergeant. He led the only party—a band of 10 men—who came through all the way to our lines from the Stoneman disaster, mounted. Was promoted 2d lieutenant of Company "C" May 8th, 1865; and was mustered out with the regiment. He was present with the regiment in every engagement. He was always ready for any duty, and while sergeant was often entrusted with the command of parties on important duties.

D.

Captain Ebenezer L. Foote, mustered as captain of Company "D" January 7th, 1863. Resigned June 7th, 1863.

Captain Henry C. Carrico; see field officers.

Captain Julius W. Miller, enlisted as private in Company "D" September 18th, 1862; promoted 1st lieutenant June 2d, 1863; promoted captain July 18th, 1865; and was mustered out with the regiment.

First Lieutenant Thomas L. Masters, mustered as 1st

lieutenant Company "D" January 7th, 1863. Dismissed from the service June 2d, 1863.

First Lieutenant Isaac H. Allen; see field officers.

Second Lieutenant John Miller, mustered as 2d lieutenant Company "D" January 7th, 1863. Resigned May 27th, 1863.

E.

Captain Benjamin Crandle was mustered as captain of Company "E" February 6th, 1863; and was mustered out with the regiment. We regret that we have no furnished biography of this excellent officer, and not even a record of his capture and imprisonment, though we are sure he was captured on the Stoneman raid.

First Lieutenant George W. Evans was mustered as 1st lieutenant Company "E" February 6th, 1863; and was mustered out with the regiment.

Second Lieutenant John Hahs was mustered as 2d lieutenant Company "E" February 6th, 1863, and resigned January 30th, 1864.

Second Lieutenant George C. Smith was not mustered, as he was promoted assistant surgeon in 5th Tennessee.

Second Lieutenant Wm. M. Duval, enlisted in Company "E" September 20th, 1862; appointed 1st sergeant; promoted 2d lieutenant March 29th, 1865; captured on Stoneman raid and died in rebel prison.

Second Lieutenant Robert P. Simmons, born in Gallatin county, Illinois, July 5th, 1842; brought up a farmer; enlisted in Campany "B," 1st Illinois Cavalry, July 4th, 1861; was twice captured at the siege of Lexington; was paroled and mustered out with regiment. Enlisted in Company "E," 14th Illinois Cavalry, December 20th, 1862; was appointed sergeant, then promoted 2d lieutenant June 2d, 1865; and was mustered out with the regiment.

F.

Captain Thomas K. Jenkins; promoted; see field officers.

Captain Wm. H. Guy, born in Fairfield county, Ohio, March 25th, 1836; emigrated to Fayette county, Illinois, in 1839, with parents; was a farmer until the Civil War broke out; enlisted and served three months under the call for 75,000; served in the 8th Illinois Infantry under Richard J. Oglesby; enlisted in 14th Illinois Cavalry and mustered as 1st lieutenant Company "F" January 7th, 1863; was promoted captain July 18th, 1865; and was mustered out with the regiment. Captain Guy was captured at Sunshine Church, Georgia, July 31st, 1864; was exchanged. Captain Guy was a brave and skillful officer.

First Lieutenant Richard M. Hughes, enlisted at Vandalia, Illinois, in Company "F" October 15th, 1862; mustered as 2d lieutenant February 6th, 1863; promoted 1st lieutenant; and mustered out with the regiment.

Second Lieutenant John Sayler, enlisted at Howard's Point, Illinois, and was mustered as 2d lieutenant of Company "F" January 7th, 1863, and resigned October 9th, 1863.

Second Lieutenant John B. Hinds, enlisted in Company "F" at Ramsey, Illinois, December 18th, 1863; appointed sergeant; promoted 2d lieutenant July 18th, 1865; and was mustered out with the regiment.

G.

Captain Wm. Perkins, mustered as captain of Company "G" January 7th, 1863; was wounded and captured on the Stoneman raid August 3d, 1864; was exchanged and resigned May 15th, 1865.

Captain Chauncey Miller; see field officers.

First Lieutenant Lewis W. Boren, born in Pulaski county, Illinois, December 11th, 1835; brought up a farmer. At manhood entered a dry goods store as clerk. Enlisted October, 1861, in Company "A," 60th Illinois Infantry; was appointed duty sergeant; was discharged for disability June, 1862. Enlisted in 109th Illinois Infantry, Company "K." In August, 1862, was transferred by promotion as 1st lieutenant Company "G," 14th Illinois Cavalry. While in Kentucky service was captured and escaped at Lafayette, Tennessee in June, 1863; was wounded at Bean Station December 14th, 1863. Lieutenant Boren was one of the most skillful and bold line officers of the regiment. He was often employed on hazardous duty. He resigned December 12th, 1864.

First Lieutenant John F. Thomas, enlisted in Company "G" in Johnson county, Illinois, September 1st, 1862; promoted 2d lieutenant March 8th, 1864; promoted 1st lieutenant March 1st, 1865; resigned May 24th, 1865. Was a good officer.

First Lieutenant John W. Sanders, born in Caroline, East Virginia, May 30th, 1825; brought up as farmer; emigrated to Johnson county, Illinois, in 1838. Enlisted in Company "H," 14th Illinois Cavalry, September 25th, 1862; transferred to Company "G" March 1st, 1863. Appointed corporal, then appointed duty sergeant. Promoted 2d lieutenant December 12th, 1864; commissioned 1st lieutenant June 8th, 1865. Mustered out with the regiment. A trusty, faithful officer.

Second Lieutenant Enoch C. Palmer, mustered as 2d lieutenant Company "G" January 7th, 1863. Resigned October 6th, 1863.

Second Lieutenant John Welch, enlisted in Company "G" in Menard county, Illinois, September 22d, 1862; was appointed commissary sergeant; then promoted 2d lieutenant June 8th, 1865; and mustered out with the regiment. Lieutenant Welch was a comrade with George W. Norris in their long and perilous journey in escaping from the Stoneman raid disaster.

H.

Captain Wm. Alexander Lord, born in Rochester, New York, August 31st, 1838. Childhood was spent in Rochester, Albany and Buffalo. In 1851 moved to Chicago, Illinois. In 1856 graduated from Judge Bell's Commercial College. In 1860 graduated from Northwestern University, Evanston, Illinois, with degree of A. B. Employed as accountant by G. and C. Union R. R. Co.; devised new system of book accounts for their shops. Went to Elkhorn, Wisconsin. Studied law with Judge Spooner. When the war broke out, enlisted 70 men; was made 1st lieutenant in Tompkins' battalion of mounted riflemen, afterward Company "H," 13th Missouri; and later 5th Missouri Cavalry. After more than a year's service the command was transferred to Illinois credit, and Governor Yates commissioned Tompkins major 3d battalion and Lieutenant Lord as captain Company "H," 14th Illinois Cavalry; were mustered February 6th, 1863. Commanded Company "H" until September 30th, 1863; was then detached as A. A. G. of 4th brigade, 4th division,

23d Army Corps. Captain Lord served on General Stoneman's staff during the raid to Macon, Georgia, and did valuable service in the battle of Sunshine Church, and led one of the columns that charged through the rebel lines after Stoneman surrendered. During the last campaign Captain Lord served on General Schofield's staff. He was mustered out with the regiment.

Colonel Capron, in his report of Stoneman raid, says: "I would here mention the valuable assistance which Captain Lord of the 14th Illinois, and assistant commissary of musters on General Stoneman's staff, rendered me, not only in the engagement of the 31st, where he exhibited great gallantry and bravery in leading a portion of my command several times in the charges made on the enemy, but also on my retreat in obtaining information in regard to the best route to be taken, and in constantly leading the advance of my command."

First Lieutenant John S. Anderson was mustered as 1st lieutenant of Company "H" February 6th, 1863, and was in command of the company much of the time, as Captain Lord was serving as staff officer. Lieutenant Anderson was a brave, active and skillful officer and deserved a more fitting biographical sketch than is here given. He was wounded December 22d, 1863. He was mustered out with the regiment.

Second Lieutenant John W. Howell was mustered as 2d Lieutenant Company "H" February 6th, 1863, and resigned February 3d, 1864.

Second Lieutenant Winfield W. Woods, enlisted in Company "H" November 15th, 1862; was appointed sergeant; was promoted 2d lieutenant November 3d, 1864; was mustered out with the regiment.

I.

Captain Francis M. Hagaman, mustered as captain of Company "I" January 7th, 1863. He resigned May 25th, 1864.

Captain Francis Bocke, mustered as 1st lieutenant Company "I" January 7th, 1863; commissioned as captain May 25th, 1864; was mustered out with regiment.

First Lieutenant DeRiley Kilbourne, mustered as 2d lieutenant Company "I" January 7th, 1863; was commissioned 1st lieutenant May 25th, 1864. He commanded the howitzer battery on the Morgan raid. He was severely wounded at the battle of Bean Station December 14th, 1863. He resigned by reason of physical disability October 19th, 1864.

First Lieutenant Washington L. Sanford was born at Liberty, near Dayton, Ohio, July 1st, 1825. In 1836 with his father removed to Noble county, Indiana, where the Miami Indians yet remained. In 1847 removed to Ogle county, Illinois. His occupation was farming and school teaching. In 1862 became convinced that it was his duty to sacrifice everything for his country; enlisted as a private in Company "I," 14th Illinois Cavalry, October 6th, 1862; was appointed 1st duty sergeant, and soon after appointed orderly sergeant. Served with the company through the Kentucky campaign, and also through the East Tennessee campaign; was commissioned 2d lieutenant of Company "I" May 25th, 1864. Served in the Georgia campaign. Commanded his company from October 19th, 1864, through all the hard service in middle Tennessee and until our last battle at Nashville, Tennessee; was promoted 1st lieutenant. The fighting in the department being ended and being broken in health he resigned and returned home about the last of March, 1865. Having kept and collected notes of the service of the regiment, he was chosen regimental historian. By the courtesy of his former cohistorian, comrade Martin West and others, officers and men of the regiment, he was permitted the use of personal notes of every important event and movement, and to these together with an elaborate and thorough examination of the government published official reports of the Union and Confederate officers, is due whatever merit his history may possess.

First Lieutenant Wm. H. Puckett, born in Fountain City, Wayne county, Indiana, June 22d, 1838; removed with parents to Jo Daviess county, Illinois, in 1848; worked on a farm. Enlisted in Company "I," 14th Illinois Cavalry, October 14th, 1862, as private; was appointed duty sergeant; was appointed orderly sergeant, vice Sanford promoted; was tendered the office of sergeant major, but declined. Was commissioned 2d lieutenant of Company "I" October 19th, 1864; commissioned 1st lieutenant

March 28th, 1865. Served with the regiment in every engagement and duty, except when absent; detailed as recruiting officer from November, 1863, to June, 1864. Was mustered out with the regiment. He is now engaged in the lumber business in Nora, Jo Daviess county, Illinois. Lieutenant Puckett was one of the bravest of soldiers, and a skillful officer and as a comrade was beloved by all.

Second Lieutenant Moses G. Hascall was enlisted at Byron, Illinois, as private, October 17th, 1862. He was appointed sergeant. In 1864 he was made leader of regimental band. He was commissioned 2d lieutenant of Company "I" March 28th, 1865, having previously served as orderly sergeant. He was with the regiment continuously, and served in every engagement and expedition. He had previously served under Grant in the 7th Illinois Infantry at Donelson and at Pittsburg landing. Lieutenant Hascall was a faithful soldier, a brave and skillful officer and a man beyond reproach, esteemed by all.

K.

Captain Wm. R. Sanford, born in Cayuga county, New York, April 12th, 1831. Finished his education at Homer Academy, Cortland county, New York. Brought up to farming; began to teach school when 18 years old; came to Bloomington, Illinois, at 22 years of age; taught school for 7 years, then engaged in dry goods business at Griggsville, Illinois, until 1861; then sold out and enlisted at the first call of troops for three months' service; then raised a company for the 12th Illinois Cavalry; declined a commission and was assigned to aid in the organization of the 14th Illinois Cavalry, and was mustered in as captain of Company "K," 14th Illinois Cavalry, January 7th, 1863. Was with the regiment in all its active work until captured. Aided in the pursuit of Morgan and in his final capture— 30 days and nights of tedious service. Was through all the hard service in East Tennessee and in the Indian fight at Quallatown, N. C. Served in the Georgia campaign; was wounded in the battle of Sunshine Church July 31st, 1864. Aided in the charge of Capron's command through the rebel lines; was captured in the night surprise August 3d, 1864, and taken to Charleston, S. C., prison, and was one of the prisoners that were placed by the enemy under the fire of our gunboats. Was exchanged and rejoined the regiment at Nashville, Tennessee, in the winter of 1864-65. Fighting in that department was ended and he resigned May 12th, 1865; preferring active life in his own business to inactive life at government expense. He has heeded the scripture injunction "Whatever thy hand findeth to do, do it with all thy might," and he has been successful. Now resides at Center, Missouri.

Captain George W. Bellows enlisted at Caledonia, Illinois, in Company "G," 14th Illinois Cavalry; was appointed quartermaster sergeant, then 1st sergeant; was then promoted as 2d lieutenant of Company "K," commissioned February 27th, 1864; was promoted 1st lieutenant May 31st, 1865; commissioned captain June 26th, 1865. Was mustered out with the regiment. The rapid rise in rank in a company to which he was transferred speaks well of the reputation and soldierly qualities of this officer. He was captured July 31st, 1864, and exchanged.

First Lieutenant John R. Garner was commissioned 1st lieutenant Company "K" February 26th, 1863; and resigned February 17th, 1864.

First Lieutenant Llewellyn D. Brown, enlisted in Company "K" February 15th, 1863; commissioned 1st lieutenant February 17th, 1864. Resigned March 7th, 1865.

First Lieutenant Alexander M. Dunbar, born in Chester, Cole county, Illinois, September 18th, 1837; was educated for the law; commenced practice in Cedar county, Iowa, in 1861. Enlisted in Company "M," 1st Iowa cavalry; was promoted 2d lieutenant in quartermaster department; was honorably mustered out under curtailment of cavalry enlistment; then enlisted in 65th Illinois Infantry May 28th, 1862; was mustered out with regiment September 26th, 1862. Enlisted in Company "K," 14th Regiment Illinois Cavalry, October 2d, 1862; was appointed duty sergeant, then commissioned 1st lieutenant June 26th, 1865; and was mustered out with the regiment.

Second Lieutenant James S. Stein, enlisted at Shelbyville, Illinois, mustered as 2d lieutenant Company "K," January 7th, 1863. Died February 27th, 1864, of wound received January 27th, 1864. Lieutenant Stein was a good officer.

Second Lieutenant James W. Beck, enlisted at Shelbyville September 21st, 1862; was appointed 1st sergeant; was captured August 1st, 1863, near Stamford, Kentucky; was paroled; was commissioned 2d lieutenant Company "K," July 26th, 1865.

L.

Captain Alvin Evarts, enlisted at Rock Island, Illinois, mustered as captain of Company "L" January 7th, 1863. Resigned November 14th, 1863.

Captain Henry C. Connelly; see field officers.

Captain Newton N. Burpee, enlisted at De Kalb, Illinois; commissioned 1st lieutenant Company "L" January 7th, 1863; commissioned captain July 11th, 1865; mustered out with the regiment.

First Lieutenant Job L. Grace, born in Springfield, Bradford county, Pennsylvania, June 14th, 1843; was raised on a farm. Emigrated to Mercer county, Illinois, in 1858; enlisted in Company "L," 14th Illinois Cavalry, in September, 1862; was appointed commissary sergeant, then orderly sergeant July 22d, 1864; was commissioned 1st lieutenant July 11th, 1865; was mustered out with the regiment.

Second Lieutenant Wm. M. Moore, born September 20th, 1835, in Armstrong county, Pennsylvania. Removed to Clarion county, Pennsylvania, in 1837. In 1860 went to Rock Island, Illinois; enlisted in Company "G," 1st Illinois Cavalry, March 27th, 1862, at Monmouth, Illinois; was mustered out with that regiment as corporal July 14th, 1862; returned to Rock Island; enlisted in Company "L," 14th Regiment Illinois Cavalry October 7th, 1862; was promoted from private to 1st sergeant January 7th, 1863; was commissioned 2d lieutenant and mustered August 12th, 1864. Lieutenant Moore was in command of the company from February, 1864, most of the time until muster out, as Captain Connelly and Lieutenant Burpee were both on detached duty. When these officers were promoted Moore was offered the 1st lieutenancy, but declined in favor of Lieutenant Job L. Grace. Lieutenant Moore served 109 days in the 1st Illinois Cavalry and 1,028 days in the 14th Illinois Cavalry, and was never absent from his company except 20 days on leave of absence to visit his home in June, 1865. Lieutenant Moore was a fine appearing soldier, and a perfect gentleman. As an officer he was cool-headed, skillful and brave. Where duty called he seemed to know no fear. A letter to the writer detailing a short account of Lieutenant Moore's escape from Stoneman raid disaster is lost. We give a few points as we remember them. With a comrade he was separated from the main body and obliged, amid a shower of bullets, to abandon their horses, and secrete themselves in a hole covered with weeds; from there they wandered on foot, secreting themselves by day in swamps and thickets, traveling by night, living on roots and berries and an occasional ear of green corn, eaten raw. For many days he thus wandered and was finally captured between the lines of the opposing armies by Union troops, who supposed that they had captured a veritable Johnnie.

M.

Captain Thomas S. Lupton was mustered as captain January 7th, 1863, and was discharged May 15th, 1865. A good officer. Captain Lupton was captured on Stoneman raid, was exchanged on Oct. 1, 1864, and again captured.

Captain Wm. W. Rowcliff was mustered as 1st lieutenant of Company "M" January 7th, 1863; was commissioned captain July 18th, 1865; and was mustered out with the regiment.

Second Lieutenant Jacob J. Ruby, was mustered as 2d lieutenant of Company "M" January 7th, 1863. Resigned January 8th, 1864.

Second Lieutenant Wm. W. Cowles, born in Hampshire county, Massachusetts, December 7th, 1830; learned the blacksmith trade; emigrated to Peoria county, Illinois, in 1856; enlisted in Company "M," 14th Illinois Cavalry, September 15th, 1862; was appointed orderly sergeant; was commissioned 2d lieutenant July 11th, 1865; and was mustered out with the regiment.

Our records give imperfect casualty lists; these we have supplemented with all we could obtain by other means. From some companies we could get nothing more, but they doubtless had the same casualties. These we have used in the biographies of officers and in the roster. We also add a list of names of wounded and captured that are not noted in the roster or biographies.

ROLLS.

Classified roster of the 14th Illinois Cavalry Volunteers, compiled from the adjutant-general's report, with such corrections and additions as it is possible to gather from all other sources. To bring the roster within the limits of the book, only the most important data is included, words are abbreviated wherever possible, as cpt. for captured; cpn. for captain; lt. for lieutenant; serg., sergeant; corp., corporal; wnd., wounded; di., died; dis., discharged; hosp., hospital; pris., prison. Time abbreviations, 64, 1864; Jan., January; Feb., February, etc. We adopt this form of roster to save space and to cheapen the cost, as the tabular form is expensive. We find the data furnished by our company records very imperfect, and sometimes erroneous. We have striven to correct all errors and to furnish missing data as far as we could. Doubtless many that died in hospitals or at home, as well as many that were discharged for disabilities, were wounded in engagements, as seldom was it noted in the records when a comrade was wounded. The record of the captured was also imperfect. Deserters and reclaimed men are omitted from the lists as not being members. All who were members are accounted for in their proper lists. The members in each class are separated into companies by their company letter preceding each class. In these lists we include only enlisted men. We are compelled to omit dates from this roster, except dates of killed and wounded.

In the great Stoneman raid the dates include the events as J. 31 for July 31st, 1864 (battle of Sunshine church); A. 3 for August 3d, 1864 (the night attack and great slaughter). For died we use d.; for died in hospital, d. h.; for died at home, d. home; for died in prison, d. p.; d. A., for died in Andersonville; d. M., died in Macon; d. R., died in Richmond; d. An., died in Annapolis, Md.; d. C., died in Charleston, etc. First list the killed. Company:

A—Cary T. Thurman, com. ser., J. 31; Theodore W. Gleason, Nov. 24, 64 (near Columbia, Tenn., in Hood campaign); John P. Holland, A. 3; Fred Henderson, Feb. 2, 64 (Indian fight); Charles M. Lindsey, A. 3; Austin Martin, A. 3; Parker Robinson, A. 3; Hamilton Henderson, A. 3; Garret Van Zandt, A. 3; George Waffle, A. 3; Thomas White, A. 3; John R. Atkinson, Dec. 14,63 (Bean Station); Wm. B. A. McKee, Dec. 14, 63; Geo. H. Jones, Nov. 24, 64; John L. Smith, J. 31; George W. Stodgell, J. 31.

B—Peter Reising, ser.; Henry Handshaw, corp.; Herman Blass, Timothy Barnett, Christian Trefty, Gotleib Ziegler, Timothy Kindly, James R. Wells, all killed A. 3.

C—Aaron W. Scott, Jul. 3, 64; John Kelly, Feb. 5, 63; Thomas Lynch, Jul. 20, 63; George H. Mason, standard bearer, Dec. 14, 63; John Sifes, Jul. 19, 63 (while sick in hospital, Scottsville, Ky.); Geo. Robinson, A. 3; John L. Maurer, d. wnd., Jul. 3, 64.

D—Thomas W. Madigan, James P. Moret, Dec. 2, 63 (Walker's ford); Charles L. Cook, Henry Plountz, Joseph Smith, A. 3; Samuel Barricks, June 13, 64.

E—John Lyons, John N. French, A. 3; Franklin Thompson, J. 31; James Dailey, May 27, 64 (Indians); Thomas Richards, Mar. 8, 64; Noah Friar, Nov. 24, 64.

F—Jacob Myer, Geo. W. Preston, Wm. Vanhorn, Thomas Vanhorn, Benjamin W. Wilson, Geo. Wiler, Peter Whitts, Albert N. Sharrott, A. 3; Wm. Bishop, May 25, 63; Wm. Clary, Jan. 18, 65; Wm. J. Fink, Dec. 2, 63.

G—Huffard Clark, James W. Hunt, Thomas Lefler, James Parker, Azariah J. Cannon, James P. Gregory, Jesse P. Ladford, Josiah McNew, Joel R. Pierson, Lander J. Passmore, Warren O. Smoot, all A. 3; Lewis W. Smith, J. 31; Francis Moon, Oct. 20, 63; Shedrick Dunn, Oct. 11, 63, wound; Edward A. Chesley, May 2, 64, of wound.

H—Geo. S. Howell, com. serg.; Martin V. Cline, Thomas H. Cooper, A. 3; Albert Anderson, Dec. 2, 63; David D. Weed, Dec. 20, 63; Joseph Wheeler, Jul. 28, 63.

I—Cassius C. Beemis, cpt., J. 31, k. escaping from pris.; Boston Brininger, John Gogan, John Mellois, James McNichols, Martin D. Rollison, Herbert Vandeburg, all J. 31; Kendrick W. Chapin, Oliver C. Douglass, Benjamin F. Welch, A. 3; James Dunn, Dec. 14, 63; Thomas Heath, Feb. 2, 64.

K—John A. Butler, Thomas J. Cox, A. 3; Joseph Ridley, Feb. 2, 64; John Little, Oct. 20, 63.

L—Patrick Cunningham, Francis Watts, John W. Kelso, John Long, A. 3, all died in rebel prisons.

M—Daniel W. York, J. 31.

Enlisted men who died in rebel prisons, where and when captured:

A—Cpt., J. 31, Zeno Hilliard, di. Wilmington pris.; cpt., A. 3, Joseph B. Skillman, di. Anp.; Swan Oleson, di. And.; Joel W. Slaughter, far. cpt., Dec. 14, 63; di. R. pris.

B—Cpt., J. 31, Charles A. Dettell, com. serg., di. Wil.; John Boehm, corp., And.; Michael Klein, A. 3, di. And.

C—Cpt., A. 3, Culberton Highland, And.; Geo. Coleman, di. Anap.

D—Cpt., A. 3, John Kreigor, And.; Charles Simpson, And.; Sherman L. Sackett, di. exchange boat, cpt. Dec. 14, 63; John Atkinson, And.; cpt., Dec. 2, 63; John Fowler, And.; cpt., J. 31, John O. Hallan, Flor.

E—Cpt., J. 31, Walker Wilmot, Anap.; Scott Await, Flor.; Jacob Borden, Flor.; Geo. Jones, exchange boat; Wm. Duval, 1st serg., Wil.

F—Cpt., Jul. 31, John K. Hanks, Anp.; Lucien Nichols, And.; Albert Philbrook, 1st serg., And.; Thomas Hamilton, Anp.; Steel Mills, And.; Charles A. Pratt, Anp.; cpt., A. 3; John B. Soiles, And.; Jacob Kent., And.

G—Cpt., Jul. 31, John Smith, And.

H—Cpt., Jul. 31, Joseph Gorbit, serg., Anp.; Isaac Boyer, serg., And.; Geo. W. Newman, musician, Anp.; James S. Perkins, Charleston; Blaxton Steward, Charleston; Francis M. Parkhurst, And.

I—Cpt., Jul. 31, Philip Meiney, And.; Joshua D. Cross, And.; Wm. Ellison, And.; Richard G. Wilson, Anp.

K—Cpt., Jul. 31, Joseph McCarty, Eli Brazington, Wm. A. Herrill, all di. And.; cpt, A. 3, Moses B. Largent, 1st serg.; Henry Senna, di. And.; Andrew J. Whitehead, Flor.; cpt., Dec. 2, 63, Wm. Clark, di. And.

L—Cpt—Jul. 31, Wm. J. Worley, di Anp.

M—Cpt., Jul. 31, Benjamin Kaufman, serg., Flor.; Henry Skinner, corp.; James A. Fernan, Theodore W. Haines, all di. And.

Total died in prison, 52. Estimating these with the killed makes lost by engagements, 150.

Enlisted men died when:

A—Frank A. Howard, Apr. 3, 63; Adam Peterson, Feb. 9, 65; Jacob Sornberger, Apr. 7, 63.

B—Jacob Froehlich, Mar. 3, 63; Harmon Huck, Mar.

15, 64; Louis Klein, May 20, 63; Henry Schneiderfritz, Aug. 29, 63; John Ziller, May 31, 63; Louis Grunckle, Mar. 15, 65; Jeremiah Sutton, May 5, 65; Samuel Trasher, Nov. 8, 64.

C—Joseph W. Clark, serg., Jul. 12, 63; Elijah Arnett, Sept. 8, 64; Jacob R. Cabel, Feb. 16, 63; John C. Crotchett, Apr. 7, 63; Leonidas Beckwith, May 16, 64; Braxton G. Plunkett, Apr. 4, 63; Earl Underhill, Jul. 19, 64.

D—Eri Meyer, q. m. serg., Dec. 63; Charles B. Goyer, Apr., 7, 63; Wm. Hughes, May 28, 63; John Harvey, May 31, 63; Hiram Washburne, Aug. 12, 63; Geo. W. Crickman, Apr. 7, 64; Joseph A. Marvlet, June 6, 64.

E—Wm. Sage, Mar. 23, 63; Richard Stone, Feb. 13, 63; Henry Artman, Apr. 10, 64; Geo. Hughes, June 18, 65; Stephen Morgan, June 6, 63; John Richards, Dec. 15, 63; Josiah F. Reagan, June 20, 64; Wm. Roleman, June 11, 64.

F—Jonatha Kitchen, Jan. 12, 63; Darby Mehan, Feb. 20, 63; William Porter, Feb. 4, 63; Alfred M. Witt, Dec. 23, 63; wnd. Dec. 14, 63; Franklin Brown, May 19, 63.

G—Joseph Miles, corp., Mar. 19, 63; Theophilus Fulton, corp., Mar. 15, 64; Robert Norris, serg. cpt. Jul. 28, 64, di. Jan. 6, 65; Wiley Fields, blksmith, June 20, 63; Wm. J. Cowan, Jan. 28, 63; Mahu Fields, Nov. 10, 63; Henry W. Hale, June 2, 63; Claiborn D. Hutchison, May 29, 63; James Marcum, Feb. 19, 63; Isaac J. Miller, Feb. 21, 63; Geo. Smith, Mar. 17, 63; Andrew J. Simpson, Feb. 17, 64.

H—Wm. H. Hosick, serg., Feb. 7, 65; John W. Baskett, Apr. 2, 63; Henry Beck, Jul. 16, 63; Geo. W. Garrison, Apr. 8, 63; John Green, Apr. 8, 63; John M. Little, Dec. 13, 63, wnd. Dec. 2, 63; Henry Young, wnd. Dec. 14, 63, di. Jan. 16, 64.

I—John J. Bonney, Feb. 14, 64; Sanders Brown, Feb. 10, 63; Francis B. Chadwick, Apr. 6, 63; Daniel M. Elliott, Dec. 8, 63; Alexander M. Gundy, Oct. 9, 64; Michael Lenan, Jan. 12, 63; Garret Niles, serg., wnd. Dec. 2, 63, di. Apr. 9, 64; John S. Pickard, Mar. 29, 63; Wm. H. Stewart, Aug. 10, 63; Erastus W. Stuart, Nov. 3, 64; Joseph R. Brown, Aug. 1, 64; Charles Palmer, Apr. 5, 63; Nelson Vandrisen, Nov. 15, 63.

K—Eli Macklin, wagn., Mar. 12, 63; Samuel Gibbs,

Jul. 21, 63; Isaac Reubensdall, Dec. 22, 63; Edwin Grant, Mar. 27, 64; Samuel J. Houston, May 8, 64; Pleasant Houston, May 18, 64; Stephen M. Moore, Nashville, Tenn.

L—Josep Aspen, Jan. 31, 63; Jonathan Cumpstem, Sept. 13, 64; Wm. S. Cavanaugh, Apr. 19, 63; James Fleming, Oct. 26, 63; James Jackson, Jan. 13, 63; Silas Valentine, Jan. 23, 64; John Young, Mar. 5, 64; Thomas Cordial, May 65; Henry E. Fleming, Oct. 12, 64; Thomas H. Nestor, May, 64.

M—Geo. Cook, Jul. 9, 63; Samuel Cleivtt, Aug. 17, 63; Thomas Connor, Feb. 2, 63; Morgan Trahern, Dec. 6, 62; Harrison S. Smith, June 19, 64.

Total number died, 92; death loss of regiment, 242.

Enlisted men discharged for disability and for other causes. When only noted "discharged" it will indicate disability. Discharged for other cause will be so noted. Many of the disability discharges were on account of wounds, though not so noted in the records. The last date is date of discharge:

A—James B. Morgan, serg., Jan. 17, 65; Wm. W. Wilson, serg., Jul. 2, 65; Walter Baldwin, serg., Jul. 1, 65; Wm. F. Plumb, serg., cpt. J. 31, 64; dis. Jul. 2, 65, prisoner; Samuel Freemale, corp., cpt. Jul. 31, 64, dis. June 16, 65; Wm. Allen, corp. Dec. 28, 64; John McHenry temst., May 8, 63; Geo. W. Woodcock, temst., Jul. 6, 63; Washington I. Jobes, wagn., June 21, 65; Milton Barton, sadler, May 21, 65; Wm. Barfoot, 64; Geo. H. Carr, Jan. 8, 64; Henry Comstock, Jn., June 4, 65; Frank A. Curtis, cpt. Jul. 31, May 30, 65, pris; Osmond T. Capron, Jul. 2, 65; Jefferson Ely, Sep. 12,'63; Charles Errick, Oct. 11, 65; Chester D. Goff, May 30, 65; John Kobb, wnd. Dec. 14, 63, Dec. 25, 63; Adam Kinser, 64; Peter Lewis, Aug. 10, 65; James McHenry, May 8, 63; David McWilliams, Jul. 8, 65; Charles Murdock, cpt. Aug. 3, 64; May 20, 65; Henry C. Nevitt, Aug. 3, 65; Alfred Somers, Mar. 18, 65; Amon Stanton, May 18, 63; Wm. Triplet, May, 63; Melville Buell, Jul. 12, 65; Samuel Frenrole, May 30, 65; Washington Fauts, May 12, 65; Edmond Groshen, Jan. 26, 65; Warren Gabriel, May 30, 65; Daniel Gilmartin, cpt. J. 31, 64, May 30, 65, pris.; Wm. B. Johnson, cpt. Aug. 3, Jan. 12, 65; Thomas Malone, cpt. Nov. 24,

64, May 30, 65; Wm. Prater, cpt. Aug. 3, May 30, 65; Benjamin Piper, Jan. 7, 63; Newton Smith, cpt. Jul. 31, May 30, 65, prisoner.

B—Albert Decker, corp., June 26, 63; Frank H. Westerman, corp., cpt. Jul. 31, June 21, 65, pris; John Oetters, temst., Jul. 6, 63; Albert Terohm, blksmith, Jul. 7, 65; Wm. Altman, Mar. 21, 64; Nicholas Barkes, Apr. 11, 63; Geo. Ebert, Dec. 9, 63; Wm. Gebhard, June 22, 65; Casper Hawser, cpt. Jul. 31, Jul. 20, 65, pris; John Hier Mier, cpt. J. 31, Jul. 8, 65, pris; John Johnson, Mar. 21, 65; Frank Kowarts, May 13, 63; Henry H. McPherson, Dec. 9, 63; Louis Mayn, cpt. Aug. 3, May 22, 65, pris; Charles Richter, May 30, 63; Geo. Ruihty, Aug. 22, 63; Joseph Shott, June 23, 65; Jacob Sansans, May 17, 64; Frederick Shramm, May 30, 63; Sebastian Wieland, May 22, 63; Joseph Seithen, May 20, 65; Thomas Varen, May 23, 63; Frederick J. Foot, June 22, 65; Frederick Farber, Aug. 13, 63; Christian Rayer, May 18, 65; Wm. Suarman, June 13, 63; Christian Stabler, Apr. 20, 65; Geo. Smith, May 27, 65; Henry Uhli, June 9, 65; Frank H. Westerman, cpt. Aug. 3, May 30, 65.

C—Wm. Gibson, serg., cpt. Jul. 31, May 30, 65, pris; Michael D. Ramey, corp., Sept. 7, 63; Elias W. Bowman, bugler, Jun. 20, 65; John Buxton, far., June 8, 65; John Linkogle, blksmith, May 30, 63; John W. Utley, sadl., cpt. Aug. 3, June 12, 65; Jerry A. Arnold, cpt. Aug. 3, May 20, 65, pris.; Morgan Dick, cpt. Aug. 3, May 20, 65, pris; Andrew K. Jones, cpt. Aug. 3, June 12, 65, pris.; Elias Lowther, Nov. 16, 63; Joseph Middleton, June 8, 65; Wm. Peeks, cpt. Jul. 31, June 12, 65; Martin Parks, June 20, 63; John H. Richardson, Jr., June 18, 65; Samuel Rogers, June 6, 63; Theodore Sample, cpt. Nov. 23, 64, Jul. 12, 65, pris.; Charles Scully, cpt. Aug. 3, Jul. 12, 65, pris.; Frederick Schener, cpt. Aug. 16, 64, June 8, 65; Geo. D. Stephen, May 13, 63; Henry Weber, cpt. Aug. 3, May 24, 65, pris; Henry Webb, cpt. Jul. 31, May 30, 65, pris.; Thomas Crimigan, cpt. Aug. 3, Jul. 12, 65, pris.; Joseph Gunning, cpt. Aug. 3, 64, Jul. 14, 65, pris.; Christopher C. Payne, cpt. Jul. 31, 65, June 3, pris.; Wm. Peck, June 25, 65; Martin Parker, June 23, 63; Barrett Sweeney, cpt. Jul. 31, May 30, 65, pris.; James B. Weaver, June 17, 65.

PLAT OF POSITIONS OF PERSONS IN THE GROUP PICTURE
OF MEMBERS OF THE

Fourteenth Illinois Cavalry Association

TAKEN THURSDAY, AUGUST 30, 1900
AT THEIR REUNION IN CHICAGO, ILLINOIS

The seats are numbered from the lower one upward. Persons on each seat are numbered from the right as we face the picture.

FIRST SEAT:

1. Lieut. W. L. SANFORD, "I"
2. Capt. WM. R. SANFORD, "K"
3. Lieut. JOHN F. THOMAS, "G"
4. Maj. WM. A. LORD, "H"
5. Maj. JAMES B. DENT, "C"
6. Capt. ALBERT B. CAPRON, "A"
7. Lieut. WM. M. MOORE, "L"
8. Capt. WM. H. GUY, "F"
9. Lieut. P. BECKWITH, "C"

SECOND SEAT:

1. MRS. J. F. STRATTEN,
   (Captain Hagaman's Daughter)
2. MRS. JANE HAGAMAN,
   (Captain's Widow)
3. Sergt. GEO. NORRIS, "G"
4. Sergt. WM. F. PLUMB, "A"
5. J. F. RANSOME, "C"
6.
7. L. A. COBB, "C"
8. E. A. NATTINGER, "C"
9. J. S. NEVINS, "A"
10. WM. MORAN, "A"
11.

THIRD SEAT:

1. WM. D. LORD, (Major's Son)
2. MISS LENA COBB
3. MRS. L. A. COBB
4. WARREN HUNT, "L"
5. CHARLES GRAVES, "L"
6. F. C. ADAMS, "L"
7.
8. WM. SMITH, "B"
9. JOHN MORSCH, "B"

FOURTH SEAT:

1. CHARLES SCULLEY, "C"
2. BRUCE PAYNE
3. MRS. C. A. FREEMAN,
   (Captain Mayo's Daughter)
4. MR. C. A. FREEMAN
5. Lieut. WM. H. PUCKETT, "I"
6. H. L. LOCKWOOD, "I"
7. GEO. KLASSY, "I"
8. WM. ENNIS, "I"

NOTE—When the picture was taken there was no thought of including it in the book; had there been, a deal of perplexity in obtaining names would have been prevented. We have done the best we could, and yet there are a number of blanks to be filled by writing names as they are learned. It was understood that only the members of the association, composed of comrades and relatives, were to be in the picture. We have included the name of Bruce Payne, not in the list, because it was pointed out by many comrades.

D—Rush Deskins, 1st serg., Aug. 1, 63; Charles E. Sackett, serg., June 20, 65; John Rogan, serg., May 18, 65; Thomas A. Hickman, corp., Jul. 18, 65; Henry Nolte, com. serg., May 3, 65; John Ingles, far., June 8, 65; John L. Dow, wagn., June 21, 65; Aaron Curry, cpt. Aug. 3, June 16, 65, pris.; Frederick W. Foote, June 8, 65; Thomas Gunn, cpt. Dec. 2, 63, June 12, 65, pris., corp.; Edward Gottry, cpt. Aug. 3, May 30, 65, pris., corp.; James W. Gardner, June 20, 65; Richmond Hammond, serg., cpt. Jul. 31, May 30, 65, pris.; Wm. Kelly, May 13, 65; Wm. Lucas, May 20, 63; Wm. H. Merit, Oct. 19, 63; Jacob Miskle, Jul. 1, 63; Dan T. McNanaman, cpt. Jul. 31, May 30, 65, pris.; Julius W. Miller, for promotion, June 25, 64; John A. McDonald, May 6, 65; John Robbins, May 20, 63; Wm. Smith, Sept. 14, 64; Joseph Smith, cpt. Aug. 3, May 30, 65, pris.; Wm. J. Williford, cpt. Aug. 3, May 25, 65, pris.; Calvin Washburn, Apr. 9, 63; Thomas Billings, June 21, 65; Aaron Curry, May 30, 65; Charles Curtis, cpt. Aug. 3, June 2, 65, pris.; Geo. Centern, cpt. Aug. 3, June 16, 65, pris.; David Cadwell, Sept. 28, 63; Hugh Crosby, May 30, 63; Charles Eckhart, V. R. C., Mar. 24, 66; David Hill, cpt. Nov. 24, 64, May 30, 65, pris.; Thomas J. Hoover, cpt. Aug. 3, May 30, 65, pris.; Samuel L. Halstead, June 1, 63; Daniel Morrison, cpt. Aug. 3, June 21, 65; Richard Oliver, June 13, 65; Julius Ruby, cpt. Aug. 3, May 30, 65, pris; Lewis N. Riggs, June 7, 65; John H. G. Shoe, Jul. 27, 65; James Stapleton, May 9, 65; Alfred S. Trobaugh, May 20, 65; Thomas Wible, cpt. Aug. 3, May 22, 65, pris.

E—Thomas R. Lawler, serg., May 29, 63; Thomas Sharp, corp., June 8, 65; Benjamin Arney, cpt. Jul. 31, June 12, 65, pris.; James M. Gather, Aug. 28, 63; John Hall, May 5, 63; John D. Hood, cpt. Jul. 31, June 16, 65, pris.; Andrew T. Walker, Mar. 22, 65; Joseph T. Bradley, June 8, 65; Michael Doyle, May 8, 64; Benjamin Davis, May 8, 63; John Ellis, May 22, 65; Benjamin F. Fuller, cpt. Aug. 3, Jul. 10, 65; John Greatorex, June 20, 63; Henderson C. Hooker, June 8, 65; James Jenkins, cpt. Jul. 31, June 16, 65; Wm. McGowan, June 19, 63; Jonathan Rowark, cpt. Aug. 3, Jul. 8, 65, pris.; John Short, Aug. 28, 63; Jesse D. Thompson, June 27, 65; Trenton Combs, cpt. Jul. 31, Jul. 10, 65, pris.

F—John Bumgardner, Mar. 27, 65; Wm. A. Barrows, serg., June 21, 64; Geo. Duquits, serg., June 21, 65; John Erving, Aug. 1, 65; Mitchell Harrison, wnd., cpt. Dec. 14, 63, May 30, 65, pris.; Geo. S. Harris, May 30, 65; Chris Hughnholts, Aug. 11, 63; Roddy Kelly, corp., Aug. 14, 63, wnd.; Pat Kennedy, No. 1, May 24, 65; Wm. Lock, cpt. Aug. 3, May 30, 65, pris.; Richard C. Lewis, Jul. 12, 65; Thomas Puckett, cpt. Jul. 31, May 30, 65, pris.; Joshua Scholes, Sept. 4, 63; Josiah Smith, Sept. 16, 63; James T. Baker, Dec. 27, 64; Samuel M. Hinds, cpt. Aug. 3, 64, Jul. 22, 65, pris.; Leonard Moby, June 21, 65; Wm. McLain, cpt. Aug. 3, 64, May 30, pris.; Jacob W. Moore, cpt. Jul. 31, May 30, 65, pris; Charles N. Oliver, cpt. Aug. 3, 64, May 24, 65, pris.; Thomas J. Smith, cpt. Jul. 31, May 30, 65, pris.; Wm. Woods, cpt. Jul. 31, May 30, 65, pris.

G—Thomas Cunningham, serg., Jul. 2, 63; David W. Lenox, corp., May 30, 63; Wm. Brooks, temst., Sept. 23, 63; Allen B. Jones, sdlr., May 30, 63; John W. Bradford, cpt. Jul. 31, May 30, 65, pris.; Wm. B. Belcher, Oct. 5, 63; John Cosgray, June 2, 65; James S. Cowan, Feb. 13, 64; Samuel Epperheimer, serg., cpt. Aug. 3, May 30, 65, pris.; James A. Farless, cpt. Jul. 31, May 30, 65, pris.; Nathan M. Gray, cpt. Jul. 31, June 7, 65; Wm. G. Graden, June 23, 65; Henry H. Hamilton, cpt. Aug. 3, Jul. 11, 65; Henry Jenkins, cpt. Aug. 3, May 30, 65, pris.; Wm. Smith, June 22, 65; John B. Scarlett, June 7, 65; Jefferson A. Travelstead, June 24, 64; David Wagoner, June 14, 65; Daniel Wood, corp., cpt. Aug. 3, May 30, 65, pris.; John Bice, cpt. Jul. 31, May 30, 65, pris.; James C. Cheek, cpt. Aug. 3, May 23, 65, pris.; Boyd Foster, June 23, 65; Geo. W. Huffman, cpt. Jul. 31, May 30, 65, pris.; Carter Jones, cpt. Jul. 31, Jul. 6, 65; Hiram Johnson, Mar. 21, 64; Joel R. McKee, cpt. Aug. 3, May 30, 65, pris.; Wm. H. H. May, May 11, 65; James H. Simpson, cpt. Aug. 3, May 30, 65, pris.; Wickliff Ward, cpt. Aug. 3, June 3, 65, pris.; John Murphy, cpt. Aug. 3, Jul. 6, 65; Albert McConnell, cpt. Aug. 3, Jul. 6, 65; Wm. G. Martin, May 3, 65; John B. Simpson, cpt. Jul. 31, June 17, 65, pris.; Barney L. Smith, cpt. Jul. 31, May 30, 65, pris.; James W. Sharp, cpt. Aug. 3, May 30, 65, pris.

H—Geo. Venters, serg., May 21, 63; Nathaniel P. Harris, sdlr., May 18, 63; Thomas J. Cook, wnd. Oct. 11, 63; Joseph Dennis, Jan. 7, 65; Morgan Deweese, Mar. 21, 64; John Giles, Jan. 7, 65; Isaac Parmer, cpt. Jul. 31, Jul. 10, 65, pris.; Viol O. Salsbury, Mar. 18, 63; Robert W. Dugans, Feb. 13, 64; Isom B. Gunn, Jul. 10, 65; Eli Hodson, June 19, 65.

I—Mattenly Addis, q. m. serg., wnd. Feb. 2, 64, dis. Oct. 3, 64; John Bardin, cpt. Jul. 31, Jul. 13, 65; Wm. D. Butterfield, Jul. 21, 63; Mathias Bretz, cpt. Jul. 31, May 30, 65, pris.; Frederick D. Buhrfiend, June 8, 63; Alexander Carmichal, May 20, 65; John Ginther, June 21, 65; Antone Miller, Apr. 5, 65; Wm. F. Morris, corp., May 18, 65; Wm. A. Michael, May 30, 65; John H. Miller, June 21, 65; Geo. A. Miller, for promotion, Nov. 1, 63; John W. Strange, Sept. 17, 63; Nana Schlimmer, May 23, 63; Wm. Strange, Sept. 25, 63; Orange Bear, May 30, 65; Youel P. Eaton, Jul. 1, 65; Geo. H. Greenman, May 13, 65; Azro W. Martin, May 30, 65; Amos W. Pardee, June 23, 65; Samuel A. Sanders, cpt. Nov. 23, 64, June 13, 65; Alfred W. Scott, Mar. 28, 65; Albert Sidstrum, Jul. 1, 65; Andrew J. Withers, cpt. Jul. 31, May 30, 65, pris.

K—Geo. F. Hutchinson, q. m. serg., May 11, 65; Julius C. Taylor, com. serg., Aug. 16, 65; James Franklin, serg., Jul. 28, 65; John Cullumber, corp., May 20, 65; John C. Hall, wnd., cpt. Jul. 31, May 30, 65, pris.; Henry Lower, blksmith, cpt. Aug. 3, Jul. 8, 65; pris.; James H. Allen, cpt. Aug. 3, Jul. 3, 65; Wm. Brown, May 28, 65; John Caughey, Aug. 27, 63; Nathan G. Curry, Jul. 2, 63; Henry H. Dibbler, Mar. 16, 63; David Klinger, June 20, 63; Wister Kime, Jul. 2, 65; Augustus G. Pratt, serg., Jan. 9, 64; Geo. P. Robinson, corp., Jul. 2, 65; L. B. Smith, Aug. 9, 65; Jacob F. Blatner, cpt. Nov. 13, 64, May 30, 65, pris.; Theodore Dennessen, cpt. Jul. 31, 64, May 30, 65, pris; Frederick Guelker, cpt. Aug. 3, May 30, 65, pris.; Frank Holden, May 29, 65; Henry Hensick, June 23, 65; Henry J. M. Johnson, May 28, 65; Geo. W. Monroe, cpt. Aug. 3, May 30, 65, pris.; Wm. G. Menlie, May 24, 65; Patrick Murphy, cpt. Aug. 3, June 20, 65; Wm. M. O'Neil, cpt. Aug. 3, June 8, 65; Barnhart Resa, cpt. Aug. 3, May 30, 65, pris.; Greenburg, B. Tally, cpt. Aug. 3, Jul. 14, 65; Albert B. Turnham, Mar. 28, 65; Frederick Varner, cpt. Aug. 3, Mar. 27, 65; Winfield S. Walker, June 23, 65.

L—Francis C. Adams, serg., Jul. 3, 65; James Bancroft, serg., June 7, 65; Bartlett H. Baldwin, cpt. Jul. 31, June 16, 65; John S. Buck, June 8, 65; Newton E. Bushnel, Apr. 31, 65; Charles E. Chapman, Jul. 2, 65; Ezekiel Cox, corp., June 21, 65; Samuel Dodge, May 15, 65; Edwin T. Field, June 22, 65; Philander Gates, Apr., 12, 65; Stephen R. Hyslop, Apr. 12, 64; Albert R. Hatch, June 13, 65; Michael Kenady, June 21, 65; Robert Kile, June 4, 65; Jerry Lynes, Apr. 1, 64; Harmon C. Morgan, Apr. 1, 64; Peter McMahan, Jan 13, 64; Obadiah Mullen, Jul, 10, 63; Terrance O'Brien, May 18, 65; Zadock C. Powers, June 8, 65; John Rector (no date); James Smilie, Apr. 5, 65; Mason Vale, Apr. 6, 63; Jasper Wagner, May 23, 65; Andrew Birkland, Apr. 12, 64, insanity; Thomas A. Clark, cpt. Jul. 31, May 30, 65, pris.; Wm. Gollars, cpt. Aug. 3, June 5, 65, pris.; Warren Stanber, Dec. 4, 64.

M—Charles E. Burt, serg., Jul. 8, 65; Thomas Putnam, serg., Jan. 10, 64; Wm. J. McEldormy, serg., Jan. 12, 63; Charles W. Fowler, corp., Jul. 12, 64; James Laughlin, temstr., Aug. 14, 65; James W. Barker, Nov. 6, 64; Thomas Clark, Jul. 2, 65; Joseph Clinderson, Nov. 6, 64; Isaac Dennis, Mar. 5, 65; Joseph L. Dodge, May 29, 65; Thomas Dunn, cpt. Jul. 31, May 30, 65, pris,; Denny Donlonie, May 16, 65; Patrick Donahue, Jul. 8, 65, pris.; Clinton Hallock, cpt. Aug. 3, Jul. 3, 65, pris.; Edward Madden, cpt. Jul. 31, May 30, 65, pris.; Emery Russell, corp., Sept. 14, 64; Henry M. Robbins, cpt. Jul. 31, Jul. 8, 65, pris.; James M. Smiley, serg., June 16, 65; Andrew J. Seed, cpt. Aug. 3, May 30, 65, pris.; John Van Klick, June 30, 64; Wm. J. Welch, May 30, 65; Ira Hiner, June 17, 65; James Holihan, June 23, 65; Wm. L. King, Apr. 2, 64; James M. Miller, June 12, 65; James S. Routh, Aug. 1, 63.

Enlisted men mustered out with the regiment July 31, 1865.

A—Henry S. Johnson, corp.; Edmund A. Gould, serg.; Fred Babcock, 1st serg.; Nathan I. Austin, corp.; Jonas Marquis, corp.; Ethan Allen, serg.; Charles Andrews, Zenrid McCulloch, corp., Wm. Moran, Joseph Nevins, Michael Parker, wnd. Nov. 12, 64; Dewitt C. Reece, cpt.

Aug. 3, 64; Geo. Sornburger, corp.; Lewis A Smith, wnd. June, 63; Jacob W. Thorp, Peter Vanarsdale, serg.; David Wimsett, corp.; Geo. Waffle, Jos. B. Agnew, serg,; Jas. H. Betty, Washington Booton, Asa Booton, Albert Brownell, John Brown, Isaac Booth, Francis E. Covert, Henry Dopp, John P. Gabriel, Robert Grant, Jacob Grace, Adam House, Jas. R. Henderson, wnd. Jul. 31; Thomas Hanihan, Benjamin Kirky, far.; James B. Lemons, corp.; Harry McLean, Jonas Marqis, Wm. Moore, John Moore, Andrew McGrew, Michael Meagher, Henry Norris, corp.; Harry Pickrel, Christian Pickrel, Wm. Price, cpt. Aug. 3; Simon Robertson, Frank Richardson, Levi Smith, James Strain, Solomon Whitaker, Alfred F. Young, Wm. J. Young, cpt. Aug. 3.

B—Paul Helmel, serg.; Louis H. Smith, 1st serg., cpt. Jul. 31; John Grove, serg., cpt. Aug. 3; Ferdinand Misselhorn, sadlr.; Wm. Huske, wagn., cpt. Aug. 3; Geo. Brown, Frank Drissler, John W. Folkers, Herman Fishbeck, Conrad Grebe, corp., cpt. Aug. 3; John H. Hoffert, cpt. Jul. 31; Matthias Hoffert, Peter Haas, cpt. Jul. 31; Henry Mehmel, John Munk, Leopold Meyer, Joseph Reiter, Hildebrand Rholes, Henry Spenk, cpt. Jul. 31; Peter Smith, corp.; Julius Seifert, wnd. Dec. 2, 63; John Tremmel, cpt. Aug. 3; Lorenz Walter, cpt. Aug. 3; Philip Weinheimer, serg., cpt. Aug. 3; Ervin Baldwin, corp.; Peter Barth, John Blaisch, Thomas Bryan, Wm. H. Brooks, cpt. Aug. 3; John Deboth, serg.; John Dorr, Charles Frederick, cpt. Dec. 2, 63; Alonzo Franklin, Michael, Kern, Joseph Kemp, Henry Luck, John Morsch, Martin Neff, cpt. Aug. 3; Wm. Ong, Abraham Pearson, Michael Peters, Wm. H. Price, Charles Roth, Wm. Schultz, Wm. Smith, cpt. Aug. 3; Henry Sierner, Wm. Vossceich, Peter Yoekel, Franklin Zeiher.

C—John B. Day, 1st serg.; Geo. T. Codding, corp.; Frederick H. Lockwood, serg.; Martin West, corp.; Charles H. Spiller, bugler; Archie Campbell, serg., cpt. Jul. 31; Wm. Danifelser, temstr., cpt. Aug. 3; James P. Breed, serg., cpt. Jul. 31; Andrew Brenner, John Bresner, Solomon P. Crow, cpt. Nov. 23, 64; Lewis A. Cobb, cpt. Jul. 31; Julius Dunnells, serg.; Aaron Dodson, James H. Henderson, Martin Hoover, cpt. Aug. 3; Samuel Hopkins, John Keller, John Kirkham, cpt. Aug. 3; Peter Larson, Jacob F. Mohr, John Mitchell, cpt. Jul. 31; Edward A. Nattinger, cpt. Jul. 31; James J. Patterson, John D. Prentice, James F. Ransom, Robert Russell, cpt. Jul. 31; John Spreves, cpt. Aug. 16, 64; August Schwocks, Geo. E. D. Weisner, serg.; James Adams, Robert Berdonner, Israel Bear, James Bartlett, Johnson Clark, Hill K. Cox, James L. Cox, Abram Ely, Robert G. Ewing, Augustus E. Foster, Simeon E. Graves, Samuel W. Hudson, Thomas K. Moore, Andrew McCormick, Thomas Newlon, Richard Pippin, cpt. Aug. 3, Thomas Pippin, Arnold Pippin, Ephraim H. Ross, Isaac Steel, Richard R. Tilton, cpt. Jul. 1, 64; Wm. B. Shields, Jacob F. Suerbuegg, Patrick Tway, Stephen T. Tarrance, Wm. Wayman, John W. Whiteside.

D—Charles Liddy, com. serg.; John M. Thompson, serg.; John F. K. Thompson, serg.; James A. Smith, serg.; Henry Gardner, 1st serg.; Jerry Ashcraft, Thomas Beaver, com. serg.; Albert O. Butler, John Dudley, wnd. cpt. A. 3; Philip Mulvaney, Joseph Madigan, cpt. Aug. 3; Wm. Percival, cpt. Aug. 3; Stephen Weaver, Henry West, Eugene Bursaw, Isaac Cook, Gideon Dill, Andrew Follett, cpt. Dec. 2, 63; John L. Hoover, cpt. Aug. 3; John Krimp, John McKinney, John Seitz, John P. Taylor, Edward Wilson, Geo. Galligher, cpt. Aug. 3; Azor Henry, serg.; John Lyons, Henry Moore, cpt. Aug. 3.

E—Jonathan H. Melvin, serg., cpt. Jul. 31; Pelige H. Spencer, q. m. serg.; James J. Russ, bugler; Thomas Clayton, far.; Joseph J. Branner, Abraham Cronk, James Danes, Charles Ingram, Joseph Ambern, Henry H. Brinkley, serg.; Harvey Bradley, John Brazier, Wm. S. Bryant, cpt. Jul. 31; Wm. Borden, Washington C. Callicott, 1st serg.; Wm. R. Cover, corp., cpt. Jul. 31; Isom B. Coleman, corp.; Wm. Dailey, Henry J. Davis, Louis Denson, Francis Dolen, James Emery, Louis F. Etherton, cpt. A. 3, pris.; Wm. A. Fields, Thomas Foster, John Gleeson, John W. Hales, serg, cpt. Jul. 31; Charles Hartman, serg.; Thomas Holland, Jacob Hester, John January, Patrick Kenneda, cpt. Jul. 31; Floyd King, John Kirkland, Elijah W. Lovering, cpt. Aug. 3; James J. McGuire, serg.; Wm. Miers, Burral Mangrum, Wm. Morgan, Silas Noblet, Wm. D. Peeler, corp.; Wilson T. Russ, corp.; Hugh Riley, corp., cpt. Jul. 31; James Reagan, John Reed, Charlton Reagan, Wm. R. Reed, Wm. Sollars, Foster Smith, James Spencer, Amos Tally, Michael Welch, James Watson, Isaiah Wallace, cpt. Jul. 31; Joseph White, James Webster, Ezekiel R. Wood, Andrew Williamson.

F—Wm. Coliver, Wash Campbell, Joseph Cochran, serg.; John Duquits, Wm. R. Eldridge, John W. Fish, Wm. F. Gardenhire, James Ginnane, Michael Hart, Riley Hicks, David Jinks, Roswell Kitchen, Wm. Little, John T. Lawrence, corp.; Oren White, Amasa H. Philips, Christopher E. Thurman, Scott White, John T. Barton, corp.; Andrew J. Buchanan, Wm. Browning, Wm. H. Betherds. Robert Campbell, Josiah Carter, Wm. P. Carlock, Jonaathan Connor, Michael Kreps, Isaiah Deel, Charles E. Dunn, Geo. Fairfax, Amasa Griffith, John B. Hinds, serg.; Jesse Kerley, James Heath, corp.; Wm. Hammond, Wm. Little, No. 2 corp,; Iverson M. Little, Samuel M. Lock, John W. Lowry, James McAdams, John McAdams, David McLanahan, Milford McDaniel, James McDaniel, Samuel Merriman, Luther P. Niles, Hiram D. C. Niles, William Parks, Samuel J. Rice, Gilbert Strait, corp.; Nicholas E. Sidney, John F. Stokes, Amos Stout, James S. Taylor, Charles H. Tucker, John A. Wesner, 1st serg.; Thomas Welch, Geo. W. West.

G —John V. Munger, serg.; John A. Neithfield, serg.; Geo. W. Norris, 1st serg.; Henry McQuarters, serg.; James W. Mayes, temst.; Asa A. Warden, far.; John E. Smith, serg.; Henry Amadon, David Bordaux, Wm. Cease, Henry Epperheimer, serg.; Amos E. Green, Joseph E. Green, David L. Jones, John Lockaby, Wm. Matthias, Sandy O'Donal, John Sooter, Thomas Tomlinson, John W. Argo, cpt. Aug. 3, pris.; Joel W. Cash, John D. Cash, John W. Dunn, serg., cpt. Jul. 31; James M. Davis, Milo Fisher, Joseph J. Freel, Thomas P. Hedgepath, John F. Mather, cpt. Dec. 14, 63; Perry Smith, Daniel C. Morgan, Wm. H. Moore, Robt. F. Mulkey, Samuel Robinson, Taylor Robinson, Samuel S. Sharp, corp.; John W. Seay, cpt. Jul. 31; Wm. H. H. Smith, Wm. H. Thomas, corp.; John Tiermeyer, Tony Wright, Caius S. Norris, John W. Harris.

H—John P Newman, 1st serg; Mathias Lamp, q. m. serg.; James M. Jordan, 1st serg.; Geo. Foster, corp.; John

W. Minton, corp.; Wm. Snider, corp.; Benjamin Gorio, corp.; Thomas C. Lum, corp.; Daniel S. Erwin, far.; capt. Dec. 2, 63; Danl. Austin, Wm. Brooks, John Young, corp.; Robert Thomas, corp.; James R. Brockett, musc.; Robert W. Boyd, Edward M. Bramblet, Thomas Bump, Wm. Cochran, James F. Collard, Moses Crabtree, Samuel C. Dale, Josiah Fulford, David M. Hosick, Charles Hayes, serg.; James M. Luther, corp.; Delos Odell, serg.; Joseph E. Polen, John C. Sanders, Albert Wells, serg.; Wm. Witcher, John M. Woods, serg.; Lewis D. Austin, Thomas Anderson, Willis Barton, corp.; Emanuel Berry, Louis Biggerstaff, John Callihan, Kelsey Curtis, Wm. H. Conniff, Wm. Doolen, Nathan Davis, Lynyear Fulford, Mathew Flaviha, Sylvester Fobar, Frank Giles, John M. Gowdy, Jonah Golden, Hutson L. Hickman, John Hoadley, Edward V. Howell, Samuel Hood, Adna Huntington, Wm. A. Jordan, James Johnson, Wm. C. Jamerson, Albert K. Minton, capt. Apr. 25, 64; Joseph N. Murphy, Israel I Murphy, Robert H. Moody, Albert A. Newman, Strawder Nance, John W. Pipper, corp.; Samuel T. Parkhurst, Isaac Parmer, Thomas Poynton, Wm. Reed, John J. Ross, Andrew Samuelson, Shubel J. Way, Taylor Weedon.

I—David S. Clare, serg.; Wm. Clair, capt. Nov. 28, 64; escaped; Richard R. Eby, Thomas Featherson, 1st serg.; Henry Glass, Charles Haggart, Henry W. Hollenbeck, corp.; Wm. O'Connor, John D. O'Sullivan, capt. Jul. 31; Thomas J. Perrine, Edward Patterson, serg., capt. Nov. 28, 64., escaped; Chester Phelps, Taylor Adams, Wm. A. Arnott, Geo. Bell, Geo. Burger, Geo. Klassy, corp.; John Bardin, capt. Jul. 31; Wm. H. Cross, Wm. Christy, Geo. W. Cooper, capt. Jul. 31; Andrew J. Cardin, Wm. J. Dyke, Wm. J. Donahoo, Robt. Donahoo, Acus M. Daniels, Wm. Ellis, Richard R. Fouke, corp.; James Fair, John Garner, Geo. W. Goldsmith, James Humphry, corp.; Danl. L. Hill, Wm. C. Hibbs, Henry L. Lockwood, Wm. Rafley, Wm. E. McCready, corp., capt. Nov. 28, 64, escaped; Hobart L. Martin, capt. Nov. 28, 64, escaped; Nathaniel Morris, Nelson H. Miller, James L. McCauley, James O'Brien, serg., Benjamin F. Puckett, corp.; David E. Rice, serg.; Andrew V. L. Roosa, Daniel Robb, Wm. J. Roland, Wm. R. Roberts, Daniel Rollan, Thomas Smith, Henry D. Smith,

Thomas Sumner, James M. Sinor, capt. Jul. 31; Henry Winter.

K—James W. Beck, serg., capt. Jul. 31, promoted 2d lt.; Francis Reichert, serg.; Daniel Lower, serg.; Henry Smith, buglr.; Allen W. McKenzie, corp., capt. Jul. 31; John Arnold, 1st serg.; Edward Barley, corp., capt. Aug. 3; Wm. Bowman, J. H. Looney, James McCann, John Mellinger, serg.; John C. Neff, John Shirk, Abraham Paul, John N. Smith, capt. Aug. 3; Daniel P. Sullivan, Wm. W. Westacott, serg.; James Bird, Elijah A. Boyles, capt. Aug. 3; Wm. M. Ball, Whatley B. Burfield, Wm. Baham, Wm. M. Carnes, Archleus M. Cochran, Richard S. Cox, capt. Aug. 3; Louis Deasel, Albert H. Gleeson, serg., Wm. Gulum, Louis Miller, Andrew J. Lynch, Isaac Hall, capt. Aug. 3; Michael A. Klintz, Wm. H. Meichler, Henry H. Palmer, August Renschlun, Swan A. Rethon, Lyn B. Short, John B. Thorn, Francis E. Williams, Wm. S. Willis, capt. Aug. 3; Charles Zimmerman, capt. Aug. 3.

L—Phineas Burlingame, Gabriel Bollman, Patrick Cahill, corp.; William Dillon, John Driscoll, corp.; Albert O'Day, Henry Ford, corp.; Charles Graves, Charles C. Green, Edmond Harrison, serg.; Uriah Harrison, corp.; Warren Hugh, serg.; Benjamin F. Jenkins, Danford Klock, Thomas Lucas, James Moore, serg.; Wm. Mullen, Hiram Ostrander, David Rogers, Jas. H. Sterling, Robert Seward, James L. Scott, Charles Scott, Wesley Taylor, Joseph M. Thompson, Wm. White, Nicholas Bodwin, Peter Bredborg, Nicholas Bradenbarger, Wm. Black, Azro K. Brown, John L. Elkins, Henry S. Featherson, Joseph Gravenhorst, Michael Heafy, James P. Knott, Cobb Loomis, James F. Loftus, Joseph J. Murry, severe wnd. Nov. 23, 64; James Morgan, John E. Moore, James O. Ross, Jacob Reaser, Geo. W. Wolf, W. S. Strong, Peter J. Sunborg, Andrew J. Wickiser, corp.; Alfred V. Wooley, Charles Whill.

M—Alexander Irvine, serg.; James Anderson, serg.; Jesse Brown, corp.; John Stulin, corp.; John S. Cleveland, corp.; John Probasco, corp.; John M. Casey, John J. Ferguson, serg.; John W. Bundy, far.; Wm. Boyd, far.; Henry M. Battles, Philip Blessington, John R. Follenwider, Thomas Hopkins, serg.; James McLay, Jonathan McKee, corp.; Ira B. Ogden, Thomas J. Shirley, corp.; Thomas Somersett, Wm. Walters, corp.; Henry Walters, corp.;

Wm. Wamsel, John J. Brown, Jesse Kreeps, Amasa L. Myers, Wm. S. Reece, Aaron Shaw, Andrew Waddell, serg.; Edmond B. Appleton, capt. Jul. 31, pris.; Ona H. Ropka, Geo. Smith, Chandler Silkworth, David H. Smith, Enoch R. Sargent.

In the following list of transferred from the regiment those not otherwise noted were transferred to the Veteran Reserve Corps.

A—Henry Geesen, corp.; Henry Jackson, for promotion in 5th U. S. C. T.; Peter Lewis.

B—Samuel Bradley, q. m. serg.; Charles Moliter, serg.; John Naeff, John Raymer, Charles Eckhart.

C—John Muligan, Wm. Sample.

D—Wm. Martin.

E—Albert M. Lacefield, serg.

F—Jonathan Short.

H—John Lamb, 45th Ill. Inft.

I—James R. Cooper.

L—Ormand Chamberlain, Charles H. Fish, John C. McElhinney, Sidney T. Robinson, 5th U. S. Col. Cav. promotion; Abraham Vancamp.

M—John D. Banks, 65th Ill. Inft.; Charles J. Williams, 58th Ill. Inft.; Thomas J. Welch, Elgin Battery.

In the following list those absent at muster out of regiment are accounted for:

A—Frank Edwards, detached; Wm. Owens, capt. A. 3, pris.; Stephen A. Rogers, sentenced.

B—Jacob Gloring, tmstr., sick; Anthony Ehmi, Joseph Smith, John Ammon, Robert E. Brady, Wm. Clark, Thomas Clark, John Cox, Wm. Gethard, corp.; Geo. B. Quainton, Samuel J. Rice, all sick.

C—John Babcock, Alonzo T. Bates, John P. Swain, all sick; Louis Reeves, arrest; Louis Stout, arrest.

D—Andrew Holder, Frederick Cook, sick; Alexander Reynolds, in confinement; Charles L. Cook, pris., capt. Aug. 3; Thomas W. Madigan, pris., Jul. 31; James P. Moret, pris., Dec. 2, 63; Henry Plountz, pris., Aug. 3.

E—Wm. J. Brown, Augustus Bartel, Francis Drone, wound; Abner R. Moore, James A. Shrives, sick; John N. French, pris. Jul. 31.

F—Henry Snowhite, sick; Wm. J. Frink, pris., Dec. 2, 63; Wm. Vanhorn, Thomas Vanhorn, pris., Jul. 31, 64;

Benjamin W. Wilson, Geo. Wiler, pris., Jul. 31; Peter Whitts, pris., Jul. 31.
G—Talifero A. Hammock, Wm. F. Crider, sick; Thomas Dailey, in arrest; Wm. D. Jones, in arrest.
H—None.
I—John Trotter, sick.
K—Anthony Heiker, Patrick Quigney, Charles V. Edwards, Edwin Grant, Robert McGrady, Wm. Moore, sick.
L—Wm. Cartwright, Morris Ingermonson, John London, Harmon Sanders, sick.
M—James Pitcher, wagoner; Edward Ross, Henry Van Hess, sick; Peter Colender, in arrest; Wm. Tucker, in arrest; Jeremiah Webb, in arrest.

Our comrades must pardon us for presenting our roster in this form; a full roster in the usual form would have cost far in excess of our means. By studying well the abbreviations and directions it can easily be understood. It contains all the names and all the essentials of our rolls, except dates of enlistment, and the individual descriptions.

The roster shows the total membership of the regiment 1,354, of this number there was at the organization of the regiment 19 field and staff and 36 line officers, leaving enlisted men 1,299. Of the enlisted men there were transferred from the regiment, 23; promoted to line officers and to field and staff, 38; leaving 1,238 men to be accounted for as follows: Killed, 98; died in prison, 52; died in hospital, in camp and at home, 92. Total deaths, 242. Many of the last enumerated deaths were doubtless the result of wounds, as well as were many of the 337 discharged. There were absent sick at the muster out of regiment, 50. Absent in prison or otherwise unaccounted for, 14. Mustered out with the regiment July 31st, 1865, 595. The lost by battle was over 12 per cent of the enlisted. The total death loss was about 20 per cent. The final muster out was 48 per cent of the whole, as against 52 per cent of those who did not enjoy that privilege. This is a showing of loss far in excess of the average in any branch of the service, which attests the severity of our service and the faithfulness and courage with which our command performed the service committed to them. The casualties of the field and staff and of the line officers are shown in their biographies. The roster shows the names of those who died in prison and also of those who remained in prison at the muster out, but there were many more captured who escaped, some soon after capture and some from the rebel prisons. Reminiscences of these adventures would form a volume of exciting interest, could they be gathered and published. Neither the history of the Rebellion, nor the world's history of wars show many, if any, raids so marked with undaunted courage, heroic adventure and sad loss as the history of the Stoneman raid to Macon, Georgia, in July, 1864, and certainly none should enlist the sympathy of the world more than this raid, undertaken with a view to release our suffering comrades from those "hells" of torture, and in spite of the most heroic battling against an overwhelming foe, ending in furnishing many more victims to the demons that ruled them. Such were the dangers that surrounded such an undertaking that, until General Stoneman and his brigade commanders conceived the project, it had never been dreamed of even by our bold commanding general, and when proposed to Sherman he consented with many misgivings and with constant anxiety for the result, as is shown by his many anxious references to it in his reports.

The following lists of casualties were furnished by our former cohistorians, comrades West and Featherson, by a personal canvass of the regiment before muster out. Some company lists are missing. We give what we have. Some included in these lists are included in our regular lists, but many are not. Some reported captured in this list are reported killed, died, discharged in other lists, at a subsequent time. Most of those marked in this list as captured subsequently escaped from the enemy:

A—J. R. Henderson, severely wnd. Dec. 14, 63; Michael Parker, wnd. Nov. 12, 64; Lewis A. Smith, wnd. June, 63. Captured Aug. 3, 64: Frank A. Howard, Wm. B. Johnson, Charles Lindsley, Charles Murdock, Austin Martin, Swan Oleson, Wm. Owens, Wm. Prater, Wm. Price, Parker Robinson, D. C. Reece, J. R. Skillman, G. W. Stodgell, Geo. Waffle, Thomas White, Wm. J. Young. Captured on other dates: J. W. Slaughter, Dec. 14th, 63; Geo. H. Jones, Nov. 14, 64; Thomas Malone, Nov. 24, 64.

B—Wnd. July 31, 64, Cpt. H. H. Mayo, Julius Seifert. Captured July 31, 64, Serg. Charles A. Dettell, Harry Handshu, Frank H. Westerman, Serg. Peter Reising, Louis H. Smith, John Boehm, Jacob Hoffert, John January, John Grove, Timothy Barnett, Wm. H. Brooks, John Forrer, Charles Frederick, Casper Hauser, John Hiermeyer, Peter Haas, Dan Kindley, Lewis Greenekle, Martin Neff, Henry Spenke, Wm. Smith, Jeremiah Sutton, John Tremmel, Christian Treftz, James R. Wells, Harman Blass, Peter Yokel, Gotleib Zeigler; captured on other dates: Capt. Paul Ditzler, Aug. 3, 64; Wm. Huske, Sept. 24, 63; Lewis Mayn, Nov. 24, 64.

C—Wounded and captured, Lt. J. M. Balderston, Aug. 3, 64, and Jan., 65; Eugene H. Levering, Feb. 2, 64; captured, Capt. J. B. Dent, Jul. 24, 64, and Oct., 64; captured Jul. 31, 64, Wm. Gibson, Jerry A. Arnold, James P. Breed, Lewis A. Cobb, Samuel Hopkins, John Mitchel, Edward A. Nattinger, Wm. Peeks, Henry Weber, Barnett Sweeney, James B. Weaver; Aug. 3, 64, Henry Webb, Archie Campbell, Wm. Danifelser, Corp. Dick Morgan, James K. Andrews, John Kirkham, Richard Pippin, Charles Sculley, Geo. Coleman, Thomas Crimigan, Joseph Gunning, Geo. Robinson.

D—The list of this company is partly destroyed. They were with Major Davidson, and thus missed the battle July 31st, 64. Wounded: John Dudley, and captured Aug. 3, 64; others captured Aug. 3, 64: Capt. Carrico and Lt. I. H. Allen, Aaron Curry, Charles Curtis, Geo. Centner, Charles L. Cook, Edward Gotry, Geo. Gallagher, Thomas J. Hoover, Henry Moore, Dan McManaman, Joseph Madigan, Dan Morrison, Wm. Percival. On other dates: John Atkinson, Dec. 14, 63; John Fowler, Dec. 2, 63; Andrew Follett, Dec. 2, 63; Thomas Gunn, Dec. 2, 63; Andrew Holden, Nov. 17, 64; David Hill, Nov. 24, 64; James P. Moret, Dec. 2, 63; Thomas W. Madigan, Dec. 2, 63; Henry Plountz, Dec. 2, 63.

E—Captured Jul. 31, 64: Lt. W. M. Duvall, Serg. J. H. Melven; wounded: Corp. Wm. R. Cover, Benjamin Arney, Wm. S. Bryant, Jacob Bordau; captured Aug. 3, 64: J. W. Hales, Charlton Reagan, Walker Wilmot, Wm. Daily, L. F. Etherton, Benj. F. Fuller, John French, James Jenkins, Patrick Keneda, John January, John Lyons, E. W. Lovering, Hughey Riley, Isaiah Wallace, Wm. Rollman, Thomas Foster, Franklin Thompson; captured on other dates: W. C. Callicott, Dec. 14, 63, exchanged; Trenton Combs, Nov. 24, 64; Harvey Bradley, May 27, 64; Joseph J. Brannan, June 29, 63; Francis Drone, wounded Aug. 24, 64; George Jones, Dec. 14, 63; Wm. Whitman, Dec. 2, 63; Jonathan Rowark, Nov. 24, 64.

F—Captured Jul. 31, 64: Serg. Albert Philbrook; Serg. John B. Sayler, John K. Hanks, Jacob Kent, Wm. Lock, John McAdams, wound.; Steel Mills, wound.; Jacob Moore, Geo. W. Preston, Charles A. Pratt, Thomas J. Smith, Wm. Vanhorn, Wm. Woods, Benjamin Wilson, Peter Whitt, Lucien Nichols, Thomas Puckett, Wm. McLain; on other dates: Wm. Clary, Jan. 18, 65; W. J. Fink, Dec. 2, 63; Rodey Kelley, wound., May 25, 63; Harrison Mitchell, wound., Dec. 14, 63.

G—Captured July 31, 64: Lt. Geo. W. Bellows, Serg. John Welch, Asa Warden; captured Aug. 3, 64: Carter Jones, Jesse R. Ladford, Capt. Wm. Perkins, wound.: Geo. W. Norris, Serg. John Welch, John W. Argo, Hazzard Clark, Samuel Epperheimer, Nathan W. Gray, James W. Hunt, Henry Jenkins, Thomas Lefler, John Murphy, Albert McConnel, Sandy O'Donnel, Leander J. Passimore, James Parker, Daniel Wood, John W. Seay, John Bice, James P. Gregory, John F. Mather; captured on other dates: James A. Farless, June 28, 64; Henry H. Hamilton, June 12, 64; John Smith, Dec 14, 63; John W. Dunn, Dec. 14, 63.

H—We greatly regret that we have no special casualty list of this splendid company. Under such leaders as Captain Lord and Lieutenant Anderson it was abreast of the other companies, as the losses reported by the adjutant general shows.

I—Lt. Kilbourne, wound. Dec. 14, 63; Serg. Mattenly Addis, wound., Feb. 2, 64; Garret Niles and Ed. Patterson, wound., Dec. 2, 63; Captured Jul. 31, 64, Matthias Bretz wound.; Andrew J. Withers, and wound.; John Bardin, Kendrich W. Chapin, Herbert Vandeberg, James O'Brien, John Ginther, Elihu M. Butterfield, Matthias Bretz, Geo. W. Cooper, Cassius Beemis, Daniel Robb, Daniel Rollins, James Sinor, Richard G. Wilson, Benjamin F. Welch, John Gogan, Geo. H. Greenman, James W. Humphrey, Antone Miller, John Mellois, Oliver C. Douglas, Aug. 3, 64: Henry L. Lockwood, Phillips Meiney,

James McNichols; on other dates Jan. 27, 64, Cassius C. Beemis, escaped. Nov. 28, 64; Edward Patterson and Wm. B. Clair, both escaped Dec. 12, 64; Wm. E. McCready and Hobart Martin, both escaped same day; John Ginther, Jul. 31, 64; Martin D. Rollison, Jul. 15, 64; Wm. A. Arnott, Nov. 24, 64, escaped; Orange H. Bear, Nov. 22, 64; James Dunn, Dec. 14, 63; James Sinor, Jul. 15, 64; Samuel Sanders, Nov. 23, 64; James Fair, Jul. 15, 64, escaped and capt. Jul. 31, 64; John Garner, Nov. 23, 64, escaped; Wm. A. Michael, Nov. 23, 64, escaped; Azro W. Martin, Nov. 23, 64, escaped..

K—Capt. Wm. R. Sanford, wound. Jul. 31, 64, captured Aug. 3, 64; Lt. James S. Stem, wound. Jan. 27, 64; John C. Hall, wounded; Allen W. McKenzie, Theodore Dennison; captured Aug. 3, 64: Henry Lower, James H. Allen, John A. Butler, Edward Bailey, Elijah A. Boyles, Thomas J. Cox, Richard S. Cox, Frederick Gulker, Wm. A. Herrill, Orderly Serg. Moses B. Largent, Geo. W. Munroe, Patrick Murphy, Joseph McCartey, Wm. M. O'Neil, John M. Smith, Henry Senna, Greenbury B. Tally, Frederick Varner, Wm. S. Willis, Andrew J. Whitehead, Charles F. Zimmerman, Isaac Hall, Barnhard Resa. Captured on other dates: James W. Beck, Aug. 1, 63, escaped; Jacob T. Blatner, Nov. 23, 64, Forrest; Wm. Clark, near Danville, Tenn.; John Little, wounded Oct. 24, 63.

L—Only a partial list of casualties of this company is found. Captured Jul. 31, 64: John W. Kelso, Wm. J. Worley, Thomas Carlile, Thomas A. Clark. Captured Aug. 3, 64: Bartlet H. Baldwin, Patrick Cunningham, Robert Kile, John Long, Francis Watts; Jul. 8, 64, Wm. Sollars.

M—No special casualty list of this company is found. Captain Lupton was captured on the Stoneman raid and was never again with us on active duty. The adjutant general's report shows the average of casualties.

A thousands thanks to those generous comrades who have made our history possible. Comrades! we have answered many roll calls. Let us all prepare for the general roll call.

PRINTED BY R. R. DONNELLEY
AND SONS COMPANY AT THE
LAKESIDE PRESS, CHICAGO, ILL.

www.ingramcontent.com/pod-product-compliance
Lightning Source LLC
Chambersburg PA
CBHW020101020526
44112CB00032B/805